# COMPETING IN THE
# AGE OF
# DIGITAL CONVERGENCE

# COMPETING IN THE AGE OF DIGITAL CONVERGENCE

*Edited by*
David B. Yoffie

HARVARD BUSINESS SCHOOL PRESS
*Boston, Massachusetts*

Printed in the United States of America

01 00 99 98 97    5 4 3 2 1

Library of Congress Cataloging-in-Publication Data

Competing in the age of digital convergence / edited by David B.
    Yoffie.
        p.    cm.
    Includes index.
    ISBN 0-87584-726-9 (alk. paper)
    1. Computer industry.    2. Microelectronics industry.
3. Telecommunication equipment industry.    4. Information technology.
5. Competition.    I. Yoffie, David B.
HD9696.C62C63    1997
338.4'7004—dc20                                        96-10890
                                                          CIP

The paper used in this publication meets the requirements of the American National
Standard for Permanence of Paper for Printed Library Materials Z39.49-1984

# CONTENTS

*Preface and Acknowledgments*                                                *vii*

CHAPTER 1                                                                        *1*
INTRODUCTION
*CHESS and Competing in the Age of Digital Convergence*
David B. Yoffie

CHAPTER 2                                                                       *37*
THE COMPUTER INDUSTRY
*The First Half-Century*
Alfred D. Chandler, Jr.

CHAPTER 3                                                                      *123*
SUN WARS
*Competition within a Modular Cluster, 1985–1990*
Carliss Y. Baldwin and Kim B. Clark

CHAPTER 4                                                                      *159*
WINNERS AND LOSERS
*Industry Structure in the Converging World of Telecommunications,*
*Computing, and Entertainment*
David J. Collis, P. William Bane, and Stephen P. Bradley

CHAPTER 5                                                                      *201*
WHAT DOES INDUSTRY CONVERGENCE MEAN?
Shane Greenstein and Tarun Khanna

CHAPTER 6                                                     *227*

CREATING VALUE AND SETTING STANDARDS
*The Lessons of Consumer Electronics for Personal Digital Assistants*
Anita M. McGahan, Leslie L. Vadasz, and David B. Yoffie

CHAPTER 7           *265*

LARGER FIRMS' DEMAND FOR
COMPUTER PRODUCTS AND SERVICES
*Competing Market Models, Inertia, and Enabling Strategic Change*
Timothy F. Bresnahan and Garth Saloner

CHAPTER 8           *301*

PATENT SCOPE AND EMERGING INDUSTRIES
*Biotechnology, Software, and Beyond*
Josh Lerner and Robert P. Merges

CHAPTER 9           *325*

ALLIANCE CLUSTERS IN MULTIMEDIA
*Safety Net or Entanglement?*
Benjamin Gomes-Casseres and Dorothy Leonard-Barton

CHAPTER 10           *371*

BEYOND THE WATERFALL
*Software Development at Microsoft*
Michael A. Cusumano and Stanley A. Smith

CHAPTER 11           *413*

MANAGING CHAOS
*System-Focused Product Development
in the Computer and Multimedia Environment*
Marco Iansiti

*Index*           *445*

*About the Contributors*           *459*

# PREFACE AND
# ACKNOWLEDGMENTS

The idea for this book originated in 1993, in discussions with my colleagues at the Harvard Business School. We noticed that a large number of us were working on different aspects of the electronics industry, and it seemed to make sense to combine forces. There were a number of projects on the computer industry already under way, and several other scholars were beginning to embark on new research that would look at the intersection of computers, communications, and consumer electronics. By integrating these efforts, we hoped that the whole would be greater than the sum of the parts.

Starting in the fall of 1993, we held periodic seminars where the authors presented the preliminary results of their research. In October 1994, we organized a colloquium at the Harvard Business School for roughly forty practitioners and forty scholars. The title of the colloquium was "Colliding Worlds: The Convergence of Computers, Telecommunications, and Consumer Electronics." Most of the papers in this volume were discussed by a wide range of participants from companies, such as Compaq, Intel, IBM, Philips, and US West, in a wide range of industries, including computers, software, consumer electronics, telecommunications, and information services. We also had several keynote speakers:

Steve Ballmer, an executive vice president of Microsoft; Walt Mossberg, the technology columnist for the *Wall Street Journal,* and Hermann Hauser, the chairman of ATM Limited of the United Kingdom. The conference convinced us that our research had uncovered a number of ideas as well as empirical data that were worth publishing in a book. In a volume such as this one, with twenty authors, it is nearly impossible to thank everyone who contributed. But a few specific mentions are necessary. Financially, neither the colloquium nor the book would have materialized without the support of Senior Associate Dean Warren McFarlan, who ran the HBS Division of Research in 1993 and 1994, and former HBS Dean John McArthur. Both recognized the value of exploring these new technologies with a diverse group of scholars. The Division of Research also gave us funds to hire numerous research assistants who helped gather data; their names are mentioned in the credits of the individual chapters. Toward the end of the process, John Sculley, the former chairman and CEO of Apple Computer, and Professor Richard Nolan, reviewed the entire manuscript and provided valuable suggestions for all of the authors on their individual chapters.

As the editor of the book, I want to thank a few additional individuals. First, I need to thank Professor Emeritus Alfred Chandler. Although Professor Chandler did not participate in the colloquium, he read significant pieces of the manuscript and gave me a number of ideas as well as very useful feedback on my first chapter. I was also grateful that he contributed his masterful historical essay on the computer industry to the volume. Second, several of the authors offered very useful suggestions for the overview chapter, including Anita McGahan, Tarun Khanna, Garth Saloner, Les Vadasz, and Josh Lerner. My thanks also to Tom Eisenmann for his comments, and Takia Mahmood, who collected some of the data cited in the first chapter. Third, Nick Philipson from HBS Press, and Lisa DeLucia, my assistant at HBS, were invaluable in helping put the manuscript together physically. Pulling together all of the pieces was not an easy task, especially with twenty authors and an editor who was three thousand miles away, on sabbatical at Stanford Business School, during the year prior to publication. And fourth, I want to thank Andy Grove and John Sculley. While doing a case study on Apple Computer in 1992, John forced me to consider the issues of digital convergence long before it was really fashionable. At the same time, I have had the pleasure of listening to Andy Grove, as an Intel director, talk about the computer and telecommunications industries for almost seven years. Andy has always stimulated my thinking on how these very diverse and complicated businesses interact.

# CHAPTER 1

# INTRODUCTION
## CHESS and Competing
## in the Age of Digital Convergence

David B. Yoffie

Separating hype from reality seems almost impossible when talking about digital convergence. Droves of start-ups are pouring into the information superhighway, best-selling books are being written about "being digital,"[1] politicians are proclaiming the age of new electronic democracy, and multibillion-dollar deals are inked almost daily in the name of digital convergence. But how much substance is behind the hype? Are we on the verge of a true technological revolution that will reshape the global economy? What should companies and managers do to prepare for such a turbulent world?

There is something real to the excitement over digital convergence. If only a small portion of the convergence-related R&D pays off, our lives could be materially altered by the turn of the century. In the consumer segment of the market, for example, firms are undertaking huge investments in video-on-demand, interactive television, on-line services, and new forms of digital entertainment content; in education, companies are exploring ways to use multimedia technology to enhance student–student learning, teacher–teacher sharing, and continuous learning; and in business, enhancements to corporate networks, and the Internet are creating opportunities for new channels of distribution, new methods of communication (e.g., personal videoconferencing), and new vehicles for delivering real-time corporate information. Some products and technologies, such as personal digital assistants, are designed to cut across segments, potentially serving as personal communicators for business while also acting as personal organizers for the home. While some firms are making big investments to enhance the personal computer as a general-purpose device that will equally serve the home, business, and education, others are proclaiming the death of the modern PC with the emergence of a ubiquitous multimedia network and cheap Internet access devices.

Our challenge in this volume is to say something meaningful about such trends, even though the technology and the market seem to change almost daily. Our solution has been to focus our research on how companies have managed previous paradigm shifts in the world of electronics and information technology. While it is too early to predict the winners and losers in the battle for the information superhighway, there is a great deal we can learn about the forthcoming battle from more than forty years of consumer electronics experience, thirty years of mainframe and minicomputer experience, and almost twenty years of experience with the microprocessor revolution.

We start with a functional definition of digital convergence and an overview of its key drivers. *Merriam-Webster's Collegiate Dictionary* defines convergence as a movement toward a point or the coming together to unite in a common interest or focus. Likewise, we define convergence as the unification of functions—the coming together of previously distinct products that employ digital technologies. The telephone and the computer, for example, both utilize digital technologies, but historically they have served completely different markets with entirely different functions. The process of digital convergence implies that a computer begins to incorporate the functionality of a communicating device, and the telephone takes on the functionality of a computer.

Our primary interest is understanding the consequences of convergence. The argument is that mastering digital convergence does not require a magical new set of technologies. Too many companies have sought, and failed, to master digital convergence with a big technological breakthrough or grand acquisition. Instead, I suggest, success will emerge by adopting a strategy that I summarize in the acronym CHESS, which stands for *c*reative combinations, *h*orizontal solutions, *e*xternalities and standards, *s*cale and bundling, and new production techniques, called *s*ystem-focused development.

A CHESS strategy means rethinking many traditional approaches to convergence. The entertainment business and telecommunications industries, for example, have focused their strategies on huge infrastructure investments or big bets that will reorganize the hardware and software industries. But the lesson we have learned from the computer industry is that success is more likely to emerge from *creative combinations* that build on complementary technologies. Moreover, mastering all aspects of digital technology appears to be beyond the capabilities of most firms. Even the world's largest electronics giants, from NEC and Fujitsu to IBM and AT&T, have failed in their efforts to internalize digital convergence through extensive vertical integration. The most successful strategies have emerged from companies adopting *horizontal solutions,* such as Microsoft in software and Intel in silicon.

Digital convergence further requires an appreciation for *externalities* and the art of creating standards. The growing importance of networks, especially of the Internet, means that no single firm or group of firms can capture all of the value embodied in the network. Some firms have discovered that Trojan horse strategies can set de facto standards, while others embrace and enhance open standards. Ironically, the firms best positioned to influence the emerging global standards may be the existing incumbents, not the start-ups who are pioneering these efforts. Today's dominant firms have the advantages of *scale economies* and the ability to bundle complementary technologies. However, incumbents can sustain their advantages only if they are willing and able to aggressively cannibalize their historic market positions.

Finally, CHESS means changing the basic organization of production. New business processes must emerge to handle the turbulence and uncertainty associated with next-generation technologies. Our research found that successful internal processes for the converging world will have to reflect at least two potentially conflicting imperatives: first, they have to be highly flexible and adaptive; and second, they must be very time-sensitive. Microsoft's *synch-and-stabilize* approach and Silicon Graphics' *system-focused product* development strategy are models to be emulated.

## DIGITAL CONVERGENCE

The topic of convergence has been around for decades. Forecasters have long predicted the coming of a digital age in which semiconductors, computing, communications, and other forms of electronics would converge into overlapping industries. In its simplest form, convergence means the uniting of the functions of the computer, the telephone, and the television set. Taken literally, the unification of functions could produce a massive reorganization of a trillion dollars in global business.

One of the corporate pioneers in evangelizing digital convergence was Japan's NEC Corporation. In 1977 the company first adopted "C&C" (Computers and Communications) as their corporate slogan and rallying cry (see figure 1-1).

NEC management foresaw many of the basic drivers pointing to convergence:

> As digital technology finds its rightful place in communications, communications technology will inevitably converge with computer functions, and communications networks will become capable of more effective transmission of information. With distributed processing systems linking a group of processing units, the computer will become highly systemized and inseparable from communications.[2]

The center of NEC's vision was semiconductor technology. Moving up the diagonal in figure 1-1, the progression from vacuum tubes to transistors to very-large-scale integrated (VLSI) circuits would drive computers toward distributed processing and communications toward digital networks. As computers became more powerful and ubiquitous, and communications became capable of handling rich data that could be digitized, such as facsimile and video, convergence would become a reality.

After NEC proclaimed the coming of digital convergence, many companies adopted similar slogans. For example, John Sculley, while chairman of Apple Computer in the early 1990s, displayed an alternative vision for information-based digital industries. Rather than focus on the underlying technology drivers from a provider's perspective, Sculley pictured convergence from the customer's perspective. In Sculley's view, telecommunications, office equipment, consumer electronics, media, and computers were separate and distinct industries through the 1990s, offering different services with different methods of delivery. But as the computer became an "information appliance," businesses would move to take advantage of emerging digital technologies, such as CD-ROMs and virtual reality, and industry boundaries would blur (see figure 1-2).

Conceptually, NEC, Apple, and many other firms have been delivering the same message: the development of key digital technologies allows companies to create new functionality and extend product features into new arenas. The problem has been predicting the appropriate time frame and the course of digital convergence. As figure 1-2 suggests, boundaries between industries are not collapsing but blurring at the edges. And while

FIGURE 1-1

## NEC's 1977 Vision of Computers and Communication

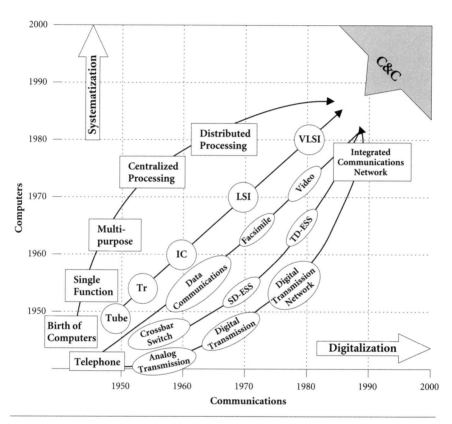

SOURCE: Adapted from NEC Corporation, *The First 80 Years* (Tokyo: NEC Corp., 1984), p. 82. © Koji Kobayashi, NEC Corporation. Reprinted with permission.

NEC's original diagram assumed convergence in the mid-1980s, later depictions moved the end point to the mid-1990s, and still later pictures show convergence at the turn of the century.

The uncertainty over time frames and industry boundaries is partly a function of different combinations of technologies progressing at different rates. Believing in long-run convergence should never imply a unilinear path. Some industries will converge before others, and some technologies will mature faster than others. Moreover, the mass acceptance of convergence requires content as well as infrastructure. Just as

FIGURE 1-2

## JOHN SCULLEY'S VISION FOR DIGITAL CONVERGENCE

Info Industry, 2001: Fusion Powered

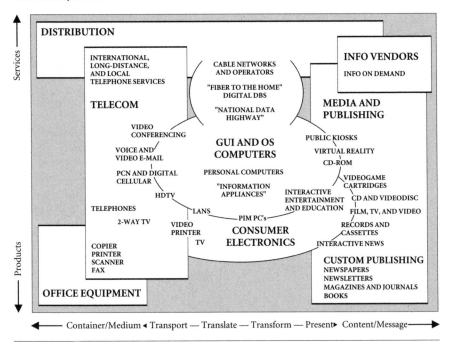

SOURCE: Adapted from a presentation by John Sculley at Harvard University, Program on Information Resources Policy, 1991.

the computer industry required killer applications to drive demand, much of the substantive content for business and consumers has yet to be delivered.

## The Drivers of Digital Convergence

The premise of this book is that we are closing in on digital convergence as we approach the twenty-first century, and three driving forces are accelerating these trends: semiconductor, software, and digital communications technologies; government deregulation; and managerial creativity. The inexorable expansion of computing power from the microprocessor, the inevitable decline in the price of bandwidth, and creative combinations of technologies and content will increasingly lead to new products and services with overlapping functionality.[3]

Most of the underlying technology and governmental drivers of this convergence are well understood. The place to begin is Moore's Law, named after Intel Corporation's chairman, Gordon Moore. In the 1960s, as a manager at Fairchild Semiconductor, Moore made a prediction that the power and capacity of integrated circuits would double approximately every eighteen months. Remarkably, Moore's Law has held true for thirty years. While the doubling cycle is now stretching out to almost two years, the basic principle remains: the price of computing power is becoming so cheap that it is virtually free. With only one chip costing a few hundred dollars, a product can perform most of the functions of a multimillion-dollar mainframe computer of fifteen years ago. Within the next ten years, microprocessors will have one hundred million transistors and will be capable of processing billions of instructions every second!

The declining cost of microprocessor power and the declining cost for memory and storage have enabled computers to become pervasive. Once the sole responsibility of the information technologist in a glass house, computers became ubiquitous on the corporate desktop and reached into thirty to forty million homes around the world. According to one estimate, 35 percent of American homes had computers by the end of 1994.[4] And America was not unique. Computers are spreading to the home throughout the world. Microsoft, for example, projected that 65 percent of the one million computers sold in Korea in 1994 went to the home.[5]

By making computing power cheap and ubiquitous, computers have already begun to envelop adjacent businesses, ranging from calculators to answering machines, and from electronic games to faxes. As semiconductors and related software become more powerful and cost less, they allow computers to take over a growing range of functions in the home and the office. In fact, computer and semiconductor technologies have an imperial nature: each new generation of chip grabs more functionality from related products, and each new generation of computer utilizes chip and software technology to conquer new businesses. For example, multimedia, once the sole domain of electronic games, has become part of the computer domain: 22 percent of all computers shipped in the world in 1994 had multimedia capabilities, up from only 1 percent two years earlier.[6]

Progress in communications has lagged somewhat behind the computer revolution. However, a combination of government deregulation and new transmission and software technologies is beginning to dramatically reduce the cost of delivering information. Traditionally, communications depended upon copper wires, called twisted pair, as conduits of information. These copper wires' limited capacity to move information (i.e., limited bandwidth) raised the costs of telecommunication services; in addition, complicated regulatory schemes around the world forced telecommunication vendors to cross-subsidize different forms of service for various customers. The dramatic reduction in costs for telecommunication services began with a global process of deregulation, which gained considerable momentum with the breakup of AT&T in the United States in 1984. As communications around the world move from monopoly provider to competitive service, prices will ultimately decline.

But just as important as deregulation is the advent of new technologies that undermine many of the traditional cost/price relationships in telecommunications and may accelerate the trends of deregulation. First, the explosion in wireless technology created the opportunity for anywhere, anytime communications. Second, coaxial cable, historically used for cable television, as well as the growing installation of fiber-optic cable, exploded the amount of bandwidth available to transmit voice, video, and data. While traditional phone lines could carry up to six million bits per second, fiber will ultimately carry more than one billion bits per second. The third technology driver is software compression, which can provide order-of-magnitude growth in bandwidth within each of these channels —copper, wireless, coaxial, or fiber. As communications companies lay fiber-optic cable and introduce software compression techniques, and as government regulatory barriers melt away the prohibitions that prevent phone and cable TV companies from meeting in the marketplace, the price of bandwidth should become as cheap as computing power. Once we can transmit all types of data, from anywhere to anyplace, at very low cost, the possibilities become virtually endless for the real-time linking of computers and communications.

Yet technology and deregulation alone will not lead to digital convergence. Computing and communication costs have been declining for decades, but the promise of digital convergence did not materialize in the 1970s, 1980s, or early 1990s. Much of the technological progress in computers, communications, and consumer electronics took place within established industry boundaries rather than across boundaries. A PC on every desk and in every home, high-bandwidth communications, or five hundred-channel television sets in every corner will not, by themselves, change the way we work, play, or organize our lives. We need creative business and home solutions to drive the market for converging technologies.

Thus the third driving force required for digital convergence is managerial creativity. Many of the early efforts by corporations to facilitate convergence relied on conventional views of technology, which stated that hardware firms needed software expertise, computer firms required communications capabilities, or communications firms needed to learn how to make computers. Like Says's Law, managers assumed that once they assembled the capabilities, "converged products" would emerge and supply would create its own demand. Yet most firms that followed this conventional approach lost spectacular sums of money in the name of digital convergence. The biggest failures have include the biggest names: IBM, with its failed acquisition of Rolm; AT&T, with its failed acquisition of NCR; and Matsushita's and Sony's disastrous acquisitions of MCA and Columbia Pictures, respectively.

Despite the large number of failures, activity to bring about convergence through brute force continues on a large scale. The most obvious indicator of this activity is the mergers, acquisitions, and alliance deals among communications, information, and entertainment companies. Collis, Bane, and Bradley catalog 508 multimedia alliances prior to 1993. Since that time, activity has increased. In 1994, for example, KMPG Peat Marwick reported that a record $27.8 billion was spent on multimedia acquisitions, and another $22 billion in the first half of 1995.[7] A partial analysis of investments and acquisitions made in the name of building capabilities for convergence during 1993, 1994, and the first half of 1995 suggests that more than $96 billion has been committed to projects in anticipation of convergence. As table 1-1 illustrates, the largest investments were made by telecommunications and entertainment companies. Almost half of these investments have been related to infrastructure and have been made by local telephone companies. Finally, while the computer companies have not been prominent among the largest deal makers to date, they have been investing aggressively in new product categories, such as personal digital assistants (PDAs),[8] PC videoconferencing,[9] and interactive television, that require substantial investments in R&D, manufacturing, and marketing. At the other end of the spectrum, start-up firms have been exploding onto the scene, looking to capitalize on technological discontinuities. Successful start-ups have focused on niche markets where established players have been too slow to respond, too tied to an existing customer base, or too committed to a single technological path.

Through the mid-1990s, start-ups have provided most of the managerial creativity for driving digital convergence. Perhaps the most powerful and widely cited example of this creativity is the Internet. Its history

TABLE 1-1

## INVESTMENTS IN MULTIMEDIA CAPABILITIES, 1993–1995 (IN MILLION DOLLARS)

| Year | Company | Amount | Details | Capital |
|------|---------|--------|---------|---------|
| | Ameritech | 4,400 | expansion project to bring switched interactive video to homes | budgeted |
| | AT&T | 5 | to Ziff-Davis for Interchange | spent |
| 1994 | PacTel, Bell Atlantic, NYNEX | 300 | with CAA to develop multimedia programs | budgeted |
| 1994 | Ameritech, Bell South, SBC | 500 | with Disney develop multimedia programming | budgeted |
| | Bell Atlantic | 11,000 | build broadband networks | budgeted |
| | Bell Atlantic | 1,500 | wire 8.5 million customers for video | budgeted |
| 1993 | Bell South | 300 | 22.5% stake in Prime Cable of Austin, TX | spent |
| | MCI | 2,000 | 13.5% stake in News Corp. over 4 years | budgeted |
| 1994 | Microsoft | 55 | investment in Mobile Telecommunications Technologies Corp. | spent |
| | Microsoft | 10 | with SBC Communications to test interactive services in Texas | under way |
| 1994 | NYNEX | 1,200 | investment in Viacom | spent |
| | NYNEX | 2,000 | per year investment to upgrade network | budgeted |
| | Pacific Telesis | 16,000 | create fiber-optic/coaxial network for interactive video in CA, NV | budgeted |
| | Prodigy | 1,000 | investment of IBM and Sears since 1984 | spent |
| 1993 | SBC Communications | 680 | purchase two suburban cable companies | spent |
| | SBC Communications | 1,000 | over 4 years to add multimedia capabilities | budgeted |
| | TCI Technology | 125 | 20% stake in Microsoft Network | spent |
| 1993 | US West | 2,500 | 25% stake in Time Warner | spent |
| | US West | 10,000 | 500,000 per year over 20 years to upgrade network capacity | budgeted |
| 1994 | US West | 1,200 | purchase two cable systems in Atlanta | spent |
| | Consortium of European railways | 600 | to build trans-European network with Global Telesystems group | budgeted |
| 1995 | Veba | 1,300 | 10% of British Telecom | budgeted |
| 1994 | Viacom | 10,000 | acquisition of Paramount | spent |
| 1995 | Disney | 19,000 | acquisition of Cap Cities/ABC | budgeted |
| 1995 | Time Warner | 8,000 | acquisition of Turner Broadcasting | budgeted |
| 1995 | MCI | 2,000 | 13.5% stake in News Corporation | budgeted |
| | Total Investment | $96,675 | | |

SOURCES: Various issues of *The Economist; Broadcasting & Cable;* and *Media Week.*

clearly suggests more about the creative drive of companies and entrepreneurs than about the role of technology and government. When Vice President Al Gore stimulated interest in an information superhighway in 1992–1993, the initial response was for government and telecommunications giants to build the highway of fiber optics, coaxial cable, and large-scale transmission systems, much like the government-sponsored interstate highway system in the 1950s and 1960s. It took entrepreneurs to realize that the technology and infrastructure already existed for most of the functionality promised by Gore's superhighway.

The Internet had very modest beginnings. Started in the late 1960s, it was an arcane technology that served as a communication vehicle for scientific laboratories and universities. As late as 1983, there were only five hundred "host" Internet sites in the world. As local area networks expanded within corporations and universities, people began to discover the power of E-mail—the ability to use computers as an inexpensive communication tool. By tapping into the Internet, more universities, research labs, and a limited number of companies recognized the possibilities of communicating with E-mail across organizations, rather than only within. However, it was not until the creation of the World Wide Web (WWW) and software tools to browse the Internet that demand exploded (see figure 1-3). The WWW is no technological breakthrough; rather, it is a simple technology built around a set of software protocols,

FIGURE 1-3

**CURRENT AND FORECASTED INTERNET USERS (IN MILLIONS)**

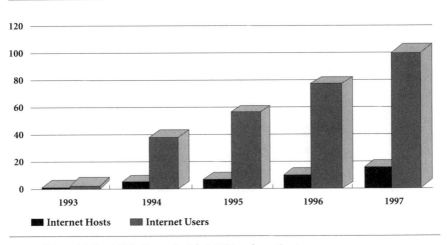

SOURCE: "Network Wizards," *The Economist*, July 1, 1995; author estimates.

called hypertext, that allow multiple documents to be linked and rich data (text, pictures, and even video) to be transmitted. When creatively combined with Web browsers, like Mosaic and Netscape, the WWW on the Internet became available to any nontechnical user who owned a computer and a modem, and could point and click a mouse. Suddenly communications, computing, and various forms of entertainment and business information were integrated into one medium.

## A CHESS STRATEGY FOR DIGITAL CONVERGENCE

The rapid acceptance of the Internet has stimulated enormous excitement in digital convergence. A database search for the word "Internet" discovered 2,475 stories in newspapers in only one month in late 1994, as well as 230 books with "Internet" in the title.[10] During the trial of O. J. Simpson, twenty-four thousand articles appeared on him, compared to thirty-nine thousand articles written about the Internet! Another indication is the excitement over companies selling Internet software and services. By August 1995, investors had bid up the price of four start-up software companies, with only $34 million in combined revenues, to a breathtaking valuation of $4.5 billion.[11] Before year-end 1995, Netscape alone had reached a market capitalization of more than $6 billion. Indeed, the Internet has made convergence feel real to many people. If it can be fully exploited, there are almost endless possibilities for hardware, software, and communication combinations. This is why Collis, Bane, and Bradley argue in chapter 4 that convergence will drive a massive restructuring of consumer electronics, entertainment, and telecommunications industries.

But in the process of restructuring, the opportunities for disappointment are equally vast. Chapters 6, 7, and 8 identify huge barriers to adoption of such technologies. Weak intellectual property regimes, inertia, and the lack of standards and compelling value-added services could greatly slow the spread of many of these new technologies. Moreover, very few companies have developed a business model that demonstrates that a firm can make money and create sustainable competitive advantages in these new intersecting technologies.

In fact, historian Alfred Chandler points out in chapter 2 that established companies in electronics have fared less well, and start-up firms have been particularly prominent, compared with other major industries like chemicals, pharmaceuticals, and aerospace.[12] During the introductory phase of new information technologies, like the creation of the personal computer, the development of the computer workstation, and the emergence of the Internet, barriers to entry seem to disintegrate for a period of time, leaving a window of opportunity for new players to pioneer new segments. Digital Equipment (DEC), for instance, was the start-up that pioneered the minicomputer in the 1960s; Apple, which started in a garage, pioneered the PC industry in the late 1970s; and Apollo and Sun Microsystems, both start-ups, pioneered the stand-alone workstation in the 1980s. During each of these discontinuities, many incumbents failed: GE, RCA, and Honeywell never completed successful transitions to mainframes or minicomputers; and Prime Computer and Wang could not make the transition from minicomputers to workstations or PCs.

But an important observation in chapter 2 is that after each discontinuity, there were always a few large incumbents that retained significant status across technological generations. In minicomputers, IBM ultimately responded to DEC, becoming the world leader; and despite a miserable record in the late 1980s and early 1990s, IBM was the world leader in PCs from 1981 until 1993. Even in workstations, only Sun Microsystems and Silicon Graphics have survived as significant players as the industry has consolidated around the former minicomputer incumbents Hewlett-Packard, DEC, and IBM.

After each of these previous transitions, a significant consolidation took place. Economies of scale, network externalities, and the need for standards, all of which are discussed later in this chapter, made it difficult for the majority of start-ups and small competitors to survive. In fact, history tells us that in similar industries characterized by many start-ups, survival rates tend to be low.[13] For example, several hundred firms entered the automobile industry in the United States around the turn of the century, but only three firms survived half a century later; and more than 150 firms entered the new television industry in its first decade in the 1950s, but no independent American players were left by 1995. Similar dynamics are likely in industries characterized by digital convergence: start-ups will pioneer a thousand niches, but we can anticipate a sea of red ink when the mania ends and the shakeouts begin.

Our research, which focuses mainly on the computer industry, suggests that incumbents and start-ups alike need a CHESS strategy to master the intricacies of digital convergence. The computer industry is a logical starting point, if for no other reason than that computers have become the centerpiece of the digital revolution. There has been considerable debate since in the early 1990s about the role of the TV set, new handheld devices, or Internet appliances as the linchpin of convergence, but computers have emerged as the dominant access and manipulation device for digital information. While the computer industry has some unique features that will not be directly applicable to all converging sectors, many of the underlying dynamics observed by the authors in this book will have substantial impact as we move toward a digital world.

## CHESS: "C" Stands for Creative Combinations

The first lesson we observed across many of our industry studies was that success in this new world is most likely to be fueled by companies that exploit "creative combinations"—of old and new technologies, old and new channels of distribution, and old and new corporate capabilities.[14] The idea of creative combinations flies in the face of strategies being pursued by many firms in the name of digital convergence. Like the start-ups pouring into the industry, numerous managers see convergence as an opportunity to redefine the battlefield through radical innovations. They see convergence delivering Joseph Schumpeter's promise of "creative destruction."[15] Following this line of reasoning, firms like Sony—with its acquisition of Columbia Pictures, AT&T—with its acquisition of NCR, and Bell Atlantic—with its failed mega-acquisition of TCI, have been seeking the great new idea or grand combination that can be used to create a new digital era, sweeping away the existing order. Early efforts to pioneer the personal digital assistant and to build the broadband, interactive television service are a few of the examples discussed in detail in this book that sought "creative destruction."

But in the search for creative destruction, we cannot lose sight of Schumpeter's equally important insight that prior to creative destruction, entrepreneurs who "have created no original means of production" will flourish by carrying out "new combinations" that take existing approaches and use them "more appropriately, more advantageously."[16] While creative destruction may be the "end" of this process, it is not necessarily the means. In fact, the lessons of the computer revolution are that many of the greatest commercial successes were creative combinations of available technologies with new models of doing business. The breakthroughs of the personal computer and the technical workstation, for example, were largely functions of managerial creativity combined with much earlier breakthroughs in semiconductor technology rather than a breakthrough in the technology itself. As *Scientific American* reminded us in its survey of twenty-first-century technologies, "Even the greatest ideas and inventions can flounder, whereas more modest steps forward sometimes change the world."[17]

Big bets on radical innovation and creative destruction have worked for many technologies in the past. The IBM System 360, which revolutionized the computer industry in the early 1960s, was a $5 billion investment that bet the company. Media firms, such as Malone's TCI and Murdoch's Fox Broadcasting and Sky TV, and Time Warner have bet billions of dollars since the 1970s to build infrastructure and programming. And billions are being invested in the 1990s to push out the technological frontier of semiconductors, software, communications, and consumer electronics. Enormous technological progress is in the offing, much of which will require large-scale investment. While the payoffs to these investments should be commensurate with the risks, the highest returns to these types of strategies seem to lie largely within existing industry boundaries.

Similar strategies are far more difficult in converging technologies because they require firms to master a far broader array of technologies and markets that often extend beyond their sphere of competence. Gomes-Casseres and Leonard-Barton describe in chapter 9 how firms try to solve this problem by building broad-based alliance networks that try to leverage the competencies of others. But as the authors found in the PDA market, alliances are no panacea for the competency problem. Coordinating and exploiting multiple competencies across multiple firms has proven extremely difficult.

The power of creative combinations of new and old technologies, new and old methods of production and marketing, and so on, is that the resulting products and services can open entirely new markets while simultaneously exploiting more leverage from existing skills and competencies. Moreover, when creative combinations start as complements to the installed base, working in concert with existing technologies, the adoption rates are likely to be faster and switching costs lower. Historically, many of the visions of convergence, such as broadband digital communications, required large infrastructure investments prior to market development. These visions assumed that if a new infrastructure existed, it would drive the market for new technologies and services. Yet chapter 5 points out that most people have assumed that convergence means substitution; that is, as technologies converge, a new technology will create substitutes for old products or services. Greenstein and Khanna explain that convergence often can begin with complements. In addition, substitutes and complements should not be seen as mutually exclusive. Personal computers began as complements to minicomputers and mainframes, only to emerge later as possible substitutes.

We have numerous examples of creative combinations winning battles for next-generation technologies. Particularly poignant is Baldwin and Clark's analysis of the workstation wars in chapter 3. They find that Sun's pioneering effort to create the workstation business was largely the result of off-the-shelf technologies' being put together in ways not previously contemplated by the existing players. Sun originally caught its competitors flat-footed: companies such as IBM, DEC, and Hewlett-Packard had grown up in a mainframe paradigm, which meant closed, proprietary systems. By utilizing existing microprocessor technology, existing operating systems (UNIX), and only a few key proprietary components, Sun was able to break the mainframe paradigm within a new segment. In the short run, Sun pioneered a new way of doing business as much as it pioneered new technology; and over the long run, Sun has helped to foment a revolution in computing that is "creatively destroying" the minicomputer business and the low-end mainframe business. A similar pattern occurred at Silicon Graphics.[18]

By contrast, the firms we studied that sought to change the rules with breakthrough technologies, looking for new products and technologies that would change the world, were far less successful. The two chapters on PDAs, for example, point out that the most successful products on the market have come from companies, such as Sharp and Hewlett-Packard, that made product line extensions of their traditional personal organizers, rather than from Apple and AT&T, which were trying to break new ground from top to bottom. The Apple Newton, in particular, was an effort to revolutionize the computer paradigm with brand-new system architecture, operating systems, and form factors. In the aftermath of the Newton's early failures, John Sculley confided that he had learned a great deal from the Newton experience.[19] First among many lessons was that creatively extending existing technologies offered much higher probabilities of success than pioneering from scratch. In fact, Sculley noted that most of Apple Computer's greatest successes had come from creative combinations of established and somewhat new technologies. After all, the heart of Apple Computer was the Macintosh, which borrowed extensively from ideas developed almost a decade earlier at Xerox PARC. And Apple's biggest success in the early 1990s was another creative combination—the Powerbook, which introduced Mac features, some software enhancements, and a new industrial design into existing notebook technologies.

Creative combination strategies that focus initially on complementary products, services, and technologies have the further advantage that they generally try to offer some degree of compatibility with the installed base. In a converging world, where communications is an essential component, some degree of compatibility becomes required. It is possible to introduce a new stand-alone computer or a new stand-alone consumer electronic product with few concerns about compatibility. Because of an installed base of prior technologies, switching costs may still be high (e.g., it took years to move consumers from records to the much higher-quality digital CDs),[20] but clear product superiority with a significant enhancement in consumer value can ultimately drive acceptance. In a converging world, the inability to communicate with an installed base, no matter how superior the product, service, or technology, greatly increases those switching costs. The Internet is a classic example of creative combinations of old and new technologies that developed a mass appeal, at least in part, because it was a complement to virtually the entire installed base of computers in the world. With only the addition of a modem, people working on a Macintosh, PC, or workstation could connect and gain comparable access to rich data. On-line services also began as complements to the Internet. While the Internet might ultimately substitute for many alternative products and services, complementarities between on-line services and the Web greatly reduce the barriers to acceptance.

## CHESS: "H" Stands for Horizontal Solutions

A second pattern emphasized throughout the volume is that scale economies, government deregulation, and technology are driving the information industry toward a horizontal structure and away from a vertical orientation. In industry after industry, the traditional vertical integration adopted by firms in the consumer electronics and computer industries is being replaced by a horizontal model, where competition is between components firms. Under the old model, a company such as IBM or Fujitsu would make the vast majority of components in-house and sell a complete package to the consumer. This model was viable in the era of the mainframe because proprietary, closed products created a one-stop shop for the customer, which in turn generated very high margins for the dominant players. These margins could be reinvested in every stage of the value chain. As long as firms had significant market share, they could build adequate economies of scale in R&D and manufacturing to remain cost-competitive. (See figure 1-4.) The vertical model was also attractive because it prevented firms with specialized and complementary assets from appropriating a disproportionate share of the value.

Several years ago, the CEO of Intel, Andrew Grove, argued that a new horizontal model had emerged (see figure 1-5). The winners in this model

FIGURE 1-4

THE "OLD" COMPUTER INDUSTRY
**Vertically Integrated Firms Competing Across All Segments**

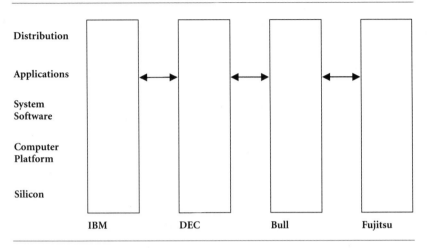

SOURCES: Adapted from Intel documents and *The Economist.*

are the firms that have a large, and usually dominant, market share within a horizontal layer. High profits are a function of the new economics of computers: growing scale economies and the rising importance of network externalities drive firms to dominate a horizontal layer, such as operating systems, disk drives, LCD screens, or microprocessors. Once a firm controls a large share of the horizontal layer, it then works through creative combinations with other complementary firms to deliver a product to the final consumer.[21] The economics that drive the horizontal structure are compelling: in active-matrix LCD screens, approximately $400 million is required to build just one high-volume, state-of-the-art factory;[22] in microprocessors, it typically takes three years to develop a new generation of chips and then costs roughly $2 billion to build just one high-volume, state-of-the-art plant; and it costs approximately $500 million, and several years, to build a state-of-the-art operating system. Few firms can justify these types of expenditures if they are serving only a vertical, captive market. Microsoft's Windows 95, for instance, has roughly eleven million lines of codes, and took more than four thousand man-years and more than four years elapsed time to develop. Beyond the up-front investment, an operating system (OS) must attract large numbers of independent software vendors (ISVs) to write applications. Microsoft alone spends more than $60 million annually, with five

FIGURE 1-5

## THE 1995 COMPUTER INDUSTRY
## Fragmented, Horizontal Competition

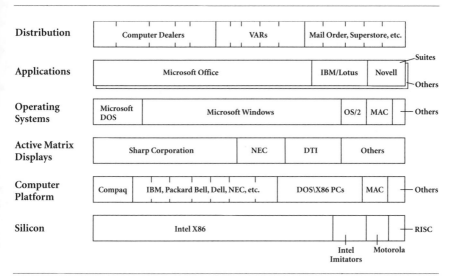

SOURCES: Adapted from Intel documents; *The Economist;* and Department of Defense, *Building U.S. Capabilities in Flat Panel Displays* (October 1994).

hundred dedicated engineers, to support one hundred thousand ISVs.[23] Apple Computer's decision to license its operating system in 1994 and pursue a more horizontal model was a belated recognition of these economics.

There is considerable debate as to whether a similar transition to the horizontal model will take place in the telecommunications, consumer electronics, and entertainment pieces of the business. On the one hand, many media and telecommunications companies have been investing large sums to increase their vertical integration in the 1990s, most notably Disney, with its acquisition of Cap Cities-ABC. Many of these efforts have been made in the name of preventing the downstream players from extracting excess profits. On the other hand, economies of scale and deregulation could drive the telecommunications and consumer electronics firms toward a horizontal structure similar to that of computers. In telecommunications, government regulations historically required vertical solutions in most countries around the world. At the same time, most consumer electronics firms integrated vertically because they were offering pioneering technologies that required unique components and software that were unavailable on the open market. Bradley, Bane, and

Collis (figure 1-6) suggest that these rationales are dissipating, just as they did in computers. Deregulation will increasingly allow telecommunications firms to offer complete solutions by creatively combining internal resources with external products and services. And growing economies of scale at the component level, and the emergence of independent semiconductor and software industries, have eliminated many of the forces compelling consumer electronics firms to make the products in-house. Indeed, AT&T's decision in 1995 to break itself into three pieces, dividing telecommunications services from telecommunications hardware and computers, is testimony to the difficulties of extensive vertical integration in an era of convergence.

If a horizontal structure does indeed emerge, several authors in the book point out that horizontally configured industries are no panacea. In fact, one of the biggest obstacles to digital convergence is overcoming the inherent weaknesses of the horizontal model. The biggest advantage to a vertical structure is that firms can usually offer the customer a highly coordinated package of goods and services. Vertically integrated firms have the advantage of lower transactions costs—that is, suppliers and customers need to deal with only a limited number of vendors. Having to contract separately for every service and component can raise the costs of doing business, raise prices to consumers, and, in many cases, produce inferior products because of the multitude of opportunities for things to

FIGURE 1-6

EMERGING INDUSTRY STRUCTURE

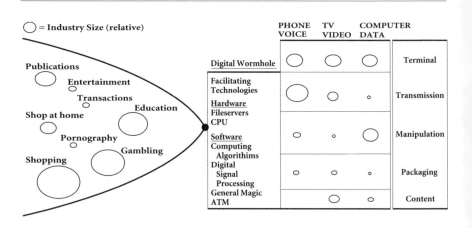

SOURCE: Figure 4-1 in this volume.

go wrong. Bresnahan and Saloner point out in chapter 7 that coordination is usually easy in a vertical market because one vendor takes responsibility. At the same time, coordination can be a nightmare in a horizontal model. While the customer can pick and choose the best pieces or components in a horizontal industry, it requires a high degree of coordination, common interfaces, and standards. Over time, consumer electronics companies solved this problem with "plug and play" standards: virtually any stereo component can be attached to virtually any speakers, CD players, and so on. However, this ability to create common interfaces across horizontal layers has not yet emerged within the PC paradigm, not to mention the broader world of communications and consumer electronics converging with PCs. If the horizontal model spreads to the new converging technologies, it stands to reason that dominant market share within a horizontal slice and the ability to "plug and play" or create standard interfaces across horizontal layers and converging technologies will become the key drivers of competitive success.

## CHESS: "E" Stands for Exploiting Externalities to Set Global Standards

It has become a cliché to pronounce that winners in this new digital world will set and control the standards. But firms that set important standards, create the dominant designs, or control a dominant architecture[24] may be even more important in converging industries than they were in PCs or consumer electronics. Unlike the stand-alone products of the early consumer electronics industry or the early personal computer industry, competition in the new digital industries will revolve around networks and communication. If there are multiple standards, there will be less ability to communicate and interact. In addition, the lack of common interfaces, particularly in a horizontal market structure, slows market acceptance. As chapters 6 and 7 suggest, customers resist adoption of new architectures, like client-server computing, or new products, like PDAs, if there are multiple, competing standards, a lack of complementary assets (software or hardware), and expectations of eventual shakeouts. In the absence of compelling strategic needs, most customers prefer to wait.

A related reason for the crucial importance of standards is the role of network effects or network externalities. To overcome consumer resistance, new converging technologies require a wide array of complementary products and services: on-line services and the World Wide Web, five hundred TV channels, and CD-ROMs need content; PDAs, PCs, and smart telephones need a wide range of software; and so on. As we learned from the histories of computers and consumer electronics, the variety and range of available software and services increase as the "network" or number of users grows. In fact, what makes network effects so crucial is that they create virtuous cycles: a growing variety of CD titles induces additional buyers to purchase CD hardware, and as the installed base of CD hardware expands, there are greater incentives to produce more CD titles. Or in the case of Microsoft's OSs, as the installed base of Windows users expands, more ISVs want to write applications for Windows, and as more applications become available for Windows, more users want to adopt the OS.

Network effects also are important because they drive down the costs of learning, distribution, and service. As the installed base of a single standard grows, friends and coworkers teach each other how to use the product. In addition, as volume goes up, distribution and service capabilities spread. With multiple standards, a higher degree of sales and service support is required. But a single standard reduces sales and support costs for the user as well as the provider. For example, before IBM set a clear standard in PCs, full-service dealers were necessary to educate the consumer and service the products. But once the IBM-compatible standard was well established in the second half of the 1980s, the channels of distribution exploded in the United States: value-added resellers, direct marketers, and mass merchandisers supplemented the full-service dealers of the early 1980s, driving down the margins for the middlemen and making the products more accessible. This pattern contrasts sharply with Japan, where multiple PC standards have existed, resulting in much less development of local software and far fewer channels of distribution.[25]

The role of standards in converging industries is further reinforced because of the threats of "lockin" and "lockout."[26] "Lockin" means that once firms and customers make a commitment to a particular path, it becomes increasingly difficult to change course. Once a standard is set, the customer sinks so much investment in complementary assets and training that it is often cheaper to stick with the known migration path than to reincur start-up costs and move down a new, and sometimes superior, technology path.[27] When companies started buying IBM's solution for mainframe computing in the 1960s, they got locked in for decades. The IBM customer built mission-critical applications around the IBM product, and any effort to move away from that one solution could, at worst, bring an operation to a halt and, at best, cost millions of dollars to change. A similar pattern has been created by Microsoft and Intel. Both companies have locked in the majority of computer users because, like corporate investments in IBM's mainframes, so much time, money, and energy have been spent on buying hardware based on Intel architecture, and training corporate personnel on DOS or Windows-based software, that few customers have been eager to switch. And, finally, much of the excitement over Netscape—the dominant provider of WWW browser software—is a function of Netscape's ability to set a de facto standard. By giving away its browser, Netscape took a page directly from Microsoft's early history to build an installed base of almost 70 percent of Internet users. If Netscape can retain market share by building more functionality and complements around its product, it, too, may lock in its customers for future generations.

The dangers of "lockout" are an equally important strategic problem for firms in converging industries. If a company is not part of a standard, it can be excluded from participating in the growth and profits that historically have been earned by standard-bearers, such as IBM and Microsoft. In addition, many of the investments required to be successful in any given technology generation are highly specific. A decision not to invest in the current generation may be much more expensive to reverse in the next generation.

The fear of lockout helps to explain the herd mentality that has been so pervasive in the battles for converging industries. When Apple first introduced the concept of the PDA in 1992, for example, there was pandemonium in computer, telecommunications, and consumer electronics circles. What if Apple could create a standard around the Newton? Could Apple become the next Microsoft of the converging world, locking out competitors? Fearing the answer, dozens of firms around the world almost immediately announced that similar products were in the offing. Semiconductor companies started designing chip sets for this unknown market; software companies began research on PDA applications and announced alternative OSs; computer companies announced that they, too, would have handheld devices at a future date. A similar pattern occurred when Apple announced its intentions to reinvent the television set with set-top boxes for televisions. Companies ranging from Oracle and Sun Microsystems to Microsoft and Intel rapidly responded.

This herd mentality and fear of lockout explain why it is so difficult for individual or small numbers of companies to set or control new standards. Most of the successful standard setters have gained control over global standards by following Trojan horse strategies: they innocently proliferate their products in the early stages of maturity, make the technology a de facto standard, and then appropriate returns once the standard grows. Intel's original strategy for its X86 microprocessor architecture, Microsoft's original DOS strategy, and Netscape's browser strategy were all reminiscent of Trojan horses. Few managers understood the importance of the microprocessor, the PC operating system, or the Web browser at the outset, and in the beginning, none of these firms was making significant profits from these products. But each hoped that its standard would catch on before the latent value of the standard attracted direct competition. In 1995, Sun Microsystems sought to give away Java, its highly touted software language for the Internet, in the same spirit that Netscape gave away its browser. Sun's challenge will be that the Trojan horse has been uncovered, and new competitors quickly emerged.

A second approach to standards has been to embrace open standards, to try to enhance them, and, in some cases, ultimately to lead them. Compaq, the world's largest personal computer company as of 1994, has largely followed this model with great success over its first ten years. While the market-share leaders in PCs, Apple and IBM, had been trying to set new standards since the mid-1980s, Compaq's success was based on embracing and enhancing the standards set by Microsoft, Intel, and others. Whenever Compaq tried to build a new standard, as it did with the ACE consortium in the early 1990s, it failed. Microsoft followed a similar strategy in response to the Internet in late 1995. After initially trying to create a proprietary approach, Microsoft management decided to embrace fully the existing Internet standards, with the hope of ultimately influencing their long-term direction.

A third approach to standards has been to proclaim the standard and try to implement it through brute force. While this worked for IBM with the original IBM PC, it has rarely worked in the last fifteen years. In the early 1980s, IBM had roughly 60 percent of the world computer market, which allowed it to set de facto standards through unilateral moves. In the 1990s, no company—not Intel, Microsoft, IBM, AT&T, or any other firm in the broad realm of information technology, communications, or consumer electronics—has the kind of market power that IBM had in the early 1980s. Moreover, ex post, everyone sees the rewards reaped by Intel and Microsoft as standard-bearers; thus, ex ante, the competition for setting new standards has become fierce.

This herd mentality has meant that virtually every effort to set a new proprietary standard in the late 1980s and 1990s has been met by ferocious resistance and countervailing movements. In consumer electronics, for example, Sony and Philips Electronics, the two losers in the VCR standard battle, tried to create a new standard for digital video disks in 1995. They were immediately challenged, however, by Time Warner and Toshiba, as well as their twenty-five partner corporations around the world. Ultimately, the warring parties compromised on a relatively open standard under which no serious contender would be locked out. In computer workstations, Baldwin and Clark describe Sun Microsystems' efforts to create a new workstation standard around its version of UNIX and its own RISC microprocessor. Although Sun charged into the lead in workstations, other major competitors refused to adopt its proposed standards. As a group, the major vendors united to oppose Sun on UNIX; and as individual companies, they tried to create their own RISC microprocessor standard. Similarly, chapter 6 reports that Apple and AT&T wanted to create new standards around their PDAs, but, like Sun, they met significant resistance: both companies proclaimed an "open" standard, but both retained significant proprietary components. The proprietary approach plus the lack of momentum behind their products reduced the appeal for widespread adoption of their standards. Even Netscape, with its spectacular success at swiftly building a huge installed base, has faced rapid responses from Microsoft and a host of start-ups that want to prevent Netscape from creating a new, potentially proprietary standard.

## CHESS: "S" Stands for Scale and Scope

Industries with standards have a unique problem, which is often described as "the tyranny of the installed base." The history of computers, telecommunications, and consumer electronics tells us that the sheer size of the installed base can generate excessive inertia and resistance to change, even when better solutions are available. As this tyranny plays out in converging industries, it leads to another imperative: firms must reach large economies of scale within core horizontal businesses, and find ways to leverage those economies into adjacent markets. Similar to Alfred Chandler's findings in his classic work on modern capitalism, *Scale and Scope*, we suggest that companies that build scale (e.g., create large numbers in the installed base) and expand their scope (e.g., bundle technologies and services into adjacent horizontal layers) can build more enduring competitive advantages for future generations.

Scale has become critical partly because of the forces driving standards and horizontal markets described above. But scale requirements are emerging from other sources as well. Perhaps most important is the reality of globalization. Computers, communications, and consumer electronics are global businesses today. The huge size of the customer base, which now numbers more than two hundred million installed personal computers with a 386, 486, or Pentium microprocessor, gives at least two advantages to incumbent companies with scale: one, it generates a huge annuity from servicing the installed base, which supports large ongoing investments; two, network externalities make defection by customers and complements very difficult.[28] The numbers supporting a particular standard can become so large, and the momentum so great, that the reasons to switch standards must be overwhelming. Thus Microsoft, owner of the dominant OS standard, can ship about ten million copies of its new OS (Windows 95) to its distributors prior to release, and expect to sell out in a few months. This allows Microsoft to break even on a roughly half-billion-dollar investment in less than a year. Meanwhile, IBM, with a technically superior product (OS/2) but less than 10 percent of the installed base, could not break even or sell ten million copies of its OS in its eight-year life. Furthermore, Microsoft's presence in the installed base is so great that many natural complements for converging industries will be attracted to Microsoft. Whether it be NBC, Wal-Mart, or MCI, most firms with complementary products that are looking for a digital partner naturally turn to Microsoft because of its scale and presence.

While scale economies may be necessary for long-run success, they are not sufficient. Convergence is about the coming together of diverse technologies and capabilities. Firms with broad scope can gain an advantage over narrowly focused firms if they can bring together competencies through bundling their products into adjacent markets. When an incumbent company dominates a standard in a horizontal layer, it will be easier for that firm to influence standards in closely related technologies. Bundling, for example, allows the incumbent to add functionality incrementally, incorporating more of the value into the dominant products or services. In a world of revolutionary technological change, bundling might not be successful: new firms and capabilities could destroy the sources of advantage for the incumbent. But in a world of creative combinations, bundling closely related products gives the incumbent a leg up. The incumbent should have superior information about existing products and demand, which should help point toward the appropriate bundle. In addition, incumbents have greater incentives to create and bundle complementary products, especially if they expand primary demand. While a de novo entrant must realize a return on a stand-alone basis, incumbents may be willing to bundle complements, as long as the complements help to generate incremental sales of the core product. Finally, as computers become more modular, a feature described in depth in chapter 3, the move to adjacent layers becomes even easier. Modularity and bundling can facilitate a strategy of fast following: start-ups may pioneer new categories and segments, but as long as those new categories and segments are in an adjacent layer, the incumbent's existing credibility with the customer base should provide it with a natural advantage.

IBM's success in the 1960s, 1970s, and early 1980s is a model of using the installed base and bundling to retain dominance in each new category of computing that emerged over the three decades. In the late 1980s and the 1990s, Microsoft is one of the best examples of a company exploiting the incumbent's advantage. In the early 1980s, Microsoft began with software tools and operating systems. Lotus Development was the leader in applications, followed by WordPerfect. Over time, Microsoft moved into applications, then applications suites, ultimately garnering close to an 80 percent market share in suites. Similarly, while not the pioneer in CD-ROMs and multimedia applications, Microsoft was able to leverage its competencies in applications, its original equipment manufacturer (OEM) relationships, and its power in the retail channel to become the overall volume leader in CD-ROMs in 1994.[29] And as Microsoft's new operating system, Windows 95, has proliferated, it has created a potential competitive advantage for the Internet Explorer, a bundled World Wide Web browser.

Scale and scope, however, do not guarantee dominance for large incumbents in converging industries, or even in the next generation of technology within an existing industry boundary. In many cases, it is unclear, ex ante, which firm is the natural incumbent and which scale and scope economies are most relevant. In PDAs, for instance, computer companies like Apple, telecommunications companies like AT&T, and consumer electronics companies like Casio all laid claim to incumbency. In PC videoconferencing, companies with core businesses in semiconductors, computers, telecommunications, and existing room videoconferencing each believe they are the natural incumbents. In both of these cases, all of them are right: each firm and industry has a set of competencies and skills it brings to the table. Yet no one has won in either arena because no firm or industry has found mechanisms for creatively combining their *existing* assets and skills with the *new* assets and skills required to develop products or services of significant value. Thus, *World Book* and *Encyclopaedia Britannica* might have been seen as the logical incumbents for the multimedia encyclopedia because they controlled a valuable existing asset: encyclopedia content. But it was Microsoft (a different type of incumbent) that emerged to dominate the segment. Microsoft won because it was more aggressive in adapting its software skills with a strategy to acquire someone else's existing asset.

This leads to another caveat: having the advantages of scale and scope does not equate with competency. IBM's failure to sustain its incumbent advantages in the late 1980s and early 1990s demonstrates how an incumbent with scale and scope can become fragile. Similarly, Microsoft's strategy to bundle Microsoft Network with Windows 95 creates an advantage by offering greater distribution. Since customer acquisition costs are among the highest costs for an on-line service, this potential advantage is significant. But Microsoft Network will fail if the company cannot find a way to exploit the Internet or match its competitors' content and ease of use.

Moreover, scale and scope can be a liability to incumbents in converging industries if the firms do not develop a capability for rapid change and a willingness to cannibalize their businesses. The history of information technology provides very clear lessons on this point: if you have the capability to cannibalize your own product lines and choose not to, someone else surely will. The danger of refusing to cannibalize your own sales is that when new products or technologies emerge as substitutes, they get locked in and you get locked out. The strategic question of cannibalization is not one of "if"; it is only a question of "when." Baldwin and Clark's discussion of Apollo's refusal to pursue a nonproprietary, UNIX-based workstation aggressively in the mid-1980s because it would cannibalize its proprietary workstation sales was a disaster; similarly, IBM's refusal to use its best technology for its first technical workstation, the PC RT, for fear it would cannibalize its AS\400 sales, was an unmitigated failure. In all of these cases, and many others offered in the book, firms that did not aggressively capitalize on new technologies found their businesses floundering and their market shares under attack. Whenever the technology was possible, other firms would find a way to utilize it. Ed McCracken, the CEO of Silicon Graphics, captures the essence of his incumbent's advantage in this quote from chapter 11:

> The source of our competitiveness in this industry is our ability to manage in a chaotic environment. But it's more proactive than that. We actually help create the chaos in the first place—that's what keeps a lot of potential competitors out.

## CHESS: "S" Stands for System-Focused Processes

So far, I have described how industries, firms, and technology strategies have to adjust to take advantage of digital convergence. The last two chapters of the book suggest that internal processes within the firm also will have to make dramatic adjustments. Highly uncertain technologies with equally uncertain market outcomes can wreak havoc on organizations. This is particularly true when significant competitive and market shifts take place during the process of development. Research, development, and market introduction methodologies that worked well within an existing paradigm, with relatively predictable cycles, are unlikely to work in highly turbulent environments. As a result, successful internal processes for the converging world will have to reflect at least two potentially conflicting imperatives: first, they have to be highly flexible and adaptive; and second, they must be very time-sensitive.

The conflict between these two imperatives is that "flexible and adaptive" is often interpreted as flexible deadlines as well as flexible projects, while hard-and-fast deadlines usually mean rigid implementation programs. In software, for example, Cusumano and Smith describe the traditional waterfall model of production, in which products were specified, detailed designs were created, and modules were constructed, tested, then reworked. This approach was highly structured, and it required a very powerful up-front process that accurately developed user requirements and product concepts. A similar development process exists within many hardware industries, described by Iansiti, that demanded clear separations between concept development and implementation.

The authors in this volume found that these types of structured processes tend to be suboptimal in highly uncertain, dynamic environments. Sequential processes are more orderly, but they do not allow the organization to react to new information and adapt quickly during implementation. The answer is a set of processes that are more *iterative* (i.e., they start with a broad vision and allow for new information to be integrated into product design) and *system-focused* (i.e., they focus on tight integration of the entire project rather than its component pieces) while retaining milestones and forcing deadlines on the organization.

Cusumano and Smith, in their study of Microsoft, and Iansiti, in his study of Silicon Graphics, found that both companies had pioneered new iterative development processes that allowed management to be much more flexible than traditional hardware and software systems did, while allowing for greater creativity and teamwork. For Microsoft, its *synch-and-stabilize* approach allowed it to gather information throughout the development process, interpret new data, and then react to manufacture products that were more feature rich and acceptable to customers than those of their competition. For Silicon Graphics, its *system-focused product development strategy* allowed for fluid specifications late into the development project, thus ultimately producing higher-performance systems. Both companies also benefited from strong project leadership, including the involvement of senior management in setting the vision for the projects, as well as a highly developed synchronization system that allowed for the coordination of large numbers of individuals and teams.

Yet for both Microsoft and Silicon Graphics, retaining fluid, adaptive development processes was not enough. Disciplined milestones were equally critical. While time-to-market is always important, new technologies in converging industries must pass through a whole spectrum of windows: there are technical windows, where standards are formulated; there are competitive windows, where competing products or services are not yet available; there are financial windows, where debt and equity markets are more accessible; and there are marketing windows, where brand, distribution, and pricing options are relatively open. The lesson of "lockout" is that these windows have limited life, and when they close, even superior products can be preempted. While Microsoft has had an incumbent's advantage that has allowed it to miss the announced release date for products like Windows 95, it also has a luxury that most other competitors could not afford.

## ORGANIZATION OF THIS VOLUME

To explore these patterns, four chapters in the book delve into the current battles for converging industries, and six chapters examine why companies have succeeded or failed in prior transitions. Most of the research focuses on the computer industry, which has experienced several major disruptions over the last three decades.

Some of the contributions in this volume are empirical. We examine a wide range of industries and companies. Our research extends from the broad data-processing sector and the whole spectrum of consumer and communications technologies, to more narrowly focused studies on personal digital assistants, workstations, PC software, and disk drives. We also have tried to lay out the conceptual and empirical foundations of convergence in digital technologies. There was a consensus among the authors that digital convergence will occur, though their contributions reflect considerable debate about the timing and difficulties of making it happen.

The first two chapters provide a historical perspective on the computer industry, with an emphasis on the transitions between various generations of computer products. Chapter 2, by Alfred Chandler, offers a sweeping overview of changes that have occurred during the past four decades in the computer industry. Chandler divides the history of computers into three chronological periods: the formative years, from World War II to the end of the mid-1960s; the dominance of the System 360 and the challenge of the minicomputer, from the mid-1960s to the early 1980s; and the personal computer, marked by the dominance of Intel and Microsoft. He concludes that computers have a very special dynamic that is important for thinking about competition in a converging world. Of particular note are the tendencies for high degrees of concentration and for companies to build extraordinarily powerful positions relative to other American industries, past and present.

The second chapter on historical perspectives is by Carliss Baldwin and Kim Clark, who take us back to the 1980s to investigate the birth of modularity in the computer industry. The empirical focus of their study is the war between Sun Microsystems and Apollo for supremacy in the technical workstation. Baldwin and Clark demonstrate that modularity produced competing paradigms in computing: a mainframe paradigm that depended heavily on closed, vertically integrated systems; and a modular paradigm that was more open, allowed components to be mixed and matched, and depended heavily on speed and preemptive cannibalization. Their research points to one of the central problems of competition in a modular, digital world: as competitive imitation becomes rampant, opportunities for sustained advantages tend to evaporate.

Chapters 4 and 5 explore the prospects and hopes for digital convergence. David Collis, William Bane, and Stephen Bradley begin this section with an analysis of the resources and capabilities that will be required to win in consumer markets converging around telecommunications, computing, and entertainment. Their principal hypothesis is that the consumer multimedia industry will be changed from three vertical businesses into five horizontal segments. Their conclusion is that content providers like Disney are in the strongest position to prosper, while computer hardware companies face limited prospects.

The chapter by Shane Greenstein and Tarun Khanna focuses on the conceptual challenges of thinking about convergence. They argue that the industries converge in a variety of ways, and they encourage the reader to consider the difference between convergence in substitutes and convergence in complements. The traditional view has always been to think about convergence in terms of substitution, where new industries emerge to replace the old. By forcing us to consider convergence in complements, that is, where two products work better together than separately, Greenstein and Khanna broaden the horizon for thinking about digital convergence.

Chapters 6, 7, and 8 explore the economic, legal, and managerial obstacles to digital convergence. The section starts with a chapter by Anita McGahan, Les Vadasz, and David Yoffie on PDAs. They analyze the early failure of PDAs in comparison with the evolution of other consumer electronic products in the twentieth century, including FM radio, color television, audiocassettes, VCRs, and digital compact disks. They conclude that the early failures of corporate strategies to introduce PDAs resulted from the lack of a compelling value proposition and the inability to set standards. Firms introducing PDAs missed many of the critical lessons of the consumer electronics revolution, where hardware and software were generally separated, standards were necessary, and, in many cases, some degree of compatibility was required to facilitate acceptance.

While McGahan et al. examine largely consumer businesses, Timothy Bresnahan and Garth Saloner research the business market. Their particular concern is central to the problems of digital convergence: how quickly new technologies will be adopted within corporate settings. More specifically, they ask why it has been so hard and has taken so long for corporate America to adopt client-server architecture, given the consensus among the information technology (IT) experts that client-server computing will ultimately win. Unlike PDAs, which have not established compelling value, client-server architectures should be cheaper and more cost-effective in the long run. Their answer is that standard interfaces have not yet emerged in the client-server model, and that only organizations that find a compelling strategic rationale will be early adopters.

The third chapter in this section examines the problems of intellectual property and its impact on an industry's structure. Since there is not a large enough body of precedent in converging industries, Josh Lerner and Robert Merges study intellectual property in the context of other emerging industries, especially software and biotechnology. Their particular concern is patent breadth. For example, when Compton's NewMedia received a patent for multimedia search systems, it gave the company the opportunity to demand royalties from the entire multimedia industry; and CompuServe used its GIF patent to try to appropriate the rents from Internet service providers. Despite the controversy over such broad patent awards, Lerner and Merges argue that they are in the interest of industries in their formative stages.

Chapters 9, 10, and 11 examine a broad set of managerial challenges facing companies in rapidly changing hardware and software environments. The first chapter examines the connections between product development and external markets, while the last two chapters delve into the process of product development itself.

Benjamin Gomes-Casseres and Dorothy Leonard-Barton look at the problems of product development and coordination in the context of great uncertainty in converging markets. The empirical focus in this chapter is the product-development, product-introduction, and alliance-building processes in the personal digital assistant market. The authors found that conventional marketing and technology development programs were difficult to employ in converging technologies. Time pressure to shape the industry and devise standards pushed companies to introduce products very rapidly, while at the same time finding ways to create or exploit a host of capabilities that already resided within the firms. They found three distinct patterns of product introduction, which they called market experimentation, market morphing, and vicarious experimentation. They also found that firms formed alliance groups, which were competing collectively as well as individually.

The last two chapters, which were described above, were written by Michael Cusumano and Stanley Smith, and by Marco Iansiti. These studies go to the heart of product development, exploring the successful transitions by Microsoft and Silicon Graphics from traditional product development paradigms to new approaches that pioneered iterative development processes while retaining development discipline and fostering greater creativity and teamwork. Both analyses also emphasize the importance of strategic and technological vision, especially the abilities to understand the technical and customer frontiers and to devise strategic guidelines for exploiting them. These two studies illustrate one of the key problems in making the world of converging technologies a reality: unless companies can find creative ways to specify, develop, and distribute products, the promise of convergence will continue to be little more than a promise.

---

### NOTES

1. Nicolas Negroponte, *Being Digital* (New York: Alfred A. Knopf, 1995).
2. NEC Corporation, *The First 80 Years* (Tokyo: NEC Corporation, 1984).
3. This point is made most forcefully in chapter 4.
4. Negroponte, 5.
5. Steve Ballmer, executive vice president of Microsoft, made this point in his opening remarks to the colloquium, October 1994.
6. *The Economist*, "The World This Week," March 18, 1995, p. 5.
7. *The Economist*, "Multimedia No-Man's Land," July 22, 1995, p. 57.

8. Discussed in chapters 6 and 9.

9. Hundreds of millions of dollars have been invested annually since the early 1990s in videoconferencing over PCs by IBM, AT&T, Picturetel, Creative Labs, Intel, and others.

10. David Churbnek, "Where's the Money?" *Forbes*, January 30, 1995, p. 101.

11. The four companies were Spyglass, Netscape, Performance Systems International, and UUNET. *Business Week*, August 21, 1995.

12. See Alfred Chandler, chapter 2.

13. Steven Klepper, "Evolution, Market Concentration, and Firm Survival," unpublished paper, Carnegie Mellon University, February 1995.

14. This idea is similar, though not identical, to the ideas of incremental versus radical innovation, and incremental versus architectural innovation, discussed in R. Nelson and S. Winter, *An Evolutionary Theory of Economic Change* (Cambridge: Harvard University Press, 1982); and Rebecca Henderson and Kim Clark, "Architectural Innovation: The Reconfiguration of Existing Product Technologies and the Failure of Established Firms," *Administrative Sciences Quarterly* 35 (1990): 9–30.

15. W. J. Abernathy and K. B. Clark, "Innovation: Mapping the Winds of Creative Destruction," *Research Policy* 14 (1985): 3–22.

16. Joseph A. Schumpeter, *The Theory of Economic Development: An Inquiry into Profits, Capital, Credit, Interest, and the Business Cycle* (Cambridge, Mass.: Harvard University Press, 1961), p. 133.

17. John Rennie, "Introduction: The Uncertainty of Technological Innovation," *Scientific American,* September 1995, p. 57.

18. Silicon Graphics is described by Iansiti in chapter 11.

19. Interview with John Sculley, April 1994.

20. Discussed in chapter 6.

21. These themes are explored in chapter 7 as well as in chapter 6.

22. Department of Defense, *Building U.S. Capabilities in Flat Panel Displays*, The Flat Panel Task Force Final Report (October 1994), p. IV-11.

23. Tarun Khanna and David B. Yoffie, "Microsoft 1995," HBS case 9-795-147 (Boston: Harvard Business School, 1995).

24. P. Anderson and M. L. Tushman, "Technological Discontinuities and Dominant Designs: A Cyclical Model of Technological Change," *Administrative Science Quarterly* 35 (1990): 604–633; Charles Ferguson and Charles Morris, *Computer Wars: How the West Can Win in a Post-IBM World* (New York: Random House, 1993).

25. Thomas J. Cottrell, "Fragmented Standards and the Development of Japan's Microcomputer Software Industry," unpublished manuscript, University of California, Berkeley, 1992.

26. For a general discussion of "lockin" and "lockout," see Pankaj Ghemawat, *Commitment: The Dynamics of Strategy* (New York: Free Press, 1991).

27. Paul David, "Clio and the Economics of QUERTY," *American Economic Review* 75 (May 1985): 332–336.

28. Joseph Farrell and Garth Saloner, "Standardization, Compatibility, and Innovation," *Rand Journal of Economics* 16 (Spring 1985): 70–83.

29. Khanna and Yoffie.

CHAPTER 2

# THE COMPUTER INDUSTRY
*The First Half-Century*

Alfred D. Chandler, Jr.

Electronic computers, the core of the information revolution, had a far greater impact on American industry, business, and way of life than did the products of other major high-technology industries that drove economic growth and transformed the processes of production and distribution in the second half of the twentieth century: chemicals, pharmaceuticals, and aerospace.

At the core of the new and evolving computer industry were the electronic transistor and its successor, the integrated chip. Probably the most important technological innovation of the twentieth century, the electronic semiconductor not only created new data-processing industries but also transformed the existing mechanical products and processes into

*This chapter provides a historical framework for a broader, more analytical historical review of the computer industry in my forthcoming study of the U.S. high-technology industries during the twentieth century, to be published by The Free Press. That study will compare and attempt to explain the very different historical evolution of several high-tech industries: aerospace, chemicals, pharmaceuticals, computers, and consumer and other electrical and electronic-based products.

I have greatly benefited from the careful reading of all or parts of the chapter, and the resulting essential comments and corrections, by John F. Ackers, James W. Cortada, Michael A. Cusumano, Zenas Hutcheson, James L. McKenney, Robert E. Kennedy, Richard M. Langlois, Kenneth Roland, Richard S. Rosenbloom, William T. Schiano, David B. Yoffie, and G. Pascal Zachary. I am also indebted to Emerson W. Pugh and especially to Takashi Hikino for assistance with the research for this chapter.

electronic ones across many industries. The coming of the computer and the chip led to the rapid growth of existing companies and the creation of thousands of new ones. The increasingly powerful chip became the central element in the continuing growth and transformation of the new computer and larger data-processing industry.

The critical differences between the computer and the other high-tech industries rested on the timing of the basic innovations on which the commercializing of new products rested. In polymer chemicals, antibiotics, and aeronautical engineering, as well as in radio and other electronic devices, the underlying innovations came before World War II, and their commercialization was force-fed by wartime military demands. Thus, in these industries, established enterprises carried out the commercialization of new technology on the basis of well-developed, industry-specific organizational capabilities. The military demands of the war led to the mass production of electronic items: radar, sonar, fire-control devices, proximity fuses, and the like.[1]

On the other hand, the first commercial use of a general-purpose digital electronic computer did not happen until six years after the war's end. The major technological innovations that replaced the vacuum tube, the initial technological core of the electronics industry—the transistor and the integrated circuit—were patented in 1948 and 1959, respectively. Their commercialization came in the 1950s and 1960s. As a result, in computers and closely related industries, start-ups played a more significant role than in the earlier high-tech industries. Even so, in these industries a smaller number of large enterprises quickly came to dominate, and their domination became more powerful than in other major American industries, past and present.

The history of the computer and closely related industries during the past half-century falls into three time periods. The first began in the early 1950s, when established electrical equipment and business machinery companies, which had begun to produce computers for military and government markets, started to use their organizational capabilities to enter a wide range of nongovernmental engineering, industrial, and commercial markets. IBM was the first company to make the large-scale investments in production, research and development, and marketing and distribution required to exploit these markets. By the early 1960s, it dominated these nongovernment markets, producing over a dozen types of computers for different customer needs.

The second period began in the mid-1960s, when IBM made its massive investment in new products and processes that created the System 360. That system was a full line of compatible, general-purpose computers that used the same architecture, components, peripheral equipment, and software, but each had different prices and performance levels for different markets and sizes of systems. These internal economies quickly gave IBM a global dominance that few industrial enterprises have ever achieved. During the period of the System 360 and its successor, the 370, not only was IBM the leading producer in the global markets but, and once again in an unprecedented manner, its computers and related products were widely cloned. By the mid-1970s, Japanese firms were beginning to produce IBM compatibles (unlicensed copies), which they sold to the leading European producers to sell under the latter's label. During this period, entrepreneurial start-ups began to commercialize minicomputers for the low-price end and supercomputers for the high end of the markets that IBM's System 360/370 dominated. The most successful were the minicomputers with low-cost, high-powered technology for scientific and engineering purposes. By the 1980s, minicomputers accounted for one-third of the U.S. computer market.

The third period started in the early 1980s as a new product, the microcomputer, began to challenge large, general-purpose systems. This challenge rested on the industry's two most significant developments of the 1970s. One was the swift proliferation of computers worldwide, especially the IBM systems and their clones. The resulting volume production of semiconductors, peripherals, software packages, and related products brought a dramatic reduction in costs and, therefore, in price and availability. The other was a commercialization of the microprocessor, the "computer on a chip," which sharply increased the processing power of the chip as large-scale production decreased its cost.

In microprocessors, IBM again took the lead by mass-producing its PC. Its outstanding success sowed the seeds of a powerful challenge to its dominance. For IBM relied, as did the pioneering start-ups, on outside suppliers for its components and software. It contracted with Intel to produce its chip and Microsoft to produce the operating system based on that chip. Since cloning PCs was far easier than cloning a mainframe, competitors swarmed into the market and IBM's share of that market dropped rapidly. But nearly all the PC clones had to use the Intel microprocessor and the Microsoft operating system. Within less than a decade, Intel, by exploiting the economies of scale made possible by this huge market, became the largest producer worldwide of microprocessors, and Microsoft, by utilizing economies of both scale and scope, achieved the same goal in software for microcomputers. By the 1990s, the only market that escaped the Intel–Microsoft grip was that served by the new workstations, the microprocessor successor to the minicomputer. By 1990 three established producers of minicomputers—IBM, Digital Equipment, and Hewlett-Packard—and one start-up—Sun Microsystems—dominated this much smaller but fast-growing market. They did so by using a new type of chip, reduced instruction set computing (RISC), and an existing nonproprietary operating system (UNIX).

Since 1990 a fourth period may be evolving. The period of IBM's dominance was an era of large machines—mainframes and minicomputers. During the microcomputer revolution, small desktop, portable, and other machines used by individuals began to replace large ones. During the early 1990s, innovations in and the growth of the industry rested increasingly on the combining of small boxes with big boxes to form multicomputer networks within which their different capabilities were simultaneously integrated and coordinated.

## THE FIRST PERIOD: FROM MILITARY TO COMMERCIAL PRODUCTION

As World War II was drawing to a close, the concept of the electronic digital computer was beginning to form. Wartime innovations in high-speed calculators, cryptoanalytic (code-breaking) devices, and servomechanisms (as used in gunfire control) set the stage for making the concept a reality. In 1944, Harvard's electromechanical Mark I, an aircraft simulator for Navy fighter aircraft, was in operation. Designed by Howard H. Aiken, its components were developed and its systems engineered by IBM. In the same year, Jay Forrester's Servomechanism Laboratories at MIT began work on what would become the Whirlwind Computer Project. In February 1946, at the Moore School of the University of Pennsylvania, J. W. Presper Eckert and John W. Mauchly, working with John von Neumann, a brilliant mathematician at the Institute for Advanced Study at Princeton, demonstrated their ENIAC, used to compute Army ballistic tables. ENIAC incorporated most of the elements of the modern digital computer. In 1945, von Neumann published a report that outlined what remains the basic architecture of the computer. In 1946, Harold Engstrom and William Norris, senior analysts at the Navy's Cryptoanalysis Unit, formed Engineering Research Associates (ERA) in St. Paul, Minnesota. Organized to serve the Navy's computing needs, it was soon building a general-purpose, stored-program computer, Atlas I.

The success of these initial efforts became a reality only in 1950 and 1951. At the end of 1950, ERA's Atlas went into full operation only a week after its delivery. It was quickly followed by a commercial version, the

ERM 1101. A few months later, Eckert and Mauchly, who had started a company of their own in 1946, assisted Northrop Aviation Company to build the BINAC for the National Bureau of Standards. In March 1951, a year after their firm had been acquired by Remington Rand, it delivered UNIVAC I to the Census Bureau. In that same year, MIT's Worldwind computer was completed.[2]

## IBM

Thus Remington Rand, and not IBM, could claim the sale of the first large, general-purpose computer for nonmilitary purposes. But IBM quickly took the lead by developing a stream of new and continually improved computer systems. Its first, the 701, "the Defense Computer," was intended for commercial as well as military needs. This first computer to be produced in volume was introduced in 1953. The 701 was followed in the next year by the 650, which was produced in even larger numbers for commercial uses, and then by the 702.[3]

From the start, IBM's management made the distinction between computers for business and computers for scientific purposes. The first called for a narrow internal data path with a fast and well-developed line of peripherals (terminals, printers, card readers and punches, tape and disk drives) to meet customers' more varied needs. The second had a wider data path with faster processors and a minimal number of peripherals to handle high-precision scientific calculations. The 650 was the progenitor of IBM's popular small business systems, as was the 704 of its scientific line and the 705 of its large business machines. The 704 and the 705 were introduced in 1956. The 704, designed by Gene M. Amdahl, was the fastest and largest general-purpose computer of its day. A second generation of computers of the 7000 series was announced in 1958, with the 7090 for the commercial market and the 7080 for the scientific market. Then in 1960 came the 1401 series, a highly successful small business system. Nearly twenty thousand 1401s were sold, an impressive record, since by 1960 only six thousand general-purpose computers had been installed in the United States.

By the early 1960s, IBM was producing fifteen different systems. By then it had transformed itself from the world's leader in producing electromechanical punch-card technology for record keeping to the world's leader in the new electronic computer technology. In 1960, over two-thirds of its revenue came from computers, software, and peripherals. After it shut down its punch-card operations, the remaining one-third came from electric typewriters and other office equipment.

The person most responsible for this strategic transformation was Thomas J. Watson, Jr. His father, Thomas, Sr., who had guided the company since 1914, had been attentive to the opportunities of the new electronic technology. By building the components and systems for Aiken's Harvard Mark I, IBM had participated in the industry's birth. The elder Watson pushed the development of the SSEC, which became operational in January 1948. A half-electronic, half-electric device, it was the first stored-program computer and the first to run on software. At this time, the elder Watson, still committed to the company's existing punch-card technology, turned over the development of the new electronic technology to his son. Thomas, Jr., who became executive vice president in 1949 and president in 1952, put together the team that developed the 701 and its successors, expanded research, and influenced the company's relations with the government—before he became chairman and CEO in 1956.[4]

The new technological capabilities developed in these pioneering years were based directly on those learned through designing and producing the earlier electromechanical machines. This was particularly true in the development of peripherals, for no other company had produced a broader range of devices by which one basic machine could be used to meet customers' needs in different industries and businesses. As Kenneth Flamm, a historian of the industry, notes:

> The card readers and punchers used with early computers, even those not built by IBM, were often IBM products. An ambitious development program for printers, magnetic tape drives, and magnetic drums and disks added strength to traditional expertise. The availability of quality peripheral equipment for IBM computers was crucial to its phenomenal growth.

At the same time, IBM programmers (about 150 during the 1950s) were developing essential software, including one of the first major high-level programming languages, FORTRAN, for the 704.[5]

IBM's half-century of working with its customers gave it an even greater competitive strength in marketing the new computer lines than it did in their development. And the edge in product design and development was reinforced after Thomas Watson, Jr., greatly increased the enterprise's investment in research and development. To head the expanded program, he brought in Emanuel R. Piore, formerly chief scientist at the Office of Naval Research. Piore had been intimately involved in wartime and immediate postwar developments in electronics and electronic computing.[6]

The U.S. government, through its massive defense contracts and its antitrust actions, further propelled IBM's transition from tabulating machines to computers. In the early 1950s, over half of its research funds came from government agencies. The SAGE air defense program, for which IBM built, beginning in 1952, fifty-six computers for $30 million apiece, provided ample funding as well as an invaluable learning experience. And another government program, Project Stretch, beginning in 1956, helped to lay the technological bases for the 7080, the 7090, the 1401, and the brilliant innovative achievement of the 1960s, the System 360.

Project Stretch grew out of IBM's development work to improve the 704. Two government agencies, the Los Almos Laboratories of the Atomic Energy Commission (AEC) and the National Security Agency (NSA), agreed to help fund the project if the final product could meet the needs of each agency. The design was then stretched to meet the high-precision "scientific" requirements of the AEC and the broader "business" ones of the NSA. Its requirements for compatibility led to advances in basic circuit logic, high-speed core memories, common interface standards, standard operating systems, and, Emerson Pugh adds, "multiprogramming, memory protect, generalized interrupt, interleaving of memories, lookahead, the memory bus, a standard interface for input–output equipment, and the eight-bit character called the byte."[7]

The government's antitrust action hastened the transformation of IBM's product line from punch card to computers through the consent decree negotiated with the Justice Department in January 1956. Since the suit focused primarily on IBM's dominance of the punch-card record-keeping business, the younger Watson, committed to computers, persuaded his father to agree that IBM would reduce its investments in plants producing tabulating cards to 50 percent of the industry's total capacity; would sell as well as lease its machines; and would do so on terms that were comparable with its existing lease arrangements. It was also to assist other enterprises in servicing installed machines. The decree had profound implications beyond tabulating cards, for IBM further agreed to license its "existing and future patents" to any "person making written application."[8]

At almost the same moment, the Justice Department had obtained a comparable clause in similar consent decrees with AT&T and RCA that had as great an impact on the future of their industries as the IBM decree had on the computing industry. As the chief of the Antitrust Division emphasized, these decrees provided the Justice Department with a way "to open up the electronics field." And indeed they did open the three major fields—data processing, consumer electronics, and telecommunications—not just to U.S. but also to foreign, particularly Japanese, competitors.

In 1961, as the sales of the low-price 1401 (rental $2,500 monthly) and the larger 7080 were taking commanding positions in their markets, IBM's management began to plan its next generation of computers. By then its different product lines bracketed the market from the smaller business machines to high-powered scientific computers, but none of these systems were compatible. They used different peripherals, components, software, and architecture. By then IBM was meeting increasing competition in several lines from companies that concentrated on only one or two lines in the performance/price spectrum. By then, too, customers often wanted a mix of business and scientific applications. In addition, growing internal rivalries between the producers of large scientific machines in Poughkeepsie, New York, and those of IBM's business lines at Endicott, New York, were delaying product development. These pressures, as well as the learned experience from Project Stretch and other developmental activities, emphasized both the need and the potential for achieving increased economies of scale and scope by making IBM systems compatible with one another.[9]

Early in 1961, Watson created a task group "to establish an overall IBM plan [for the third generation] of data processing products." In its final report of December 1961, the task group recommended that a family of completely new products be developed to bracket the performance/price spectrum, along with standard interfaces for input/output equipment, tapes and disk storage, card readers, printers, terminals, and other peripherals. The new System 360 was to consist of five (then six) new processors spanning a two hundred-fold range in performance and priced accordingly. This plan had similarities to one devised by Pierre du Pont and Alfred P. Sloan at General Motors in 1922 as they reorganized their existing lines into a family of products "for every purse and purpose." But the technological challenge of creating compatability at IBM was far greater than that at General Motors of achieving economies through using comparable parts, materials, and accessories in the production of its several lines.[10]

The execution of the task group's charge demanded an unprecedented innovation in both product and process. Most daunting was the senior managers' decision to rely on the untested integrated chip technology rather than the existing transistor technology for the source of computing power. Previously the company had purchased transistor-based processors from outside suppliers, primarily Texas Instruments (TI). Now it agreed not only to the development of a new solid logic technology (SLT) but also, in order to meet the large anticipated output of these chips, to design and then to build a giant works to produce them. In the words of James Cortada, "The decision to base the System 360 on this new technology was perhaps the riskiest ever taken by the company, but it paid off."[11]

The investment in other innovations called for by the planners was less risky, for they rested more on the capabilities IBM had learned during the previous decade. One was to have its systems meet the needs of both the scientific and the commercial markets. This led to improvement and expansion of the company's ferrite high-speed core memories. Input/output (I/O) interfaces were standardized, and a new and improved set of peripherals was developed. Still another challenge was the standardization of software so that it was compatible not only between the new family of machines but also, where possible, with existing ones.

To meet these unprecedented challenges and daunting risks, Watson poured all the services and financial resources available to the company into the creation of the new family of compatible computers. Implementation required the hiring of sixty thousand new employees. The project quickly fell behind schedule, and costs soared. Those of developing the SLT logic chips outran all estimates. The creation of new software was even more costly. In 1964, the critical year for development, more than a thousand persons were involved in developing the new operating system. In that year, more money was spent for software development than had originally been planned for the entire project.[12]

Nevertheless, on April 4, 1964, the date originally scheduled for completion, the company announced the appearance of the System 360. It did so at the insistence of the sales organization, which feared the loss of customers to competitors if the announcement were delayed. The first products began to emerge in 1965. But the manufacturing and software crisis continued. In 1966, $600 million was tied up in work-in-process inventory. By 1967, however, the multitude of new products began to pour into the market. By the end of the decade, IBM had 70 percent of the world's general-service computer market.

By the late 1960s, IBM enjoyed powerful competitive advantages that would assure its dominance in global markets until the next transforming innovation—the microprocessor—again revolutionized the industry. As Flamm points out: "The introduction of the concept of compatibility proved a turning point in the economic history of the industry." The competitive strength of the compatible System 360 lay in the exploitation of both the economies of scale and those of scope. In production, its scale economies came not only from a greater output of products but also from the volume production of parts and accessories. In R&D, as in the production of hardware, "The unit cost of designing a product therefore declines with the number of units sold. All other things being equal, the firm with the largest share of the market will then have the lowest unit cost." Of more importance, Flamm points out, "were the economies of scope in product development in order to use the results of fixed investments in R&D in the widest array of products." But it was software that "emerged as the primary areas in which to exploit the economies of scope." Because software had to be written for specific hardware, "the fixed cost of writing a complex program could now be spread over a much wider market, and the cost of implementing such an application for an individual user greatly reduced." This critical relationship between hardware and software differentiated the electronic data-processing industry and its historical evolution from all other major industries.[13]

A second source of IBM's competitive strength lay in its learned marketing capabilities; the largest commercial market for the new electronic data-processing systems was the users of the mechanically driven punch cards. Through the renting and servicing of its machines, IBM's marketing organization had direct contact with more potential buyers of computers than did other business machine companies, and certainly more than any entrepreneurial start-ups. Its intimate knowledge of the requirements of different types of customers, both commercial and scientific, permitted it to bring to market products to meet the needs of a larger number and a broader range of customers than did its competitors. Moreover, because computers were more complex to use than the electromechanical products, those customers whom IBM had long serviced welcomed the new services provided to bring them into the computer age.[14]

In these ways, the IBM System 360 ushered in the second period of the industry's history. That achievement required half a decade of intense development work and a cost of $6–$7 billion. In addition to developing hardware and software, these costs included the construction of five new plants that cost $4.5 billion. Surely no other company or government agency in the world had the learned technological and marketing capabilities, and the financial resources to carry out such an immensely innovative project.

In 1961, IBM was the world's largest and most profitable maker of computers. It acquired this position by building on the capabilities in development, production, and marketing that it had learned well before World War II as the leading producer of punch cards and related products. During the 1950s, its engineers, managers, and workers learned the intricacies of the new electronic technologies through its government contracts; but so did those of its competitors. More than any of these competitors, IBM concentrated on the potential of the nongovernment market, bringing out a series of new products whose performance surpassed those of previous ones. So successful was this strategy by the end of the 1950s that it had shut down the production of its punch cards and more recently developed electronic calculators. To appreciate better the significance of IBM's initial strategy and the resulting competitive advantages created during the first period of the new electronic data-processing industry, the histories of IBM competitors need to be examined.

## Sperry-Rand and Control Data

In 1953, when IBM delivered its first military Defense Calculator, Remington Rand was the new industry's leader. During the 1930s, Remington Rand had become the largest American business machine company, followed by National Cash Register (NCR), IBM, and Burroughs (Adding) Machine Company. It achieved that status in 1927, when James Henry Rand merged the Remington Typewriter Company, the nation's largest typewriting enterprise, with several smaller companies that produced adding machines, punch cards, accounting forms, and similar products.[15]

After the war, Rand, who still headed the company, moved boldly into the embryonic computer industry. Whereas the senior Watson at IBM, a consummate organization builder, carefully probed the company's entrance into the new technology, Jim Rand, an empire builder, moved in on a grand scale. In 1949, he hired General Leslie R. Groves, who as head of the Manhattan Project, which developed the atomic bomb, was considered one of the nation's foremost technological experts, to set up the Remington Rand Laboratories close to the company's headquarters at Norwalk, Connecticut. Groves hired a group of senior engineers from Eckert-Mauchly. Then in 1950, as that company's UNIVAC was nearing completion, Rand purchased the enterprise. Two years later Rand acquired Engineering Research Associates (ERA), the other major pioneering firm, located in St. Paul, Minnesota, where William Norris's Atlas had become fully operational the year before. "Thus Remington Rand had no less than three different computer development groups," Flamm points out, "together accounting for a good part of the stock of knowledge and experience with computers in the world at that time. It also had a three-year head start over any other firm in shipping a commercial computer product."

Yet within three years this head start had evaporated. As has so often occurred in industrial history, the empire creator was not an organization builder. The three research teams remained located in Norwalk, Philadelphia, and St. Paul. Their work was not coordinated or integrated. They continued to have "fragmented, rivalrous and squabbling relationships with one another." The Remington sales force had little interest in or understanding of the operations or uses of the new machines. Rand and his senior managers were reluctant to invest heavily in developing a successor to UNIVAC I.

Not surprisingly, James Rand's response to the rising challenge from IBM was to rely on acquisition rather than internal investment. In 1955 he merged his company with Sperry, the country's leading instrument maker, to form the Sperry-Rand Corporation. Sperry had been established in 1910 to produce Elmer Sperry's gyroscope. It turned to making torpedoes and bombsights in World War I, and produced gunnery fire control and aviation equipment in World War II. The rationale for the merger was that Sperry would provide research capabilities, as well as funds, and Remington Rand offered access to business markets. Although three development units were placed in a single division headed by William Norris, they remained in their separate locations. Conflicts continued. In less than two years, a disgruntled Norris and several engineering associates left to start Control Data.

The Rand Division of Sperry-Rand continued to be organized on functional lines, with the production and sales managers responsible for all office products (of which the computer was only one). The sales force failed to develop close relationships with either the production or the development department. It had little understanding of computer technology and how such technology might be used by customers. Few computer-oriented capabilities were created. There was no stream of new products. UNIVAC II came in 1957 and UNIVAC III in 1960. The next generation, UNIVAC 1004 and UNIVAC 1008 II, were announced in 1963 and 1965, respectively.

Thus, as IBM moved to capture the commercial markets, Sperry-Rand continued to rely on designing and building computers for the government, particularly the Air Force and the Atomic Energy Commission. It did little exploratory work along the lines of IBM's Poughkeepsie research laboratory. Its strategy became one of concentrating on government contract work and then spinning off commercial products when the opportunity presented itself. By 1963, before the System 360 was announced, Sperry-Rand was still second after IBM, but its revenues from data-processing products were $145.4 million, compared with IBM's $1,224 million.[16]

If the senior managers at Remington Rand and then Sperry-Rand had failed to transform the capabilities of individuals into organizational ones, William Norris at Control Data succeeded brilliantly. In the fall of 1951, when Jim Rand offered to acquire ERA, Norris, who headed operations, opposed the move. The company was badly capitalized, however, so its president, James Parker, who had been responsible for raising much of the initial capital, insisted that the acquisition by Rand was necessary if the Norris team was to make its way in the new computer world. After five years, however, frustrated by the failure of senior managers at Rand and Sperry-Rand to support his activities, Norris and most of his team departed.

When Norris established Control Data in 1957, with $600,000 and twelve employees, he laid down two strategies for building this fledgling start-up into a major computer enterprise. The first was to acquire funding and continued learning, as he had done at Sperry-Rand, by developing machines for government agencies at the high end of the price/performance spectrum, then spinning off commercial products from them. In Norris's words: "We picked out a particular niche of the market—the scientific and engineering part of the market—by building large, scientific computers with a lot more bang for their buck." This was achieved primarily by very-high-performance hardware with the customer doing most of the software. His second strategy was one of vertical integration. His company was to produce its own components—processors, memories, peripherals, and the like—and to build a computer-knowledgeable sales force in the United States and abroad. In addition, it expanded the use of its computers by setting up its own data service bureaus and time-sharing facilities.[17]

The new company's major initial commercial products, the CDC 1604 and 160, were spin-offs of computers shipped to military customers in 1960. Its Series 3600 followed in 1963. In that same year, the company enlarged its scientific and engineering lines through the acquisition of Bendix Aviation's computer business and General Instrument's Liberscope division. The G-15 was the major product of the first, and the LGP-30, of the second.

The year before, Control Data had announced its first supercomputer —the 660, to be designed by Seymour Cray (who had joined ERA in 1950, immediately after graduating from the University of Minnesota) and to be delivered to the Atomic Energy Commission's Livermore Laboratory. IBM immediately responded by announcing that it would produce an even more powerful system. The announcement of the 660 was made as the contract was signed, but its first product was not delivered to the Livermore Laboratory until 1966. Nevertheless, since IBM was in the throes of creating the System 360, it was unable to follow through on its challenge—a challenge that was later the source of a major lawsuit involving the two companies. The 660 and its successors gave Control Data and its designers dominance of the supercomputer market until 1972, when Cray left to start his own company.

In transforming this pioneering entrepreneurial start-up into a powerful industrial enterprise, Norris and his associates relied on acquisitions. They differed strikingly, however, from those of James Rand. In the production of the initial 1604 and the 160, the company had had to rely on outside suppliers, including IBM, for nearly all its peripherals, and on NCR to market its 160 in the United States and Ferranti to sell the 1604 abroad. Between 1963 and 1969, Control Data purchased thirty-eight small producers of data-processing equipment. Nearly all were entrepreneurial start-ups. Their careful integration into the design and production activities of the larger operating units provided the company with its initial learning base.

By so doing, Control Data became, by the end of the 1960s, a major producer of display terminals, printers, disk drives, storage units, tape transports, disk files, and other peripherals, not only for itself but also for GE, RCA, NCR, Honeywell, Germany's Siemens, Britain's ICL, and other original equipment manufacturers (OEMs). In 1966 it began to produce its own integrated circuits, which until then had been purchased primarily from Texas Instruments. To expand the market, Norris began providing customized software applications—solutions to specific customers' needs—as well as expanding service bureaus and time-sharing activities.

In these ways, this entrepreneurial firm became the most successful challenger in the industry's initial years to its first mover, IBM. It did so by focusing on a niche that the first mover had not entered and by vertically integrating through the acquisition of small start-ups. This careful strategy of consolidation provided the "critical mass" necessary for the scale economies and a broad learning base that permitted Control Data to become a global leader in the production of peripherals and services as well as high-end computers.

## NCR, Burroughs, and Honeywell

NCR, Burroughs, and Honeywell were the three other challengers to IBM during the 1950s. General Electric and RCA entered the production of general-purpose commercial computers in the mid-1960s, just as IBM's System 360 was coming onstream. Another potential challenger, Philco, quickly lost its competitive capabilities after being acquired by Ford in

1961. AT&T was barred from producing commercial computers by a consent decree signed with the U.S. Department of Justice in 1956 (only a day after the signing of IBM's consent decree). The three challengers that entered in the 1950s all did so through acquisitions. None had made serious inroads into the market when the System 360 was announced.

NCR gingerly moved into the new business in 1952, when it purchased the Computer Research Corporation, a California company producing small machines for military markets. Its initial model, the 303, was designed in California and produced at the company's central factory in Dayton, Ohio. Next, after temporarily taking over the marketing of Control Data's 160, NCR developed the 315 and 390, primarily for its banking customers. NCR continued to sell these products through its cash register sales force. By 1962, only 2 percent of its revenue came from electronic data-processing products. In 1963, these revenues stood at $36 million, compared with the five-year-old Control Data's revenues of $84.6 million. Moreover, in these same years, NCR's management held back on making a commitment to transform its electromechanical cash register and related processes of production into electronic ones. In 1964, NCR was still much the same company, producing much the same products, in much the same manner as it had before World War II.[18]

Before World War II, the Burroughs Machine Company was the fourth largest business machine maker in the United States in terms of sales. The first mover in adding machines, it broadened its line during the 1930s to cash registers and accounting and bookkeeping devices. Its initial involvement with computers began in 1953, with the production of a static magnetic memory for ENIAC. It experimented in building small computers for the government before it purchased Electrodata in 1956. Like NCR's acquisition, Electrodata was a small California producer. It had built, in collaboration with the Jet Propulsion Laboratory of the California Institute of Technology, a computer named Datatron. In 1957, its first attempt at a commercial product—its vacuum-tube-based Datatron—was a failure; but its transistor-based follow-up was more successful. Sold largely to Burroughs's bank accounting customers, it was soon losing out to IBM's 7070 and 1400. In 1963, Burroughs's total revenues from electronic data processing were $38.6 million. As was the case at NCR, before 1964, Burroughs had made no serious attempt to transform its primary products and processes into electronic ones.[19]

Honeywell's story differs largely in that its move into computers came through a joint venture with Raytheon, a prewar producer of radio tubes that had grown enormously during World War II by making radar and other military electronics. After the war, Raytheon began to work on computers for the Navy. In 1953, it designed a commercial computer that became the Datamatic, which was to sell for $2 million. In 1955, Raytheon joined with Honeywell (60 percent Honeywell and 40 percent Raytheon) to complete and market the machine; but it performed so poorly that in 1957, Raytheon decided to pull out of the venture and the industry. More successful were the next transistor-based systems, the 800 series and the 200 series (the 290, sold to chemical, oil, and other energy-related producers, did particularly well). In 1963 came the 400, a revised 800 at half the price. In 1962, the company negotiated an arrangement with Japan's Nippon Electric Company to manufacture and sell Honeywell's computers in Japan. Nevertheless, the total revenues from the data-processing products reached only $27 million in 1963, 5 percent of the company's total revenues. In 1964, like the two business machine companies, Honeywell still considered itself a producer of electromechanical products by mechanical processes.[20]

In 1963, the total revenue for these three established machinery firms that pioneered in the electronic data-processing industry was just over $100 million, compared with IBM's $1,244 million, Sperry-Rand's $145.5 million, and Control Data's $84.6 million. Nevertheless, small as their share was, they were able to survive the impact of IBM's System 360, whereas the nation's two electrical/electronics giants—RCA and GE—were not. They did so because during the second period in the history of the U.S. electronic data-processing industry, they transformed their primary products and processes from electromechanical to electronic ones. By relying on product-specific learned development and, particularly, marketing capabilities that neither RCA nor GE had acquired, they quickly regained their dominant positions in their original markets. Their computer business remained profitable because their design, production, and sales organizations focused on customers whose businesses were the closest to their core business—the banking and retail industries for NCR and Burroughs, and regulating and control systems for Honeywell.

## THE SECOND PERIOD:
## THE DOMINANCE OF THE SYSTEM 360

IBM dominated the U.S. and world computer business for a decade and a half after the System 360 came into full production in 1967. Its broad range of products and the increased performance of its processors, memories, peripherals, chips, and consumables made possible an explosion in the use of computers throughout the world. Few other modern industries ever grew so fast or became such a powerful agent of transformation. The motor vehicle industry during the 1920s provides the closest historical parallel. An infant industry in 1900, it grew from middle size by 1915 to the nation's largest in 1935, in terms of revenues, value added in manufacturing, and wages, and the third largest in employment. Motor vehicles transformed other industries—oil, rubber, glass, metals, chemicals, and modes of transportation. Computers did even more during the late 1960s and 1970s in transforming the ways of providing and processing information, which in turn revolutionized the processes of production and distribution.

But there were significant differences. The designing and producing of computers and their numerous essential components was technologically much more complex than the making of automobiles, trucks, other motor vehicles, and their parts and accessories. Of more importance, the use of the computer required the creation of two new industries: software in great variety, to produce usable information, and "service bureaus," to provide computer services to a vast number of customers who preferred not to buy or even lease computers or to take the time to learn the intricacies of their operation. Indeed, as the size of this nonhardware sector grew in the 1960s, the term "electronic data processing" began to replace the term "computers" to identify the industry.

Another difference was the role of the first movers in the two industries. In automobiles, Ford was one of a multitude of start-ups until Henry Ford began building the Highland Park, Michigan, plant in 1911. The introduction of the moving assembly line there in 1913 and 1914 led to a massive increase in output of motor vehicles, engines, components, and other ancillary products by the Ford Motor Company. But others quickly followed Ford's lead. Within less than a decade, Ford was being effectively challenged by General Motors, Chrysler, and several smaller companies in the United States and abroad. In computers and allied electronic information-processing equipment, IBM dominated the U.S. industry before it carried out the transforming innovations of the System 360. That gave the products it designed a worldwide position that almost no other company has ever achieved. Indeed, its strongest competitors were those that built IBM machines—IBM plug compatibles or clones, as they came to be called.

The tables on the electronic data-processing industry collected by James Cortada and Kenneth Flamm document its unprecedented growth after the mid-1960s. Table 2-1 gives information on the data-processing shipments and revenues during these explosive years; table 2-2, on the value of computer systems; table 2-3, on expenditures for computer

TABLE 2-1

DATA-PROCESSING INDUSTRY SHIPMENTS AND REVENUES BY U.S. FIRMS, 1955–1979, SELECTED YEARS (BILLIONS OF DOLLARS)

| Year | Domestic | Worldwide |
|------|----------|-----------|
| 1955 | less than 1 | less than 1 |
| 1960 | 0.5 | 1.0 |
| 1965 | 2.0 | 2.5 |
| 1970 | 7.0 | 10.0 |
| 1975 | 15.0 | 21.0 |
| 1979 | 28.0 | 37.0 |

SOURCE: Montgomery Phister, Jr., "Computer Industry," in Anthony Ralston and Edwin D. Reilly, Jr., eds., *Encyclopedia of Computer Science and Engineering* (New York: Van Nostrand Reinhold, 1983), 335. Reprinted by permission of International Thomson Computer Press.

Data represent estimations only, with a reliability variance of approximately 10 percent.

TABLE 2-2

VALUE OF COMPUTER SYSTEMS IN THE UNITED STATES, 1955–1979, SELECTED YEARS (BILLIONS OF DOLLARS)

| Year | General Purpose | Minis | Small Business | Total |
|------|-----------------|-------|----------------|-------|
| 1955 | 0 | 0 | 0 | 0.5 |
| 1960 | 0 | 0 | 0 | 1.0 |
| 1965 | 5.0 | 0 | 0 | 5.0 |
| 1970 | 18.0 | 1.0 | 0 | 24.0 |
| 1975 | 30.0 | 5.0 | 0 | 35.0 |
| 1979 | 50.0 | 7.0 | 2.5 | 59.5 |

SOURCE: Estimated figures extracted from Montgomery Phister, Jr., "Computer Industry," in Anthony Ralston and Edwin D. Reilly, Jr., eds., *Encyclopedia of Computer Science and Engineering* (New York: Van Nostrand Reinhold, 1983), 337, fig. 4. Reprinted by permission of International Thomson Computer Press.

hardware; and tables 2-4 and 2-5, on the growth of the software and service sectors.

During the decade that followed the introduction of the System 360, when foreign competition was beginning to invade other U.S. markets, net exports of the American data-processing companies soared (see table 2-6). By 1971, 45 percent of the computers made in the United States had been sold abroad, for a total value of $3.3 billion. In addition, their output was supplemented by an increasing production of U.S. plants in foreign lands. By the mid-1970s, U.S. firms produced most of the computers

TABLE 2-3

EXPENDITURES FOR COMPUTER HARDWARE IN THE UNITED STATES,
1954–1973, SELECTED YEARS

| Year | Million Dollars |
|------|-----------------|
| 1954 | 10 |
| 1958 | 250 |
| 1963 | 1,500 |
| 1968 | 4,500 |
| 1973 | 7,000 |

SOURCE: James W. Cortada, *Historical Dictionary of Data Processing: Organizations* (Westport, Ct.: Greenwood, 1987), p. 18. Reprinted with permission of the author.

TABLE 2-4

ESTIMATED SOFTWARE REVENUES, 1964–1980, SELECTED YEARS
(MILLIONS OF DOLLARS)

| Year | Custom Programming | Packages | Total |
|------|--------------------|----------|-------|
| 1964 | 150–175 | 50-100 | 225–275 |
| 1968 | 300 | 100 | 400 |
| 1970 | 300 | 200 | 500 |
| 1972 | 350 | 300-350 | 650–700 |
| 1974 | 400 | 300-350 | 700–750 |
| 1976 | 400–425 | 750 | 1,150–1,175 |
| 1978 | 500 | 1,000 | 1,500 |
| 1980 | 600 | 1,500 | 2,100 |

SOURCE: James W. Cortada, *Historical Dictionary of Data Processing: Organizations* (Westport, Ct.: Greenwood, 1987), p. 23. Reprinted with permission of the author.

Based on available data, statistics for custom programming in the 1960s cited above may be 10 to 25 percent too low, and for packages 10 to 15 percent too high; for the 1970s, all data may be 15 to 25 percent too low. By the mid-1980s, software amounted to $4 billion per year in the United States. All data above are for U.S. market only.

installed in France and West Germany, close to two-thirds of those in Britain, and nearly 40 percent of those in Japan.[21]

Again only the motor vehicle industry provides a comparable example of U.S. dominance abroad. In 1928, of all cars exported to foreign markets, 72 percent were made in the United States, 6 percent in France, 5 percent in Britain, and 1 percent in Germany. But a striking difference between the motor vehicle and the computer was that General Motors

TABLE 2-5

ESTIMATED REVENUES FROM SERVICE SECTOR OF DATA-PROCESSING
INDUSTRY, 1955–1979, SELECTED YEARS (BILLIONS OF DOLLARS)

| Year | Total |
|------|-------|
| 1955 | 0.3 |
| 1960 | 0.4–0.5 |
| 1965 | 0.5–0.7 |
| 1970 | 1.1 |
| 1975 | 3.2 |
| 1979 | 5.5 |

SOURCE: Montgomery Phister, Jr., "Computer Industry," in Anthony Ralston and Edwin D. Reilly, Jr., eds., *Encyclopedia of Computer Science and Engineering* (New York: Van Nostrand Reinhold, 1983), 342–343. Reprinted by permission of International Thomson Computer Press.

Facilities management (service sector) revenues remained almost minuscule until after 1970; then they grew, reaching nearly $500 million by the late 1970s; on-line services grew from several hundred million dollars in the late 1960s to over $3 billion by the end of the 1970s; batch processing experienced a less steep growth rate than on-line processing but rose from approximately $400 million in 1965 to over $2 billion in 1980.

TABLE 2-6

ANNUAL EXPORTS AND IMPORTS OF COMPUTER EQUIPMENT IN THE U.S.
MARKET, 1967–1971 (MILLIONS OF DOLLARS)

| Exports-Imports | 1967 | 1968 | 1969 | 1970 | 1971 |
|-----------------|------|------|------|------|------|
| Exports | 475 | 530 | 786 | 1,237 | 1,262 |
| Imports* | 20 | 18 | 37 | 60 | 119 |
| Net exports | 455 | 152 | 749 | 1,177 | 1,143 |

SOURCE: James W. Cortada, *Historical Dictionary of Data Processing: Organizations* (Westport, Ct.: Greenwood, 1987), p. 21. Reprinted with permission of the author.

*Parts not included.

and Chrysler shared the global market with Ford, and as the share of the two challengers rose, Ford's declined sharply. Nearly all major capital-intensive industries have been dominated within a decade or so after their establishment by a small number of first movers and challengers, with market share and profits shifting among the members of the oligopoly. But in the computer industry, a single firm not only dominated production and distribution but also often led the way in the development of new products.[22]

On the other hand, as the number of computers produced expanded exponentially, so did the number of producers of components, peripherals, and other ancillary equipment, quickly reducing IBM's share in those businesses. Again, there is a parallel to the decline in market share of the "Big Three" in the production of motor vehicle parts and accessories. The reason, of course, was that parts and accessories used in motor vehicles and their engines were essential in many other industries, ranging from aircraft to industrial and agricultural equipment. As these industries grew, so did the demand for replacement parts and other equipment. In the same way, transistors, integrated circuit chips, peripherals, and other components were used in industries besides computers, including telecommunications, a wide variety of consumer and nonconsumer electronic products, motor vehicles, industrial products including machine tools, medical equipment, and other products employing so-called embedded systems.

## IBM

In keeping with their commitment to continuing product development, the senior managers at IBM began to focus on their next line of computers even before the first 360 reached the market. In January 1965, John W. Haanstra, who had headed the Spread Committee, was appointed president of the new Systems Development Division. He immediately began to plan for the creation of a system as revolutionary as the 360 had been, one based on the concept of putting several circuits on a single chip. At a time when the challenge was to fabricate a chip with five circuits, Haanstra set a goal of ten to one hundred. That great leap forward in chips would require entirely new operating systems. But 1965 was the year of crisis at IBM. In the management reshuffling that resulted, Haanstra was dropped as the head of product development. When planning was renewed in the following year, his successor and senior managers agreed that evolution, not revolution, was the most promising course.[23]

So the System 370, the first models of which were announced in June 1970, was an evolutionary extension of the 360. Monolithic integrated circuits, and a small, high-speed cache memory in the central processing unit to enhance the performance of low-cost main memories, brought a fourfold increase in performance and a much greater reliability to the processors. All semiconductor memories replaced the ferrite core ones. The improved peripherals included faster printers, greater disk storage capacity, and virtual memory (a combination of hardware and software that expanded the capacity of the main memory).[24]

The 370 enlarged the number of lines IBM produced, particularly at the high end. However, at the low end the designers were still unable to produce a computer that was compatible with the System 370's basic operating system. The technological complexities remained too challenging. In October 1969, the company established its General Systems Division to manufacture its noncompatible System 3 that would rent for less than $1,000 a month.[25]

As the System 370 entered the marketplace, senior management created the Future Systems (F/S) task force, with John R. Opel as its chairman, to meet the challenge of future growth. A business recession had brought a sharp decline in orders. At the same time, long-term projections indicated that because of the continuing drop in costs and prices of computers, new products and new applications were needed if the company was to maintain its goal of 15 percent annual growth. Among the goals set by the task force were the reduction of the costs to customers of developing their own application software and the development of more user-friendly interfaces for professional programmers and novices alike. More radical was the goal of consolidating all memories and memory storage so that information stored anywhere in the system could be retrieved more quickly and easily. Central to the program was the development of high-powered, high-density, very-large-scale integrated (VLSI) chips that Haanstra proposed in 1965. But despite intensive and continuing efforts, the developers were unable to overcome the technical challenges involved. As one consultant reported in June 1973, "Complexity is the fatal foe."[26]

In the spring of 1974, the expected time before formal announcement was forty-five months, precisely what it had been in the fall of 1971 when the Opel task force completed its work. Top managers then agreed to terminate the F/S and instead "to extend the architecture of the System 360/370." Although much of the hardware developed for the F/S was used in later models, Pugh points out, "most of the system designs, microcode, and software were discarded. It was the most expensive development failure in the company's history." It was often referred to as IBM's Vietnam.[27]

During these years when IBM was fighting a losing battle to develop innovative architecture for its mainframe computers, competition increased. Although it remained the global giant, IBM's market share declined from 1970 on. Competition came less from its rivals of the 1950s and early 1960s and more from entrepreneurial start-ups using different architectures for more specialized markets. But the most serious threat, from IBM's perspective, was the companies that marketed their own versions of the computers and peripherals of the System 360/370, those that produced IBM "plug compatibles" or clones. These manufacturers could undersell IBM because they did not have the first movers' costs of developing the hardware and related software, and of building the market for the products at home and abroad.

Leading producers of peripherals quickly moved into making IBM compatibles. They usually started by producing them on an OEM basis, that is, selling directly to other manufacturers for use in their final products. Soon, however, they were selling them to computer users as replacement parts. In 1967, Telex, a prewar hearing aid producer that began to manufacture tape drives in 1962, marketed its first IBM plug-compatible tape drive, which it sold at a 50 percent discount. In 1968, Memorex, established in 1961 as a maker of magnetic and then tape drives, began making plug-compatible disk packs and drives. In the same year Ampex, a tape drive maker established in the early 1950s, began producing plug-compatible disk drives, and in 1969, core memories. In addition, in 1967, twelve engineers left IBM to form Information Storage Systems, and shortly thereafter four others started Storage Technology Corporation. In the 1970s, the number of producers of plug-compatible peripherals increased substantially.[28]

The most aggressive of such competitors were Control Data and the Amdahl Corporation. Control Data, which in the early 1960s produced a full line of peripherals for its own computers, and then sold them to others on an OEM basis, quickly began to make IBM plug-compatible disk drives, then "add-on memories," and soon a full line of peripherals. Each time IBM announced a new peripheral, Control Data quickly brought one out at a lower price. Through the practice of retroengineering and making slight changes, it could stay abreast of IBM without incurring similar development costs.[29]

Although Gene M. Amdahl was the first to produce a successful IBM-compatible mainframe, RCA was the first to try. RCA did so by announcing its Spectra series immediately after IBM announced the System 360, but its computers "were totally different machines."[30] On the other hand, Amdahl, one of the chief architects of the System 360 and the 370, began to design the first true plug-compatible computer in 1970, when he left IBM to form his own enterprise. He left because in the development of the System 370, top management insisted that its high-end computer had to conform to the price/performance relationship defined for the rest of the 370. Amdahl was certain that the high-end computer could be produced at profit, but not at what IBM considered its "normal" (that is impressively high) profit level. He wrote that he recognized "that

IBM's desire to optimize its financial return represented an Achilles heel, which I could exploit if I were to leave and go into the large computer business in competition with IBM." His firm would build the central processor and obtain the peripherals from the rapidly growing plug-compatible market.[31]

Amdahl's challenge, however, was finance. His business plan called for $33 million to $44 million, far too much to be met by the existing venture capital industry. Thus, in 1972, Amdahl turned to the leading Japanese computer maker, Fujitsu, which with other Japanese companies and a government agency, MITI, was attempting to develop competitive computer technology. Fujitsu acquired 24 percent of Amdahl's equity in return for an exchange of technical information. Three years later, Fujitsu announced that it would make computers in Japan for Amdahl to sell in the United States. As Flamm notes, "This was the turning point for the Japanese computer industry. At last it would acquire the ability to produce computers competitively with the latest IBM models."[32]

Working with Hitachi, Fujitsu developed the M Series of IBM-compatible computers and peripherals. By 1976, Fujitsu had committed $54 million to Amdahl, and in 1979 it increased its share of the American company to 49 percent. That year, Amdahl departed to establish the Triology Systems Corporation, which would build a faster, less expensive computer using VLSI chips. One of the industry's largest start-ups in terms of funding, it quickly failed.

By 1986, four computer companies—Fujitsu, Hitachi, IBM's Japanese subsidiary, and Nippon Electric (NEC)—accounted for three-fourths of the computers sold in Japan. Of these, NEC concentrated on its production for the telecommunications market—a market that IBM had left largely to AT&T. As Marie Anchordoguy, the historian of the Japanese computer industry, notes, "The M series today [1988] remains the mainstay of Fujitsu's and Hitachi's offerings." By the mid-1980s, the leading European producers were selling Japanese-made plug compatibles under their labels. Siemens' and Britain's ICL mainframes were made by Fujitsu; those of Olivetti and BASF, by Hitachi; and those of France's Bull, by NEC. To quote Flamm again: "The market for large business machines is now [1987] mainly between IBM and other American and Japanese products." Thus, by that time, IBM's basic 360/370 architecture may have accounted for as much as two-thirds of the mainframe computers operating worldwide (see figures 2-1 and 2-2).[33]

IBM had to compete with its own machines on another front. In the mid-1960s, independent companies began to purchase computers and then lease them to customers. With large-scale production of the System

360 after 1967, leasing immediately became a big business. These firms purchased IBM machines, leasing them at a lower price and offering more financing alternatives than did IBM. They did so by depreciating them over a longer period. When the 370 appeared, they sold their 360s as they bought the new machines. Some of the leasing companies were units of large conglomerates such as Greyhound, but most were start-ups, including Itel, Diebold, Leasco, Levin-Townsend, and MAI. The increase of Diebold's revenues from $268,000 in 1967 to $30.8 million in 1969, of Itel's from $1.4 million in 1967 to $38.7 million in 1969, and of Leasco's from $8.5 million in 1967 to $37.7 million in 1969 documents the astonishingly swift growth of these companies.[34]

What, then, are the implications of the unprecedented global dominance of IBM's major product line? First, it emphasized IBM's role as an innovator. IBM developed much of the mainframe, semiconductor, peripheral, and software technologies from which other companies learned and upon which they built, first in the United States and then in Japan. Not surprisingly, because IBM and IBM compatibles (particularly those of Japan) dominated the European market, no strong learning base essential to the nurturing of mainframe, semiconductor, peripheral, and software technologies evolved in Europe.

Second, the IBM story indicates the role the U.S. government played in the development of the industry. The initial learning experience for the industry as a whole came from government contracts during the 1950s, but government agencies had less direct impact on the transferring of the learned knowledge to development of the products for the increasingly larger and, for the long term, more significant commercial markets. It played almost no part in the planning and executing of IBM's most profound learning experience, the creation of the System 360, the innovations of which transformed the industry worldwide.

The U.S. government may have played a greater part in the history of IBM and the computer industry through its antitrust actions than by directly encouraging and funding the growth of commercial products as governments in Japan and Europe did. Its greatest impact reflected the provisions of the 1956 consent decree. More indirect was the influence of the antitrust suit carried on for thirteen years by the Justice Department against IBM. That case cost both parties millions of dollars in legal fees. Its immediate impact was to push IBM to "unbundle" its software and peripherals.[35]

The Justice Department had begun to prepare an antitrust case in 1965, but it took no direct action until December 1968, when Control Data brought a suit against IBM for unfair business practices, not for

FIGURE 2-1

## RELATIVE SHARES OF THE TOP COMPUTER COMPANIES IN THE EUROPEAN MARKET

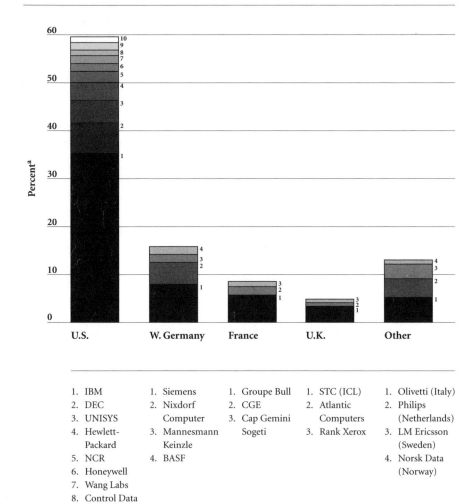

| 1. IBM | 1. Siemens | 1. Groupe Bull | 1. STC (ICL) | 1. Olivetti (Italy) |
| 2. DEC | 2. Nixdorf | 2. CGE | 2. Atlantic | 2. Philips |
| 3. UNISYS | Computer | 3. Cap Gemini | Computers | (Netherlands) |
| 4. Hewlett- | 3. Mannesmann | Sogeti | 3. Rank Xerox | 3. LM Ericsson |
| Packard | Keinzle | | | (Sweden) |
| 5. NCR | 4. BASF | | | 4. Norsk Data |
| 6. Honeywell | | | | (Norway) |
| 7. Wang Labs | | | | |
| 8. Control Data | | | | |
| 9. Commodore | | | | |
| and Apple | | | | |
| 10. Data General | | | | |

SOURCE: Adopted from Kenneth Flamm, *Creating the Computer: Government, Industry, and High Technology* (Washington, D.C.: Brookings Institution, 1988), fig. 5-1, p. 168. Reprinted by permission.

a Percentage of data-processing sales (hardware, software, services) in European markets by the twenty-five largest vendors. The top twenty-five accounted for $44.5 billion of a total European data-processing market estimated at more than $70 billion.

FIGURE 2-2

RELATIVE SHARES OF THE TOP COMPUTER COMPANIES IN THE JAPANESE MARKET

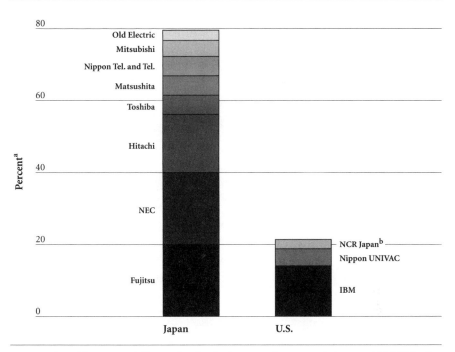

SOURCE: Adopted from Kenneth Flamm, *Creating the Computer: Government, Industry, and High Technology* (Washington, D.C.: Brookings Institution, 1988), fig. 6-2, p. 201. Reprinted by permission.

a Percentage of data-processing sales (hardware, software, and services) in the Japanese market by the eleven largest vendors. The top eleven accounted for $26.4 billion of a total Japanese data-processing market estimated at $30.4 billion.

b Estimate.

violating the 1956 consent decree. Control Data's complaint was that in 1963, IBM had announced the introduction of its supercomputer before it had begun any research on the design of the project. IBM's "phantom computer," Control Data argued, took potential customers away from its recently announced 660. The Justice Department then began its antitrust suit on the grounds that IBM had "impaired" the development of independent electronic data-processing companies.[36]

Hoping for a quick settlement, IBM announced the following June that it would respond to one of the major charges—that it sold hardware, software, and services only as a single package—by unbundling these products. It would now sell, in Watson's words, "engineering services, customer training and some of our software at à la carte prices."

The government's suit opened the door for litigation by a number of companies. Of the plaintiffs in these cases, more were leasing companies than makers of computers or peripherals. IBM won all but one of the sixteen suits that were filed. The most significant settlement was that made out of court to Control Data. IBM sold its service business to Control Data at a price that was well below its worth and included the value of over $100 million in cash and contracts. The government case dragged on until June 1982, when the solicitor general agreed that the case was "without merit."

Except for the very significant unbundling of its peripherals and its software, the government suit and the other resulting legal battles had little direct impact on industry competition. But its cost in terms of management time and stress, as well as an "annual legal bill [that] went up into the tens of millions of dollars," had an indelible impact on the top management of IBM. In the 1980s, antitrust considerations had an impact on defining the company's relationships with its smaller suppliers and competitors.

## The Mainframe Competitors

By the 1960s, IBM's major competitors numbered seven, "the Seven Dwarfs." For two, GE and RCA, the move into computers was short-lived. Both began to produce for the commercial market in the early 1960s, before the 360 came onstream. But with the announcement of the 370, both realized that they could not catch up. GE sold its computer division to Honeywell in 1970, and RCA sold to Sperry-Rand in 1971. By that time, RCA's computer losses were close to a half a billion dollars. The two firms' precipitous withdrawal provides powerful evidence of IBM's role as the industry's technological leader.[37]

Of the remaining five, Control Data was the most successful. Not only was it a major rival in plug-compatible peripherals and services, but it continued to hold the lead in large-scale supercomputers. In the high-end scientific market, IBM was unable to catch up. Control Data's 7600 followed the 6000. Then came the Star in 1969 and the Cyber 205 in 1981. As in the past, the first models were delivered to government customers. Control Data's major competitor in the superconductor market became, and remained, its brilliant designer Seymour Cray, who left in 1972 to form Cray Research.[38]

With the coming of the System 360, Sperry-Rand's UNIVAC Division continued to lose market share. As in the 1950s, it did little exploratory research and continued to rely heavily on government agencies, particularly the Air Force, for the sale of its products—its UNIVAC system and then its general-purpose computer, the 1100, announced in 1970. The acquisition of RCA's computer business in 1971 made Sperry-Rand the nation's second largest computer maker. But its performance did not improve. Little effort was made to integrate the two operations. The company continued to produce RCA's Spectra and its own 1100 family. By the end of 1974, only 5 percent of RCA's customers had installed UNIVAC equipment, and 77 percent still had their RCA machines. By 1973, Sperry-Rand, which a decade before had been second in revenues, had dropped to fourth place despite the increase in size through the RCA purchase. Merger brought no new capabilities and diluted existing ones.[39]

On the other hand, the late 1960s and 1970s saw a resurgence of the fortunes of NCR and Burroughs. In both cases, however, the revival was based more on a readjustment of their core businesses than on expanding their lines of computers. For both, continuing success rested on applying the new electronic technologies to the businesses they knew best. In incorporating these technologies, they reshaped their existing product-specific capabilities, particularly in research and development and, to a lesser extent, marketing, and did so with existing personnel and conservative external financing. The strengthening of the core, path-dependent capabilities, in turn, permitted them to produce competitive computers for markets they had long served.[40]

Burroughs began its corporate restructuring immediately after IBM's announcement of the System 360. A team headed by Ray W. MacDonald, who later became the company's CEO after heading its marketing organization, was formed "to establish a set of clearly defined product development objectives" and to reshape its functional activities so as to implement the new definition. In defining the company's strategy, the team took "the line of business approach," focusing on the needs of its specific business markets in industry, banking, and government. Its accounting machines were transformed from electromechanical to fully electronic products with electronic memories. Manufacturing was decentralized through the building of several new plants, each producing different machines for the different markets. The sales force was reshaped along the same lines. Computers were no longer sold by accounting machinery salesmen, but only by those trained in electronic data processing and procedures. Burroughs improved its computer lines by using new monolithic integrated circuits, and at the end of the 1960s, it produced a new generation of low-end, general-purpose computers.

Restructuring paid off. Revenues almost doubled between 1963 and 1969—from $392 million to $760 million—and net earnings rose more than fivefold, from $10 million to $55 million. R&D expenditures more than doubled, growing from $15 million to $35 million (and to $102 million in 1977). Over $670 million had been raised through increases in debt and equity. The renewed earnings permitted the debt–equity ratio to drop from 52 percent at the end of 1970 to 20 percent in 1976. During the same period, assets had risen over 75 percent and income, over 110 percent. By 1973, Burroughs' revenues from electronic data products were the third largest of the mainframe producers, just behind Honeywell, which had more than doubled its income through the acquisition of GE's computer hardware business in 1970. During the 1970s, Burroughs continued to grow through the development of a new 700 series and then its 900 series of general-purpose computers, as well as low-cost smaller computers, and word-processing and facsimile communication systems. At the same time, continuing government work made it a major producer of computers for the Army's ballistic missile systems. For Burroughs, the road to profit was one of continuing the development of improved and new products for much the same well-defined, closely related markets that it had long served.

NCR waited almost a decade before refining its competitive strength with a comparable strategy. Indeed, if its board had not named William F. Anderson, who headed its Japanese subsidiary, as CEO in 1972, the company might well have gone under. By then Singer, Pitney-Bowes, Litton, and other firms had, largely through acquisitions, become powerful competitors in the new electronic point-of-sale cash registers. In 1972, Singer already held 50 percent of the market. Within two years Anderson transformed the company from a mass producer of high-precision machines with mechanical parts into a high-quality assembler of purchased electronic components. Manufacturing, which had been centered in Dayton, was spread out in the United States and overseas in small new plants. The marketing organization also was transformed in the Burroughs manner.

In 1973, NCR delivered seventy-five thousand of its new electronic cash registers. The next year, Pitney-Bowes exited from the industry. By 1975, as it rounded out its complete line of electronic point-of-sale cash registers and closed down the production of its electromechanical machines, NCR's market share had risen to 61 percent. Given NCR's existing worldwide marketing strength and its new technological abilities, Singer and two other smaller competitors abandoned the market. By 1976, comparable changes in the production and distribution of accounting machinery were completed. A new line of computers with its own peripherals, software, and services for retailing and banking customers was coming into production. That year, Anderson turned the company over to Charles Exley, Jr., a twenty-two-year Burroughs veteran.

If the experiences of Burroughs and NCR indicate the value of maintaining growth and competitive strength by moving into a new technological paradigm through internal investment in products intended for long-held major markets, the story of Honeywell, like that of Sperry-Rand, underlines the weaknesses of attempting to do so by acquisition. Honeywell's initial response to the System 360 was an attempt to market its 200 and then its 800 line to users of IBM's 1400, which had been displaced by the 360. The strategy was not successful. Most of Honeywell's sales continued to come from providing updated versions to users of its earlier models.[41]

In 1966, it turned to the strategy of growth through acquisition. First came its purchase of Computer Control Products, a producer of small computers for scientific and communication switching devices. The acquired company then developed a low-end general-purpose computer as well as a full line of peripherals. In 1970, Honeywell doubled its electronic data-processing business by acquiring GE's computer hardware unit. That purchase brought with it a 66 percent interest in France's Machines Bull. Honeywell then continued to maintain GE's lines for its existing customers in parallel with its lines for its own long-term users. The acquisition of Xerox's Scientific Data Systems (SDS) followed much the same pattern. SDS, one of the most successful of the new minicomputer companies, declined rapidly after Xerox purchased it in 1970, and continued to do so after Honeywell acquired Xerox's computer activities in 1975. After that year, Honeywell continued to handle three noncompatible computer lines but made little attempt to develop improved lines in any of the three.

Not surprisingly, Honeywell, which in 1973 had the second largest data-processing revenues, had dropped by 1982 to seventh place, and in 1984, to ninth. In 1986, it exited altogether from the computer business. On the other hand, during the same years, Honeywell, like Burroughs and NCR, did successfully make the transition from electromechanical to electronic products and processes. By 1993 it held leading positions in computer-based industrial and building control systems.

For IBM's competitors in the production of mainframes, the paths they embarked upon in the 1950s and 1960s shaped their business portfolios of the 1970s and 1980s. Continued profitability came not by buying existing enterprises but by reshaping and building internal capabilities. Indeed, acquisitions, as in the case of SDS by Xerox and then Honeywell, and (somewhat earlier) of Philco by Ford, destroyed the capabilities of the acquired company as well as diminishing those of the acquirer. Once again, a lesson was learned. The path to continuing vitality came through building, not acquiring, learned organizational capabilities.

## Minicomputers: Entrepreneurial Start-ups

During the initial period of growth of the computer industry, large, established enterprises, with the exception of Control Data, were the primary players, as was the case in other postwar high-tech industries: chemicals, pharmaceuticals, aerospace, telecommunications, and consumer electronics. But in the early 1960s, as IBM was moving full force into the development of the System 360, entrepreneurs began, in the manner of Control Data, to build new global enterprises. These start-ups at first did not directly challenge IBM's basic lines. As Control Data was moving into the high end of the price/performance range, the pioneering minicomputer firms were entering the low end with high-powered machines specifically for scientific and engineering markets. These pioneers—Digital Equipment Corporation (DEC), Scientific Data Systems (SDS), Data General, and Prime Computer—made extensive investments in technically advanced production facilities, quickly created national and then international marketing and servicing organizations, and recruited large labor forces and technically trained teams of top-, middle-, and lower-level managers.

Such patterns of initial growth were very similar to those of the entrepreneurial firms that became dominant in the new capital-intensive, scale-dependent industries during the 1880s and 1890s, as well as those that did so somewhat later by exploiting the potential of the internal combustion engine. One major difference was that the entrepreneurs in computers were technically trained specialists in the field. A second was that the initial pioneering firms often bred other entrepreneurial ones. As was true of the founders of Control Data, Amdahl and Cray, the pioneers of new minicomputers had participated in the operations and management of the pioneering enterprises, including IBM.

Kenneth H. Olsen, who established Digital Equipment at Maynard, Massachusetts, in 1957, one of the industry's most impressive technological innovators, was even more successful than high-end producers in transforming individual capabilities into organizational ones. Olsen entered MIT in 1947, after completing his service in the Naval Reserve. While still a student, he began to work on Jay Forrester's Navy Whirlwind Project. Between 1953 and 1956, he was at IBM as liaison for Forrester's Lincoln Laboratory in the development of the SAGE computer.

At DEC, Olsen's first product, the Programmed Data Processor (PDP

1), went on the market in 1961. This and the next three products were "little more than tailor-made devices, assembled almost to order." In 1963 came the PDP 5, which in Flamm's words "quickly carved out a whole new market," because it permitted the placing of computers on the shop floor and in engineering and research laboratories. It was quickly followed by the PDP 6, the first computer with commercially available time-sharing systems, and the PDP 8. The first mass-produced minicomputer, and the first to use integrated circuits, the PDP 8 sold for the extraordinarily low price of $18,000.[42]

Thus Olsen, like Norris, designed his product line for a niche, for the specific needs of specialized engineering and scientific markets. He provided computers of very high performance at very low cost. DEC computers were made for a small number of applications—indeed, many had only a single application. Customers therefore developed most of their own software. Indeed, 30–50 percent of PDP 8 and its successors were sold to OEMs that embodied them in their own data-processing systems or mechanical devices, or to value-added resalers (VAR) that combined them with other components to produce their own specialized products. The rest went to university laboratories and companies. The higher-priced PDP 6 included a significant software innovation that permitted multiple users of a single computer through time-sharing.

The strategy of low price/high performance succeeded brilliantly. In one year, 1966, DEC's revenues soared from $15 million to $23 million, and its profits multiplied six times between 1965 and 1967. Although its marketing force was much smaller and more specialized than IBM's, DEC had twenty-four sales offices in six countries by 1966. By then, Olsen had brought together an impressive management team and designed a matrix organizational structure to integrate the activities of the functional and product departments.

By 1970, DEC had become the third largest computer company, with revenues exceeded only by Sperry-Rand and IBM. In the late 1960s, it moved into larger machines targeted to compete with the lower end of the IBM line. But after 1970, it pulled back to concentrate on its initial market by developing the PDP 11 family of compatible, more powerful, and versatile computers. In 1977, DEC introduced a new product line, the VAX 11/780, to compete with the larger IBM 3031 and 3032. This enhanced minicomputer quickly made impressive inroads in the low end of IBM's mainframe markets.

Scientific Data Systems, initially DEC's strongest competitor, was formed in 1961 by two engineers, Max Palevsky and Robert Bell. They had worked on Army missile development at Bendix, and then organized

Packard-Bell's military computer manufacturing operations. Their production of a low-cost scientific machine permitted SDS to grow even faster than DEC until 1966. But it continued to rely more on government contracts, with 40 percent of its production going to NASA. Its SDS 940, first marketed in 1966, effectively challenged DEC's PDP 6. SDS was beginning to move into larger machines with broader commercial applications when Xerox acquired it in 1970. Then its capabilities atrophied.[43]

After 1970, DEC's major rival was one of its progeny. Data General was formed in 1968 by Edwin de Castro, a key designer of the PDP 8, who took with him a group of DEC's most talented engineers. Its primary product, the low-cost NOVA, which sold for $8,000, was the first 16-bit processor with improved memory capability. It was followed in 1974 by the larger and more sophisticated Eclipse series. The systems could be linked together and had interfaces for linkages with IBM's System 360. Like Control Data, Data General sold peripherals and some software and services, and focused on VARs.[44]

Prime Computer was established in 1971 by a group headed by William Poduska; they had been with the Computer Control Products when it was acquired in 1966 by Honeywell. Frustrated by Honeywell's loss of interest in CCC's products, the group formed their own company to produce computers they had developed. Prime grew quickly during the 1970s, commercializing the state-of-the-art systems, but its competitive strength declined after Poduska and much of its top management, disturbed by the failure of its board to invest in product development, left the company to start Apollo, the first producer of microprocessor-based workstations.[45]

In the early 1970s, other firms began to crowd the market. The most successful was Hewlett-Packard, a producer of electronic computer-like analytical instruments that had been formed in 1938 and expanded the output of the initial line during the war. In the following years, new products were commercialized, including, in 1966, its first processor to provide computational support for its instruments; it then led the way in handheld calculators. In 1968, Hewlett-Packard entered the field cautiously, bringing out in early 1972 its HP 3000, a highly successful minicomputer that performed broader general-purpose computations than its rivals. Upgraded in 1976, it did time-sharing, multiprocessing, batch processing, or on-line processing, and supported various languages used by large mainframes. Another was Wang Laboratories, formed in 1951 by an MIT engineer, An Wang. The company produced several specialized electronic products before entering the office equipment machine business with desktop calculators. In 1976, the company introduced the first screen-based word processor. In the following year, it began to make its U.S. series, a line of compatible business minicomputers.[46]

During the 1970s, as the minicomputer firms began to successfully challenge mainframes in broader commercial markets, both IBM, with its 4300 computer family, and Burroughs entered the minicomputer business, and did so aggressively. So aggressively, in fact, that by 1982, according to the trade journal *Datamation*, IBM was first and Burroughs was third in revenues generated by production of minicomputers; Digital was second and Data General was fourth, followed by Hewlett-Packard, Wang, and Prime Computer. Together these seven accounted for more than 75 percent of the revenues generated in the minicomputer market. By 1982, that market accounted for 30 percent of the total computer revenues.[47]

## Service Bureaus and Software

The operation of the electronic digital computer created two new ancillary businesses—the production of software and specialists in providing computer services. Unlike the products of other major industries, the computer had no value until application programs were written for the machine, and those applications required specialized skills. Both businesses exploded with the introduction of IBM's 360 (see tables 2-4 and 2-5). IBM, and then Control Data and the other smaller competitors, had developed their own service bureau and software businesses before the mid-1960s, as did the minicomputer companies after 1965. But the massive increase in computer use—driven by the global spread of the IBM System 360 and, as important, IBM's decision in 1969, under antitrust pressure, to unbundle its services and software—brought a swarm of new competitors into the business.[48]

Well before the IBM decision, however, the number of independent producers of custom-made software and then software packages, and of providers of computer time and other specialized services, had been growing rapidly. Entry into the service bureau business required little more than purchasing a computer. In addition to start-ups and computer leasing companies, banks, aerospace, and other industrial enterprises with unused capacity entered the market. The time-sharing possibilities of the mainframes and especially of minicomputers provided attractive opportunities.

Revenues in the service bureau industries rose as swiftly as they did in leasing. Those of Automatic Data Processing, the pioneer established in 1948 to handle payrolls in firms using existing methods and machines, went from $187,000 in 1957 to $2 million in 1963, to $20 million in 1968, and to $37 million in 1970. Those of Tymsharing, formed in 1966, soared from $1 million in 1967 to $10 million in 1970. H. Ross Perot, an IBM employee who left to start Electronic Data Systems in 1962, became a multimillionaire in the 1970s. By 1975, 1,560 service companies were producing revenues of well over $3.2 billion (see table 2-5).[49]

The production of software enjoyed a comparable growth in the decade after the introduction of the System 360. It had even fewer barriers to entry than the service bureau business: 85 percent of the production costs were for salaries to programmers and system analysts; 5 percent, for developing new programs; and 10 percent, for buying software packages and services. By 1985, in addition to the software produced by computer makers, service bureaus, leasing companies, and in-house units of industrial, commercial, and military enterprises, over one thousand independent firms were producing two thousand different products with sales of over a billion dollars.

The major development of the 1970s, hastened by IBM's unbundling in 1969, was the shift from software designed specifically to meet a customer's need to packaged software to handle specific functional activities such as payrolls, ledgers, income tax preparation, and the like. While revenues from custom programming rose from $300 million in 1968 to $600 million in 1980, those for packaged software applications rose from $100 million to $1,500 million in the same years (see table 2-4). Individual companies grew even faster than those in leasing and services. For example, the revenues of Computer Sciences Corporation (CSC), established in 1959, rose from $5.7 million in 1965 to $82 million in 1970 and to $452 million in 1980 (and $709.4 million in 1984).[50]

## PERIPHERALS AND SEMICONDUCTORS

During the era of the System 360/370, the growth of the component industry was as rapid as that of the computer's unique software, services, and leasing businesses. As in all major capital-intensive industries, the first movers in computers became the core of a network of companies of all sizes that provided essential components—processors, memories, and input-output peripheral equipment. In addition to such hardware, computers required "consumables," primarily the media by which data were stored in machines in readable form—computer cards, paper, disk packs, magnetic tapes, and diskettes.

The output of these consumables and of peripherals soared as dramatically as did output of software and services, although the jump in revenues and profits was probably less. The makers of IBM's clones—Memorex, Ampex, and Storage Technology—continued to grow rapidly during the 1970s, and numerous entrepreneurial start-ups came into the market. In disk drives, for example, such firms included Intercomp, OEMEC, Caelus, Community Computer Corporation, and BDC Computing Corporation.

By far the most critical components were those that made up the "engine of the computer," the central processing unit with its logic elements for computing devices and its main memory units. What differentiated this electronic power source from that provided by the internal combustion engine in other mechanical industries was that the components making up this "engine" became a far greater source of innovation than did the design—the architecture—of the computer itself. Innovations in the semiconductor far more profoundly transformed the machines it drove than those in the internal combustion engine ever did in the machines it powered. The first such innovation, the solid-state transistor, was central to the initial growth of the computer industry in the 1950s. In the 1960s, the integrated circuit, which placed transistors, resistors, and other components on a single silicon chip, not only expanded the performance of the general-purpose mainframe computers but also was central to the rise of the more specialized, highly powered minicomputers. And in the 1980s, the microprocessor, "the computer on a chip," became the critical element in the appearance of the microcomputer and the transformation it wrought.

Semiconductors came to be used in most all electronic final products. In addition to computers, they were employed in consumer electronics, automotive devices, communication equipment, medical equipment, analytical, test, and measurement instruments, and industrial equipment. This chapter focuses only on the development of those used in computers: digital integrated memories, logic families, and microprocessors in both bipolar and metal oxide semiconductor (MOS) technologies. Also, AT&T from the industry's start, and IBM from the commercializing of the System 360, became the largest makers of such products—but only for their own internal use. Thus the briefest review of the activities of the leading makers of semiconductors is essential for understanding the evolution of the computer industry.

The semiconductor industry began early in 1952 when AT&T's Western Electric, which had just begun to manufacture the transistor invented by Bell Laboratories in 1948, signed an agreement with twenty companies to make the new device that would transform telephone switching equipment. It did so in part because of its own needs, but also because the Justice Department had filed an antitrust suit against the company in 1949. The producers of radio transmission and reception equipment, including GE, Westinghouse, RCA, Sylvania, Philco, and Raytheon, soon began to produce and improve the transistor and related diodes and rectifiers. These firms, however, remained committed to the older vacuum tube technologies, in part because RCA, GE, and possibly others received greater income from the sale of their tubes than from their radio and other electronic consumer products.[51]

The more aggressive pioneers in the application of the new transistor technology were smaller firms that had not produced vacuum tubes. These included Motorola, a maker since 1928 of car radios, and during World War II of walkie-talkies and other radio communication products; Texas Instruments (TI), since 1930 a producer of electronic geodetic instruments and during the war of airborne magnetic detectors; Hughes Aviation, another wartime producer; and two start-ups, Transitron, established in 1952, and Fairchild Semiconductor, formed in 1957. The last was an offshoot of a company that William Shockley, one of the transistor's inventors, had organized in 1954. By 1963, Hughes had dropped out and Transitron, which had 20 percent of the market in 1957, had fallen to only 3 percent. Texas Instruments enjoyed 18 percent; Motorola, 10 percent; and Fairchild, 9 percent. GE, RCA, and Westinghouse together accounted for another 20 percent (8 percent, 7 percent, and 5 percent). By 1957, TI and Motorola were the industry's two world leaders, and they remained so until the 1980s.

Both TI and Motorola had the advantages of retained earnings, which Transitron and Fairchild did not, and of capabilities learned in the manufacture of electronic products during and after the war, which Hughes did not. Finally, they had a far more focused production line than GE or Westinghouse; and had no dominant position to maintain, as did RCA.

Of the two, Texas Instruments was the more innovative. From 1946 on, it enhanced its electronic capabilities by producing airborne radar and sonar systems for the Navy. In 1952, after signing the agreement with AT&T, it began to volume-produce transistor radios. As the first to commercialize the silicon junction transistor (in 1954) and the diffused transistor (in 1956), it quickly dominated silicon-based products. In December 1957, its success led IBM to enter a joint licensing and development agreement that, for all practical purposes, made TI the component supplier (until the System 360 began to be shipped) for the computer industry's fastest growing enterprise. Its position was further strengthened in 1959, when Jack Kilby, one of its engineers, patented the integrated circuit.[52]

During the 1960s, TI, after making large investments in production and marketing facilities at home, began to expand rapidly by building plants and marketing networks abroad—an expansion financed almost wholly by retained earnings. By 1965, it was operating fifteen plants in ten countries, all wholly owned. Those in Europe placed manufacturing close to the customers, but, of more importance, had the advantage of skilled technicians and workers to build and operate complex fabrication plants; those in Latin America and Asia used cheap labor for assembling the machines. By 1968, TI was the largest producer of semiconductors in Britain (with 23 percent of the market) and France (with 20 percent) and third in Germany (with 6 percent). Throughout the 1970s, TI led the industry with worldwide market shares of 11.5 percent in 1972, 12.8 percent in 1974, 11.4 percent in 1976, and 11.2 percent in 1980.[53]

This overseas expansion was carried out by direct investment through the creation of wholly owned subsidiaries. Japan was the sole exception. There TI was forced to enter a joint venture. Negotiations for such an arrangement with Sony lasted from November 1963 until April 1968. They were completed only after TI agreed to license the Kilby patent and other integrated circuit technologies, not just to Sony but to *all* Japanese firms. The delay and the deal itself, Anchordoguy writes, provided the Japanese producers of electronics with "a crucial opportunity to build up economies of scale before encountering foreign competition."[54]

Motorola was less of a radical innovator than TI, but more successful in maintaining its technological leadership in product development through continuous learning. The 1952 agreement with AT&T freed it from its dependence on RCA for radio tubes. It immediately began to produce transistors both for internal use in its production of commercial and consumer radio and television sets and for external sales. After 1958, under the leadership of Robert Galvin, the son of the founder, the company's senior managers began to move into telecommunications. Motorola expanded abroad somewhat more slowly than TI. By 1968, it had 5 percent of the market in Britain and 4 percent in West Germany, where it had built no plants, and 5 percent in France, where it had. By 1970, it had factories in Britain and West Germany as well as in Latin America and Asia. As with TI, all these overseas operations were wholly owned except in Japan, where Motorola had an even more difficult time than TI in gaining entry through a joint venture. Thus by 1972, Motorola was the second largest producer worldwide, with 9.0 percent. In the U.S. market, according to the estimate of Mariann Jelinek and Claudia B. Schoonhoven, Motorola and TI held just over 70 percent, with Motorola having 33.3 percent and TI having 37.4 percent for the five-year averages of 1975–1979.[55]

These same estimates of the U.S. market gave their closest competitors—the leading California start-ups, Fairchild, National, and Intel—only 8.3 percent, 7.5 percent, and 5.9 percent, respectively. Although Fairchild failed to keep up with the industry's two first movers, it was responsible for creating many of the entrepreneurial start-ups that took advantage of the opportunities engendered by the massive growth of the electronic data-processing industry after the IBM 360 came into full production. In fact, Fairchild failed in good part because, by becoming an entrepreneurial seedbed, it was unable to continue to enhance its own organizational capabilities, so necessary to maintaining its competitive strength.

Fairchild Semiconductor had a most auspicious beginning. This spin-off from William Shockley's Laboratories, Inc., formed in 1954 near Palo Alto, was established in 1957 when eight engineers, headed by Robert Noyce, departed to form their own firm with the financial backing of Fairchild Camera and Instrument. After getting his Ph.D. at MIT, Noyce had spent three years at Philco before he joined the Shockley team in 1956. In 1959 he patented the integrated circuit chip almost simultaneously with Jack Kilby of Texas Instruments. By 1963, Fairchild had 5 percent of the semiconductor market, and by 1966 its 13 percent put it ahead of Motorola (12 percent). It moved overseas as quickly as Texas Instruments. In 1961, it entered a joint venture with Olivetti and another Italian business machine company. In 1963, it built a plant in Hong Kong, followed by one in Singapore. In 1965, it restructured its marketing organization with separate units for the four major markets it had entered: military, industrial, consumer, and computers.[56]

But where Motorola continued to grow, Fairchild declined. In 1968, it sold its share of its Italian joint venture to Olivetti. Its market share fell off. In 1979, it was acquired by the French firm Schlumberger. By 1982, Fairchild, as the tenth largest producer worldwide, had fallen well behind National Semiconductor (which would acquire it in 1987), which was fifth, and Intel, which was seventh.[57]

As James C. Williams has written, with the coming of Fairchild, "Silicon Valley was born." Fairchild became a "corporate vocational school for young engineers." Once trained, most moved on "to replicate the founders' experience in new ventures." By Williams' count, forty-one new companies were established by employees of Fairchild. At a 1969 conference in Sunnyvale, California, Annalee Saxenian reports, "fewer than two dozen of the 400 men there had never worked for Fairchild."[58]

Of Fairchild's numerous progeny, only a tiny number became significant players in global or even national markets. Very few were able to transform individual capabilities into organizational ones in the manner of Norris or Olsen. Those that did, did so by explicitly using the opportunities to exploit the cost advantages of scale made possible by the massive growth of the computer industry beginning in the late 1960s.

For just as that growth transformed the production of software from custom design to packaged products, it transformed the production of custom-designed chips into standardized, volume-produced devices. At the same time, the cost of fabricating plants soared, rising from $500,000 in 1960 to $2 million in 1972, $5 million in 1978, $10 million by 1980, and $200 million by the mid-1980s. (By 1991, Intel's new plant cost was set at $1.3 billion, and in 1995 that of its projected works was $3 billion.) The rising cost of facilities reflected the increasingly complex technology involved in chip production and the rising need for close supervision in coordinating the processes involved, from the design to the delivery of the final product. By 1980, the industry had become, as Saxenian notes, "one of the nation's most capital-intensive industries—seven times more than the U.S. average." As costs of facilities soared, so did output, and the prices of semiconductors dropped dramatically. Many entrepreneurial enterprises disappeared. *Dataquest* reported in 1980, "of the 35 semiconductor companies started between 1966 and 1975, only seven remained independent in 1980."[59]

In Silicon Valley, firms that first made the investments necessary in building fabricating plants to minimum efficient scale and in creating national and international marketing organizations between 1967 and 1973—National Semiconductor, Intel, and Advanced Micro Devices— quickly challenged Fairchild's leadership. In 1967, Peter Sprague, heir to Sprague Electric Equipment and owner of National Semiconductor Corporation, with a small plant in Danbury, Connecticut, hired Charles Spork, the general manager at Fairchild, as National's president. By building a large fabricating plant in Silicon Valley, one authority wrote: "National Semiconductor positioned itself as the low-cost, efficient producer of integrated circuits," both linear memories and logic chips. In 1969, W. Jeremiah Sanders, formerly a salesman (not an engineer) at Fairchild Camera (not Fairchild Semiconductor), formed Advanced Micro Devices (AMD). Sanders moved into the volume production of chips designed and licensed by other companies.[60]

The third of these start-ups, Intel, was established a few months before AMD by two cofounders of Fairchild, Robert Noyce and Gordon Moore. Noyce became CEO and focused on management, and Moore was director of research, assisted by Andrew Grove, who had joined Fairchild in 1963, after receiving a Ph.D. from the University of California. The challenge at Fairchild was, as Moore has written, not invention but manufacturing the innovations developed and getting them to market before a spin-off did. The fact that his laboratory's "new ideas were spawning new companies rather than contributing to the growth of Fairchild was immensely frustrating." Intel's founders began by volume-manufacturing complex random access memories (RAMs) based on the MOS technology developed at Fairchild. Its success was followed by the production of dynamic RAMs (DRAMs) and then the first erasable programmable read on memories (EPROMs).[61]

Intel also pioneered in commercializing the microprocessor. In 1971, its Ted Hoff combined central processing circuitry, two types of memory chips, and an input/output register on a single chip. This "computer on a chip" was, like the earlier integrated chip, a multiple discovery. But, as Moore points out, until 1980 the microprocessor was used primarily as a microcomputer in dedicated control systems in automobiles, appliances, automated production lines, and the like. During the 1970s, when Intel's revenues from memory systems were much greater than those from microprocessors, the company expanded its marketing organizations and capabilities, and improved and speeded up its manufacturing processes. The resulting scale economies reduced cost and prices. The price for its 8-bit 8080A in 1975 was $110; in 1977, it was $20. By 1980, a standard 8-bit processor sold for between $5 and $8. The rapid growth of these three companies and their suppliers, Saxenian reports, "contributed to the creation of more than 200,000 new technology jobs in the region during the 1970s, more than quadrupling local technology employment."[62]

By 1976, TI and Motorola, using comparable mass-production techniques, had surpassed Intel in share of the DRAM market. Motorola concentrated more on the new microprocessors. Soon its 6800 processor was considered superior to Intel's 8080. In 1980, TI and Motorola were still the world's largest producers of semiconductors, with 11.2 percent and 7.8 percent shares of the global semiconductor market.[63]

By 1980, however, the major challengers to TI and Motorola were not American start-ups but long established, very large Japanese producers of both consumer electronics and information-processing equipment. None of these companies produced semiconductors as their major line. Instead, they designed and manufactured them internally for their related product lines, which were more numerous than those of either Texas Instruments or Motorola. With Japanese firms' rapid conquest of global markets for consumer electronics in the early and mid-1970s, and the simultaneous rapid expansion of Japanese computer sales in Europe as well as the continuing growth in the home market, such firms as Sony, Matsushita,

Hitachi, Toshiba, Fujitsu, and NEC had, from the early 1970s on, developed new mass-production techniques. Their internal demands provided not only an assured volume but also, and of more importance, the learning base for making incremental refinements in semiconductor design and production, particularly in the development of the far more powerful VLSI chip. Profits from established lines assured ample funding for such development.[64] As one Intel manager explained, "they build large plants that are organized with large clean rooms and more automation" than those in the United States. The particular strengths of these companies rested, as they did in automobile production, on close ties with suppliers and careful coordination of the process flows within the plant so as to maintain high throughput with minimum defects, as well as to assure close coordination of design and manufacturing capabilities with customer needs.[65]

By the end of the 1970s, the semiconductor divisions of these firms were operating at a minimum efficient scale that spewed forth high-performance products at prices that permitted them to sweep global markets. In 1980, Hewlett-Packard sounded the alarm for the American industry by announcing that the Japanese 16-K DRAMs were of far higher quality than those made in the United States. "At first glance the impression is that the Japanese are using low-cost and domestic production as levers to build a strong base for exports. On closer inspection, this premise [about Japanese "dumping"] does not hold up. The Japanese semiconductor companies are using superior product quality to gain competitive advantage of enormous magnitude." The impact was indeed devastating.[66]

From 1980 to 1984, the Japanese share of world markets for semiconductors rose, according to one estimate from 26 percent to 40 percent, while that of U.S. companies dropped from 57 percent to 44 percent. By 1985, Motorola, Intel, National Semiconductor, Advanced Micro Devices, and MOSTEK (a spin-off from TI based in Colorado Springs) had dropped out of the memory chip business except for EPROMs. Only a weak TI and a tiny start-up, Micron Technology, hung on. The Japanese firms' astonishingly swift success provides a dramatic example of the competitive power of large enterprises in the capital- and knowledge-intensive industries that effectively exploit the economies of learning, scale, and scope.

The semiconductor story also dramatically emphasizes the urgency of transforming individual capabilities into organizational ones. The competitive advantage of the Japanese firms rested on technological, managerial, and workforce capabilities based on constant learning within long established enterprises, learning that continued as individuals moved in and out of the organization. The Silicon Valley challengers to TI and Motorola were single-product start-ups that were only beginning to create comparable global competitive competencies.

In Silicon Valley, individual capabilities were prized and organizational ones downplayed. Fairchild Semiconductor remained a model. The initial success of its spin-offs and the urging of venture capitalists encouraged designers and engineers to leave recently formed enterprises to set up firms of their own. At times, companies were dismantled even before the new product came onstream, because members of the founding team were lured away by eager venture capitalists. "Vulture capitalism" was the term used in the Valley. Long-lived firms were rare; the death rate of start-ups was high. As a result, the Valley continued to be a dynamic force in innovative design, especially in software, and in filling of specialized niches, especially in chipmaking equipment; but often its products were profitably commercialized by existing integrated organizations that had created the production and distribution capabilities necessary to reach global markets.[67]

## THE THIRD PERIOD: THE MICROCOMPUTER REVOLUTION

Two of the most significant developments of the 1970s ushered in the microcomputer revolution that transformed the industry in the 1980s as profoundly as the System 360 had in the 1960s. One was rooted in the global spread of the System 360/370. The resulting proliferation worldwide of the volume production of standardized semiconductors, peripherals, software packages, and other related products brought a dramatic reduction in the costs of their production and, therefore, in their price—and a dramatic increase in their availability. In this way, the internal economies of scale, of scope, and of incremental learning, developed by the leading U.S. and Japanese firms over a quarter of a century, created the external economies that permitted the rise of the new industry.

The other development was the commercialization, and then volume production, of the microprocessor by Intel, TI, and Motorola that so sharply increased the processing power and decreased the price of the computer's engine. By 1975, amateur "hobbyists" were assembling cheap, readily available components into small, inexpensive computers. Then kits—the MITS Altair and IMSAI 8080—were sold to buyers who could construct their own computers.

The availability of low-priced parts and a high-powered engine led to the spontaneous beginnings of the microcomputer industry. Within a single year, 1977, three widely separated firms introduced their initial offerings: Apple Computer in California, Radio Shack (the leading U.S. retailer of consumer electronics) in Texas, and Commodore (producer of electronic calculators) in Pennsylvania.

The story of Apple is well known—the classic one of a garage-born enterprise combining the brilliance of a computer designer and the creativity of an entrepreneur. The beginnings of the other two are less well known. The achievement of Steve Wozniak and Steven Jobs was not in designing a technologically advanced machine but, as Richard Langlois wrote, "rather one that was a compromise between technology and marketing, the Apple II." Apple II used an MOS 6502 chip designed and produced by Chuck Paddle, who had helped develop the successful Motorola 6800 before establishing his own enterprise, MOS Technologies, outside Philadelphia. For Apple II, Wozniak wrote a version of BASIC, a nonproprietary operating system. Nearly all the components except its disk and disk drives were outsourced. As Adam Osborne, a less-than-triumphant pioneer noted, Apple's key to success was "that this company was the first to offer real customer support and to behave like a genuine business." In addition, the Visi Calc spreadsheet, invented by Daniel Bricklin, a Harvard MBA and former DEC employee, provided entry into the low-end business market.

Commodore's PET computer, announced in January 1977, had, like Apple II, an MOS 6502 microprocessor. Indeed, in 1975, Jack Tramiel, Commodore's founder, had acquired Chuck Paddle's MOS Technologies. In the early 1970s, Tramiel's company had entered and increasingly prospered in the handheld calculator business; it purchased Paddle's enterprise in order to have an assured supply of chips. Paddle, in turn, urged Tramiel to begin producing microcomputers. From the start, Tramiel and Paddle focused on the low end, the "home computer" market.

In 1977 the Tandy Corporation of Fort Worth, Texas, was the largest mass retailer of electronic goods in the United States. Established in 1927, it became a national chain retailing leather craft products after World War II. In 1962, Charles Tandy, the son of the founder, decided to enter the electronics business by acquiring the Boston-based mass retailer Radio Shack. By 1973, Radio Shack had grown from 1,174 stores to 2,294, and by 1979, to 7,353 (compared with McDonald's fast-food chain of 5,353 stores). In response to the suggestion of one of its buyers, Don French, Tandy decided to enter the market. French brought an engineer who had worked for National Semiconductor to Fort Worth to assist in producing the TRS model, using a Z-80 chip (produced by Zilog, a Motorola spin-off formed in 1974). Like Commodore and Apple, Tandy developed its own proprietary software system. It sold this product primarily through the company's outlets at low prices, for home and amusement use.

After 1977, the three firms improved their product lines: Apple's improved spreadsheet and a customer service organization enhanced its strong competitive advantage in the business markets. By one estimate, the three firms enjoyed 72 percent of the market in 1978—Radio Shack with 50 percent, Commodore with 12 percent, and Apple with 10 percent. Others began to enter the industry. By 1980, Apple led with 27 percent, followed by Commodore with 20 percent, Radio Shack with 21 percent, Hewlett-Packard with 5 percent, and Japan's NEC with 9 percent. Nevertheless, when IBM's management decided to enter in the spring of 1980, the industry was still in its embryonic stage.[68]

Entering with an impressive, brilliantly executed strategy, IBM almost immediately brought the industry into young adulthood. But that very act gave a huge impetus to a product that in a short time would begin to destroy the worldwide dominance of the mainframe by IBM and its clones. That move began when the senior managers at IBM directed William Lowe, the manager of its Entry Level Systems (i.e., small computers), based in Boca Raton, Florida, to organize, in the usual IBM manner, a task force to study the feasibility of producing a low-priced, mass-produced desktop computer in as short a time as possible. In early July, Lowe carried the task force's report to Armonk, New York.[69]

The report stressed that a completely autonomous unit operating outside of IBM's existing organization and its business culture had to develop, produce, and market the new system. The task force began by recommending "an open architecture." The computer would not be protected, as its competitors were, by patents. It would use a modular bus that would permit the customer to use desired add-ons. As Langlois has written, "The IBM PC was a system, not an appliance; an incomplete package, an open box ready for expansion, reconfiguration and continuing upgrading."

The implementation of the report called for a totally new approach. IBM would not, as it had in the past, build its own components, peripherals, and software. Instead, in the interest of speeding the product to the mass consumer market, and in order to benefit from the recently created external economies, all these items would be purchased from outside suppliers. In addition, the software would be developed independently of the hardware. Once the prototype was completed, the software would be developed; the plant to assemble these products was being built at Boca Raton. At the same time, the unit would create its own sales and service force to support a national, and then a worldwide, network of franchised dealers as of well as large, conventional mass retailers.

IBM's Central Management Committee approved Lowe's report, upgraded the task force to a full-scale project development group (and then to an independent business unit), appointed Philip D. "Don" Estridge its chief, and gave him precisely one year to have the product on the market. Estridge quickly recruited the management team, including heads of engineering, materials, production, and marketing units.

For its microprocessor, Estridge's team chose Intel's older 8-bit chip rather than the state-of-the-art chips of Motorola or their clones—then used by Apple, Tandy, and Commodore—or even Intel's new, much more powerful 16-bit chip, the 8086. The IBM task force agreed that the PC did not need the computing power of the 16-bit processor. The cheaper 8-bit 8088 could accommodate nearly all the application software then available for small computers. Estridge then asked Intel to sign a standard nondisclosure agreement and, in addition, stated that Intel should license the chip out so that the Boca Raton plant could be sure of a second source. Intel, as a contemporary noted, "readily accepted the offer" for its "commercially unpopular chip" that was losing out to competing products from Motorola, Zilog, and others. And, as Gordon Moore has pointed out, that decision "changed the entire course of Intel's history."[70]

Once the chip decision had been made, Estridge approached Gary Kildall, whose Digital Research had written the pioneering control program for microcomputers (CPM), which by 1981 had become the dominant operating system for microcomputers. Kildall, however, was unwilling to sign the standard nondisclosure agreements on which IBM insisted. Estridge therefore turned to William Gates, whose Seattle-based Microsoft had pioneered in writing a version of BASIC, a widely used programming language, for microprocessors. Gates quickly accepted the offer with its nondisclosure clause. His firm then purchased the operating system of a nearby fellow computer buff, Ron Brock, whose Seattle Computer Products had developed it for the Intel 8088, but did not reveal the reason because of its nondisclosure agreement with IBM. Gates then converted Brock's SCP-DOS into MS-DOS. Once it was fully developed, IBM agreed to let Microsoft license its product to others. The reasoning was that although the move would allow competitors to enter, it not only would assure the availability of software but also would make that software the industry's standard.

In this way, Microsoft and Intel received what became the most lucrative franchises in the history of American industry. If Kildall had been willing to accept the nondisclosure clause, and if Motorola's chip had been the first choice rather than Intel's commercially unpopular one, the underlying history of the microprocessor industry during the critical decade of the 1980s might have remained much the same. But the two most powerful players in the 1990s would not have been Microsoft and Intel.

Once those two had been signed on, Estridge completed contracts with peripheral suppliers. Tandon made the disk drives in California; Zenith, the PC power supplies in Michigan; the Silicon Valley Division of SCI Systems (a contract manufacturer), the circuit boards; a Japanese firm, Epson, the printers; IBM's Charlotte, North Carolina, plant, the board assemblers, and its Lexington, Kentucky, plant, the keyboards.

The marketing and servicing of the new low-cost, mass-produced computer obviously had to be as different as its manufacturing. As directed, Estridge's group made arrangements with such mass retailing chains as ComputerLand and Sears Business Centers, and built a national (then international) marketing unit to recruit and support a network of franchised dealers. Nevertheless, they did agree to let the sales forces of other IBM divisions sell PCs to corporate and government customers and to service them. This impressive implementation of Lowe's proposal within the allotted year made possible the fulfillment of, as two members of Estridge's team, wrote, "The long-term strategy [that] called for IBM's entry in the market to cause a dramatic explosion in demand for personal computers [so] that its operating system would be the internationally accepted standard for all desktop computing."[71]

Demand soared far above anticipated sales. Though its automated production lines were spewing out one PC every forty-five seconds, IBM was unable to keep up. In 1983 its Management Committee created an entirely new Entry System Division to manage this explosive growth. The announcement of this organizational change noted that "more systems [were] shipped over the first five months of 1983 than in all of 1982. Daily manufacturing volumes increased 600% with high quality. Retail outlets have doubled. Sales have risen to the point that would rank ESD eligible for the Fortune 500 index." It further stated that "Some 6,000 application programs for the IBM PC were being written by more than 2000 software houses. . . . Meanwhile, plans were being completed to sell the division's products in 74 countries." In 1984, revenues had reached $4.0 billion, equivalent to those of the seventy-fifth largest company on *Fortune*'s list, and leveled off at $5.5 billion in 1985. The organizational and management challenges, driven by a $5 billion increase in revenue in four years, were truly unprecedented.[72]

The huge unanticipated demand that quickly transformed the

microcomputer industry intensified these challenges. Companies—established and start-ups—swarmed into the market because cloning the PC was simplicity itself in comparison to cloning IBM mainframes. Nor was the minimum efficient scale of the PC production plant high enough to create an effective barrier to entry. Most of the cloners sold products under their own names, but a good number built them on an OEM basis for leading manufacturers to sell under their own logo.

Late in 1984, as output began to catch up with demand, an industry shakeout occurred. Many of the start-ups disappeared, including the initially profitable Sinclair, Osborne, Corona, and Timex. Texas Instruments left the field (returning in the late 1980s by putting its label on clones made in Taiwan), and Hewlett-Packard began to concentrate on producing workstations (the other new microprocessor-based product line). Nevertheless, when demand began to grow again, the opportunity to build clones with improved performance and lower price reappeared. By July 1986, *Business Week* reported: "Now more than 200 clone suppliers... use the same software and work with the same hardware" to challenge the standards' progenitor, IBM. By the end of the decade, IBM's market share worldwide had dropped to 22.3 percent. By then the PC industry was no longer concentrated.[73]

As the PC market became increasingly competitive, the production of microprocessors and operating software for personal computers was becoming as concentrated as any industry in the United States. Nearly all the producers of clones had to use Intel microprocessors (or one of the small number of its clones) and Microsoft's operating system (or one of the small number of its clones). The IBM franchise assured Intel of the powerful competitive advantages of the economies of scale, and Microsoft those of the economies of both scale and scope. Before reviewing that story, it is essential to examine the two most significant developments in the swiftly expanding microprocessor industry—the rapid growth of the PC clones and then the coming of the microcomputer workstation.

Although in 1980, IBM's managers were not aware of the far-reaching implications of the mass production of microcomputers, several sensed that the "microprocessor based PC was a very real threat to the core of IBM's business." They saw it as "a Trojan horse within the Big Blue walls." Their opposition was strong enough to force John Opel, the CEO, constantly to protect the project during its development. In one way the critics were right, for the coming of the PC did mark the beginnings of the disintegration of IBM's core mainframe business. On the other hand, if IBM had not moved into PCs, it could have missed the personal computer revolution altogether.[74]

Of the clones, the most successful, in terms of market share, revenues, and profits, were those that were able to transform, or had already transformed, individual capabilities into organizational ones. Of these, none was more successful than Compaq Computer. Compaq was founded in 1982 by Rod Canion and two other engineering managers from Texas Instruments. The three were frustrated not only by their company's failure in the PC market but also by its loss to large, integrated, diversified Japanese companies of the bulk of its electronics business: the pocket calculators and digital watches it had pioneered, and its memory chip business. They were also well aware of Motorola's capabilities, which had permitted it to move successfully into new electronic products and to maintain a competitive position in microprocessors as the primary supplier to Apple and other proprietary PC makers.[75]

Canion stressed that their goal was not to start a little company and expect it to grow large, but to begin by laying the foundations of a big company. He explicitly rejected the Silicon Valley model. Instead, Compaq would focus on developing and maintaining the organizational capabilities of the company as a whole. "Above all," he insisted, "we want team members and not individualists." The founders raised a record amount of venture capital, $30 million, and developed strong financial controls and a forecasting system even before production began. They recruited design and production engineers from TI and lured "Sparky" Sparks and James D'Arezzo, who had built Estridge's marketing organization, to do the same at Compaq. Such preparations made possible rapid growth in 1983, from production of two hundred machines a month in January to nine thousand by the end of the year.

Compaq's strategic goal was as straightforward as its organizational one: to build an IBM clone, add extra features to the finished model, and sell it at a higher price. Its first product was a portable rather than a desktop PC, a niche that IBM had not yet entered. This strategy permitted it to have R&D costs of 4 percent of revenue, well below those of IBM and Apple. The national retail organization that Sparks and D'Arezzo created consisted principally of a network of authorized dealers supported by a strong marketing and distribution organization with an impressive market research staff. Unlike IBM, it had no salespersons of its own, so dealers were assured that they did not have to fear competition from company sales reps. A former TI executive, Eckhard Pfeiffer, built a comparable dealer network abroad by setting up subsidiaries in eleven European nations in 1983 and 1984.

In 1985, as Compaq developed its new desktop, Deskpro 386, its engineers worked closely with Intel and Microsoft. At Intel's request, it had tested that company's next-generation, 32-bit chip, the 80386, to assure that it met all software requirements written for systems already using the 80286, including IBM's new PC/AT. Canion then persuaded Intel to adjust the chip to meet Compaq's requirements. At the same time, Gates spent a year assisting Compaq, as *Fortune* reported, "mainly by writing software that increases the amount of computer memories current programs can use when they run on a Deskpro 386." That operating system became Microsoft's Windows 386.[76]

Introduced in September 1986, the new product provided Compaq with revenues that made it the third largest microcomputer company (behind IBM and Apple). In Europe, where it was number two, ahead of Apple and Olivetti, its sales soared from $20 million in 1984 to $733 million in 1988. In 1987, Compaq built a large plant in the Glasgow/Edinburgh area, Britain's so-called Silicon Glen (which then housed plants of IBM, Honeywell, Digital, NEC, Motorola, and Sun Microsystems), the first U.S. overseas PC clone works. By then it was one of the Fortune 500—the fastest a start-up had ever made that list.

During the mid-1980s, Apple's management was effectively transforming its individual capabilities into organizational ones. In 1981, A. C. Markulla, who had worked for Fairchild and then Intel, and was the major initial investor in Apple, with one-third of its equity, took over the administrative reins as CEO. In 1983, Markulla and Steve Jobs persuaded John Sculley, the president of PepsiCo, to become Apple's president. In 1985, Sculley became chairman and CEO. That same year the founding engineers, Jobs and Wozniak, left. As Langlois notes, "It was only under the administration of John Sculley that the Macintosh [Apple's most successful product] took off." By then, the company's strategy was to concentrate on the business market, and to focus on user-friendly technology to achieve a modularity and accessibility better than IBM's, to rely on outside suppliers, to expand its software capabilities, to encourage third-party application software, and to continue to build a strong national and then international marketing organization.[77]

As Compaq and Apple began to build their global enterprises, IBM's Early System Division was becoming integrated into the centralized operating structure of one of the world's largest industrial enterprises. As a child of IBM, the PC division benefited from its parent's powerful financial and managerial strengths. No start-up could have generated $5 billion in revenues in four years. On the other hand, the division remained somewhat of a sideline of the mainframe business, which in 1985 had revenues of $14.0 billion and much higher profit margins.

This difference between IBM's ESD and its major start-up competitors seems to have been reflected in new product development. In 1983, overworked and overconfident designers at Boca Raton had their first failure, an inexpensive PC Jr. that was to compete with Commodore in the home market. But the PC/AT, introduced a year later for the business market and based on a 16-bit rather than an 8-bit Intel chip, quickly became the industry's standard.

It was in the development of its next generation, the PS/2, that the conflicts within IBM and uneasy relationships with its suppliers, particularly Microsoft, plagued product commercialization in ways that rarely existed in small start-ups. One error was the decision, made partly at Gates's urging, to use the Intel 286 instead of its 32-bit 386. Another was the failed attempt to develop a new proprietary bus, a dud that Compaq and other competitors quickly overcame with a 32-bit bus of their own.[78]

By 1988, IBM, Apple, and Compaq were the world's three largest producers of microcomputers. Together, by *Datamation* estimates, they received 43.4 percent of total revenues. IBM's share was 25.5 percent; Apple's, 10.5 percent; and Compaq's, 7.4 percent. Their competitors were, with the exception of Tandy/Radio Shack and a British firm, Amstrand, still large companies that produced other products besides PCs. Fifteen firms accounted for 85 percent of the revenues of that sector. Of these, the U.S. firms included, besides those just listed, Hewlett-Packard, Unisys (a merger of Burroughs and Sperry-Rand in 1986), AT&T (which sold Olivetti products under its own label), and Zenith, which had acquired the start-up Heath Company in 1979 (and sold it in 1989 to France's Bull). The remaining six were foreign firms, four Japanese—Toshiba, Fujitsu, NEC, and Matsushita—and two European—Olivetti and Amstrand.

Nevertheless, given the competitive structure of the industry and the limited potential for exploiting the economies of scale and scope, these multiproduct firms had relatively few competitive advantages. IBM, Apple, and Compaq would continue to be the industry's "Big Three," but start-up firms continued to push aside companies that produced more than just personal computers. These start-ups, however, entered the market more through innovations in marketing and distribution than in design and production.

By 1992, marketing, not technological, innovations had become the key to growth. Michael Dell of Austin, Texas, was the pioneer in developing a direct marketing business in the mid-1980s. Dell machines, ordered over the telephone, were designed to meet the customer's specific needs. Customers were assured of twenty-four-hour telephone service for advice. Repairs were guaranteed in twenty-four hours. The saving of the retailer's markup assured lower prices. In 1992, Dell's revenues placed it among the top fifteen PC producers. But the barriers to entry were low.

Of the three most successful followers, Gateway 2000 of Des Moines, Iowa, copied Dell's direct marketing strategy; Packard Bell of Sacramento, California, sold through Wal-Mart and other mass retailing discount stores; and AST marketed through multiple channels, including PC dealers, computer chains such as Sears Business Systems, and value-added retailers.[79]

By 1992 the turnover among the top fifteen was greater in personal computers than in any other sector of the data-processing industry. IBM, Apple, and Compaq still led in worldwide market shares. Dell was seventh with 4.1 percent, AST was ninth with 2.6 percent, Gateway 2000 was tenth with 2.5 percent, and Packard Bell was fourteenth with 2.0 percent. All the large U.S. computer companies except AT&T had dropped off the list. Although AT&T no longer relied on Olivetti for its personal computers, its PC business remained unprofitable. The remaining five large companies on the list were foreign—four Japanese (NEC, Toshiba, Fujitsu, and Hitachi) and one European (Olivetti), plus a start-up, Acer of Taiwan, which was thirteenth with 2.0 percent.[80]

Design continued to be a competitive weapon used to develop smaller and smaller platforms relying on the increasing power of the microprocessor. Here the pioneers were Japanese companies, including Sharp, Sony, and especially Toshiba, as well as Tandy in the United States. Others quickly followed their lead. By 1989, Compaq, Apple, IBM, Dell, AST, and others were flooding the market with laptops, notebooks, and the like. Indeed their R&D investment was primarily in the designing of such products, and leapfrogging product innovation became central to maintaining market share in the 1990s.

## Workstations

The personal computer quickly became a commodity by reaching a mass market of individual users. But it rarely met the needs for high-powered, complex data processing required by scientific, engineering, industrial, medical, financial, and some commercial institutions, the market that the minicomputers were created to serve. That need brought forth another technology based on the microprocessor, that of the workstation. The new technology rested on the networking of high-end computers using a minicomputer, even a mainframe or a specially designed microcomputer, to act as a "server" to store and transmit data to a network of workstation microcomputers, the "clients," within a single department, enterprise, or institution having similar computing needs. Much of the innovative work done by AT&T and other telecommunication companies in developing switches, modems, terminals, and other electronic devices constantly improved such networking capabilities. Indeed, the creation of network devices and systems to be transmitted over telephone lines quickly became a major industry in itself.

Precisely because of the organizational capabilities learned in the development and continuing improvement of products for their specialized and highly sophisticated markets, the first movers in the new microcomputer workstation technology were, with one exception, the leading producers of minicomputers—DEC, Hewlett-Packard, IBM, and the senior management team at Prime Computer who left to form Apollo. The one exception was the highly successful start-up Sun Microsystems. The capabilities of the other four, based on the learning trajectory that began with DEC's PDP systems, permitted the workstation sector of the microcomputer industry to remain outside the grip of the de facto standards set for PCs by Intel and Microsoft. These inherited capabilities permitted these same firms to defeat a powerful attempt by the newcomer to become the de facto standard in their sector.

As they had for their initial line of products, these minicomputer companies created their own operating systems based on their own chips. Increasingly, however, their chips used a reduced instruction set computing (RISC) technology, and their operating systems used software based on nonproprietary UNIX systems. John Cocke of IBM had initially developed the RISC processor in the 1970s, but IBM only began to produce it in the late 1980s. It was further developed at Stanford in the early 1980s. The RISC technology increased the power of the chip and reduced its costs by simplifying and streamlining the instructions set so as to meet the more specialized power needs of workstations. AT&T's Bell Laboratories had initially developed the UNIX operating system. Released in 1969, it was licensed to all comers and could be used with both mainframes and minicomputers. By 1982 over three thousand computers, largely in universities and government agencies, were using the UNIX operating system.[81]

William Poduska was the first to exploit the potential of the new network technology. One of the engineers who had left Honeywell to form Prime Computer in 1971, he and his senior management team had become frustrated with the failure of that minicomputer company to invest in new product development. They therefore departed en masse to start a new company that would more effectively exploit the opportunities created by the microprocessor. Apollo used its own processors (based on Motorola's) and wrote its own proprietary operating system, but purchased most of its peripherals from outside sources. Before it was acquired by Hewlett-Packard in 1989, it had responded to the loss of market share by turning to the production of a RISC processor and a new Parallel RISC-based Multiprocessing (PRISM) operating system that improved its networking capabilities.[82]

Apollo was quickly overtaken by Sun Microsystems, largely because Sun's founders began with an ambitious plan to dominate the new technology by developing an open UNIX operating system and a low-cost microprocessor. In 1982, two young Stanford MBAs, Scott McNealy (who became its CEO) and Vinod Khosla, had formed the company to commercialize the workstation that a Stanford graduate engineering student, Andreas Bechtolsheim, had designed. They then recruited William Joy, Berkeley's UNIX expert, to develop the operating system. Like the founders of Compaq, they explicitly began by laying the foundations—the structure—of an industry leader. McNealy's father had been vice chairman of American Motors, so the young CEO had witnessed at first hand the powerful competitive capabilities of the large, well-managed Japanese automobile companies that so successfully entered the U.S. market. From the start the founders' strategy was to become the industry's standard by relying, like the IBM PC, on an open system. The authors of *Sunburst: The Ascent of Sun Microsystems* wrote in 1986:

> Sun tenaciously pursued the vision of open systems because it gave the company an immediate distinction over its competition. The company also saw that riding the open system wave was the most effective way to become a long term major player in the computer industry. . . . In the view of Sun's management, if the company were [*sic*] to survive into the next century, it would have to establish itself as a multi-billion dollar organization that offered a clear and desirable alternative to the competition. In the minds of some at Sun, with McNealy as the most vocal and visible proponent, the workstation's arena would be reduced to four, maybe five, serious players consisting of IBM, DEC, Apple, Sun, and perhaps Hewlett-Packard.

Like Apollo, Sun purchased peripherals from outside suppliers and used Motorola-based chips, but it began with a UNIX that relied heavily on third parties for applications. Also like Apollo, and DEC (especially in its early years), a large portion of Sun's sales went to value-added resalers (VARs) who added their own software applications and specialized equipment, as well as to third-party software application developers.[83]

In 1985, Sun advanced toward this goal by forming a strong alliance with AT&T to integrate their UNIX systems, and then began to work on a new RISC microprocessor, SPARC, for which that integrated UNIX system would be written. In 1987, the year the SPARC was introduced, AT&T

promised financial support to the extent of $450 million through the purchase of Sun stock. Sun immediately licensed its new chips (and operating systems) to Fujitsu and NV Philips, and in the United States to Cypress Semiconductor, Bipolar Integrated Technology, LSI Logic, and TI, because McNealy believed that to invest in the production of the chip would divert resources essential to the building of national and international marketing organizations. More important, the licensing of the chips and operating systems would rapidly expand the market for software applications. It would make Sun's products the industry's standard.

Except for the last, McNealy's strategy worked. Supported by aggressive financial moves, Sun quickly became the industry's leader. By the end of the 1980s, 2,800 software packages had been written for its machines, and 51 percent of the company's sales were outside the United States. It had built a plant in Scotland's Silicon Glen even before Compaq did. By 1987, Sun led with 29 percent of the industry's revenues, compared with Apollo's 21 percent. By then McNealy's prediction had, with the exception of Apple, been fulfilled. After Hewlett-Packard acquired Apollo in 1989, four firms—Hewlett-Packard, Sun, DEC, and IBM—accounted for more than 70 percent of the U.S. companies' revenues from workstations.[84]

Nevertheless, by 1987 it may have been too late for Sun to achieve its underlying goal of becoming the de facto setter of workstation standards. By the time it had received financial support from AT&T, the leading minicomputer companies, using retained earnings, had established strong positions in the workstation market. Their response to the AT&T-promised funding of Sun was to form the Open Software Foundation, with the goal of wresting UNIX from AT&T, in 1988. Little came of that alliance, however; it fell apart as each of its members continued to produce its own variation of UNIX written for its own RISC chip. In workstations no enterprise had the overwhelming first-mover advantages for setting standards comparable with those of IBM in mainframes and the recipients of IBM's franchises in semiconductors and software in PCs.[85]

DEC had entered the market in 1983, with a line of VAXstations. The first were modifications of its larger minicomputers that added power to desktop and work group stations and were compatible with DEC's existing lines. As Sun's market share grew, DEC, like Apollo, turned to the RISC chip. It had purchased 20 percent of the equity of MIPS, a California computer chip designer, and had it develop a RISC chip that could run a variant of a UNIX operating system. The result was VAXstation 2000. At the same time DEC introduced the more powerful VAXstation 3100 with its proprietary operating system, claiming that with its new Alpha chip, it could operate twice as fast as its open system. By 1990, *Datamation* ranked DEC second, but well behind Sun, in revenues from workstations.[86]

In the early 1990s, IBM and Hewlett-Packard became stronger competitors, and DEC fell back. In 1990, while Hewlett-Packard was preoccupied with absorbing Apollo into its organizational structure, IBM finally, after a succession of mishaps, brought out an impressive new product. It had entered the market in 1986 with its RT-PC workstation. With its weakly powered chip, it attracted few customers. In 1990 it had only 4.0 percent of U.S. shipments to workstation markets worldwide.

In 1987, IBM's senior managers, Jack Kuehler and Jack Bertram, formed another independent business unit project similar to the one that created the PC. With their strong support, its chief, Andrew Heller, designed a RISC chip to be produced by the IBM chip plant in Burlington, Vermont. That chip was expected to give IBM RS 6000 workstations twice the power of the next most powerful competitor. Placed on the market in February 1990, the RS 6000 came with IBM's version of UNIX or an IBM OS/2 operating system. In 1991, IBM's workstation sales amounted to $1.4 billion, accounting for 10 percent of the world market and representing a 40 percent growth, moving IBM into second place behind Sun. In 1992 its performance, as recorded in *Datamation,* was $1.89 billion in revenues and a 35 percent growth with 13.7 percent market share.[87]

In the early 1980s, Hewlett-Packard was producing a highly profitable minicomputer, the HP 3000, but was having less success with its personal computer. It entered the workstation market in November 1982 with its HP 9000, investing $250 million in the development of its own UNIX Spectrum operating system written on its own RISC chip. It then licensed that chip to Hitachi and Samsung to expand the use of the Spectrum applications. By 1987, with 12 percent of the sector's total worldwide revenues, it was well ahead of IBM. In October 1991, after it had absorbed Apollo's personnel into its operating organization, Hewlett-Packard restructured that organization in the classic manner by placing its computer business into two units delineated by different markets—one for minicomputers and workstations that were sold by the company's sales force to corporations and other institutions, and the other for mass producers of PCs, calculators, and printers that were sold through retailers. Then, using an improved RISC chip and a "New Wave" software (which Apple legally challenged), its workstation revenues continued to grow impressively, rising from $1.0 billion in 1990 to $1.52 billion and a market share of 22 percent in 1992.[88]

In 1992, Sun, IBM, and Hewlett-Packard were the top three producers of workstations in terms of revenues worldwide. DEC was fifth. By then three other U.S. firms were listed in the top fifteen. Silicon Graphics, a niche producer of three-dimensional graphics, moved into that market in 1987. After it acquired MIPS, the leading RISC chip designer that had designed its processor chip, in 1992, Silicon Graphics quickly expanded its lines and output, becoming the most serious challenger to the industry's leaders. Intergraph, formed in Huntsville, Alabama, in 1969 and a pioneer in commercial graphics, became a major producer of computer-aided design and computer-aided manufacturing (CAD/CAM) products. In 1984 it moved into workstations using RISC chip and UNIX software. Another entrant was Prime Computer (renamed Computervision after its financial reorganization), which also had gone to MIPS in 1986 to develop a RISC chip for workstation computers. These three ranked seventh, ninth, and thirteenth. Unisys entered in 1989 by purchasing a small UNIX-based workstation company, Convergence, and was eighth. The remaining seven were, except for Siemens-Nixdorf, Japanese firms.[89]

By 1992 the U.S. leaders among the top fifteen accounted for close to two-thirds of the fast-growing workstation revenues; the Japanese had only 16 percent; and the one European company, 2.8 percent. U.S. firms still led the way in the much larger personal computer market, with the top fifteen holding 51.6 percent; the Japanese producers accounted for 32.8 percent of revenues, and Olivetti for 3.0 percent. These figures indicate that although the Japanese firms remained strong producers of large-scale systems, of memories, and of other commodity chips, the United States led the way in the products of the microcomputer revolution, including peripherals, microprocessors, and software, as well as workstations and PC.

## Peripherals

The swift growth of the microcomputer in the early and mid-1980s had as great an impact on the component industries as the IBM 360 had in the late 1960s and 1970s. Indeed, by creating a huge new mass market, the new microcomputer industry may have saved the U.S. semiconductor industry from its Japanese competitors. Its swift expansion in the United States meant that American producers were the first to acquire the cost advantages of scale. However, since minimum efficient scale in production for peripherals was often lower than in semiconductors, the microprocessor revolution increased the number of small and medium-sized producers in the United States and East Asia (and much less so in Europe) making modems, network interface boards, accelerator boards, co-processors, ancillary chips, and the like.

On the other hand, the explosive demand brought new large-scale mass producers in printers and disk drives. Before the early 1980s the major producers of printers for the merchant market had been the giant first movers in copiers—Xerox in the United States and Canon in Japan. Since the early 1970s these firms had produced printers for mainframes, primarily IBM clones, and minis. Although Epson, a Japanese firm, received the initial franchise from IBM, Hewlett-Packard, an established producer of peripherals, seized the opportunity as a much-needed second source. Working with Canon, it brought out the first low-priced laser printer (at $3,500) for the new PC market. After making the investment necessary to assure the cost advantages of scale, it continued to work with Canon to introduce the Laser Jet II. Since then it has remained the leading producer. Xerox continued to lag behind; and Apple, using a Canon engine, continued to make its own printers. By the early 1990s, Hewlett-Packard had a 60 percent share of global production of printers, Epson was in second place, and Canon produced 70 percent of laser printer engines.[90]

The coming of the PC transformed the disk drive business in the same manner. By 1992, three makers of disk drives for PCs—Seagate Technology, Quantum, and Conner—were among the top fifteen peripheral producers worldwide. Although Tandon had received the initial IBM franchise, IBM's second source, Alan Shugart's Seagate Technology, quickly took the lead. Shugart had been one of the team that invented the floppy disk. He left IBM in 1969, taking more than a hundred IBM employees to Memorex, one of the first producers of plug-compatible IBM equipment. In 1973 he formed Shugart Associates, which Xerox purchased in 1977. In 1979 he and others of his team, including Finis Conner, founded Seagate Technology. The firm was thus positioned to miniaturize mainframe hard disks for PC compatibles in a way that permitted the drive to have thirty times more storage than a floppy disk. By 1984, Seagate, exploiting economies of scale, became the nation's high-volume, low-cost producer.[91]

The two other leading disk drive producers that grew rapidly in the 1980s were Quantum and Conner Peripherals. Both did so because of the franchises they had received from the second and third largest producers of PCs. Apple called on Quantum, a small start-up, to be its supplier. In 1990, Apple still accounted for 41 percent of Quantum sales, but Quantum was soon selling to Matsushita as well as to IBM and IBM clones. In 1985, when Compaq's output began to soar, Rod Canion asked Finis Conner, who had left Seagate, to form a company of his own to supply Compaq, and provided $12 million to assist the start-up. At first, 90 percent of Conner's output went to Compaq, but soon it was, like Quantum, supplying other PC makers.[92]

## Semiconductors

Of all the industry's sectors, the microcomputer revolution had its most dramatic impact on semiconductors. Here the franchise that IBM had given Intel permitted the latter to become the largest producer of microprocessors in the world and, therefore, to set de facto standards for personal computers and, in turn, to play a major role in reviving the U.S. semiconductor business. At precisely the moment when the giant Japanese producers had succeeded in driving the U.S. makers out of the DRAM markets, the PC and its clones were creating a totally unexpected huge demand for microprocessors. As demand soared, so did Intel's revenues and income, rising to $1,629 million and $198 million, respectively, in 1984. Andrew Grove, Intel's CEO, noted in the company's 1986 Annual Report:

> In 1983, demand for semiconductors exploded, fueled in large part by the expansion of the personal computer business. No one could get enough semiconductors, especially Intel Microprocessors, which had emerged as the standard for personal computers. . . . We licensed other semiconductor manufacturers to produce Intel microprocessors, peripherals and microcontrollers. We met our customers' needs and helped expand the total market for our products, though we lost control over a generation of our products and created our own competition.

Again, as in disk drives, IBM called for a second source, specifically Advanced Micro Devices. Soon that firm and eleven others were producing the 8088 and the 8086. Of these, the most aggressive, Advanced Micro Devices, came to have a larger share of this older 8-bit processor than did Intel itself. Intel's second sources ultimately commanded 70 percent of the 8088 and the 8086 market.[93]

The combination of competing microprocessors, rising costs for designing and building new large-scale capacity, and the one-time costs for shutting down the DRAM operations brought on a financial stringency. By 1984, Intel had only one DRAM plant still in operation, and that was shut down in 1986. In addition to requiring funds to build costly new fabricating plants, the company planned to spend $250 million "on a massive program to build design expertise and CAD tools." The designing and the manufacturing of volume-produced microprocessors required different equipment and skills than did the designing and producing memories.[94]

IBM, which in 1982 had provided $250 million to acquire 15 percent of Intel's equity, in 1984 raised the ante to close to $400 million for a total of 20 percent of Intel's stock. That aid permitted Intel to transform its product lines despite a drop in net income from $198 million in 1984 to $2 million in 1985, and to a loss of $173 million in 1986. Once Intel's future seemed assured, IBM sold off its Intel stock for a profitable $625 million.[95]

By 1985 all agreed that Intel's future depended on the success of its investment in the new volume-produced, far more powerful 80386 32-bit microprocessor. In that same year of financial tightness, IBM, after negotiations, agreed to have Intel continue to provide the 386 microprocessor for its PC, on the condition that IBM could develop compatible versions for its own use. According to a senior IBM executive, the company decided not to take up the option because Intel was already far ahead in the development of the new chip. Thus the development of an Intel clone that used Microsoft operating system software would not warrant its costs.

Intel's managers then asked Compaq to test the chip to meet the requirements of all existing PC software. That chip, used by Compaq and nearly all the PC clones as well as IBM's second generation PS/2, assured Intel's dominance. Revenues doubled from just under $2 billion in 1987 to just under $4 billion in 1990, and net income rose from $248 million to $650 million. In 1989 the company brought out a still higher powered microprocessor, the 486. By then it was producing over 70 percent of microprocessors for PCs—desktops, portables, notebooks, laptops, and other computer products. The *New York Times* reported in April 1992 that Intel's increase in revenue between 1986 and 1991 was "a gain that alone is responsible for the American market share [worldwide] being 5% higher than it would have otherwise been." Intel was then fighting legal battles with AMD, its major competitor, which had cloned the 386 and 486 as well as the 288 and 286. The only other strong competitor was Motorola, which made a noncompatible processor for Apple.[96]

Thus, although American firms began to regain their lost market share only in the early 1990s, IBM's transformation of the microprocessor industry, and then its infusion of capital into Intel at a critical moment, permitted U.S. companies to take and maintain the lead in microprocessor-based PCs and workstations. The continued market growth permitted Intel and Motorola to use their earnings and to enhance their skills and knowledge in order to maintain the technological lead by developing new generations of complex instruction set computing (CISC) products. In the RISC microprocessors, the United States also had taken the lead, as the licensing of these chips to such leading Japanese firms as Fujitsu, Toshiba, and Hitachi by Sun, Hewlett-Packard, and the leading RISC designer, MIPS, indicates.

By the late 1980s the RISC microprocessor with its UNIX software was the most obvious challenge to Intel's standard-setting dominance. But it has been slow to become a serious one, in good part because the companies failed to agree on a single hardware or software standard. As soon as Sun and AT&T completed their alliance in 1987, DEC, IBM, and Hewlett-Packard formed the Open Software Foundation, in hopes of taking UNIX from AT&T by establishing such a de facto standard. However, as mentioned earlier, little came from the alliance. Each of its founders continued to develop its own proprietary RISC chips and relied on its own version of a UNIX operating system.

In 1991, Compaq made another try at creating a RISC chip/UNIX standard. Its first move was to acquire 13 percent of Silicon Graphics, a pioneer in three-dimensional graphic products, and pay $50 million for access to its technology. In April 1991, Compaq and DEC, supported by Gates's Microsoft (which had acquired a 20 percent share of the UNIX developer, the Santa Cruz Operation), joined Compaq in announcing the formation of the Advanced Computer Environment to establish a standard to compete with those of Sun, IBM and Hewlett-Packard (HP) in both workstations and PCs.[97]

Although Control Data, Prime, Tandem, and several foreign computer makers joined the alliance, it collapsed within a year. Compaq's technology deal with Silicon Graphics quickly fell apart. To assure its ability to meet its rapidly expanding 3-D market, Silicon Graphics bought back Compaq's stake for $150 million, and then acquired MIPS for $231 million. DEC developed its own Alpha chip, and Sun, IBM, and HP continued to use and license their own proprietary chips and versions of UNIX operating systems for workstations as the enlarged Silicon Graphics became a major competitor.

Also in 1991 a potentially more serious challenge came from another quarter. An alliance of IBM, Apple, and Motorola, announced in October, struck at Intel's primary CISC product (the total RISC business still amounted to less than 5 percent of the unit volume of the CISC market). The alliance was the result of extended negotiations that began when

Apple, interested in developing a faster processor for its Macintosh, became impressed with IBM's workstation RS 6000. By the agreement, IBM was to design its workstation processor to meet the needs of Apple's PC, and Motorola was to become a second source for manufacturing the chip—the Power PC—for IBM, Apple, and the open market. In addition, two new joint ventures were formed. One, Taligent, was to produce a next-generation operating system, facilitating object-oriented database management software that purportedly permitted customers to design their own software to meet their particular needs. The other, Kaleida, was to produce next-generation multimedia systems and software. But by 1995 neither had succeeded.[98]

With this 1991 alliance IBM reshaped its decade-old relationship with Intel. Intel's major chip competitor was now Motorola's Power PC. It quickly responded to that challenge. In 1993, Intel released the Pentium, a far more powerful and more costly chip, to be fabricated in plants that cost $1.3 billion. It was to run all major operating systems, including UNIX and those developed by Microsoft. In 1994, Intel held 74 percent of the worldwide market for microprocessors, followed by Motorola with 12 percent, Advanced Micro Devices with 7 percent, and Texas Instruments with 3 percent.[99]

Intel's brief history provides a striking example of the powerful competitive advantages created by scale and learning economies. These advantages rested on the organizational capabilities developed within the firm and were further enhanced by the continuing reinvestment in physical and human capital—in building large capital-using plants and in molding and integrating the activities of teams for research and development, production, and marketing. Intel's initial commercialization of the microprocessor was a team effort. The development of the 386 and the 486 required the funds, the knowledge, and the skills that were not available to entrepreneurial start-ups. Moreover, Intel enjoyed another powerful first-mover advantage as its 386 became the de facto market standard, locking in customers because of their need to be compatible with existing applications produced by Microsoft that rested on its operating software.

## Software

The history of Microsoft, the other prime beneficiary of IBM's venture into personal computers, provides as stunning an example of the creation of competitive advantages based on the economies not only of learning, scale, and de facto standard setting but also of scope. Gates's comment on his company's strategic strength was "It is all about scale economics and market share. When you are shipping one million units of Windows software a month, you can afford to spend $300 million a year improving it and still sell it at a low price." Cusumano and Selby have described Microsoft's benefits from the economies of scope in much the same terms that Flamm described those of the System 360. In addition, Microsoft's strength in setting technical standards for operating systems software that, in turn, defined standards for application software gave it first-mover advantages even greater than those of Intel.[100]

The microcomputer revolution realigned the roster of leading players in the software industry. In 1982, before IBM's PC had transformed the microcomputer industry, the top fifteen leaders worldwide in software were makers of mainframe computers and minicomputers. By 1987, Microsoft was eleventh, Lotus (the producer of spreadsheets) was twelfth, and Computer Associates, a merger of several third-party vendors of applications software, was seventh. Five years later Microsoft was third, behind IBM and Fujitsu (both still producing software for the older, large-scale systems), Computer Associates was fifth, Novell (maker of networking software) was seventh, Lotus was ninth, and Oracle (database software) was eleventh. Of these, Microsoft was the only new entrant to produce major operating systems. The others were makers of specialized applications software.

Microsoft's startling growth lay, of course, in its franchise from IBM. Just as Intel, at IBM's request, was to license out its chip to meet the unprecedented demand for the PC and its clones, so Bill Gates was to license out MS-DOS to an even larger number of makers. By the mid-1980s, having licensed to close to one hundred, it had become the de facto standard for the industry. In 1984, Microsoft's revenues were over $100 million and its profits $15 million. Early in 1985 senior IBM managers, headed by William Lowe, who took over the Entry System Division following Estridge's death in an airplane crash, began negotiations with Gates to decide Microsoft's role in the development of the next generation of software. Under the joint development agreement signed that June between the two companies, Gates was to participate in the development of OS/2, the new operating system for IBM's next-generation PC, the PS/2. In addition, he would receive the OS/2 royalties from all other manufacturers of PCs besides IBM. At the same time IBM turned down Gates's offer to acquire his Windows, a graphical user interface project, still in an early developmental stage.[101]

Tensions quickly arose between the signers of the agreement. The underlying reason, Ferguson and Morris argue in *Computer Wars,* was that each had a different goal: "Microsoft's ambition was to become the software standard setter; to do so, it needed to treat all software platforms equally. But IBM was aiming at hardware supremacy that served its own ambitions, not Microsoft's." Other irritations occurred. For Gates these included IBM's internal confusions, bureaucratic struggles, and resulting delays and mistakes. IBM managers were, in turn, troubled by Gates's aggressive, petulant attitude and, most important of all, his concentration on Microsoft's own software products.[102]

This last concern reflected the different goals. Gates had tied the development of the new OS/2 operating system to Intel's older 8-bit 286 rather than the 16-bit 386, for which his Windows 386 had been developed in close conjunction with Compaq and Intel in 1985. Why, then, write OS/2 in a 286 assembler program? Ferguson and Morris suggest two reasons. One, its development would be a "learning" experience essential to the development of his own Windows system. Two, "Bluntly, if Gates expected ultimately to break with IBM, he had every interest in ensuring OS/2's failure."[103]

Gates's strong protests against IBM's negotiations with the other firms concerning software further reflected their different goals. Gates was incensed when, in the spring of 1988, IBM joined with DEC, Apple, and Hewlett-Packard in the Open Software Foundation. Fearing that the association might bring into being a single UNIX standard that would challenge DOS, OS/2, and ultimately Windows, Gates "mounted a brief spirited counterattack against IBM's involvement." The following October he returned to IBM's headquarters at Armonk, where he "blew up again" because IBM had paid Steve Jobs, who after leaving Apple had formed NeXt, $50 million for the rights to Jobs's innovative operating systems for workstations. In the summer of 1990, Gates was again at IBM headquarters outlining his plans to challenge, with IBM's support, Novell, a start-up that had quickly become the dominant firm in the new networking software technology and was leading the way in developing operating systems for client-server systems. Again he was rebuffed.[104]

Later in 1990, Gates broke openly with IBM, about six months after Microsoft introduced Windows 3.0. IBM's OS/2 had appeared in late 1987, receiving a chilly reception. By 1990 it had only about 1 percent of the installed base of operating systems. It was clearly a failure. Windows 3.0 became an instant success. It had "a vast array of supporting third-party software, including a long list of excellent applications from Microsoft that somehow never got developed for OS/2." Gates had achieved his goal. Windows emerged as the standard for personal computer operating system software worldwide. Revenues and net income soared from $804 million and $171 million in 1989 to $1,843 million and

$400 million in 1991. Microsoft's growth of 53.8 percent in 1991 made it the fastest-growing firm in any of the industry's several sectors.[105]

During the 1980s, software, one of the most knowledge-intensive industries, found product development increasingly costly. It took Microsoft's large teams of designers six years and at least two tries before the successful launch of Windows 3.0. Windows NT, the workstation operating system, required five years and hundreds of millions of dollars. In 1993, Microsoft spent $470 million on research and development and $1.2 billion on marketing and sales, creating as powerful a barrier to entry as Intel's $1.3 billion chip plant.[106]

In the early 1990s, Microsoft was using its retained earnings and enlarged capabilities not only to develop next-generation operating systems, such as Windows 95 for PCs, but also to commercialize operating systems for workstations (Windows NT) and a wide variety of third-party software applications. In 1990, Gates sought to secure a position in workstations by his investment in a UNIX designer, the Santa Cruz Operation, and by alliances with Hewlett-Packard and Tandem. The Windows NT operating system was aimed at acquiring dominance in networked industrial and office markets.

At the same time Gates was using Microsoft's learned internal capabilities to intensify his moves into closely related software applications markets and to do so by a frontal attack on the nation's largest producers in these markets. As early as 1991, 51 percent of Microsoft's revenues came from applications software, 36 percent from operating systems, and 13 percent from books, hardware, and the like. By 1995, Microsoft had made inroads into the corporate networking software market dominated by Novell, the PC database market of Borland, and the database for large computers of Oracle. Microsoft also overwhelmed Lotus in spreadsheets, WordPerfect in word-processing software, and many of the more specialized markets served by Computer Associates.[107]

In the early 1990s, U.S. firms were world leaders in making the products of the microcomputer revolution. Although the Japanese still dominated the production of memory chips and some peripherals—engines for printers and flat panels, among others—the United States had the technological lead in personal computers, workstations, microprocessors, and the software applications related to them. Such Japanese diversified electronic data-processing firms as Fujitsu, NEC, Toshiba, and Hitachi remained powerful competitors in global markets, and producers in Korea and Taiwan were coming on behind them. In Europe only Olivetti and Siemens continued to have a substantial but weakening presence, one that relied on close ties with Japanese firms. The failure of European firms to compete successfully with IBM and IBM clones in mainframes, and with other U.S. companies in minicomputers, deprived them of the opportunity to develop the critical learning bases and the essential networks of ancillary firms necessary to maintain their competitive strength as the microcomputer revolution reshaped the industry.

## CONCLUSION: THE COMPUTER INDUSTRY AT FIFTY

A review of table 2-7, *Datamation*'s list of the ten largest revenue producers in the industry's major market segments—large systems, mid-range systems, workstations, peripherals, and software—provides a useful conclusion to this fifty-year history. (*Datamation* does not list semiconductors, but the pattern is much the same.) The table documents that the industry's leaders in the mid-1990s are the firms that have driven innovation and growth over the past half-century. All but three of these firms have been mentioned in the history just presented. The table thus emphasizes the continuity of technological leadership. Further, it suggests that this continuity will exist during what may be the emergence of a fourth period in the history of the industry.

Once the computer industry had made the shift from military to commercial markets, it witnessed two waves of technological and organizational innovation, each marking the beginning of a new historical period. By the late 1960s the mainframe, the minicomputer, and the supercomputer—big boxes—used by institutions ushered in the second period. By the mid-1980s these big boxes were being replaced by small ones—PCs and workstations—used by individuals. In the mid-1990s a new wave may be under way through coordinated activities of networks of computers, both small and large. Such combinations include client-server networks and large-scale parallel processing networks.

A very brief and tentative review of the current activities of the companies listed in each of these segments, including semiconductors, indicates how they are adjusting to and participating in the transformation to a possible new era of multicomputer networks. The makers of mainframes, shattered in the late 1980s by the PC revolution, face the greatest challenge. All have undergone massive restructuring, financial write-offs, and reductions in employment. IBM, by far the largest producer of mainframes, had by far the largest losses—$15 billion over three years—and the most dramatic restructuring, including a 40 percent reduction of employees. That restructuring permitted it to show a reasonable 4.6 percent net return on revenues in 1994—$3 billion on $64 billion. Its revival

TABLE 2-7

## The Ten Leading American Vendors, by Market Segment, 1994

| Rank | Company | Revenue (million $) | Rank | Company | Revenue (million $) |
|---|---|---|---|---|---|
| **LARGE SYSTEMS** | | | **MIDRANGE SYSTEMS** | | |
| 1 | IBM | 5,956.8 | 1 | IBM | 5,764.7 |
| 2 | Unisys | 1,243.2 | 2 | AT&T GIS | 5,042.0 |
| 3 | Amdahl | 819.3 | 3 | Hewlett-Packard | 2,688.0 |
| 4 | Cray | 571.4 | 4 | Tandem | 1,538.9 |
| 5 | Intel | 460.8 | 5 | Digital | 1,174.5 |
| 6 | Silicon Graphics | 163.1 | 6 | Motorola | 616.8 |
| 7 | Convex | 76.4 | 7 | Data General | 536.5 |
| 8 | Digital | 40.5 | 8 | Sun Microsystems | 534.8 |
| 9 | Control Data | 5.2 | 9 | Unisys | 497.3 |
| | | | 10 | Apple | 477.5 |
| **WORKSTATIONS** | | | **PCS** | | |
| 1 | Sun Microsystems | 3,262.0 | 1 | Compaq | 9,018.8 |
| 2 | IBM | 3,206.6 | 2 | IBM | 8,775.1 |
| 3 | Hewlett-Packard | 2,880.0 | 3 | Apple | 7,161.8 |
| 4 | Silicon Graphics | 1,223.2 | 4 | Dell | 2,870.0 |
| 5 | Digital | 1,080.0 | 5 | Gateway 2000 | 2,700.0 |
| 6 | Intergraph | 833.1 | 6 | Packard Bell | 2,600.0 |
| 7 | Motorola | 593.1 | 7 | AST Research | 2,311.0 |
| 8 | Unisys | 435.1 | 8 | AT&T GIS | 1,718.9 |
| 9 | Control Data | 31.5 | 9 | Digital | 1,350.0 |
| 10 | Data General | 22.8 | 10 | Hewlett-Packard | 1,152.0 |
| **PERIPHERALS** | | | **SOFTWARE** | | |
| 1 | IBM | 8,583.0 | 1 | IBM | 11,529.4 |
| 2 | Hewlett-Packard | 6,336.0 | 2 | Microsoft | 4,464.0 |
| 3 | Seagate | 3,465.0 | 3 | Computer Associates | 2,454.7 |
| 4 | Quantum | 3,286.0 | 4 | Novell | 1,918.1 |
| 5 | Xerox | 3,126.8 | 5 | Oracle | 1,901.6 |
| 6 | Conner Peripherals | 2,352.0 | 6 | Lockheed Martin | 1,242.0 |
| 7 | Western Digital | 1,900.0 | 7 | Digital | 1,215.0 |
| 8 | Digital | 1,620.0 | 8 | AT&T | 916.7 |
| 9 | Lexmark | 1,215.0 | 9 | Lotus | 873.6 |
| 10 | StorageTek | 1,121.2 | 10 | Unisys | 683.8 |

SOURCE: Compiled from "Datamation 100, 1995," *Datamation,* June 1, 1995, pp. 47, 48, 57, 61, 62, 66. Excerpted with permission of *DATAMATION* Magazine, June 1, 1996. © 1996 by Cahners Publishing Company.

NOTE: Revenue figures represent worldwide revenue for each segment.

rested in good part on the reshaping of its high-end products—mainframes, minicomputers, data storage systems and other peripherals, and related software—to become servers in corporate and other networks. In the large-system market its revenues of almost $6 billion account for two-thirds of the segment's total revenues. "For now, at least," notes *Datamation*, "IBM's biggest problem was making enough System 390s to keep up with 35% growth in capacity demand." But the other mainframe companies, although still among the top ten, are no longer significant players. Unisys (the merger of Sperry-Rand and Burroughs) has shifted to providing services. Control Data has come under the wing of Silicon Graphics, and NCR, after being acquired by AT&T in 1991, has steadily recorded losses.[108]

In supercomputers the pioneers in massive parallel processing, Intel and Convex, quickly challenged Amdahl and Cray Research. For Intel the i860 RISC chip, introduced in 1989, provided an entry through the production of such systems for oil companies, government agencies, and financial firms. Convex, a 1982 start-up that first produced mini supercomputers, moved into parallel processing in the early 1990s. At about the same time IBM began to develop comparable products. The supercomputer pioneers, Cray Research and Amdahl (the latter still controlled by Fujitsu, its major supplier of components) in 1994 reported respectable returns of 6.4 percent and 4.6 percent, respectively. Nevertheless, Cray's losses in 1995 led to its acquisition in February 1996 by Silicon Graphics.[109]

As in mainframes, the major survival opportunity for the makers of minicomputers was the creation of such client-server networks. The firms best prepared for the development of such mid-range systems were those that in the 1980s had successfully commercialized workstations: IBM, HP, and DEC. The other minicomputer makers all endured heavy losses from 1987 on. Wang declared bankruptcy in 1993. Prime Computer, now Computervision, began to break even only in 1994. That year Data General still reported losses. Tandem, continuing to focus on its specialty, no-fault computers, began to show profits after a major write-off of assets and reduction of personnel. Finally, AT&T's General Information Systems (GIS), formerly NCR, by concentrating on becoming a mid-range vendor, produced impressive revenues but no profits. So when the AT&T management decided in 1995 to break the company into three units, it was made clear that it would immediately put the computer business up for sale.[110]

The evolution of IBM, HP, and DEC into mid-range multicomputer network producers demonstrates how companies can effectively reshape their product lines. They did so by making the most of the capabilities created in the production and marketing of minicomputers in the 1970s and the commercializing of workstations in the 1980s for much the same set of customers. One of IBM's most successful products in the early 1990s was its AS/400. Introduced in 1988, it was based on the earlier S/38 minicomputers, in which major components, including central processors and data storage units, could be changed without disrupting the system as a whole. Becoming "the most popular multiuser system," it has been revamped continuously. This experience was reinforced by the successful development of the RS 6000 workstation, introduced in 1990.

Hewlett-Packard's mid-range system was developed in a comparable manner, based on its highly successful HP 3000 family, introduced in 1972 and continuously upgraded during the 1980s, and its HP 9000 workstation, with its own RISC chip and version of UNIX. By 1994 it was producing new lines that used simultaneous multiprocessing (SMP) software and hardware. The story might have been the same for DEC after it developed its VAX 3100, which could run UNIX software on its proprietary Alpha chip. But in 1991 Kenneth Olsen made a disastrous strategic decision to return to the production of mainframes with the VAX 9000. Losses that began in 1989 soared to $617 million in 1991 and have continued until today (1995).[111]

For the sectors of the computer industry created by the microcomputer revolution, the patterns of firm growth and competition that evolved in the 1980s have continued into the mid-1990s. In workstations, where by 1994 the growth of shipments was somewhat faster than of PCs —25 percent versus 23 percent—Hewlett-Packard and IBM continued to catch up with Sun; Sun's market share was 36 percent, HP's was 20 percent, and IBM's was just under 13 percent, while DEC fell further behind. Sun had moved into the middle-level market with new chips to run on its Solaris operating system, in much the same manner as Silicon Graphics had entered the market for large systems. The new entrant on the 1994 list of the top ten, Motorola, used its organizational capabilities in chips and a variety of computer-related products to develop multicomputer systems for both workstations and client-server mid-range systems.[112]

In PCs the clustering of leaders has remained much the same. In 1994, Compaq, IBM, and Apple together accounted for $25 billion in PC revenues, and had roughly equal market shares. The marketing innovators Dell, Gateway 2000, Packard Bell, and AST Research formed a second-tier cluster having total revenues of $10.2 billion, with each of them in the $2 billion range. Compaq's rapid rise from third to first place in two years dramatically underlines the significance of this shift from technology to marketing as the instrument of competitive success in PCs. In the autumn of 1991, Compaq's board removed Canion, an engineer, as CEO and replaced him with Pfeiffer, a marketer. Within eight months Compaq introduced twenty-nine new models, launched its low-priced marketing strategy, and sold through mass retailers and other outlets besides its franchised dealers. Price competition and low margins have forced both Packard Bell and AST Research to go abroad for financing. The first sold just under 20 percent of its equity to France's Groupe Bull, in addition to offering a $300 million issue of stock. (An attempt to sell another 20 percent to Japan's NEC fell through.) The second sold 40 percent of its equity to Korea's Samsung. AT&T is planning to sell off its PC operations as well as its mid-range products.[113]

In the production of disk drives, printers, data storage, and other peripherals, the new multicomputer systems have rapidly expanded demand and intensified the need for innovation. The largest revenue producers in the mid-1990s were those of the 1980s. Five had become leaders before the microcomputer revolution. (Lexmark was a 1993 leveraged buyout spin-off of IBM's printer division.) Of the other five, Western Digital, the one new entrant, has been a producer of disk drives since 1983. In 1995, Quantum expanded its business by purchasing DEC's component and drive business. At about the same time Seagate and Conners merged to become the world's largest maker of disk drives.[114]

The development of multicomputer network systems brought comparable market growth and technological innovation in U.S. semiconductors and software. The overall growth of the production of microprocessors played a major role in increasing the U.S. lead over Japan in semiconductors. Estimates of U.S. market share worldwide in semiconductors rose from 36 percent in 1990 to 47 percent in 1994, while Japan's fell from 48 percent to 36 percent in the same years. At the same time the surging demand for DRAMs brought their production in the United States back to life. For example, early in 1995, Micron Technology, one of the very few U.S. firms to stay in DRAM production, announced plans to build a $1.3 billion plant in Utah.[115]

For the makers of both chips and related software, the challenge of the early 1990s has been the development of technologically advanced products essential to coordinate simultaneously the operations of different computers within a single network. The companies meeting this challenge remain established firms. Intel's new-generation Pentium P6 microprocessor, with twice the speed of its Pentium processor, has the capability of supporting four instructions in parallel. IBM and Motorola are developing comparable chips for PCs and workstations as well as for larger systems. Hewlett-Packard in 1994 delivered three thousand of its SMP machines. In August 1995, DEC made an arrangement with Microsoft to support Windows NT on workstations powered by DEC's Alpha chips.

In software, Novell, not Microsoft, became the pioneer by leading the way in developing local area networking (LAN) during the 1980s. In 1989 it introduced a "multithread" SMP system that worked on major operating systems, including IBM's OS/2, UNIX, and Apple's Macintosh, to run different tasks or applications simultaneously. In 1991 a marketing alliance with IBM and a joint development and marketing arrangement with Apple gave Novell a strong edge over Microsoft's LAN Manager. Gates's response was Windows NT, initially developed for workstations. By 1994, according to Dataquest, Windows NT had 13 percent of the market, Novell had fallen to 43 percent (from 63 percent in 1991), IBM's OS/2 had 17 percent, UNIX producers (HP, Sun, and others) had 13 percent, and mainframe systems, largely those of IBM, had 10 percent. Microsoft's recent introduction of the upgraded Windows NT 3.5 and its alliance with DEC for the use of its Alpha chip have Dataquest and others predicting that Microsoft will become the dominant player in this, as in many other software arenas. But for the present, IBM's software production for large and middle-range systems, workstations, and PCs gives it revenues from software of $11.5 billion, versus Microsoft's $4.5 billion.[116]

This review, by providing a snapshot of the industry's leading enterprises at a moment in time—a half-century since it began—emphasizes that the industry's leaders in all sectors were first movers. That is, they were among the first to exploit fully the economies of scale and scope in terms of commercializing the opportunities of a new technological paradigm by making investments in production and distribution necessary to compete globally, and in R&D necessary for further development of products and processes. This was true for the development of mainframes, minicomputers, and semiconductors, especially in the late 1960s and early 1970s. It was also true for microcomputers, especially in the first half of the 1980s.

The review also suggests why the chapter might be subtitled "A Schumpeterian Tale," a story first of creativity on an unprecedented scale, followed by one of dramatic "creative destruction." Tables 2-1 to 2-6 emphasize the extraordinary growth of the industry's output and revenues as the IBM System/360 and DEC's PDP series came onstream, marking the beginnings of the industry's second historical period. In addition, as table 2-8 indicates, an explosion of new enterprises, created

TABLE 2-8

## NET PROFIT RATIOS OF COMPUTER AND RELATED COMPANIES, 1994

| Company | Net Income/ Total Revenue | Rank[a] | Date of Establishment | | |
| --- | --- | --- | --- | --- | --- |
| | | | PERIOD I | PERIOD II | PERIOD III |
| Microsoft | 24.7% | 10 | | | 1979[b] |
| Intel | 19.9 | | | 1968 | |
| ComputerAssociates | 16.5 | 18 | | | 1980 |
| Oracle | 14.2 | 21 | | | 1977 |
| Advanced Micro Devices | 13.8 | | | 1969 | |
| National Semiconductor | 13.8 | | | 1967 | |
| Novell | 10.3 | 28 | | | 1980 |
| Silicon Graphics | 9.5 | 31 | | | 1982 |
| Compaq | 8.0 | 5 | | | 1982 |
| Tandem | 8.0 | 26 | | 1974 | |
| Western Digital | 7.5 | 29 | | | 1983 |
| Motorola | 7.0 | | 1928 | | |
| Hewlett-Packard | 6.4 | 2 | 1938 | (1968)[c] | |
| Seagate | 6.4 | 13 | | 1970 | |
| Cray Research | 6.1 | 46 | | 1970 | |
| IBM | 4.6 | 1 | 1911 | | |
| Conner Peripherals | 4.6 | 20 | | | 1985 |
| Amdahl | 4.6 | 30 | | 1972 | |
| Sun Microsystems | 4.2 | 9 | | | 1982 |
| Dell | 4.8 | 12 | | | 1984 |
| Packard Bell | 3.6 | 17 | | | 1985 |
| Gateway 2000 | 3.6 | 16 | | | 1985 |
| Apple | 3.4 | 7 | | | 1977 |
| Quantum | 2.4 | 14 | | | 1980 |
| AST Research | 2.3 | 23 | | | 1980 |
| StorageTek | 2.0 | 32 | | 1969 | |
| Unisys (Burroughs/Sperry-Rand) | 1.4 | 8 | 1880s | | |
| Intergraph | -0.0 | 40 | | 1969 | |
| Data General | -0.0 | 39 | | 1972 | |
| Lotus | -0.0 | 44 | | | 1982 |
| DEC | -15.9 | 3 | 1957 | | |
| Control Data | -17.8 | 61 | 1957 | | |

SOURCE: Compiled and calculated from "The Datamation 100, 1995," *Datamation*, June 1, 1995; and *Hoover's Handbook of American Business, 1996: Profiles of 500 Major U.S. Companies* (New York: Hoover, 1996).

a Rankings in terms of gross revenues are those of "The Datamation North American 100" which covers information-technology companies in general but excludes semiconductor firms. The following enterprises are excluded from the list because of the lack of comparable data: Convex, Lexmark, AT&T-GIS, Xerox, and Lockheed Martin.

b Establishment in Seattle (incorporated in 1981).

c Entry in minicomputer market.

to exploit the new mainframe and minicomputer technologies, occurred during the same years, particularly between 1968 and 1972. In this same period computer-based electronic data processing was beginning to transform profoundly the processes of production and distribution of nearly all the nation's industrial and service sectors.

The impact of the computer on industry and commerce, and indeed on American life, continued into the 1980s because its use was moving far beyond mere data processing. But in the 1980s continued growth rested on the creative destruction of the minicomputer and mainframe markets by the new microcomputer technology. Ironically, the primary instrument of change was the very enterprise that had been the prime mover in the creative years of the industry's initial growth. As table 2-8 indicates, IBM's $5 billion increase in PC revenues between 1981 and 1985 helped to bring an even larger new explosion of start-ups exploiting the microcomputer technologies than had occurred in the first wave between 1968 and 1972. Table 2-8 also documents the destructive impact of microcomputer technology in terms of income as a percent of revenue of the existing companies. Nevertheless, that destruction has been in no way complete. As table 2-7 shows, in 1994 a substantial number of the older enterprises remained major players in all sectors of the industry listed.

Table 2-7 further suggests that the enterprises established by the mid-1980s are becoming the leaders in what may be a new period of technological change and industry growth based on the commercialization of multicomputer networks. Innovative technologies and strategies will bring new start-ups to the top. Indeed, if the mid- and late 1990s mark the beginnings of what may be a new period in the industry's history comparable with that ushered in by the System/360 and DEC's PDP series, and that launched by the PC, start-ups should flourish, much as they did in the first years of those two periods. If not, the industry may follow the patterns of other high-tech industries where start-ups are few and much of the commercializing of new products and processes has been carried out by large, existing industrial enterprises.

## NOTES

1. The history told here is strikingly different from that of the other high-technology industries after World War II—aerospace, chemicals, and pharmaceuticals. These differences are indicated in my chapter, "The United States: Engines of Economic Growth in Capital- and Knowledge-Intensive Industries," in Alfred D. Chandler, Jr., Franco Amatori, and Takashi Hikino, eds., *Big*

*Business and the Wealth of Nations* (New York: Cambridge University Press, 1997), ch. 3.

2. The coming of the first digital computers is told in detail in two outstanding historically oriented studies by Kenneth Flamm: *Creating the Computer: Government, Industry, and High Technology* (Washington, DC: Brookings Institution, 1988) and *Targeting the Computer: Government Support and International Competition* (Washington, DC: Brookings Institution, 1988). The information in this and the following paragraphs comes from chapter 3 of *Creating the Computer*. The digital computer processed bits of data in parallel; an analog computer did so serially.

3. The information in this and the next two paragraphs comes from Flamm, *Creating the Computer*, 182–184, 94, 106; James W. Cortada, *Historical Dictionary of Data Processing: Organizations* (Westport, Ct.: Greenwood Press, 1987), 160; Emerson W. Pugh, *Building IBM: Shaping an Industry and Its Technology* (Cambridge, Mass.: MIT Press, 1995); chs. 12–16.

4. For the Watsons' roles, see Cortada, 159–160; Thomas J. Watson, Jr., and Peter Petre, *Father, Son & Co.: My Life at IBM and Beyond* (New York: Bantam Books, 1990), 190–192 and chs. 18–22; Pugh, 135–136 and chs. 12–13. Internal records show, Pugh points out, that by turning over the electronics to Thomas, Jr., "a father who enticed his son into taking responsibility for the new technology" as a way to indicate its importance for the company and as a means to smooth the coming transition at the top (149–150, 165).

5. Flamm, *Creating the Computer*, 83. For FORTRAN, James W. Cortada, *Historical Dictionary of Data Processing: Technology* (Westport, Ct.: Greenwood Press, 1987), 172–174.

6. Flamm, *Creating the Computer*, 84–85; Pugh, 237–242.

7. For IBM's defense work, Flamm, *Creating the Computer*, 88–94; Pugh, 236–237, quotation from 237.

8. Pugh, 253–256; the quotations and the next paragraph are from 255.

9. Flamm, *Creating the Computer*, 96–97; Pugh, 263–270.

10. The task group, named SPRED (an acronym for System Programming, Research, Engineering, and Development), and its report are covered in Pugh, 270–273.

11. This and the following paragraph are based on Cortada, *Technology*, 212–220, quotation from 214; Flamm, *Creating the Computer*, 97–100; Pugh, 275–277, 282–291, 301–304.

12. This and the next paragraph are from Watson and Petre, ch. 27; Charles H. Ferguson and Charles R. Morris, *Computer Wars: How the West Can Win in the Post-IBM World* (New York: Times Books, 1993), 7–10; Pugh, 291–296. Pugh, 294, states: "[O]ver a thousand persons were employed during the peak year"; and Watson, 353, writes: "[B]y 1996 we had two thousand people working on"

the basic software. Watson adds that the total cost of creating the software operating system came to half a billion dollars. Three types of operating systems were developed. BOS (basic operating system), TOS (tape operating system), and DOS (disk operating system). Pugh, 295–296.

13. Flamm, *Creating the Computer,* 210–214.

14. For IBM's marketing, see Robert Sobel, *IBM: Colossus in Transition* (New York: Times Books, 1981), 79–86. In a letter to Chandler dated February 14, 1996, Professor James McKenney, a specialist in computer development since the 1950s, emphasizes the "prowess and ubiquity of IBM's marketing strategy." Its strength, he argues, rested on close collaboration during the 1950s with industry leaders—Procter & Gamble in groceries, American Airlines in air transportation, and Union Pacific in railroads—to develop industry-specific systems; its provision of twenty-four-hour assistance, and the creation of an outstanding sales force of industry specialists who maintained close contact with the product designers. For an example of the effectiveness of this strategy in the insurance industry, see JoAnne Yates, "Application Software for Insurance in the 1960s and Early 1970s," *Business and Economic History* 24 (Fall 1995): 123–133.

15. The information on Sperry-Rand comes from Flamm, *Creating the Computer,* 107–111, quotations from 107–108. See also Cortada, *Organizations,* 235–240, and *Technology,* 366–371; Watson and Petre, 199–241; James C. Worthy, *William C. Norris: Portrait of a Maverick* (Cambridge, Mass.: Ballinger Publishing, 1987), 23–32.

16. Franklin M. Fisher, James W. McKee, and Richard B. Mancke, *IBM and the U.S. Data Processing Industry: An Economic History* (New York: Praeger, 1983), 65.

17. For Control Data, see Flamm, *Creating the Computer,* 111–112; Cortada, *Organizations,* 101–105; Fisher et al., 90–94, quotations from 91; and most detailed of all, Worthy, 26–32, and chs. 3 and 4. See also Watson and Petre, 283–284. For an instructive summary of the debate within the firm over the move to develop the OEM business, see Worthy, 60–62.

18. For National Cash Register, Flamm, *Creating the Computer,* 118–119; Cortada, *Organizations,* 204–205; and Richard S. Rosenbloom, "From Gears to Chips: The Transformation of NCR and Harris in the Digital Era," *Harvard Business History Seminar,* February 18, 1988, 7–15, and "A Comparison of NCR's and Burroughs' Entry into Computers," *Harvard Business History Seminar,* October 2, 1989, 1–6.

19. For Burroughs Corporation, see Flamm, *Creating the Computer,* 116–117; Cortada, *Organizations,* 87–89; Fisher et al., 79–85; Ray W. MacDonald, *Strategy for Growth: The Story of Burroughs Corporation* (New York: Newcomen Society, 1978), 12–18.

20. For Honeywell, see Flamm, *Creating the Computer,* 113–114; Cortada, *Organizations,* 147–148; Fisher et al., 68–71.

21. Flamm, *Creating the Computer,* 135; ch. 5 has an excellent review of competition in Europe, and ch. 6, on competition in Japan.

22. See Alfred D. Chandler, Jr., *Scale and Scope: The Dynamics of Industrial Capitalism* (Cambridge, Mass.: Belknap/Harvard University Press, 1990), 209, for motor vehicle exports.

23. Pugh, 302–204. The all-semiconductor main memory introduced in September 1970 made IBM the leader in that product. Another innovative device was the virtual memory developed shortly after the initial IBM System 360 announcement.

24. Ibid., 304–307.

25. Ibid., 312–313.

26. Ibid., 307–311, quotation from 310. Ferguson and Morris, 31–35, is an excellent survey of Project F/S in which they argue that "F/S was absurdly ambitious." Marie Anchordoguy, *Computers Inc.: Japan's Challenge to IBM* (Cambridge, Mass.: Harvard University Press, 1989), 135–140, indicates how in 1975, knowledge of IBM's work in VLSI led Japan's MITI and its leading computer companies to form the first VLSI development project, which lasted from 1976 through 1979 and cost $360 million.

27. Pugh, 309.

28. Fisher et al., 286–303; Cortada, *Organizations,* 164–165, 191–194; Pugh, 299–300.

29. Fisher et al., 288; Worthy, 63–64; Cortada, *Organizations,* 48, 105–106.

30. Quoted in Fisher et al., 204; see also Cortada, *Organizations,* 228.

31. For Amdahl, see Cortada, *Organizations,* 47–49; Flamm, *Creating the Computer,* 193–196; and Gene M. Amdahl, "The Early Chapters of the PMC Story," *Datamation,* February 1979, pp. 113–119, quotation from 113. IBM developed a competitive supercomputer in the late 1970s that became the System 390 family.

32. Flamm, *Creating the Computer,* 195.

33. Anchordoguy, 113–116 (quotation from 115), 147. For sales of computers to European manufacturers on an OEM basis, see Flamm, *Creating the Computer,* 170–171, quotation from 171. In 1975, IBM had the largest market share in Japan (28 percent), followed by Fujitsu (24 percent), Hitachi (14 percent), and NEC (11 percent). By 1982, the figures were IBM, 22 percent; Fujitsu, 24 percent; and Hitachi and NEC, 16 percent each (Flamm, 185).

34. Fisher et al., 303–316; Cortada, *Organizations,* 165. In 1969, leasing companies purchased $2.5 billion worth of IBM products.

35. A most useful review of these legal wars is Sobel, ch. 12, "A Generation of Litigation," quotation from 262; see also Watson and Petre, 380–389; Fisher et al., 379–380, 448–449. In the one case IBM lost, the plaintiff, Telex, also was heavily fined.

36. Worthy, 69–75. For the details outlined in this and the next three paragraphs, see Watson and Petre, 378–389, quotations from 381, 386.

37. For GE and RCA, see Flamm, *Creating the Computer,* 124–126; Pugh, 296–297.

38. The activities of Control Data and Cray Research are briefly summarized in Flamm, *Creating the Computer,* 112–113; and Cortada, *Organizations,* 105–106, 134–137, 227–231. In 1972, Control Data made a joint venture with NCR, and in 1975 with Honeywell, to produce new lines of peripherals.

39. For Sperry-Rand, see Flamm, *Creating the Computer,* 108–111; Cortada, *Organizations,* 251–252.

40. For Burroughs, see MacDonald, 18–25, quotations from 18–21; Cortada, *Organizations,* 90–91; and Fisher et al., 242–249, 382–383. The two paragraphs on NCR are based on Rosenbloom, "From Gears to Chips," 19–27, and "NCR and Burroughs," 6–12.

41. This and the following paragraph are from Flamm, 114–115, 130–131; and Cortada, *Organizations,* 150–151; see Gary Hoover et al., eds., *Hoover's Handbook of American Business* (Austin, Texas: The Reference Press, 1993), 328, for Honeywell's position in control and sensing systems.

42. For DEC, see Flamm, *Creating the Computer,* 127–129; Cortada, *Organizations,* 116–120, and *Technology,* 296–299, quotation from 297; Fisher et al., 271–273. Glenn Rifkin and George Harrar, *The Ultimate Entrepreneur: The Story of Ken Olsen and the Digital Equipment Corporation* (Chicago: Contemporary Books, 1988), chs. 8–9, describes the swift growth of the company in the mid-1960s; the revenue and profit figures and the OEM sales are given on 71–72. Cortada has somewhat different, but comparable, revenue and profit figures, with the revenues rising from $4.1 million in 1961 to $142.6 million in 1970—a growth rate of 44 percent per year (p. 119).

43. For SDS, see Flamm, *Creating the Computer,* 129–131; Cortada, *Organizations,* 243–255; Fisher et al., 263–277.

44. For Data General, see Cortada, *Organizations,* 109–111; Fisher et al., 409–410; Rifkin and Harrar, ch. 10.

45. For Prime, see Flamm, *Creating the Computer,* 114–131; Fisher et al., 411–412; Cortada, *Organizations,* 222–223.

46. For Wang, see Fisher et al., 414. For Hewlett-Packard, see Cortada, *Organizations,* 142–143; "Hewlett-Packard Corporation," Graduate School of Business, Stanford University, S-M-150R (1973); *Datamation,* June 15, 1981, p. 110. Between 1972 and 1979 HP's revenues from data processing products rose to nearly 50 percent. Other companies that sold more specialized mini-computers included Tandem, a maker of "fault tolerant" computers (1976); Datapoint, with its 600 "advanced business processor" (1977); Perkins-Elmer, an instrument maker, with its 7/32 computer (1975); and Harris, a maker of printing equipment with a high-performance series 500 (1978).

47. *Datamation,* June 15, 1983, p. 90. IBM led with $3,000 million, followed by Digital with $1,680, Burroughs with $800, Data General with $603.8, HP with $588.0, Wang with $584.7, and Prime with $315.0. See also Cortada, *Organizations,* 119.

48. Fisher et al., 316–320; Cortada, *Organizations,* 18, 19, 72–73.

49. Automatic Data Processing (ADP) also sold computers on an OEM basis; Fisher et al., 320–321, 425–427.

50. For software, see Cortada, *Organizations,* 22–24; and for the Computer Science Corporation, Fisher et al., 322–323. For the peripherals mentioned in the next paragraph, see Fisher et al., 289–303.

51. These and the following paragraphs are from John E. Tilton, *International Diffusion of Technology: The Case of Semiconductors* (Washington, D.C.: Brookings Institution, 1971), 66–67; Cortada, *Technology,* 59–60.

52. Cortada, *Organizations,* 261–263, also 54–55, and *Technology,* 60; Pugh, 280–284; Tilton, 25. In the early 1960s the Justice Department was filing suits against these large firms for price-fixing.

53. Tilton, 115; Cortada, *Organizations,* 263–264; P. R. Morris, *A History of the World Semiconductor Industry* (London: Peter Peregrinus, 1990), 91–94; Mark Mason, *American Multinationals and Japan: The Political Economy of Japanese Capital Controls, 1899–1980* (Cambridge, Mass.: Harvard University Press, 1992), 174–176. Mariann Jelenik and Claudia Bird Schoonhoven, *The Innovation Marathon: Lessons from High Technology Firms* (Oxford: Basil Blackwell, 1990), has valuable information on TI, Motorola, National Semiconductor, Intel, and other semiconductor companies discussed here. See Frank Malerba, *The Semiconductor Business: The Economics of Rapid Growth and Decline* (Madison: University of Wisconsin Press, 1985), 159, for market share, and 100–122 for the role of U.S. firms in Europe.

54. The negotiations are described in detail in Mason, 176–187; see also Anchordoguy, 28–29.

55. Tilton, 115; Morris, 91–94. Mason, 218–231, discusses Motorola's extended negotiation with the Japanese government. For worldwide market share, see Malerba, 159. The U.S. market share information comes from Jelinek and Schoonhoven, 126. They note: "These figures are difficult to obtain, and more difficult to substantiate. Estimates vary substantially by product and by market, and figures from different sources are seldom truly compatible." However approximate, they do indicate the market strength of TI and Motorola.

56. For Fairchild see Tilton, 66; Cortada, *Organizations,* 123–128; *Biographies,* 193, 237–238; Jelinek and Schoonhoven, ch. 4; Michael R. Leibowitz, "Founding Father: Robert Noyce," *P/C Computing,* May 1989, pp. 95–100.

57. Morris, 98–100, 125; Malerba, 109, 117–119, 168–169.

58. James C. Williams, "The Rise of Silicon Valley," *Innovation and Technology,* Spring/Summer 1990, 24; Annalee Saxenian, *Regional Advantage: Culture and Competition in Silicon Valley and Route 128* (Cambridge, Mass.: Harvard University Press, 1994), ch. 2, has an excellent review of the extensive literature on the growth of the Valley and its culture (quotation on Fairchild is from 31).

59. Saxenian, 85–88, reviews the shift to mass production. The quotation from *Dataquest,* June 15, 1980, is in Morris, 85. For capital cost, see Malerba, 18. The cost of Intel's projected plant was given to me by David Yoffie.

60. Cortada, *Organizations,* 126–127; Jelinek and Schoonhoven, 99–103, 106, and quotation from 123–124.

61. For Intel, see Gordon E. Moore, "Intel—Memories and the Microprocessor," *Daedalus* 125 (Spring 1996): 55–80, (quotation from 59.) Cortada, *Organizations,* 155–156; Jelinek and Schoonhoven, 112–114, 143–156; Saxenian, 85–86; Robert A. Burgleman, "Fading Memories: A Process of Strategic Business Exit in Dynamic Environments," Working Paper, Stanford University, June 1993, 4–5, 13–20.

62. Moore, 69–77. The quotation is from Saxenian, 88.

63. For global market shares, see Burgelman, fig. 3; and Malerba, 159. For TI's early efforts toward large-scale production, see Morris, 93–94. Two smaller start-ups located outside of Silicon Valley began to produce standardized chips in the 1970s. MOSTEK was established in 1969 in Colorado Springs by a TI engineer, R. Petritz. In the late 1970s it had a market share of 1.3 percent. The other, Analog Devices, moved into an even higher-end product at 1.0 percent. Morris, 85 and 117; and scattered references in Jelinek and Schoonhoven, ch. 4, on Advanced Micro Devices. The market share figures are from 126.

64. Charles H. Ferguson, "Sources and Implications of Strategic Decline: The Case of Japanese-American Competition in Micro-electronics," Working paper, Center for Technology, Policy and Industrial Development, Massachusetts Institute of Technology, revised June 30, 1997; and Ferguson and Morris, 108–109. See Anchordoguy, 137–148, for the development of the VLSI chip. This shift from ten thousand to at least one hundred thousand circuits per device, which the companies used to develop the 64-bit DRAM, assured Japan's almost complete dominance in memories by the early 1980s. Burgleman, fig. 4, gives the market share figures for DRAM producers from 1974 to 1986.

65. Martin Fransman, *Japan's Computer and Communications Industry: The Evolution of Industrial Giants and Global Competitiveness* (Oxford: Oxford University Press, 1995), 161–163; M. Theresa Flaherty, "Strategic Organizational and Technological Reasons for Slow Learners in Semiconductor Factories," unpublished paper presented at the Prince Bertel Symposium, Stockholm, June 1994.

66. Andrew S. Grove, "Silicon Valley: The Next Techno-Colony?" speech at Semiconductor Industry Association forecast dinner, September 26, 1990, on Intel Corporation; see also Saxenian, 88–95, quotation from 90. In addition to Burgleman's fig. 4, the estimates of changing market share of Japanese and American companies from *Dataquest* have often been reprinted; see, e.g., *Boston Globe,* December 3, 1986, p. A-28.

67. See Grove. Saxenian, ch. 2, describes the Valley's practices and culture. *New York Times,* January 16, 1996, p. D-2, reviews the Valley's industrial activities in the mid-1990s.

68. Richard M. Langlois, "External Economies and Economic Progress," *Business History Review* 66 (Spring 1992):13–19, under the heading "The industry begins in 1977," has an excellent review of these three companies; it is supplemented by the outlines of their historical growth in Cortada, *Organizations,* 60–64, 94–95, 255–258. The quotations from Langlois are on 15 and 16. (The Osborne quotation is on 16.) Market share statistics are from John Friar and Mel Horwitch, "The Emergence of Technology Strategy: A New Dimension of Strategic Management," *Technology in Society* (1985):152.

69. The following account is based on James Chposky and Ted Leonsis, *Blue Magic: The People, Power, and Politics Behind the IBM Personal Computer* (New York: Facts on File, n.d.), chs. 3–8, supplemented by Langlois, 20–23 (quotation in next paragraph from 20). *Blue Magic* was written by members of the project development group that commercialized the PC, based on lengthy interviews with other participants and documentary data. The authors point out that the story would have been far less complete if several of the group's leaders had not left the company. The brief review of the development of the PC is in Ferguson and Morris, 23–27.

70. For Intel, see Chposky and Leonsis, 26–27. The quotations are from Leibowitz, 100, and Moore, 77. For Gates, see Chposky and Leonsis, chs. 9–10; Stephen Manes and Paul Andrews, *Gates: How Microsoft's Mogul Reinvented an Industry—and Made Himself the Richest Man in America* (New York: Doubleday, 1993), chs. 11, 12.

71. For suppliers, see Chposky and Leonsis, 66; for marketing, servicing, and also advertising, 75–77, 98; for the quotation on strategic goals, 120.

72. Ibid., 145. See also *Datamation*'s annual review issue, June 1983, p. 198, for 1982; June 1984, p. 55, for 1983; June 1985, p. 38, for 1984; and June 1986, p. 45, for 1985.

73. Langlois, 23–28, has an excellent review of the rise of the clones worldwide. A good contemporary account is "The PC Wars: IBM vs. the Clones," *Business Week,* July 28, 1996, pp. 62, 68 (quotation on 62); see also *Datamation,* June 1, 1984, pp. 37–38. For market share in 1989, see *Datamation,* June 15, 1990, p. 184.

74. Quotations from Chposky and Leonsis, 105.

75. The information for this and the two following paragraphs on Compaq are based on "Compaq's Compact," *Management Today,* May 1985, pp. 92–98. As that analyst noted, "Whatever TI's recent troubles, it is a wonderful training ground for hard-headed, rather conservative managers, very different from the West Coast, Silicon Valley types" (92); see also "The PC Wars" (note 73); and "How Compaq Gets There Firstest with the Mostest," *Business Week,* June 26, 1989, pp. 146–150; Chposky and Leonsis, 162; and Moore, 79.

76. The information for this and the next paragraph is from "Take That, Goliath," *Business Month,* June 1987, p. 25; "Compaq Bids for Leadership," *Fortune,* September 29, 1986, pp. 30–32 (includes quotation on Gates's contribution); "Soft Dollars, Hard Choices," *Forbes,* September 4, 1989, pp. 106–109. Manes and Andrews, 203, 234, 348, describes the relationship between Compaq and Microsoft. Compaq had no service force; like automobiles, machines were serviced by franchise dealers (109). See also *New York Times,* January 10, 1988, p. F-14; "Compaq's Conquest in Europe," *New York Times,* July 9, 1989, p. F-4. Ferguson and Morris, 52–53, indicates how Compaq reverse-engineered the PC/2 proprietary motherboard, a device IBM hoped would protect its PCs from being cloned.

77. Langlois, 45–46, 31–33, summarizes the Apple experience; see also Cortada, *Organizations,* 60–63. John Sculley with John A. Bryne, *Odyssey: Pepsi to Apple. . . A Journey of Adventure, Ideas, and the Future* (New York: Harper & Row, 1987), chs. 8–12, reviews in detail the company's 1985 crisis and the resulting changes in command. Its excellence in graphics quickly made it the leader in publishing and educational markets.

78. Ferguson and Morris, 56–58; Langlois, 29–30. For comparative revenues in 1988, see *Datamation,* June 15, 1989, p. 154.

79. For Dell and its rivals, see *New York Times,* July 21, 1991, pp. F-4 and F-5; March 13, 1993, p. D-1; May 28, 1993, p. D-3; July 15, 1993, p. D-4; August 2, 1993, p. D-2; August 22, 1993, p. F-10. See also *Business Week,* March 22, 1993, pp. 83–86. For Gateway 2000, see *New York Times,* May 27, 1993, pp. D-1 and D-6, and September 27, 1995, p. D-10; for Packard Bell, *New York Times,* October 12, 1994, pp. D-1 and D-7, July 6, 1995, pp. D-1 and D-3, September 12, 1995, pp. D-1 and D-3; for AST Research, Hoover et al., 133, 235, 396, 678; *New York Times,* September 13, 1995, pp. D-1 and D-2.

80. For market shares, see *Datamation,* June 15, 1993, p. 22.

81. For a useful review of the development of workstations, see David Yoffie and Ben Huston, "Note on Microcomputers: Overview of PCs and Workstations," Harvard Business School, Case N9-389-136 (1990), 7–9. Ferguson and Morris, 37–50, has an excellent review of the development of the RISC chip. By becoming increasingly powerful with an increasing number of instructions, the RISC chips became hard to distinguish from the other complex instruction set

computing (CISC) chips. For the development of UNIX, see Ferguson and Morris, 103–105; Cortada, *Technology,* 289–290.

82. For Apollo, see Saxenian, 126–128, 141–143; Carliss Baldwin and Jack Soll, "Sun Microsystems, Inc. 1987 (A)," Harvard Business School, Case N9-290-051 (1990), 3.

83. For Sun, see Saxenian, 126–127, 134–135; also Mark Hall and John Barry, *Sunburst: The Ascent of Sun Microsystems* (Chicago: Contemporary Books, 1986), 26, for quotation. Also valuable are Jonathan Khazam and David Mowery, "The Commercializing of RISC: Strategies for the Creation of Dominant Designs," *Research Policy* 23 (1994):89–102; and Raghu Garud and Arun Kumasway, "Changing Competitive Dynamics in Network Industries: An Exploration of Sun Microsystems' Open Strategy," *Strategic Management* 14 (1993):351–369. A biographical sketch of McNealy, *New York Times,* January 29, 1996, p. D1, emphasizes the impact of his Detroit background on his strategic thinking.

84. *Datamation,* June 15, 1988, p. 154; June 15, 1991, p. 222; April 1, 1992, pp. 3–6.

85. See the Baldwin and Clark chapter in this book, and *New York Times,* December 31, 1989, p. D-5.

86. For DEC, HBS, see Yoffie and Huston, p. 10; *Datamation,* April 1, 1992, pp. 34–36. For a history of DEC's VAX and Prism, see Ferguson and Morris, 103–105.

87. For IBM, Ferguson and Morris, 45–50; *New York Times,* April 23, 1989, p. F-1, and February 9, 1990, p. D-1; and *Datamation,* June 15, 1993, p. 26, for revenues and market share.

88. For Hewlett-Packard, see Ferguson and Morris, 49–50; *Datamation,* June 15, 1983, p. 106; *Business Week,* September 11, 1989, pp. 106–112 (fast-growing workstations and desktop peripheral business), August 15, 1990, pp. 22–26; April 1, 1991, pp. 76–79; March 23, 1992, pp. 88–89; *New York Times,* March 21, 1991, p. D-1.

89. *Datamation,* June 15, 1993, p. 22. Information on Silicon Graphics, Intergraph, and Computervision comes from Hoover et al., eds., *Hoover's Handbook 1993,* 503, 338, 211. For Intergraph, see also *Datamation,* June 11, 1985, p. 38, and June 15, 1986, p. 118; for Silicon Graphics, see also *Business Week,* July 18, 1994, pp. 56–63. Data General entered the market in 1989 with its AViiON RISC-based servers, *Hoover's Handbook, 1994,* 232.

90. *Business Week,* October 1, 1990, pp. 103–104; October 6, 1991, pp. 79–80. Ferguson and Morris, 157, describes HP's strategy of fighting off Canon on the one side and U.S. cloners on the other.

91. Pugh, 299–300; Fisher et al., 397; Hoover et al., 1994 ed., 498. As a major supplier for IBM's PC, Seagate reported that it quickly acquired half of the small disk market.

92. For Quantum, *Business Week,* July 8, 1991, pp. 84–85; for Conner Peripherals, Hoover et al., 1994 ed., 213; *New York Times,* May 27, 1990, pp. B-1 and B-3. In 1988, Conner acquired 49 percent control, and in 1991, 51 percent, of Olivetti's disk drive business. By 1990, 29 percent of sales came from Compaq, 12 percent from Olivetti, and 10 percent from Toshiba.

93. Ferguson and Morris, 142–143. The quotation is from Jelinek and Schoonhoven, 97; AMD's marketshare, from Hoover et al., 1993 ed., 93. I am indebted to David Yoffie for the information on Intel's second sources.

94. Burgleman, 22–24, quotation from 24.

95. Ferguson and Morris, 60–61; David Yoffie, Rolinda Lurie, and Ben Huston, "Intel Corporation, 1988," Harvard Business School, Case 1-389-063 (1989), p. 14, for income figures. Motorola continued to be the leader in microcontrollers and other chips used in electronic products other than computers.

96. Quotation from *New York Times,* April 9, 1992, pp. A-1, D-4. See Yoffie, Lurie, and Huston, 1–12, 14; and *New York Times,* February 14, 1990, p. D-1, for income figures. See Paul Carroll, *Big Blues: The Unmaking of IBM* (New York: Random House, 1993), 131, for the sale of Intel's stock. Intel also sold DRAMs made by Samsung under its own label, and PCs, add-on boards, and platforms on a similar OEM basis. In 1989 these lines accounted for 26 percent of its revenues.

97. The information for this and the following paragraph is from *New York Times,* February 9, 1991, p. 29, and April 8, 1991, p. D-1; Manes and Andrews, 423–428; and Hoover et al., 1993 ed., 209, 240, 503, for Compaq, DEC, and Silicon Graphics. Also for Silicon Graphics, see *New York Times,* February 8, 1991, p. D-1; *Business Week,* July 18, 1994, pp. 62–63. Useful, too, is Khazam and Mowery, 93–97. They point out that only 30 percent of MIPS' revenues came from the designing and licensing of chips; the remaining 70 percent was from producing workstations on an OEM basis. Hence its output was listed under the final manufacturer's name (93). For comparative size of market, see *New York Times,* February 8, 1991, p. D-1.

98. *New York Times,* April 8, 1991, p. D-1; July 14, 1991, p. F-1; October 3, 1991, p. D-1; May 11, 1993 (no page); January 1, 1996, p. 47. See also Carroll, 293–298; Ferguson and Morris, 213–214.

99. *New York Times,* April 4, 1993, p. F-11; May 11, 1993 (no page); November 14, 1993, p. F-10. For market share data, see *New York Times,* February 20, 1994, p. F-13. Ferguson and Morris date the Intel–IBM "friendly divorce" in mid-1992: "IBM would henceforth diversify the base of microprocessor vendors and supply more of its needs internally. Intel has always sold its chips to all comers" (60). The relationship during the PC years is reviewed on 61–65.

100. Michael A. Cusumano and Richard W. Selby, *Microsoft Secrets: How the World's Most Powerful Software Company Creates Technology, Shapes Markets, and Manages People* (New York: The Free Press, 1995), 157–158, 401–402,

quotation from 158. Also see David Yoffie's chapter in this book. For market share rankings in the next paragraph, see *Datamation,* June 15, 1988, p. 162, June 15, 1993, p. 22.

101. Carroll, 88–91; Ferguson and Morris, 69–71; Manes and Andrews, 285–288.

102. The continuing story of the relationships between Gates and IBM is told in Ferguson and Morris, ch. 5 (quotation from 75), and Carroll, especially 182–185 and 233–234. Their brief versions need to be checked against the complex details of this complicated story presented in Manes and Andrews, chs. 21–30. Carroll, 119, indicates that Gates offered to sell 10 percent of Microsoft's shares to IBM. He notes that Gates talked with one senior IBM manager who "never got very specific." Since no offer was made, no offer was discussed and then rejected by IBM's top management.

103. Ferguson and Morris, 78–81; quotation from 78–79.

104. Carroll, 182–185, 233–235, quotations from 183–185; Manes and Andrews, 369, 375–377.

105. Ferguson and Morris, 80–83, quotation from 81; Carroll, chs. 12–13. A post-Microsoft OS/22.0, a realigned OS/2, did make a modest comeback (*New York Times,* July 31, 1994, p. D-1). For Microsoft's revenue and income, see Hoover et al., 1993 ed., 406.

106. The expenditure figures are from David Yoffie. By fiscal 1995, Microsoft's R&D expenditures were $830 million. Cusumano and Selby, 158.

107. *New York Times,* September 22, 1992, p. D-1; *Datamation,* June 15, 1994, pp. 54–56. For Lotus, *New York Times,* June 21, 1994, p. D-1; Ferguson and Morris, 152. For Oracle, *Fortune,* November 29, 1993, pp. 39–50. For Computer Associates, *New York Times,* August 16, 1992, p. F-5. Also see references to these companies in Hoover et al., 1993 ed., 372, 436, 210.

108. Information on mainframe firms comes from *Datamation's* annual review, June 1, 1995, quotation from 95. For IBM, *Business Week,* October 30, 1995, pp. 142–152; for Unisys, *New York Times,* January 5, 1995, pp. D-1 and D-10 and October 7, 1995, p. 36; and for Control Data, January 31, 1989, pp. D-1 and D-6 and May 28, 1992, p. D-4; and Hoover et al., 1996 ed., has information on revenues, income, and income as percent of revenue annually for the preceding decade.

109. For supercomputers, in addition to *Datamation,* annual review, June 1, 1995, *New York Times,* December 3, 1988, pp. D-1 and D-3, May 21, 1989, pp. F-1 and F-8, June 15, 1992, pp. D-1 and D-3, August 7, 1994, and August 25, 1995, pp. 47 and 49, *Boston Globe,* March 28, 1995, p. 69; Hoover et al., 1996 ed., 66, 77b. Leading start-ups, including Kendall Square Research and Thinking Machines, filed Chapter 11 petitions in 1994. For Cray Research's 1995 losses and the resulting takeover by Silicon Graphics, see *New York Times,* February 26, 1996, pp. D-1 and D-6.

110. For the less successful minis and mid-range enterprises, in addition to *Datamation*'s annual review, see *New York Times*, March 1, 1989, and January 5, 1995, D-1 and D-10, and, for Tandem, *New York Times*, July 21, 1993, p. D-4.

111. For IBM, *New York Times*, March 5, 1995, sec. 3, p. 10; and Pugh, 312; for HP, *Datamation*, June 1, 1995, p. 57; for DEC, *New York Times*, October 22, 1990, pp. D-1 and D-4; and Ferguson and Morris, 103–104.

112. For market share, see *New York Times*, March 5, 1995, p. 10; for Silicon Graphics, *Business Week*, July 18, 1994, p. 56 and passim, and *Fortune*, October 30, 1995, pp.113–126.

113. I am indebted to Kenneth Roman for information on Compaq. For Packard Bell and AST Research financing, see *New York Times*, October 12, 1994, pp. D-4 and D-8; July 6, 1995, pp. D-1 and D-2; September 12, 1995, pp. D-1 and D-2. Packard Bell acquired Tandy in 1993, *New York Times*, May 27, 1993, pp. D-1 and D-8. For HP's improving position in PCs, *New York Times*, February 17, 1995, p. D-4; for Gateway 2000's activities, *New York Times*, September 27, 1995, p. D-10.

114. For Lexmark, *New York Times*, March 29, 1993, pp. D-1 and D-3; for Quantum's purchase of Digital and Seagate's merger with Conner, *New York Times*, July 6, 1994, D-3, and September 21, 1995, pp. D-1 and D-7.

115. For memory chips and worldwide market share of U.S. and Japanese companies see *Business Week*, January 10, 1994, p. 83; for Micron Technology, *New York Times*, September 5, 1995, pp. D-1 and D-8; for Intel, *New York Times*, February 26, 1995, p. F-23. In a preliminary 1993 estimate of worldwide ranking in semiconductors, Intel was first, Motorola was third, TI was sixth, and IBM was tenth. Five of the others were integrated Japanese electronics enterprises, and the remaining one was Samsung of Korea. *Electronic News*, December 20, 1993, pp. 7–8.

116. For software, *New York Times*, February 5, 1995, p. F-9, August 7, 1995, p. D-5, October 31, 1995, pp. D-1 and D-22; Cusumano and Selby, 144–145.

# CHAPTER 3

# SUN WARS
## *Competition within a Modular Cluster, 1985–1990*

Carliss Y. Baldwin

Kim B. Clark

## INTRODUCTION:
## THE EMERGENCE OF A MODULAR CLUSTER

Computers have been designed as modular systems with interoperable components since the advent of IBM's System/360 in 1964.[1] A modular design separates the design parameters of particular product into visible and hidden subsets. Visible design parameters are embodied in the system architecture and its interfaces—designers must take account of this information when designing individual components that function within the system. Hidden design parameters, in contrast, are "buried" in components. The designers of other parts of a system do not need to know in detail how a single component works so long as it conforms to system interface specifications.[2] As a corollary, hidden parts of a system can be changed to optimize their performance without compromising the system as a whole. Thus experimentation and improvement can proceed at

*We thank Jack Soll, Ellen Stein, Todd Pulvino, Partha Mohandas, Brent Omdahl and Joanne Ching for invaluable assistance in preparing this paper. The financial support of the Division of Research of the Harvard Business School is gratefully acknowledged. Mistakes, errors, or omissions are ours alone.

the component level while the overall system architecture and interface designs remain intact.[3]

In the decades following the introduction of the System/360, the modular design of computers gave rise to a modular cluster of companies. In the early years (1966–1980), most new entrants to the cluster competed on the basis of hidden design information. That is, they offered superior hardware and software products designed to function within another vendor's system. From this era of plug-compatible peripherals comes the quote "IBM is not the competition, it is the environment."

However, as fundamental technical knowledge expanded, it became possible to reconfigure known elements to make new systems. The computer workstation, for example, represented a fundamentally different conceptualization of the product and its relationship to the user. While it was based on many of the same components—electronic circuits, circuit boards, semiconductors, disk and tape drives, keyboards, and monitors—as traditional mainframes or minicomputers, it was smaller (and less expensive) than its predecessors, and it organized the elements of the system in a different way.

Such architectural innovations created new patterns of use for computers and, consequently, new markets. As a result of this evolutionary process, by the mid-1980s competition in the computer industry was essentially among platforms.[4] Then a new set of rivalries emerged that set the stage for a collision between two contrasting paradigms of firm behavior.[5] One pattern—which we term the "mainframe paradigm"—was initially invented by IBM and was a mode of behavior appropriate to the early stages of a modular cluster's formation. Many other computer companies, including DEC, Data General, and Prime, achieved great success by adopting this paradigm. But as the cluster of firms participating in the industry grew larger and denser, another pattern—which we call the "modular paradigm"—came into play. The purpose of this paper is to describe how these two paradigms collided in the competition between Sun and Apollo in the period 1985–1990.

The plan of the paper is as follows. The second section describes the two opposing paradigms. The third describes the competition between Sun and Apollo between 1985 and 1987. The fourth explains the rationale behind the Sun–AT&T technical alliance and describes the formation of the Open Software Foundation (the competitive response to the Sun–AT&T joint initiative) and its effect on AT&T's commitment to Sun. The fifth section concludes.

# EXPLOITING MODULARITY: TWO PARADIGMS

## Modularity and Its Consequences

The workstation environment of the mid-1980s had its roots in the early 1960s, when IBM first tackled the problem of compatibility among computer systems. The challenge was to design a family of computers that spanned a wide range of size, cost, and operating performance parameters and yet could run the same programs and use the same printers and disk drives. The key to solving the challenge was modularity, a technical principle embodied in IBM's System/360 (a family of computer systems first conceived in 1961 and brought to market in 1965).[6]

Modularity is a principle of design in which a complex system is broken down into independent modules that are linked together through standard interfaces. The antithesis of a modular product is one in which every component—down to the smallest screw—is unique and can function in only one context. There are in fact several different types of modularity: a product may be modular-in-production, modular-in-design, or modular-in-use. Modularity-in-production rationalizes a product into components and allows parts to be standardized (e.g., all screws the same size) and produced independently before assembly into the final system. Modularity-in-design goes a step further: with an overall architecture and standard interfaces, the modules can be designed independently, and mixed and matched to create a complete system. Finally, a product is modular-in-use if consumers themselves can mix and match components to arrive at a functioning whole.

The benefits of modularity-in-production are scale and scope economies, and the reduction in complexity of manufacturing and materials handling systems. The benefits of modularity-in-design are mix-and-match flexibility and efficient innovation, arising from the fact that all parts do not have to be redone to improve one element. The benefits of modularity-in-use are the ability to achieve customized designs and ease of maintenance, reliability, and piecemeal upgradability.

For IBM, which in 1961 was faced with an overwhelming proliferation of incompatible computer models, the flexibility inherent in a modular product line held tremendous potential. Realizing that potential, however, required a strategy for marketing, operations, pricing, and finance that capitalized on the power inherent in the modular concept. In short, IBM needed a technical, financial, and competitive paradigm suited to a modular family of computers.

The mainframe paradigm IBM adopted was not, as we shall see, the only paradigm it could have used to exploit modularity, but it did prove highly effective. It solved a fundamental problem inherent in all modular designs: how to capture (at least some of) the value generated by the underlying efficiency of modularity. In the short run, the originator of a modular design will be able to make the product more cheaply and with greater variety than is possible for those relying on less modular designs. But in the long run, an "architect firm" will have trouble earning superior returns. When the basic design is modular, there are simply too many ways for suppliers to link up with one another and with users without paying the architect's "fee."

IBM solved the problem (at least for a while) by using its traditional strengths in sales and operations, and by developing new capabilities in software, finance, and component production.[7] These initiatives together became the core of the mainframe paradigm.

## The Mainframe Paradigm

Table 3-1 summarizes the main elements of the mainframe paradigm. Modularity is at its heart. The central processor, memory, printers, tape drives, and terminals that made up the product system were all modular in design and use. Furthermore, the manufacturing arm of the company had a long tradition of using common parts and of encapsulating components in hierarchical subassemblies. Such modularity in production proved invaluable as IBM began to cope with rapid innovation and cost reductions in electronic components and hardware.

Although IBM's hardware systems were highly modular, its software was not. IBM's mainframes were designed around a monolithic core of proprietary software consisting of the instruction set, the operating system, and compilers that translated high-level languages (like FORTRAN or COBOL) into machine-readable code. Thus, whereas hardware improvements could be incorporated into the system rapidly and economically, instruction set and operating system changes and software conversions were extremely difficult and expensive. The opacity of the software core (and of most applications programs developed in this era) had an important economic effect: it locked users into their existing systems and software.

In the mainframe paradigm, therefore, compatibility and hardware modularity created valuable user options, but once a user committed to a particular family of machines, a complex instruction set and operating system made it expensive to switch to a different platform. Moreover,

TABLE 3-1

### THE MAINFRAME PARADIGM

| Key Elements | Impact |
| --- | --- |
| 1. Compatible family of computer systems, modular in design and use, covering a wide product range | Modular upgradability; mix-and-match flexibility; one-stop shopping |
| 2. In-house manufacturing of components, peripherals, and systems; modular in production | Control over technical change and quality |
| 3. Proprietary software (operating systems, compilers) and interfaces | Tie users to platform; preempt entry by producers of modules |
| 4. Direct sales force, technically competent, focused on solving problems | Strong, enduring customer relationships; deep knowledge of customer's system |
| 5. Own the equipment, rent it to customers | Facilitate product innovation; control over customer configuration of system |
| 6. Preemptive cannibalization | Users get system upgrades as technology changes; preempts competitors |
| 7. Conservative financial strategy | Capacity to cope with the unexpected; arsenal to withstand competitive attack |

IBM's excellent service and support, and the option to upgrade piecemeal over time or reconfigure to meet changing needs, made such a switch unnecessary. Thus the mainframe paradigm tied the customer happily— but tightly—to IBM.

The paradigm also worked to deter competition on individual modules. In particular, selective pricing and product introductions were an effective disciplinary device and a deterrent to prospective entrants. Proprietary and secret interfaces made it technically difficult (and perhaps illegal) to attach a new module to the system. Finally, a conservative financial strategy gave IBM the wherewithal to cope with unexpected technical developments or competitive moves. In general, a firm's capacity to withstand competitive attack can be measured in terms of its financial slack. High internal cash flow, high cash balances, and low debt all signal potential competitors: "Don't tread on me!"

Since the 1960s, most firms that have succeeded as system designers and manufacturers in the computer industry have done so by adopting the mainframe paradigm.[8] Firms such as DEC, HP, Fujitsu, and NEC combined modular hardware with monolithic software; they offered relatively extensive product lines and maintained proprietary interfaces; they practiced selective pricing[9] and controlled cannibalization; and most maintained a high level of financial slack. Partly to exercise control over their own systems and partly as an outlet for their high internal cash flow, these firms have tended to incorporate more components and interfaces within their own boundaries over time. With some modifications, this was the model Apollo Computer adopted as it pioneered in the work-station industry.

## The Modular Paradigm: Choosing Where to Compete

A company operating under the mainframe paradigm expands outward, aiming to make enough parts proprietary to gain monopoly power over some group of users. Through vertical integration, the outward-bound innovator seeks to become the "environment" for a captive group. A quite different paradigm for competing as the "architect" in a modular cluster is to internalize the narrowest possible set of design decisions. If the cluster of firms providing design and production services to the architect is dense, then a system architect may reap significant performance gains by exercising its options to select the best implementation of each compo-nent of the system (see table 3-2).

The modular paradigm laid out in table 3-2 is virtually the polar opposite of the mainframe paradigm. While it is true that design modu-larity, compatibility, and cannibalization are features of both paradigms, these ends are pursued by very different means. Under the modular par-adigm, a system architect seeks to use divisible rather than monolithic software, and standard rather than proprietary interfaces. Architects do not attempt to make everything under one roof; they assemble and test systems made of components supplied by specialist firms; they rely on resellers and distributors for sales; they sell, not lease, equipment; and they may pursue a more aggressive financial strategy.

In addition, two other elements—technical leverage and speed—play a critical role in the success of the modular paradigm. To see why this is so, and how the elements of the paradigm fit together, consider the pressures the system architect faces in pursuing the modular strategy. To achieve high profitability without a significant degree of vertical integra-tion, the modular architect's design must be attractive enough to con-vince suppliers of complementary parts of the system to invest in making components compatible with the new architecture.[10] But to earn superior returns, the architectural innovator also must control some critical ele-ment of the overall system—a key module, subsystem, or interface.

To solve the problems of attraction and profitability, the architect firm must seek to create technical leverage. That is, it must develop knowledge of a few key elements of the design, and through these, it must

TABLE 3-2

## THE MODULAR PARADIGM

| Key Elements | Impact |
|---|---|
| 1. Compatible family of computer systems, modular in design and use, covering a wide product range | Modular upgradability; mix-and-match flexibility |
| 2. Little in-house manufacturing; reliance on a network of specialized suppliers | Need for dense network of specialists and well-defined interfaces |
| 3. Modular software, standard interfaces | Third-party software crucial; alliances on standards |
| 4. Sales through resellers and distributors; some direct for large accounts | Reseller relationships crucial; need for other channels for customer information; alliances key |
| 5. Sell, don't lease, equipment | Fosters customer creativity in system configuration (see 4) |
| 6. Preemptive cannibalization | Push envelope on performance; preempt competitors |
| 7. Aggressive financial strategy | Rely on unconventional sources and instruments; alliances, venture capital crucial |
| 8. Speed in technical development, market entry, and growth | Fast and flexible systems; keen sense of opportunity and timing |
| 9. Technical leverage through highly focused knowledge of system, interfaces, and hidden/visible information | Premium on gurus with specialized skills in architecture and interfaces; learning crucial |

substantially affect the performance of the system as a whole. Such knowledge and insight into systemic behavior does not come cheap.

But even with such knowledge and insight, control over the critical design parameters is likely to be tenuous and short-lived. In a modular cluster there will be incessant pressure to find more powerful or lower-cost solutions. Similarly, an architecture that succeeds in improving system performance will inspire relentless efforts to remodularize—that is, to carve the pieces up in different ways so that what was proprietary and hidden will be public and visible.[11]

In sum, an architect firm operating in a modular cluster can never slow down—it must transform new knowledge into a sequence of new designs over time. With an ongoing stream of designs embodying highly leveraged insight and knowledge, the architect can push the envelope of performance and create momentum in the market and in the court of cluster opinion. By doing so, for a while at least, it may earn superior returns.

This is where speed becomes critical. The time it takes competitors to copy a design or equal its performance gives the architect a window of opportunity. In fast-moving markets, however, competition is intense and windows close quickly—within eighteen to twenty-four months in the workstation industry, for example. To succeed over the longer term, the architect must move quickly to open successive windows with new, ever better designs built on leveraged technology. In effect, pursuing the modular paradigm is like riding a tiger—you've got to stay on or risk the consequences.

In summary, the mainframe and modular paradigms are business models that can be applied to products that are modular in design and use. In the mid-1980s, these two paradigms came into direct competition in the computer workstation market. Apollo adopted the mainframe paradigm—a natural step, given the company's roots in the world of minicomputers and DEC's success. Sun, on the other hand, pursued the modular paradigm, which emphasized standards, UNIX, and a dense network of component suppliers in Silicon Valley. The competition between Sun and Apollo is a natural episode in which to examine the two paradigms, their relationship, and their relative success.

## SUN AND APOLLO

### Similarities

Much has been written about the different strategies pursued by Sun and Apollo as they battled in the workstation market in the mid-1980s. In reading contemporary descriptions (particularly prospectuses), however, one is struck by how similar the two companies were. Both emerged from the same technical, business, and financial environment.

From their inceptions, Apollo and Sun pursued the same opportunity. Developments in semiconductor memory, microprocessors, disk drives, and operating systems had created the possibility of putting significant computer power—including eye-popping graphics and hyper-fast computation—on an engineer's desk. Moreover, with the emergence of low-cost networking technology, it was possible to link the desktop machines (soon called workstations) into a network where engineers could share memory and peripherals, and communicate rapidly and effectively—all at a fraction of the cost of a competitive minicomputer system.

Though Apollo was the leader in recognizing the opportunity, it was soon followed by a host of competitors, including Sun Microsystems. Both Apollo and Sun operated within a dense modular cluster. Each based its products on Motorola microprocessors. As one Sun engineer noted, they were equally hostage to Motorola's design and development cycle: if Motorola introduced a new, higher-capacity chip, Apollo and Sun had no choice but to design new systems around it. Both companies also sourced peripheral equipment (disk drives, printers, file servers, and monitors) from outside suppliers. Although there is some indication that Apollo did more to tailor peripherals (especially monitors) to its own operating system, neither company was eager to integrate backward into components or peripheral manufacturing. Their prospectuses contained the following statements (about manufacturing):

> The Company intends to continue to buy standard parts and components (rather than to integrate vertically its manufacturing operations) because management believes that in this way the Company may more quickly integrate advances in technology into Apollo products and take advantage of the research and development efforts of component manufacturers. (Apollo, 3/4/83 and 2/7/86)
>
> The Company intends to continue to purchase standard parts and components because it believes that this practice enables the Company to integrate advances in technology into its products more quickly and to take advantage of the cost reduction and research and development efforts of the component manufacturers. (Sun, 3/19/86)

The dynamics of a modular cluster were so taken for granted in the computer industry by the mid-1980s that the logic of constant improvement and cost reduction had found its way into the standard boilerplate of stock-offering documents.

On the consumer side, both Apollo and Sun depended on third-party developers to write specialized application software. Their initial public offering prospectuses contained a list of applications packages operable on their machines.[12] Moreover, large portions of the sales of both companies were to so-called system builders or original equipment manufacturers (OEMs). OEMs purchased systems (sometimes at the board level), added applications software and specialized equipment, and resold the systems (often under their own names) to end users. System builders were thus another link in the chain that stretched from components to end users.

The existence of this large set of system builders was further evidence of the density of the modular cluster Sun and Apollo inhabited. As providers of complementary goods, the system builders, component and peripheral manufacturers, and software developers all wanted "their" workstation manufacturer to succeed, but not too well. Each member of the cluster sought to garner some share of a stable stream of rents for itself. To the extent that the relevant hardware and software interfaces were not perfect (hence there were costs of changing vendors or finding new customers), the members of the cluster depended on each other for reliable inputs or a stable demand for output. But firms making modules (whether hardware or software) were vulnerable to a reduction in rents if the provider of a critical, complementary piece of the system grew too strong. Therefore, each was always looking to identify alternative sources of critical inputs and to diversify its customer base. Each was also looking for ways to become the sole supplier of one or more critical parts of the system as a whole.

Thus, in terms of their general position within the greater cluster, Apollo and Sun were very similar. Both designed and manufactured workstations and had no plans to integrate backward into components or peripherals. Both sold large quantities to system builders: their products were components of still larger systems. Both were actively involved in the development of system software but relied on third-party developers to write specialized applications software. Both gave at least lip service to the need for standards and promised to conform with industry standards where they were relevant.

## Apollo's Product Definition and Design

In spite of these similarities, Apollo and Sun exhibited distinctly different approaches to product definition and design. The differences were most evident in the areas of network design, the operating system, and modularity. Apollo presented users with an indivisible bundle consisting of (1) a network management system, (2) a single operating system, and (3) hardware. The first element was implemented through its proprietary DOMAIN network architecture; the second, through its proprietary Aegis operating system software (although by 1986 it was supporting both Aegis and an internal version of UNIX); and the third, through its workstations and associated peripherals, controllers, and storage devices. Each element required the other two in order to function; the DOMAIN architecture was inextricably tied up with the DN series of workstations, which in turn functioned best under the Aegis operating system.

This intertwining of network architecture, operating system software, and computer hardware was characteristic of the technical and commercial milieu from which Apollo emerged. Essentially all of Apollo's senior executives came from the minicomputer industry, and their explicit strategy was to exploit workstation technology to compete directly against the dominant players in the microcomputer world: IBM, DEC, and HP. The established manufacturers not only served as targets but also provided the paradigm for design, management, and competition. Edward Zander, Apollo's marketing vice president at the time, aptly summed up Apollo's position:

> The competition I worry about is IBM, DEC, Hewlett Packard. The start-ups aren't a threat to our existence—which is not to say we don't look over our shoulder to see what technology they have. IBM has taught us over the last 20–30 years that the whiz-bang product isn't always the winner. What counts is having the best price and performance at the right time, with the sales and service to back it up, and a good understanding of applications and end users.[13]

The design of Apollo's workstations reflected its roots and primary targets: minicomputers. The new workstation technology—16- and 32-bit microprocessors; high-speed, low-cost memory; small, high-capacity disk drives—gave Apollo an inherent cost advantage over minis, but its product was no bare-bones machine. Indeed, Apollo's design philosophy was to offer a high level of functionality, elegance, and quality. The Aegis operating system, for example, was chosen over UNIX (a choice actively debated within Apollo) because it offered significant advantages in networking functionality. Aegis managed network resources so that any user could transparently access memory and processing power on other nodes and servers, which meant that a single user could run bigger programs faster than would be possible with a single workstation.

In addition to its proprietary network and operating systems, Apollo emphasized advanced graphics capability and high-speed number crunching in a compact, desktop package with only a few printed circuit boards (typically three or four). While Apollo did no component manufacturing, it did build a state-of-the-art manufacturing facility to handle automated component insertion, wave soldering, assembly, and testing.

The key minicomputer manufacturers in Apollo's genealogy—Prime, Data General, and DEC—approached computer design in a similar fashion. IBM (except in the case of the PC) and DEC carried design integration even further—back to the level of chips. Many designers believed that this high degree of specialization and integration among the core elements of the machine was necessary to achieve high levels of processing speed and efficient management of memory and the central processing unit (CPU).

Moreover, proprietary operating systems and networking technology created user lockin—a loyal base of customers guaranteed a continuing stream of rents. Apollo's focus on its proprietary operating systems was hailed in the financial community. The following comment by Peter Labe, an analyst with Barney Harris Upham & Co., was typical of Wall Street's view of Apollo in 1984:

> Its proprietary operating system will keep users with Apollo. The company has responded to UNIX demand by running versions of UNIX as a subset. Users will get more performance with Apollo's operating system and it keeps it from being a commodity product. Some users prefer UNIX, and that segment Apollo won't get. But I don't see any problem; the market will grow 50% a year the next few years.

Thus Apollo followed all the major precepts of the mainframe paradigm. The company combined modular hardware with proprietary, monolithic software, and gave users options in the form of an extensive product line of compatible machines connected by proprietary interfaces. Apollo counted on users' becoming locked into their platforms. Finally, it charged high prices (relative to its costs), practiced controlled cannibalization, and tried to maintain high levels of financial slack. In 1984 Apollo had 60 percent of a market that was growing at 50 percent per year. By the conventional wisdom of the mainframe paradigm, its strategy was impeccable.

## Sun's Product Definition and Design

It was Apollo's bad luck to be in a head-on collision with a different paradigm. The founders of Sun Microsystems viewed the market opportunity from a very different vantage point: their goal was to get a powerful but low-cost workstation to market quickly. Sun pursued and—through the agency of Andreas Bechtolsheim and William Joy—managed to achieve two historically conflicting objectives of computer design: (1) low cost through standard, off-the-shelf parts and (2) superior speed and performance. Sun did not simply build a computer based on standards; it built a fast, high-performance computer based on standards. To do so, the hardware and software architects and designers at Sun reconceptualized and remodularized the design of the computer.

To achieve their low-cost objective, Sun's designers adopted two principles: standard parts and a single board. Even at the outset of their work, Sun's architects tapped into a dense modular cluster of component suppliers and thus benefited from the large volumes, R&D, and expertise of very experienced electronics companies. Standard components, including a Motorola microprocessor and an Ethernet networking chip (not to mention power supplies, disk drives, monitors, connectors, and capacitors), were widely available, relatively inexpensive, and required little development investment. The single board design was chosen to simplify logistics, materials management, testing, and manufacturing, and to eliminate the cost of designing and producing multiple boards.

The pursuit of standard solutions had the virtue of minimizing upfront investment and eliminating delays associated with developing proprietary components. Sun applied the same logic in choosing UNIX as the operating system. Bechtolsheim had used UNIX in developing a Sun workstation prototype; given the founders' strategy of simplicity and standardization, it made little sense to invest in a costly, time-consuming development effort to develop a proprietary operating system.

Designing a computer with standard parts and a single board was one thing. Making it fast and powerful in order to appeal to a technical community was quite another. To get speed and power out of standard parts, Sun's architects built on recent research in computer science to remodularize the design. In the spirit of the modular paradigm, they searched for a narrow set of design parameters they could control (all the rest would be standard). The set they hit upon was the interface between the CPU and internal memory.

In the 1970s, John Hennessy and his colleagues at Stanford (where Andreas Bechtolsheim was a graduate student) helped to pioneer research on the frequency with which instructions in different computer architectures were actually used in running programs. Hennessy's work, along with that of John Cocke at IBM and David Patterson at Berkeley, led to the introduction of commercial RISC (reduced instruction set computer) architectures in the 1980s. Hennessy established the principle that instructions or operations used frequently should be very fast.[14] In the kinds of applications Sun had targeted (e.g., computer-aided design and software engineering), implementing that principle meant running the CPU at maximum speed all the time. This in turn meant making operations to put things into and take things out of internal memory as fast as possible.

Sun developed two proprietary hardware components to couple the CPU and internal memory. The first was direct memory for the CPU, called the memory management unit (MMU). Sun patented a special "no wait state" MMU that eliminated situations where the CPU had to wait to access memory because memory was not available.[15] The second proprietary component was a high-speed, 32-bit internal memory bus. Unlike its competitors, Sun put its internal memory chips (1–4 megabytes of DRAM) and the video controller chips for its bit-mapped graphics display on a proprietary, high-speed internal bus. All other input–output operations used a standard multibus setup (see figure 3-1 for details).

The internal bus and the MMU were crucial not only to memory–CPU coupling but also to the single board design. The bus, for example, allowed Sun's designers to closely link memory and video chips and locate them on the same board. The MMU allowed Sun to avoid using cache memory (a special set of very fast memory chips designed to eliminate wait states), and thus reduce chip cost and eliminate an additional board. By effectively managing the CPU–memory connection, Sun achieved a "no wait state" design on a single board.

Software—particularly Sun's in-depth knowledge of UNIX—also played an important role. William Joy, the principal architect of the Berkeley version of UNIX, who joined Sun shortly after its founding, was a recognized master at manipulating UNIX to run efficiently on a variety of different hardware platforms. Joy and the other UNIX "kernel designers" at Sun formed a critical mass of UNIX hackers who not only understood the operating system but also could advise the hardware designers on how to take advantage of the software. When Sun encountered glitches as a result of using standard components, for example, the UNIX hackers simply wrote code to get around the problem. Furthermore, Sun exploited some of UNIX's idiosyncrasies to enhance the machine's speed. For example, the operation of the "no wait state" MMU fit perfectly with UNIX's conventions for establishing the hierarchy of operations (e.g., determining which address gets accessed first): the MMU produced exactly what UNIX wanted, when it wanted it. The result was a meshing of hardware and software critical to overall performance.

## The Impact of Remodularization
## on Competitive Performance

Sun's approach to computer design produced a fast, high-performance, surprisingly affordable workstation. Moreover, it was a product architecture in which traditional sources of dominance in the modular cluster (the operating system, high-profile components, critical applications software) either were standard products themselves, or were based on standards that allowed others to hook into the architecture and reap the

FIGURE 3-1

## SIMPLIFIED SCHEMATIC OF THE SUN-2 WORKSTATION

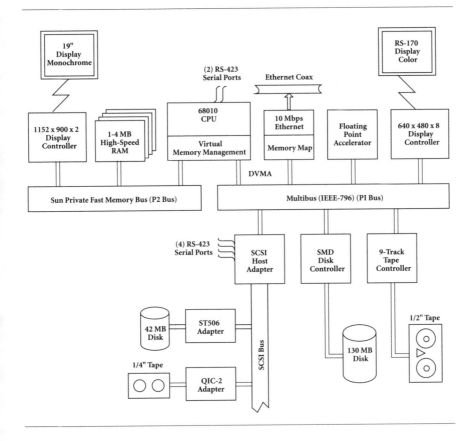

rewards outside of Sun's control. Indeed, in the area of software, Sun went out of its way to make it easy for third parties to develop new products for the Sun platform. A crucial step was the introduction of a suite of powerful software tools that hid details of the hardware and eliminated much of the drudgery in software development. While writing for Sun meant writing for UNIX-based products more generally, having great tools meant that developers had an incentive to write for Sun first.

Reconceptualization and remodularization gave Sun three important competitive advantages. First, Sun workstations were capable of running a full-fledged version of UNIX—a significant selling point to an important group of users.[16] Apollo offered a version of UNIX on its workstations from the outset (see the 1983 prospectus), but its systems did not run well under UNIX until much later, and not all features of UNIX were offered. Second, because they ran UNIX, Sun workstations could participate in networks of heterogeneous machines. This meant that users could link Sun machines into their existing DEC minicomputer networks at low cost.[17] Therefore, in stark contrast to a fundamental tenet of the mainframe paradigm, purchasing Sun workstations did not entail an irreversible commitment to Sun's product line. These two advantages were important selling points for Sun.

The third advantage was often overlooked by the trade press and investment analysts. Sun's remodularization of workstation design and its pursuit of the modularity paradigm in production as well as engineering design greatly increased its efficiency and reduced its capital requirements. Thus, a dollar of funding at Sun went approximately twice as far as a dollar at Apollo. In the long run, Sun's efficiency was as important to its success as its espousal of open systems or its implementation of UNIX on a desktop machine.[18]

Part of Sun's efficiency advantage was rooted in its strategy of relying on the dense modular cluster of suppliers for almost every aspect of manufacturing. Capitalizing on its reliance on standard components, Sun did even less in-house manufacturing than Apollo (see figure 3-2 for a comparison). The single board design accentuated that difference. With a single board, Sun greatly simplified the materials flow it had to manage, reduced the amount of work-in-process, made testing boards and systems much easier, and eliminated the need for associated overhead and facilities. The impact was a substantial increase in Sun's capital efficiency relative to Apollo.

For example, figure 3-3 shows that from mid-1985 (the earliest time for which comparative figures are available) through the end of 1988, Sun's net working capital[19] averaged about 50 percent of quarterly sales, while Apollo's was never less than 100 percent. A detailed breakdown of the components of working capital reveals that the main difference was in inventory turnover: Sun produced and shipped its product in about half as much time as Apollo. Since the evidence suggests that Sun's delivery performance was equivalent to Apollo's, this difference in throughput time underscores the power of the modular paradigm. Indeed, during this time Sun built to order, whereas Apollo built to stock. Apollo's intent was to optimize production flow at the new, highly efficient factory it brought on line in 1985. But, interestingly, Sun suffered no cost disadvantage from its "inefficient" production method: the companies' prices were comparable (Sun's were actually somewhat lower), and gross margins were almost equal.[20]

FIGURE 3-2

## SIMPLIFIED WORKSTATION PROCESS FLOW

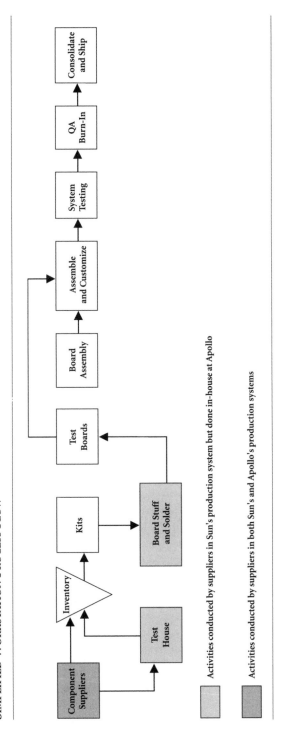

FIGURE 3-3

Productivity of Net Working Capital

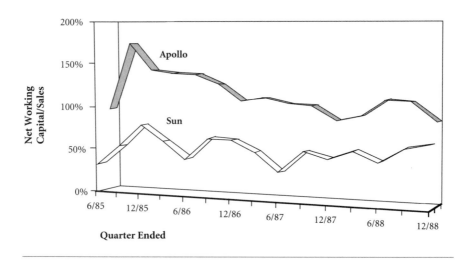

Turning to fixed assets (see figure 3-4), Sun's property, plant, and equipment never exceeded 60 percent of quarterly sales, whereas Apollo's peaked at 157 percent of quarterly sales in the third quarter of 1985 and declined to 95 percent of sales by the fourth quarter of 1988. Part of the explanation here may be Apollo's new plant. When lumpy capacity is brought onstream, there is often a period of excess capacity with correspondingly low productivity. In fact, some of Apollo's lower productivity was caused by being at less than full capacity from 1985 through the end of 1987. But the increases in property, plant, and equipment at Apollo from June 1985 to March 1987 amounted to 89 percent of incremental sales, whereas increases at Sun were only 53 percent of incremental sales.[21] Thus, even allowing for the underutilization of capacity, the figures clearly show that Sun had a system that allowed it to produce computers with substantially less fixed capital than Apollo.

What Sun's efficiency meant in financial terms is summarized in figure 3-5, which plots the return on assets employed for the two companies. The numerator of each series equals internally generated free cash flow;[22] the denominator equals the sum of net working capital and fixed and other assets. The ratio is a rate of return on the operating assets in each business. (Quarterly rates of return have been annualized so that the scale is comparable with an ordinary interest rate.)

FIGURE 3-4

## PRODUCTIVITY OF FIXED ASSETS

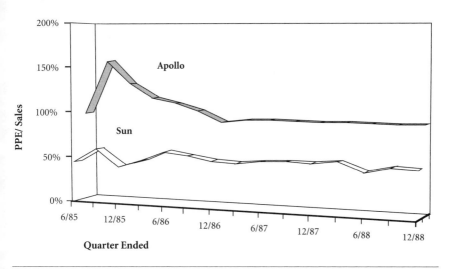

FIGURE 3-5

## RETURN ON ASSETS EMPLOYED

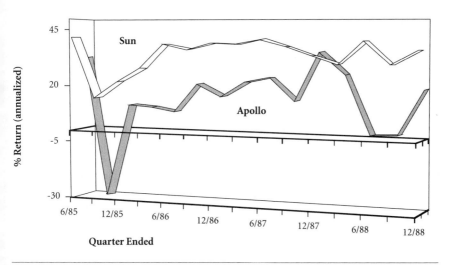

Figure 3-5 shows both companies to be very attractive businesses. After suffering a loss in the third quarter of 1985, Apollo recovered to earn between 15 percent and 20 percent on operating assets by the second half of 1986.[23] But in the same time frame, Sun was earning 35 percent to 40 percent on its operating assets. Sun's greater productivity was evidenced by the fact that although its margins were similar to Apollo's, it returned about twice as much on assets actually used in the business.

Here, then, is the power of the modular paradigm. By remodularizing around a narrow but powerful subset of design elements, using standard components and operating software, and exploiting deep knowledge of the system and interfaces, Sun could offer the market a superior product at an attractive price, earn excellent margins, and employ much less capital in production. It was a sharp departure from the mainframe paradigm, and it spelled trouble for Apollo.

## SUN'S GROWTH AND THE SUN–AT&T ALLIANCE

### Hypergrowth: Using an Aggressive Financial Strategy to Exploit Modularity

What did Sun choose to do with the capabilities derived from its more efficient systems of design and production? In principle, upon reaching a certain market share (say 50 percent), it could have adopted the same pricing and product innovation targets as Apollo. The two companies would then have grown at approximately the same rate, but Sun would be twice as profitable. The two might then have sought to differentiate their customer bases in order to maintain margins and minimize head-to-head competition. If both companies had been competing under the mainframe paradigm, their respective customers would soon have been locked into different proprietary architectures, and competition would occur only at the margin (with new customers).

But Sun was promoting open systems and a universal, nonproprietary operating system.[24] And rather than settling for high margins and positive cash flow, Sun held its margins down and grew very fast, putting continual competitive pressure on Apollo and other companies seeking a foothold in the workstation market. Sun financed its hypergrowth with massive amounts of funding raised in the public capital markets and later from AT&T.

## Financing Hypergrowth

Finance played a crucial role in the interaction between Sun and Apollo in the mid-1980s. Both firms had access to the capital markets, but they approached their capital suppliers very differently. Indeed, in 1986 and 1987, Sun embarked on a financial strategy radically different from that of Apollo. Sun went to the capital markets five times in the course of eighteen months. The money it raised was used to finance growth at the rate of 25 percent to 30 percent per quarter. As a result, in less than two years, Sun's revenues went from 60 percent to 144 percent of Apollo's.

Throughout this period, Sun put enormous downward pressure on prices, making it hard for anyone to make a profit or achieve positive cash flow in the workstation industry. In essence, Sun combined its technical productivity and efficiency with very aggressive financial tactics to buy market share in its business.

Sun's opportunity to unseat Apollo arose partly as a result of the latter's mistakes. In 1985, Apollo greatly overestimated the demand for its products in the face of a general industry slump. It brought a new high-capacity production facility onstream just as demand for its products was evaporating. In the third quarter of that year, Apollo was forced to write off $30 million in obsolete inventory and underutilized capacity, and suffered an $18 million after-tax loss. Moreover, operating losses, combined with capital expenditures on the new plant, obliterated the $50 million cash cushion Apollo had at the start of the year. The company survived by using sale and leaseback financing and drawing down a $75 million line of credit it had negotiated early in the year.

These events caused a major shakeup in management. In the fourth quarter, William Poduska, the founder, left, and David Lubrano, the chief financial officer, was ousted. Three (out of seven) members of the board resigned, and four new ones were added in the wake of the crisis. The result was to consolidate the position of Thomas Vanderslice, who had been hired as president and CEO in 1984. With Poduska's departure, Vanderslice became chairman of the board as well as president and CEO.

One of Vanderslice's first moves was to replenish the company's cash by issuing $115 million in convertible subordinated debentures. About a third of this money was used to repay existing debt; thus Apollo ended the first quarter of 1986 with $75 million in cash and investments and a $75 million unused line of credit. The 1985 Annual Report (published after the debenture sale) stated:

> [Apollo] anticipates that the proceeds from the sale of the Debentures, together with internally generated funds, will be sufficient to meet the Company's capital spending requirements and liquidity needs until mid-1987.

In other words, Apollo was not contemplating the sale of equity or further borrowing in the near term. It was already in the process of implementing major cost-cutting measures and planned to live on the cash it had in hand. The issuance of convertible debentures also indicates that Apollo was reasonably confident of its short-term profitability, and optimistic enough to bet on the future conversion of the debentures to equity.

Thus, in early 1986, Apollo's managers did not anticipate that they would soon be fighting a battle for survival against a superior rival. Even then, Apollo was losing sales to Sun in head-to-head competition and was being forced to change its stance on UNIX and open systems. But the threat posed by Sun's superior technical capabilities was not yet apparent. Sun was still a privately held, venture-capital-backed startup; its revenues were 60 percent of Apollo's; its cash balance was a mere $15 million; and it had $18 million of senior debt outstanding. In almost every way imaginable, Apollo appeared the stronger, better-capitalized company.

Sun went public in March 1986, raising $46 million of new equity in its initial public offering. It used this infusion of funds to grow: its cumulative internal funds deficit in the first three quarters of 1986 was almost $50 million, but sales more than doubled. At this point, the power of Sun's more productive business model became apparent: each dollar invested in Sun supported twice as much revenue as the same dollar invested in Apollo. Thus, although Sun's and Apollo's internal funding deficits were about the same in the first nine months of 1986, Sun's quarterly sales went from $42 million to $92 million, while Apollo's quarterly sales climbed from $71 million to $100 million. In other words, the same amount of money financed a sales ramp-up of $50 million per quarter ($200 million annualized) at Sun, but only $29 million per quarter ($116 million annualized) at Apollo.

By the third quarter of 1986, Sun's sales were almost equal to Apollo's. However, internal deficits caused by high growth eroded its cash balances: by September, Sun was down to $23 million in cash and investments, and consuming money at the rate of $10 million per month. Confronted with a potential liquidity crisis, Sun arranged four financings in quick succession. In October, it borrowed $25 million from two banks; in November, it issued $90 million of new common stock; in December, it arranged a $50 million revolving line of credit; and in February 1987, it sold $100 million of convertible subordinated debentures.

Thus, in six months, Sun's and Apollo's financial positions were dramatically reversed. In September 1986, Apollo had twice as much cash as Sun ($52 million to $23 million) and a substantial unused line of credit. By March 1987, Sun had cash in excess of $216 million, and another $70+ million available in bank lines. At this time, almost half of Sun's reported assets consisted of cash and marketable securities. Sun was now not only twice as profitable as its chief rival, but had five times as much cash to spend on building market share (see figure 3-6).

But Sun's war chest was large only relative to Apollo's. Compared with its potential need for cash, Sun's cash balances in mid-1987 were sufficient for only twelve to eighteen months of continued growth. Of course, Sun's rate of cash consumption—colloquially known as its "burn rate"—depended on its pricing strategy. If Sun were to raise prices, its growth rate and correlated need for cash would diminish. The $200 million war chest would then last a long time, and Apollo and the rest of Sun's competitors would breathe easier.

However, Sun's executives built the war chest for a purpose. They proceeded to use it, and the balances began to decline. New financing would be needed before very long, but new cash was unlikely to come from the public capital markets for two reasons. First was the stock

FIGURE 3-6

## CASH BALANCES

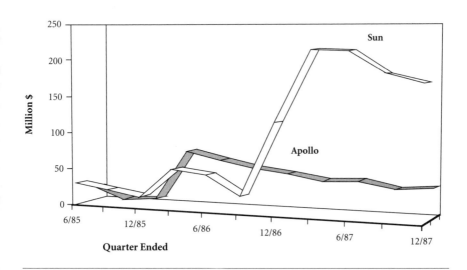

market's reaction to the introduction of the Sun-4 product family in June 1987. Consistent with the modular paradigm, Sun introduced its fourth-generation product long before the third generation had run out of steam. The Sun-4 clearly cannibalized the Sun-3, and its introduction required significant infusions of cash for phase-out/phase-in expenses. Wall Street's reaction was immediate: Sun's stock price dropped 18 percent in the two trading days surrounding the Sun-4 announcement. In contrast to its steady upward progress from September 1986 to May 1987, the stock fell from its peak of 44 and settled in the mid-30s by October 1987. And then came the second problem: Black Monday. Following the crash of the stock market on October 19, 1987, Sun's stock dropped to the low 20s and then rebounded to the low 30s. At this point the outlook for new equity issues by small, risky companies was quite uncertain. But at the same time, following a very enthusiastic response to the Sun-4, Sun was consuming cash at the rate of $15 million per month.

In the midst of this uncertain financial environment, Sun sought new cash from a familiar source: the corporate investor.[25] Sun had already worked out a technical agreement with AT&T covering the development of UNIX; an equity investment would complete the package. But this was to be no "plain vanilla" deal. Not only were the amounts of cash sizable, but the deal was structured to give Sun valuable flexibility in its battle for supremacy in workstations.

In late 1987, Sun and AT&T completed a financial agreement that allowed Sun to "put" its common stock to AT&T at a premium over the market price (25 percent over the twenty-day trailing average). The agreement, described in a filing with the Securities and Exchange Commission, gave Sun the right to demand that AT&T purchase up to six million new shares of Sun stock over the next six years. (Sun had thirty-four million shares outstanding at the time.) Sun could trigger a sale by sending a notice to AT&T, which then had thirty days to complete the transaction.[26]

The direct effect of the AT&T financing was to increase Sun's war chest by an amount proportional to its stock price. At the time the deal was announced, a conservative estimate of the total amount of money Sun could obtain was 140 percent of the value of six million shares. Sun's shares were then trading at around $38 per share, and thus the AT&T financing gave Sun access to more than $300 million of additional cash. (The technical details of the valuation of the agreement are in a separate appendix, available from the authors.)

Figure 3-7 shows the implicit effect of the AT&T financing on the relative cash balances of Sun and Apollo through the first quarter of 1989.

FIGURE 3-7

## Cash Effect of AT&T Financing

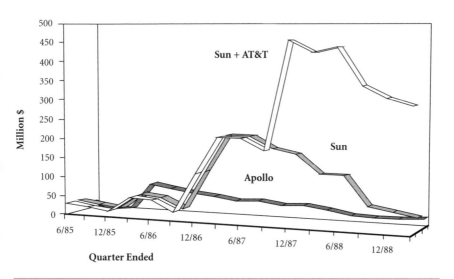

Sun + AT&T

Sun

Apollo

Million $

Quarter Ended

(This was the last quarter Apollo existed as a freestanding company.) The difference in resources between the two companies is staggering. By the end of 1987, Apollo's cash resources had dwindled to $40 million—a small sum compared with the $177 million in cash on Sun's balance sheet, and dwarfed by the $458 million Sun could raise by exercising its rights to issue shares to AT&T.

The difference in financial resources was mirrored in the two companies' spending rates. By the first quarter of 1989, Sun's internal quarterly cash deficit was in excess of $130 million, and sales were increasing by about $50 million per quarter.[27] In stark contrast, Apollo was attempting to grow with no new cash infusions. The pressure Sun was putting on industrywide margins made it hard for Apollo to show a profit, and to break even, it was forced to cut back on selling, general, and administrative expenses. Throughout this period Apollo managed to maintain its R&D spending in proportion to sales. Unfortunately, Apollo's engineers had to design and engineer a line of products as complex and extensive as Sun's on about 40 percent of Sun's R&D budget. Toward the close of 1988, it became clear that Apollo could not survive as an independent company without a massive funds infusion, but by then the total market value of its equity had dropped to around $300 million. At this point, a 100 percent dilution of Apollo's existing equity would have allowed it to match Sun's spending for two or three quarters at most.

## THE AFTERMATH: CONCLUSIONS AND IMPLICATIONS

The battle between Sun and Apollo is testimony to the power of modularity, both as a principle of design and as the basis for a new paradigm for competition. Sun's experience shows the decisive impact on productivity when a modular design creates a dense modular cluster of companies competing on independent modules. As the architect, Sun could exploit the variety of parallel initiatives to push knowledge of components deeper, performance higher, and cost lower. Moreover, by relying on standard interfaces, Sun could mix and match components to achieve what we have called the best of the best.

In principle, this flexibility was available to Apollo—it was even touted in its public statements and pronouncements. But Sun took the principle of modularity much further than Apollo, extending it to the operating system, networking hardware, and software. And Sun's bet on the capabilities inherent in the modular cluster paid off in one respect: in terms of customer acceptance and machine performance, Sun's full-blown modularity beat Apollo's limited modularity. Mixing and matching designs across the full modular cluster delivered systems with lower cost, higher perfomance, and more user options than mixing and matching designs within a single firm. This was true even though Apollo's proprietary solutions were regarded as "elegant" and "superior."

Modularity was the source of power behind Sun's strategy, but it was Sun's specific choice of a design (the memory–CPU interface and a single board), its approach to manufacturing, and its aggressive financial strategy that allowed it to exploit that power in competition. However, Sun's victory over Apollo turned out to be no guarantee of supranormal profits, nor even of a quiet life with average returns. Indeed, what happened to Sun illustrates precisely the difficulty an architect has when it attempts to convert a successful design into a dominant market position within a modular cluster.

Sun's first problem was that the niche it sought to dominate (networked workstations) was being invaded from all sides. Large, well-financed, capable players—Hewlett-Packard, IBM, and DEC—realized that Sun's products not only would be attractive to engineers and software designers, but also would be competitive in business applications. They had to develop directly competitive products or lose the business. At the same time, personal computer manufacturers, designers, and distributors had already discovered the power of the modular paradigm, and were rapidly increasing the power and range of their products. They, too, saw servers, networks, and workstations as targets of opportunity. Framed in these terms, what Sun won in its battle with Apollo was the opportunity to play in a larger game against bigger players.

The good news was that the big game was potentially very valuable. The bad news was that many important players had good reason not to let Sun achieve a dominant position in UNIX-based, RISC-powered, high-performance workstations. This became crystal clear soon after Sun announced the AT&T financing agreement. Although the technical agreement with AT&T, announced in October 1987, brought little reaction (almost everyone had some kind of technical agreement with AT&T), the announcement of the financing agreement in January 1988 set off a firestorm of protest from other UNIX licensees. This group feared that Sun's deal with AT&T would cut them out of UNIX development and give Sun both a lead time and a performance advantage. Eventually, they believed, UNIX would be optimized for Sun's processors and systems.

AT&T tried to placate the licensees, but to little avail. In May 1988, DEC, Apollo, Hewlett-Packard, IBM, and others established the Open Software Foundation (OSF) to create an independent UNIX standard. To Sun's dismay, AT&T then abandoned the idea of setting a single standard with Sun. In December 1988, AT&T and other companies that had supported the AT&T–Sun alliance set up their own independent UNIX development group, UNIX International (UI). In 1989, UI forced Sun and AT&T to shut down their joint development lab. Sun (which joined UI) would have no exclusive access to any part of the development process.

The concerted reaction of competitors prevented Sun from dominating UNIX, which would have given the company control over a powerful element of the modular cluster. But even without such control, Sun was in a relatively strong position. Hewlett-Packard was occupied with trying to absorb Apollo (which it acquired in May 1989) and was attempting to develop a coherent product line. DEC was struggling with multiple platforms in its workstation lineup (VAX-VMS and MIPS-UNIX), and IBM was trying to develop a real workstation product after the embarrassing failure of its RT entry. Thus, the big players were strong enough to prevent Sun from dominating UNIX, but they were not particularly formidable in the marketplace.

But the dynamics of the modular paradigm implied that Sun had to move quickly and hit successive windows of opportunity. Instead, Sun lost its technological focus—a not uncommon occurrence in the late

1980s. At the time, Intel's X86 line of processors was expanding in power and PCs were invading workstation turf. RISC technology (to which Sun was closely connected in history and in technical philosophy) was emerging from the laboratory. And Sun had built a huge business around Motorola's 68000 product line.

Sun's answer to this quandary was to pursue all options at once. It first tried to develop a RISC chip jointly with Motorola (Sun would bring ideas on RISC architecture, Motorola would bring expertise in design and processing). But Motorola was not interested, so Sun then proceeded to design its own processor (SPARC), which it licensed to chipmakers and other computer companies. Meanwhile, another group at Sun developed a workstation built around Intel's 80386 processor and, of course, there was the mainline product family built around Motorola's CPU. The upshot was that Sun had to support three platforms, all the while confusing its customers.

Sun executives soon realized this strategy was unsustainable, and refocused the company around SPARC. (Internally, this move was described as "we need to get all our wood behind a single arrow.") But then, Sun stumbled again. After initial success with its line of SPARCstations, it was late to market with the next generation of its processor. This gave Hewlett-Packard and IBM an opportunity to reenter the competitive arena with their own products. Sun could no longer claim price–performance leadership. With its installed base, its strong reputation, and its ability to market and price aggressively, it was able to maintain a sizable market share in workstations. But its opportunity to lead and dominate the workstation market evaporated, and its financial performance and market value stagnated.

In summary, Sun's experience underscores both the power and the peril of the modular paradigm. Moreover, it raises fundamental questions about the longer-term evolution of an industry such as computers, where modularity is fundamental and modular clusters emerge as the primary mode of competition.

## NOTES

1. SPREAD Report: Charles H. Ferguson and Charles R. Morris, *Computer Wars: How the West Can Win in a Post-IBM World* (New York: Times Books, 1993).

2. Of course, no modularization is ever perfect. To partition and decouple design tasks requires knowledge, and thus modularization typically proceeds by

stages as knowledge accumulates and is applied to system design. Some systems are technically easier to modularize than others: systems based on electricity, for example, involve a one-dimensional flow of electrons, and seem easier to break apart than mechanical systems (a car or an airplane) that contain two- and three-dimensional surfaces and must have structural integrity as well.

3 . Christopher Alexander, *Notes on the Synthesis of Form* (Cambridge, Mass.: Harvard University Press, 1964); D. L. Parnas, "A Technique for Software Module Specification with Examples," *Communications of the ACM* 15 (1972): 330–336, and "On the Criteria to Be Used in Decomposing Systems into Modules," *Communications of the ACM* 15 (1972): 1053–1058; Carliss Baldwin and Kim B. Clark, "Modularity and Real Options," Harvard Business School Working Paper #93-026 (1993).

4. Timothy F. Bresnahan and Shane Greenstein, *Technological Competition, and the Structure of the Computer Industry,* CEPR Publication no. 315 (Stanford, Calif.: Center for Economic Policy Research, Stanford University, 1992).

5. Collisions in rapidly changing technologies and markets are especially interesting because so much happens so fast. What might have taken decades to work out in an industry such as steel happened in a few years in the computer industry.

6. The 360 achieved upward, downward, peripheral, and intertemporal compatibility, but it was a major engineering gamble at the time. Few in the industry thought it could be done. Notwithstanding the naysayers, the concepts of information hiding and interoperability of parts were rapidly developing in the technical literature of that time. If IBM's implementation of the 360 had failed, the same technical goals would almost certainly have been pursued at other companies, but the evolution of the computer industry in the 1960s and 1970s would have been different. SPREAD Report; Emerson W. Pugh, Lyle R. Johnson, and John H. Palmer, *IBM's 360 and Early 370 Systems* (Cambridge, Mass.: MIT Press, 1991).

7. The paradigm that evolved around the 360 was deeply rooted in IBM's history. In its traditional tabulator business, IBM had developed a system of engineering design, finance, and sales that gave users the options they valued while preserving their investments in processing methods and data. The system was based on modular, interoperable pieces of equipment that processed a universal, standard type of data (eighty-column punched cards). IBM also developed a contractual system that effectively limited users' options to those provided by IBM. The key elements of this "nexus of contracts" were (1) IBM manufactured all physical parts of the system; (2) the IBM sales force was in constant contact with the customer's establishment; (3) IBM salesmen were technically competent and motivated to solve customer problems by incrementally reconfiguring their systems; (4) IBM owned all equipment and merely rented it to users.

8. Perhaps the most successful application of the paradigm outside IBM was accomplished, ironically, by DEC. DEC got its start in the business by producing electronic modules, and for many years defined itself as the antithesis of everything that was IBM. Yet in the late 1970s, with its VAX family of computers, DEC adopted the mainframe paradigm with great success. Its main competitors—Prime, Data General, and, to a lesser extent, Hewlett-Packard—also pursued market success through modular designs, proprietary software, a broad line, direct sales, and preemptive cannibalization.

9. Within the constraints established by antitrust law.

10. There is an inherent conflict between the goal of acceptance and the goal of dominance within a cluster. The suppliers of complementary components do not want a disproportionate share of profits to flow to another firm; each would like to dominate the cluster itself (or, failing that, prevent anyone else from doing so). Thus one of the keys to having one's design accepted is to appear unthreatening. But it is also useful to be attractive: complementary suppliers would like to be part of a winning team. Acceptance of the architect's design thus rests on its attractiveness and the absence of threats to capture a disproportionate share of the rents. Operationally, this means that acceptance and dominance cannot be pursued openly at the same time; acceptance must be nailed down before dominance can be asserted. Intertemporal inconsistency is one of the things that makes the modular paradigm complex and hard to implement.

11. When remodularization occurs (as when Compaq cloned the IBM PC), the hidden interior of the former interface becomes a component, and hence prey to competition from alternative versions that conform to the now-separate interface definitions. In this fashion a seemingly secure competitive advantage may evaporate very quickly.

12. Interestingly, Apollo's 1986 convertible subordinated debenture prospectus did not contain such a list—perhaps because enough developers had dropped Apollo that publishing an updated list would have been embarrassing to the company. Sun's initial public offering (IPO) prospectus, published one month later, listed available applications, large OEMs, and end users by name, indicating that such information was competitively relevant.

13. *Electronic Business*, April 1, 1984, p. 79. Zander later left Apollo to join Sun.

14. This principle is sometimes referred to as "Amdahl's Law."

15. Note the need for intellectual property protection for what was a fairly simple and visible change in the design.

16. One of UNIX's advantages seems to have been its high degree of modularity relative to other operating systems, which made it somewhat portable across hardware platforms. Also very important was the fact that new features could be added to UNIX very easily without compromising the basic system (this is typical of a modular design). Thus UNIX itself came to have a cluster-type

structure, with many small modifications and improvements being made everywhere, with little central control.

17. Most UNIX-based networks were implemented on DEC hardware.

18. The appeal of open systems and UNIX is explained by complementary asset externalities typical in networks. But existing network theories do not explain how a different design approach can yield a dramatic advantage in terms of overall efficiency. An understanding of the efficiency gains from modularity is needed to complete the theory.

19. For purposes of comparison, we defined net working capital as current assets, excluding cash, minus current liabilities, excluding short-term debt. Levels of cash and short-term debt reflect the firms' strategic and financial choices, and are not indicative of the operating efficiency. Detailed financial comparisons are available on request from the authors. See also Jack Soll and Carliss Baldwin, *Sun Microsystems, Inc.—1987 (A), (B), and (C)* (Boston: Harvard Business School Publishing, 1990).

20. Sun's net income over sales was higher than Apollo's because of Apollo's higher depreciation charges.

21. This period approximates the product life of the Domain 3000 and Sun-3 families. It includes the initial ramp-ups of plant and equipment in anticipation of the introductions of the Domain 4000 and Sun-4. After mid-1987, Apollo's spending was constrained by cash conservation measures.

22. Free cash flow equals net income plus depreciation expenses plus the change in deferred taxes. It approximates the cash flow available at the end of each quarter that can be reinvested in the business or, at the discretion of management, deployed elsewhere.

23. Apollo earned 36 percent on assets employed in the fourth quarter of 1987. However, the income and asset figures in that quarter were influenced by year-end asset sales and related increases in depreciation expense. Thus the high rate of return shown was anomalous; in reality, Apollo's profitability was deteriorating, as the very low returns in the second and third quarter show. (In terms of net income, Apollo lost money in the second and third quarters of 1988.)

24. UNIX was the closest thing to a universal, nonproprietary operating system that existed at this time.

25. In 1984, when Sun was faced with rapid growth and the need for additional capital, it negotiated a deal with Kodak (an important OEM buyer of Sun workstations) for $20 million in equity. After holding the equity for thirty months, Kodak cashed out at $97 million, an annualized return of 88 percent.

26. There were a number of other provisos in the agreement. In a single sale notice, Sun could not demand that AT&T purchase more than 25 percent of the six million shares reserved, and Sun could not send more than one notice in any ninety-day period. Finally, Sun had to place half the direct placement

shares before July 5, 1989 (two and a half years after the start of the agreement), or lose its right to require purchase of the shares. The rest of the shares had to be sold by January 5, 1993, the date the agreement expired. AT&T also had the right to purchase 5 percent of Sun's shares in the open market, and to participate in up to 17.65 percent of any other offering of Sun's stock. However, AT&T's voting power was strictly limited: it received a seat on Sun's board, but could not vote against management except in special circumstances. Furthermore, AT&T could not acquire more than 20 percent of Sun's voting shares without Sun's consent unless Sun became the object of a third-party takeover bid.

27. This indicates that competition was taking its toll. In 1986, $50 million of incremental spending at Sun had supported about $50 million of incremental sales per quarter ($200 million annualized). Now the same $50 million of incremental sales per quarter needed outlays of $130 million. This erosion of performance was caused by a reduction in margins and by a decrease in Sun's efficiency with respect to net working capital and property, plant, and equipment.

## REFERENCES

Alexander, Christopher. *Notes on the Synthesis of Form.* Cambridge, Mass.: Harvard University Press, 1964.

Baldwin, Carliss, and Kim B. Clark. "Modularity and Real Options." Harvard Business School Working Paper #93-026. 1993.

Bhide, Amar. *Vinod Khosla and Sun Microsystems (A).* Boston: Harvard Business School Publishing Division, 1989.

Besen, Stanley M., and Garth Saloner. "The Economics of Telecommunications Standards." In R. W. Crandall and K. Flamm, eds., *Changing the Rules: Technological Change, International Competition, and Regulation in Communications.* Washington, D.C.: Brookings Institution, 1989.

Black, Fischer, and Myron Scholes. "The Pricing of Options and Corporate Liabilities." *Journal of Political Economy* 81 (1973):637–654.

Bresnahan, Timothy F., and Shane Greenstein. *Technological Competition, and the Structure of the Computer Industry.* CEPR Publication no. 315. Stanford, Calif.: Center for Economic Policy Research, Stanford University, 1992.

Brooks, Frederick W. *The Mythical Man Month.* Reading, Mass.: Addison-Wesley, 1975.

Christensen, Clayton M. "The Rigid Disk Drive Industry: A History of Commercial and Economic Turbulence." *Business History Review* 67, 4 (1993): 531–538.

Clark, Kim B. "The Interaction of Design Hierarchies and Market Concepts in Technological Evolution." *Research Policy* 14, 5 (1985): 235–251.

Clark, Kim B. "Knowledge, Problem Solving, and Innovation in the Evolutionary Firm." Harvard Business School Working Paper. 1988.

Constantine, L. L., G. J. Myers, and W. P. Stevens. "Structured Design." *IBM Systems Journal* 13, 2 (1974): 115–139.

Dixit, Avinash K., and Robert S. Pindyck. *Investment Under Uncertainty.* Princeton: Princeton University Press, 1994.

Dorfman, Nancy S. *Innovation and Market Structure: Lessons from the Computer and Semiconductor Industries.* Cambridge, Mass.: Ballinger, 1986.

Eppinger, Steven D. "Model-Based Approaches to Managing Concurrent Engineering." *Journal of Engineering Design* 2, 4 (1991): 283–290.

Eppinger, Steven D., and Kent R. McCord. "Managing the Iteration Problem in Concurrent Engineering." MIT Working Paper 3594-93-MSA. August, 1993.

Eppinger, Steven D., Daniel E. Whitney, Robert P. Smith, and David Gebala. "A Model-Based Method for Organizing Tasks in Product Development." *Research in Engineering Design* 6, 1 (1994): 1–13.

Farrell, Joseph, Hunter K. Monroe, and Garth Saloner. "Order Statistics, Interface Standards and Open Systems." Berkeley: University of California, 1993. Mimeo.

Farrell, Joseph, and Garth Saloner. "Economic Issues in Standardization." In James Miller, ed., *Telecommunications and Equity: Policy Research Issues.* New York: North Holland, 1986.

Farrell, Joseph, and Carl Shapiro. "Optimal Contracts with Lock-in." *American Economic Review* 79, 1 (1989): 51–68.

Ferguson, Charles H., and Charles R. Morris. *Computer Wars: How the West Can Win in a Post-IBM World.* New York: Times Books, 1993.

Freeze, Karen, and Kim B. Clark. *Sun Microsystems, Inc. (B).* Boston: Harvard Business School Publishing Division, 1986.

Garud, Raghu, and Arun Kumaraswamy. "Changing Competitive Dynamics in Network Industries: An Exploration of Sun Microsystems' Open Systems Strategy." *Strategic Management Journal* 14, 5 (1993): 351–369.

Gill, Geoffrey, and Steven C. Wheelwright. *Sony Corporation: Workstation Division.* Boston: Harvard Business School Publishing Division, 1989.

Greenstein, Shane. "Markets, Standards and the Information Infrastructure." *IEEE Micro* 13 (December 1993): 36–51.

Harrison, J. M. *Brownian Motion and Stochastic Flow Systems.* New York: John Wiley and Sons, 1985.

Henderson, Rebecca M., and Kim B. Clark. "Generational Innovation: The Reconfiguration of Existing Systems and the Failure of Established Firms." *Administrative Sciences Quarterly* 35 (1990): 9–30.

Iansiti, Marco. "Technology Integration: Managing Technological Evolution in a Complex Environment." Harvard Business School Working Paper 93-057. 1993.

Iansiti, Marco, and Kim B. Clark. "Integration and Dynamic Capability: Evidence from Product Development in Automobiles and Mainframe Computers." Harvard Business School Working Paper 93-047. 1993.

Katz, Michael L., and Carl Shapiro. "Network Externalities, Competition and Compatibility." *American Economic Review* 75, 3 (1985): 424–440.

Katz, Michael L., and Carl Shapiro. "Product Introduction with Network Externalities." *Journal of Industrial Economics* 40, 1 (1992): 55–83.

Kogut, Bruce, and Nalin Kulatilaka. "Options Thinking and Platform Investments: Investing in Opportunity." Wharton School, University of Pennsylvania, 1992. Mimeo.

Langlois, Richard N., and Paul L. Robertson. "Networks and Innovation in a Modular System: Lessons from the Microcomputer and Stereo Component Industries." *Research Policy* 21 (1992): 297–313.

Langowitz, Nan, and Steven C. Wheelwright. *Sun Microsystems, Inc. (A)*. Boston: Harvard Business School Publishing Division, 1986.

Lindgren, B. W. *Statistical Theory*. New York: Macmillan, 1968.

Marples, David L. "The Decisions of Engineering Design." *IEEE Transactions on Engineering Management* 2 (1961): 55–71.

Mason, Scott P., and Robert Merton. "The Role of Contingent Claims Analysis in Corporate Finance." In E. Altman and M. Subrahmanyam, eds., *Recent Advances in Corporate Finance*. Homewood, Ill.: Richard D. Irwin, 1985.

Merton, Robert C. "Theory of Rational Option Pricing." *Bell Journal of Economics and Management Science* 4 (1973): 141–183.

Merton, Robert C. *Continuous Time Finance*. Cambridge, Mass.: Basil Blackwell, 1990.

Milgrom, Paul, and John Roberts. "The Economics of Manufacturing: Technology, Strategy and Organization." *American Economic Review*. 80, 3 (1990): 511–528.

Morris, Charles R., and Charles H. Ferguson, "How Architecture Wins Technology Wars." *Harvard Business Review* 71 (March–April 1993): 86–96.

Myers, Glenford J. *Reliable Software Through Composite Design*. New York: Van Nostrand Reinhold, 1975.

Nelson, Richard R., and Sidney G. Winter. *An Evolutionary Theory of Economic Change*. Cambridge, Mass.: Harvard University Press, 1982.

Nevins, James L., and Daniel E. Whitney. *Concurrent Design of Products and Processes.* New York: McGraw-Hill, 1989.

Parnas, D. L. "A Technique for Software Module Specification with Examples." *Communications of the ACM* 15 (May 1972): 330–336.

Parnas, D. L. "On the Criteria to Be Used in Decomposing Systems into Modules." *Communications of the ACM* 15 (December 1972): 1053–1058.

Parnas, D. L., P. C. Clements, and D. M. Weiss. "The Modular Structure of Complex Systems." *IEEE Transactions on Software Engineering* SE-11 (March 1985): 259–266.

Pugh, Emerson W., Lyle R. Johnson, and John H. Palmer. *IBM's 360 and Early 370 Systems.* Cambridge, Mass.: MIT Press, 1991.

Reinganum, Jennifer F. "The Timing of Innovation: Research, Development and Diffusion." In Richard Schmalensee and Robert D. Willig, eds., *Handbook of Industrial Organization,* volume 1. New York: Elsevier Science Publishers, 1989.

Sahlman, William A., and Howard H. Stevenson. "Capital Market Myopia." *Journal of Business Venturing* 1 (1985): 7–30.

Sanchez, Ronald A. "Strategic Flexibility, Real Options and Product-based Strategy." Ph.D. dissertation, Massachusetts Institute of Technology, 1991.

Schach, Stephen R. *Software Engineering,* 2nd ed. Burr Ridge, Ill.: Richard D. Irwin 1993.

Simon, Herbert A. *The Sciences of the Artificial.* Cambridge, Mass.: MIT Press 1969.

Shaked, Avner, and John Sutton. "Natural Oligopolies." *Econometrica* 51 (1983): 1469–1484.

Soll, Jack, and Carliss Baldwin. *Sun Microsystems, Inc.—1987 A, B, and C.* Boston: Harvard Business School Publishing Division, 1990.

Stigler, George. "The Division of Labor Is Limited by the Extent of the Market." *Journal of Political Economy* 59 (June 1951): 3.

Stulz, Rene M. "Options on the Minimum or the Maximum of Two Risky Assets." *Journal of Financial Economics* 10 (1982): 161–185.

Sutton, John. *Sunk Cost and Market Structure: Price Competition, Advertising and the Evolution of Concentration.* Cambridge, Mass.: MIT Press, 1991.

Ulrich, Karl T. "The Role of Product Architecture in the Manufacturing Firm." Working Paper no. 3483-92-MSA. Sloan School of Management, MIT, 1992.

Ulrich, Karl T., and Steven D. Eppinger. *Methodologies for Product Design and Development.* New York: McGraw-Hill, 1994.

Ulrich, Karl T., and Karen Tung. "Fundamentals of Product Modularity." Working Paper no. 3335-91. Sloan School of Management, MIT, 1991.

Von Hippel, Eric. "Task Partitioning: An Innovation Process Variable." *Research Policy* 19 (1990): 407–418.

CHAPTER 4

# WINNERS AND LOSERS

*Industry Structure in the Converging World of*
*Telecommunications, Computing, and Entertainment*

David J. Collis
P. William Bane
Stephen P. Bradley

## INTRODUCTION

The emerging multimedia industry will include some of the largest business opportunities of the next two decades. Formed from the convergence
of the telecommunication, computer, and television industries, and facilitated by the digital revolution, it holds out the promise of creating and
capitalizing on an interactive "information superhighway." Yet, beyond
the hyperbole, there is no clear picture of how this futuristic industry will
evolve.[1] In the presence of such uncertainty, players who articulate a consistent strategy to exploit the opportunities and address the risks will
shape the evolution of industry structure and participate profitably in
its bounty.[2]

Much has been written about the strategic implications of the multimedia industry's evolution.[3] This paper builds on existing literature
incorporating insights arising from "industry analysis,"[4] the "resource
based view of the firm,"[5] and economic analyses. Perhaps more important, it reflects the experience of authors working for, and researching,
the industry.[6]

This paper has four main sections. The first makes the central argument that the structure of the consumer multimedia industry, the focus of this paper, is changing from three discrete vertical businesses (telephone, television, and computer; see table 4-1) to five horizontal industry segments. Moreover, as digitization enables ever-increasing kinds of content to be distributed through the same system, other industries are likely to be transformed. The second section postulates how the structure of each of these five new industry segments might appear, and the likely participants in each. It also explains how, as the industry evolves, segments will to some extent realign vertically but will not be technologically hardwired together, as in the past. Rather, they will be joined by softer "glue" that will enable each vertical business to respond to the requirements of different customer groups. The third section identifies future key success factors in each industry segment and, by matching them to the current participants' capabilities, suggests which types of firms will be winners and losers. The fourth section discusses the implications of these fundamental changes and offers some conclusions about what can be expected for the multimedia industry in the near future.

To enable readers to quickly identify those aspects of the analysis that most directly affect them, we state our conclusions as hypotheses about the evolution of industry structure and the relative success of individual firms. While these hypotheses are speculative, we hope that the analytic approach and conceptual framework employed will sharpen the ongoing debate.

## INDUSTRY STRUCTURE

Today, the multimedia industry is being formed by the convergence of three industries that originated roughly fifty years apart: telephone in the 1890s, television in the late 1930s, and personal computing in the 1980s. Originally, their product content and technologies were as distinct as those of, for example, the airline and pipeline industries. Convergence was precipitated by the rapid increase in computer processing speed and a concomitant dramatic decline in the cost of processing and memory capacity, together with parallel advances in transmission technology— notably, vast improvements in bandwidth capacity through the use of fiber optics and compression capabilities.[7]

Digitization techniques have rendered analog signals, transmitted by telephone and television, indistinguishable from digital signals generated by personal computers, thus enabling the same infrastructure to accommodate manipulation and transmission—if not yet the input and display

—of voice, video, and data. All three types of information can now be distributed on the same network, and even input and display are converging as videoconferencing combines voice and video in one transmission, and voice and handwriting recognition capabilities combine—albeit somewhat primitively—voice and data.[8]

The importance of the digital revolution is that it alters, in fundamental ways, the availability of information in time and place, and the cost of that information. The potential now exists to make information available at any time the consumer desires (rather than when it is convenient for the producer to distribute it); consider, for example, the difference between a continually updated on-line news service and traditional home delivery of a daily newspaper. Through the use of improved wireline and, particularly, wireless networks (such as the global telephone capability promised by the Iridium satellite network), information can be available in any and every place the consumer desires.[9] Digitization also promises to reduce the cost of information transmission as it exploits steep learning curves in the design and production of standardized electronic components, and enormous economies of scale in network systems.

Even if its effects were limited to voice, video, and data, digitization would represent a powerful revolution. But it also has the potential to transform an array of other businesses and industries. In effect, the forces of digitization act like the gravity of a "wormhole" in *Star Trek,* pulling recognizable industries through it and transforming them into something unrecognizable on the other side (figure 4-1). In fact, as entertainment and shopping are already being pulled through the digitization wormhole, newspapers, education, gambling, and advertising, among other businesses, are beginning to be pulled into its gravitational field.

---

**Hypothesis (1):** Convergence implies the creation of a common distribution network that will replace previously discrete telephone, television, and personal computing networks, and will transform the distribution of many other products and services (see figure 4-1).

---

## Product Evolution

To determine which markets and products are most likely to enter the brave new world of multimedia, we start by examining markets already

TABLE 4-1

DISCRETE INDUSTRIES AND FUNCTIONS

|  | Phone (Voice) | TV (Video) | PC (Data) |
|---|---|---|---|
| **Content** | Talk<br>Music<br>  records<br>  CDs<br>  tapes | Film<br>  box office<br>  cable<br>  video rental<br>  TV | Data<br>  Yellow Pages<br>  Databases<br>  Bulletin boards |
| **Packaging** | Videoconference<br>1-900<br>Radio station | Syndicator<br>Network TV, indie<br>Cable channel<br>PPV | Time-share<br>Outsourcing (EDS)<br>App Software<br>  workgroup (notes)<br>Handwriting<br>  recognition<br>Delphi<br>Investment<br>Prodigy<br>America Online<br>Lexis/Nexis<br>Dialog<br>CompuServe<br>Minitel |
| **Manipulation** | Switch Aim<br>AIN<br>  microwave<br>ISDN<br>Frame relay | Cable decoder box<br>Navigator<br>  cable GUI | CPU<br>  semiconductor<br>Mainframe<br>  parallel<br>  RISC<br>  workstation<br>  PC<br>NOS<br>  WAN/LAN<br>Internet<br>OS<br>Adobe<br>Xerox DocuSP<br>General Magic |

affected by the convergence of the telephone, television, and personal computing industries.

Figure 4-2 breaks out average household expenditures for product categories currently undergoing transformation. It indicates, first, that content and transmission are currently more important to households than hardware and software, and, more important, that the share of

TABLE 4-1 continued

## DISCRETE INDUSTRIES AND FUNCTIONS

| | | Phone (Voice) | TV (Video) | PC (Data) |
|---|---|---|---|---|
| **Transmission** | **Long** | IXCs<br>Fibre<br>Satellite (Iridium)<br>Satellite | DB Satellite<br>Satellite | |
| | **Local** | RBOC<br>CAPs<br>Wireless<br>  cellular<br>  PCS<br>  paging<br>  mobile radio dispatch<br>  (SMR) | CATV<br>Local station | Radio-based data<br>  (Ram, Audio) |
| **Storage** | | Audiotape<br>CD<br>Record | Videotape<br>Cassette | Fileserver<br>CD ROM<br>Disk<br>  optical<br>  hard<br>  soft |
| **Terminals** | | Phoneset<br>  office<br>  mobile<br>PDA<br>Paging<br>PBX<br>Picture phone | Radio<br>Cassette player<br>CD player<br>TV set<br>  tube<br>  flat panel<br>HDTV<br>Video-game player | Keyboard<br>Monitor<br>Printer<br>Photo<br>  camera<br>  print<br>CCDs<br>Photo CD<br>Fax<br>Scanner<br>Answering machine |

household income available to new multimedia markets may be largely limited to the share already expended on existing multimedia activities, because at 7 percent of household income ($1,850 per annum), there is not much additional discretionary income available. This latter observation is supported by research on discretionary time, which shows that the average household watches seven hours of television per day[10] and spends more than one hour on the telephone. It is clear that early multibillion-dollar multimedia investments will have to be supported by substitution from existing users, not by new markets. Indeed, conversion to

FIGURE 4-1

## EMERGING INDUSTRY STRUCTURE

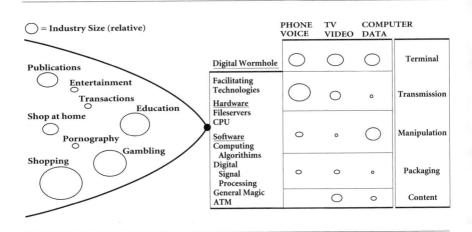

FIGURE 4-2

## MULTIMEDIA HOUSEHOLD EXPENDITURE

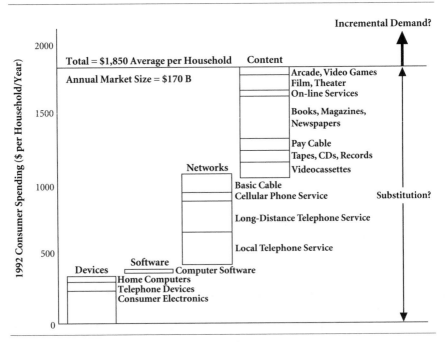

SOURCES: EIA; Morgan Stanley; Bear Stearns; Mercer Analysis.

multimedia is in progress; cable and telephone services are already, in effect, multimedia products.

Looking ahead, we can forecast the rate of multimedia substitution for other products, such as on-demand video programming substituting for videocassette rentals, by considering four key variables (see figure 4-3).

1. "Substitution economics" refers to the economic benefit of multi-media over current distribution—for example, the difference between the on-demand programming charge and the per-night movie rental fee.

2. Changes in user behavior depend on the relative ease of using alternative distribution mechanisms (e.g., using a handheld remote or the telephone to order a movie, versus a trip to the movie rental store).

3. Technological criteria that will affect speed of substitution focus on the existence of a stable standard that will minimize consumer investment risk.

FIGURE 4-3

## FACTORS DETERMINING INDUSTRY SUBSTITUTION

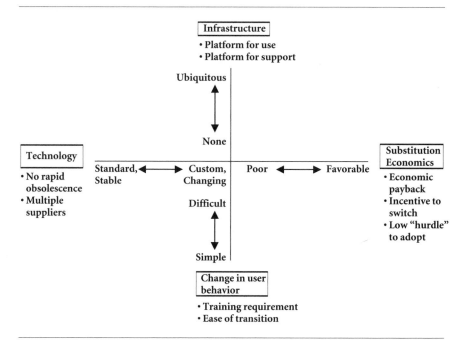

SOURCE: Mercer Management Consulting.

4. Substitution will depend on having the requisite infrastructure in place.

Figure 4-4 arrays five applications along these four dimensions, to assess the feasibility of their conversion to multimedia. This array shows that the first large markets for new multimedia household products will be, to no one's surprise, E-mail, on-demand movies, and interactive shopping. The early emergence of these markets will facilitate later substitution for other products by improving the technological infrastructure and leading changes in consumer behavior.

New multimedia product categories, such as wireless E-mail and long-distance learning, will certainly appear, but will follow current products is gaining significant market penetration (see figure 4-5).

---

**Hypothesis (2):** On-demand movies, interactive shopping, and E-mail are the applications most likely to take immediate advantage of the convergence of telephone, television, and personal computing.

---

## Business Structure

Whatever the rate of substitution or the specific products developed, the essence of the industry transformation is that content-specific distribution, provided by unique technologies, hardware, and methods, is being transformed into content-independent distribution provided by a common infrastructure. Thus, the multimedia industry is emerging not as a set of three vertical businesses but as a collection of five horizontal activities that together deliver content to consumers (see figure 4-1). These activities correspond to the industry segments identified in table 4-2:

- Content, the products and services transmitted by the medium

- Packaging, the bundling of, or selecting from among, massive arrays of available content, and the addition of integrative and presentational functionality to create a finished product for consumers

- Transmission network, the physical infrastructure that supports the transport of information

- Manipulation infrastructure, which provides intelligence to the distribution system—historically this included the processing/storage

FIGURE 4-4

SUBSTITUTION POSSIBILITIES

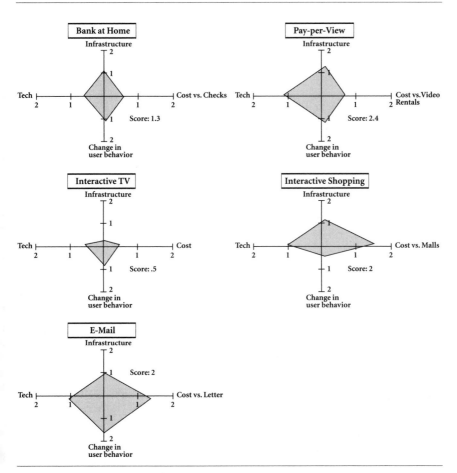

SOURCE: Mercer Management Consulting.

hardware and various types of software in computer and telecommunications systems, but in the multimedia industry it will also include a new type of manipulation software that will perform the required interactive multimedia network tasks

- Terminals, which can be any of a variety of local devices employed to capture and display information.

FIGURE 4-5

PRODUCT SUBSTITUTION POSSIBILITIES

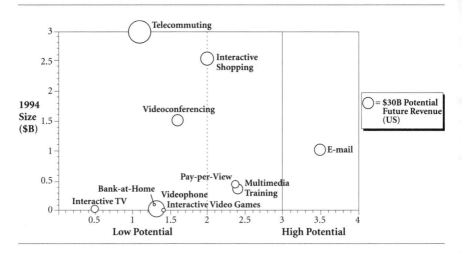

## STRUCTURE WITHIN INDUSTRIES

Although we focus on each horizontal industry segment in turn, we do expect some vertical linkages to reappear. However, these linkages will depend much less on discrete technologies than on the marketing and distribution packages that successful players (or alliances of players) install to serve distinct sets of customers.

### Content

The content segment will probably remain as fragmented and specialized as it is today, but potentially will have more economic leverage. The unique requirements of each type of content produce minimal scope economies. Reporting television news requires fundamentally different logistics than does, for example, retailing jewelry or gathering stock market quotations. Thus, even though the three forms of content (voice, video, and data) may be provided along the same pipeline to the home or office, actual content production will remain separate. Since the nature of creative or data-gathering tasks will be little changed by multimedia, the content industry will remain specialized and relatively fragmented according to content type.

Content producers can today, and will even more in the future, sell to multiple markets. Disney merchandises *Aladdin* as a movie, video game, soft toy, and home video on its cable channel, for example. In the future, such broad distribution will be facilitated by the convergence of previously discrete distribution channels, and content providers will continue to control markets in which their products are sold. Indeed, because access to quality content will have an unusual value to other industry participants during the transition period, providers will be positioned to earn abnormally high returns.

**Hypothesis (3):** Content will remain a collection of largely independent businesses, each with its own key success factors, but will capture more of the total industry value.

TABLE 4-2

INDUSTRY SEGMENTS

| Business Structure | Typical Players |
| --- | --- |
| Content | Disney<br>Washington Post<br>Dun & Bradstreet |
| Packaging | L.L. Bean<br>Time Warner<br>Disney<br>Bloomberg<br>America Online |
| Transmission | Cablevision<br>NYNEX<br>MCI<br>McCaw<br>AT&T |
| Manipulation | IBM<br>Digital<br>Apple<br>Microsoft<br>AT&T<br>Novell<br>Oracle |
| Terminals | Apple<br>Sony<br>Panasonic<br>Sega<br>Sharp |

## Packaging

There will be two types of packagers in the retail multimedia industry. The first will be the technically oriented systems integrators (the consumer analog of EDS, and Information technology (IT) consulting firms) that install turnkey systems for businesses or households. A current simple consumer example of systems integrators are "power" retailers that sell entire multimedia packages assembled from various suppliers' components—monitors, printers, computers, software—and may even include training and service in the bundle. Today systems integrators are less important in the consumer market than in the business arena, but they will be able to create a viable niche in the short and medium terms as they exploit customer uncertainty and the lack of standards. Longer term, they will gradually disappear as standards are set or as upstream suppliers offer complete systems.

The other type of packager will deliver content to businesses or households, in the way that television networks, cable channels, and America Online do today. These packagers (we will refer to them as "distribution packagers") will be more durable. They will exploit marketing scope economies by bundling various types of content—from sports, movies, and comic books, to shopping, information, and advertising—into a single package. These distribution packagers that will be a force for "soft" reverticalization, since they will contract for, or otherwise provide access to, transmission, processing, and manipulation in order to deliver an entire content package to specific sets of users. Because the intermediaries that provide these latter services will be invisible to consumers, packagers could end up "owning the customer," at least for a while.

Initially there will be a profusion of players in the distribution packager business, including existing competitors and new entrants. The novelty of the role will create opportunities for competitors with new skills, such as Michael Ovitz and CAA, the Hollywood talent agency, branching out into advertising and television programming.[11] "Edutainment" software companies, such as Davidson, Electronic Arts, and Learning Associates, will also bring the creative capabilities needed to develop new packaging forms that fully exploit the potential of multimedia. Initially, these entrants will merely adapt existing content to new distribution channels. Over time, they will become more sophisticated and separate from pure content providers. The industry will then consolidate to a greater or lesser extent as leading players exploit scope economies and bundle content from various sources.

The future structure of this industry segment could range from monopolistic to fragmented. It will be monopolistic if one player gains control of the gateway function (the Graphical User Interface, GUI, that allows access to the information superhighway) and sets monopolistic standards. This could occur if, for example, America Online or Microsoft —through its Windows 95 interface—became the universal entry ramp onto the information superhighway. As a bottleneck provider, such a monopolist could extract a toll from users and even squeeze content providers.[12]

At the other end of the spectrum, we might see a widely differentiated set of distribution packagers, each specializing in a particular vertical market accessed through a common open network such as Internet, or 800 and 900 telephone numbers. In this scenario, any distribution packager could freely access the network to make its services directly available to consumers, bypassing the need for superpackager intermediaries.

Where on this spectrum will the packaging segment actually shake out? That will depend on three factors. The first is the extent of economies of scope at the packager level, with respect to bundling content, and at the customer level, where the question is what value consumers place on one-stop shopping, receiving one invoice for all multimedia activities, and one gateway onto the information highway. If substantial scope economies exist across all the industries that will be sucked through the wormhole, then a concentrated packager industry will emerge, with a few firms competing to provide access to a huge range of products and services. But if significant demand differences emerge between, for example, shopping for shoes and booking a vacation, we will likely see a concentration within segments (as in today's cable network industry, with only three music networks, three sports networks, etc.) but industry fragmentation as a whole (there are more than one hundred cable networks). In the latter case, there may still be a single software GUI from which players such as Microsoft will make substantial royalties, but there will also be a profusion of packagers licensing that GUI.

The second factor shaping the packaging segment structure will be whether a superpackager can preemptively establish a dominant quality reputation and a large installed customer base. Such a position would give this packager an advantage over future entrants because most content providers would want to link with the packager having the most extensive distribution. To gain such an advantage, a packager would have to become the exclusive distributor of much of today's highly desirable content, which is unlikely. A number of well-funded competitors are already approaching superpackager status—Prodigy, America Online, CompuServe, the ATT-owned Ziff start-up Interchange, and Microsoft, for example. In addition, content providers will want to prevent a single superpackager from becoming too powerful by limiting the exclusivity of distribution deals. Finally, today's transmission infrastructure players still have considerable control over access to multimedia. As they roll out their new services, they can influence the choice of packager.

The third consideration shaping the future structure of packaging is technology. In the emerging multimedia industry, consumer needs will be continuously redefined by new product innovations. Virtually any segment of the industry chain, therefore, has the potential to develop a "bottleneck technology"—unique displays, terminals, algorithms, codes, or speed—that it can leverage to become a superpackager until the next hot technology appears. Thus, technical instability is likely to prevent any particular superpackager from dominating the industry.

An example is wireless terminal technology. Currently, no inexpensive, proven wireless data standard exists. If a player could successfully market a proprietary terminal with the desired feature/cost trade-offs for a particular market segment (examples might have been Bell South's EO and the Apple Newton), it could become, at least temporarily, a superpackager. On the other hand, if no specialized wireless data terminal market existed, or an open standard was established, industry pressure to consolidate would not exist.

Overall, it seems reasonable to expect the same industry structure to emerge in packaging as exists in other channels of distribution: three or four main broad superpackagers and a host of specialized vertical market packagers. Whether these packagers endure long term will depend on developments elsewhere in the industry chain, since the manipulation segment may one day produce software that provides the same function as packagers.

---

**Hypothesis (4):** Packaging will evolve much like other distribution businesses, with a few broad line suppliers (superpackagers) surrounded by a host of fragmented and specialized providers.

---

## Transmission

The transmission infrastructure will remain a common shared function —a public network. This is not to say that there will be only one monopolistic, and therefore regulated, transmission network, but rather that each network, once digitized, will be physically able to carry any content. Such a network will have inherent scope economies and unlimited, or at least very low-cost, incremental capacity.[13]

The two most important questions concerning the future structure of the transmission segment are

- How many local networks, of what type, will emerge?

- Will local and long-distance services remain separate?

*How many local networks, of what type, will emerge?*

At the local level, it is possible for the multimedia industry to operate with only one broadband provider (one local loop). This will probably be common in Western Europe and could also evolve in the United States under the so-called Rochester Plan, in which a single broadband loop is made available (by a regulated entity) to any and all firms wishing to provide telephony and other multimedia services, including the regulated entity's own unregulated subsidiary.[14] However, it is unlikely that single-loop solutions will be widely adopted in the United States given the current activity and the positions taken by major players.[15]

Assuming this situation, and based on our understanding of the current economics of system investment, operating costs, and maintenance costs, we assess the likelihood that each type of player—wireless, cable, and wireline telephone—will upgrade current facilities to broadband networks.

**Wireless.** Wireless already has a more or less saturated geographic coverage for narrow-band (limited digital transmission rates), dial-tone voice, and data services. ATT McCaw offers close to national coverage;[16] NYNEX, Bell Atlantic, US West, and Air Touch have aligned their cellular operations; and other such partnerships are possible. The next-generation, complementary personal communication systems (PCS) licenses, have been auctioned to encourage competition and provide national service.[17] Indeed, Sprint and several cable TV companies have bid for, and won, very close to a national footprint.

As competition increases and usage costs decline, wireless will penetrate the mass consumer market. In 1993, the wireless penetration rate per person was about 6 percent versus wireline's roughly 56 percent. Our analysis projects that over the next five to eight years, wireless prices will drop from the current 60¢–70¢/minute to 10¢–20¢/minute,[18] and penetration will rise to 30 to 40 percent. Hence, wireless will become a very competitive domestic telephone service supplier.

Even with increased penetration, however, it is unlikely that wireless companies will upgrade to broadband, since wireless technology lacks the capacity to economically convey more than trivial amounts of high-volume data (such as moving pictures and large files). There is no significant new product research activity on the multimedia wireless front, a testament to the absence of an infrastructure and the uncertainty of user interfaces and applications. Therefore, in the foreseeable future, we expect the structure and profits of the wireless industry to be driven by the economics of stand-alone, dial-tone-only service.

*Cable.* Broadband technology is currently available to cable television systems that enables them to provide interactive telephone service; it is a matter of upgrading from the current tree-and-branch configuration of coaxial networks to switched-star fiber/coaxial configuration networks. The issue is whether the economics are favorable.[19] On the demand side, the evidence from the United Kingdom suggests that cable television providers of telephony can capture over 20 percent of the market at prices 20 percent below those of incumbent monopolist providers.[20] On the investment cost side, estimates vary from $500 to $1,500 per subscriber for cable companies to build interactive multichannel systems switched to offer telephony.[21] Considering maintenance cost savings of fiber, new revenues from telephony, and incremental income from offering the promised eight hundred channels and interactive entertainment, it is likely that cable companies will upgrade to offer telephony, unless higher-end cost estimates prove accurate.

*Wireline.* Local telephone exchange companies (LECs) face similar economic decisions regarding upgrading to offer broadband capabilities—from twisted pair loop to fiber/coaxial hybrid loop facilities. The economics of these decisions vary according to assumptions made about how near to a residence the fiber cable must be laid.[22] Unfortunately, LECs may be forced to make the investment for defensive purposes, in order to avoid being cherry-picked by cable competitors, even if stand-alone upgrade economics are unattractive. High-volume telephone users (over $50 per month) are the most profitable customers; in effect, they subsidize money-losing, low-volume, high-cost-to-serve customers covered by the mandate to provide universal service.[23] This will become a problem when LEC monopolies on local loops are challenged, since the first targets of new entrants will be high-profit, high-volume users. This has already happened in some downtown business districts where competitive access providers (CAPs) have compelled LECs to invest in fiber loops to prevent erosion of their most profitable high-volume business customers.[24] Thus, it appears that LECs will have to upgrade their residential networks, or count on the general adoption of some form of the Rochester model of regulation to protect their revenue base and market share.

We therefore expect most cable and wireline players to upgrade, and competitive and complementary networks to proliferate. Most neighborhoods will then have at least four local service providers: two wireless, one wireline broadband local loop, and one cable broadband local loop. In densely populated areas, there could be as many as nine: two cellular, three or more new PCS entrants (ignoring two possible satellite wirelesses), the LEC, a cable company, an out-of-region LEC or cable company, and a CAP. This degree of competition, combined with the considerable capacity of any one of these networks, suggests that there will be much excess capacity in the local loop for a long time—and that many players who rush to participate in this business will be substantial losers.

**Hypothesis (5):** Absent regulation, there will be at least two wireline and two wireless networks in any urban community. For a considerable period of time, there will be substantial excess capacity in the local network.

*Will local and long-distance services remain separate?*

There is essentially no difference between local (intra-LATA) and long-distance (inter-LATA) transmission; in fact, under some circumstances it may be more economical to call across a state by sending a digital signal across the nation. Recognizing this, regulators are now considering allowing LECs and interexchange carriers (IXCs) to compete[25]—which will erase current artificial geographic restrictions on competition.

But the end of the artificial divide between the inter- and intra-LATA markets will not necessarily mean the end of either type of competitor; both can in principle survive (see the section on key success factors). Nor will it necessarily mean the end of the local/long-distance dichotomy. Local service providers may well use other providers for long-distance transmission between switches that aggregate output from wireline and wireless local loops. With the exception of 100 percent satellite-based systems (somewhat speculative due to their great expense), almost all of that long-distance traffic is likely to be routed over trunk lines because of their scale economies. However, LECs will almost certainly not create their own long-distance networks outside of their territory, but will enter into alliances with each other or with existing IXCs.[26] This will bring the aforementioned four to nine local loop competitors into direct competition with the considerable transmission capacities of IXCs in long-distance markets.

Unfortunately for current long-distance service providers, this new competition most likely will substantially reduce profitability. Excess capacity may not lead to poor industry returns with only the three current major participants, but it almost inevitably does so when the number of competitors increases.[27]

---

**Hypothesis (6):** Artificial inter/intra-LATA regulatory segmentation will be replaced by a segmentation based on underlying long-distance versus local cost economics and technologies. Excess capacity in long-distance service will lead to poor industry attractiveness for simple voice traffic.

---

## Manipulation

Historically, computer hardware and software have been tightly integrated in closed systems. As the day of open systems approaches, a real distinction has arisen between processing and storage hardware (i.e., equipment that physically transforms data) and the intelligence of the software that governs the manipulation of that data (i.e., controls how user requests are handled and digital data are transformed). In the multimedia industry, two kinds of software will be needed. The first, which we might call "information highway software," is being developed to enable the information superhighway to function as more than a simple data transmitter. This software is a hybrid, combining elements of both manipulation and transmission. It is also a battlefield on which two current vertical industries are vying for position. The second, which we might call "traditional manipulation software," includes operating systems software and stand-alone application software.

*Information Highway Software.* The telecommunications and computer industries are engaged in a fundamental conflict over the evolution of the structure of this industry subsegment. The issue is whether, and to what degree, software intelligence for transmission/manipulation (including data limitation, control, and amplification) should reside on the network or off-line, on local terminals. We believe this is the single most important and difficult issue surrounding the future structure of the manipulation and transmission segments.

The telecommunications industry is trying to shift the balance toward intelligent networks with standards and architectural approaches, such as Integrated Service Digital Network (ISDN), Data Connection Network (SS7), and Advanced Intelligent Network (AIN). In this model, networks operate as an "agency," with computers being smart servers acting on behalf of network users. The simplest example is the "follow-me" functionality that would enable the network to locate any person, anywhere, by capturing and managing that person's signal as he or she travels from place to place. In general, a more, rather than a less, intelligent network would proactively manage activities, such as verification, security, access limitation, and credit checks, that allow messages to flow and transactions to be executed. Terminals would be freed of these connectivity tasks and/or would exploit/amplify these services.

Naturally, the traditional computer industry ascribes a higher value to intelligent terminals, with standards and architectural approaches, such as asynchronous transfer mode (ATM), frame relay, and the Internet. In this model—in the Internet, for example—the transmission infrastructure is not much more than a big, dumb pipeline blindly switching messages from one location to another, manipulating them only minimally and mindlessly. All intelligence resides in users' computer terminals or other independent servers that are off, and independent of, the network. This network-independent intelligence would initiate and manage all agency tasks.

Each approach might deliver similar functionalities to the customer —for example, one would deliver a smart picture phone linked to telephone company networks, while the other would deliver videoconferencing on the Internet. Each approach has technical advantages and disadvantages, and embodies quite different consumer behavior models; neither is a priori superior. As a consequence, it is difficult to predict which model will prevail. Success will depend on consumer preference functionalities that do not yet exist; in fact, the technology is still developing.

Today, the telecommunications industry offers applications such as call waiting, voice mail, and caller ID on a broad basis, and is rapidly building deeper and broader experience bases. In addition, the cost of technical investment can be amortized over huge numbers of subscribers on the network. Moreover, to the extent that other segments require network performance of supervisory, security, and communications functions that are invisible to end users, the telecommunications industry's experience in real-time-response software and connectivity problems in general will be an advantage.

For its part, the computer industry, with a history of rapid technical innovation as well as some budding superpackagers, has offerings that could pull together complete solutions for the medium term and thus establish positions that would be difficult to overcome. To the extent that the multimedia industry evolves in ways that require users, rather than networks, to manipulate data, the computer industry will have an advantage with its deep experience bases in human/computer interfaces.

Finally, since the rate of technical progress will depend on the size, habits, and equipment of consumer installed bases, current and medium-term market shares also will determine winners.

The results of this competition will lead to products sold to content packagers. Some products will be complete applications, such as software that enables video servers to dispense movies to home set-top boxes (today ATT, Oracle, and Microsoft, among others, are working on components for this application). Other products will be more "middleware" —stand-alone tools to construct end user applications or embed code in resold applications. These will include tools that facilitate network use (e.g., intelligent agents, such as those of General Magic that can search the network for data on specified topics) and tools that make the network more accessible (e.g., the GUIs being offered by Microsoft and Bell Atlantic).[28]

The precise nature of these products is still uncertain; their design depends in part on the continuing debate about where network intelligence will reside, and on the speed with which workable solutions are offered to the marketplace. But it is certain that a new tier of software tasks and functionality is emerging that will define the information elements of the superhighway. Like all prior software developments, this new tier will build on established software standards and approaches; progress will be uneven, as befits an intrinsically evolutionary and experimental process. Eventually, standards will emerge—and as they do, the competitive structure of this new segment will shake out. However the network-level intelligence is finally partitioned, it will be marked by the emergence of standard network offerings with at most three offerings surviving in any middleware or application area.

**Hypothesis (7):** Manipulation will involve concentrated wholesale applications standards for telecommunications and computer networks. Whether telecommunications or computer networks become the dominant model for the information superhighway is more uncertain.

*Traditional Manipulation Software.* The layer below hybrid manipulation/transmission software will be operating systems for individual components of those systems. These will remain as concentrated as they are now. Microsoft dominates operating systems for stand-alone personal computers, and Novell dominates local area network (LAN) operating systems. In each case, scale economies and network externalities lead one firm to effectively set the standard, even if its technology is inferior.

Below these layers are specific retail applications that, by definition, are specialized. From simple spreadsheets and databases to more complicated applications, such as CAD/CAM, these are markets with unique requirements. Although they are less sensitive to network externalities than more systemic standards, they are still subject to the typical scale economies of software development. Therefore, they will likely become relatively concentrated businesses, although the potential for superior applications to drive out inferior ones will be higher than for tools, operating systems, or network standards.

**Hypothesis (8):** The operating systems, tools, and applications programs industry will become standardized and concentrated, even if there is a profusion of specialized applications.

*Processing/Storage Hardware.* Since digitization allows all content to be processed and stored in the same way, the same hardware will be used to manipulate all content. As the mainframe passes into history for most uses except real-time processing of huge amounts of data (as in airline reservations or bank transactions), because of flattening scale curves in memory and processing power, the cost of distributed computing becomes competitive.[29] The issue then becomes whether data and applications are held and processed centrally, or stored and manipulated locally, as with personal computing and video games today.

We suspect the answer will be a combination of the two, with the choice dependent primarily on frequency and volume of usage. For example, in the predicted move from videocassette rental to video on demand, best-sellers will probably be held on local file servers that can meet high demand without incurring long-distance transmission charges, while art movies that are viewed less frequently will be held at more central locations to optimize the mix of storage and transmission costs. Similarly, computer databases will be stored locally if they are used regularly and not updated often, and held centrally if they are searched infrequently or updated very regularly.

Wherever processing power is held, the industry is heading toward the commodity supply of hardware boxes. Intelligence will reside either in the manipulation software or in specialized components (microprocessors). Producers of processing and storage equipment will, therefore, be in an unattractive industry.

**Hypothesis (9):** Manipulation hardware will become commoditized, with specialized functions being provided on and off the network at an economically appropriate level of decentralization.

## Terminals

Market fragmentation is also likely at the terminal end of the functional chain. In the consumer market, the need to optimally meet differentiated customer requirements will probably lead to a profusion of terminal types serving various segments. Portable versus fixed, small versus large screen displays, high versus low quality, and cheap single function versus expensive multifunction are just some potential terminal market segments. Probably the most important functionality difference that will produce segmentation is the wireless (portable) versus wireline (fixed location) dichotomy.

**Hypothesis (10):** Terminals will become multifunctional, but differentiated consumer demands will support large numbers of specialized competitors.

Our predictions for the structures of various segments of the emerging multimedia industry are summarized in table 4-3.

TABLE 4-3

## Summary of Industry Structure

| Value Structure (Typical players) | Industry Structure |
|---|---|
| Content | • Fragmented and specialized<br>• Convergence represents a new distribution channel |
| Packaging | Systems integrator<br>Distribution packager<br> • 3–4 superpackagers with scale economies<br> • Remainder fragmented and specialized<br> • Simple content linking to systems integration, including GUI selection and promotion |
| Transmission | Local loop (4–9 players) including<br> • Wireless<br> • Cable<br> • Wireline<br>Long distance:<br> • More players than today<br> • Overcapacity<br> • Commodity pricing |
| Manipulation | Information highway software<br> • Specialized<br> • Providers of wide-area software platforms<br> • Based on Telco standards (Video dial tone, SS-7, AIN, etc.) OR<br> • Based on computer standards (Internet, ATM, MPEG, client/server, etc.)<br>Traditional manipulation software<br> • Fragmented<br>Proprietary hardware replaced by component functionality |
| Terminals | • Fragmented and specialized<br> • "Client" and stand-alone devices |

## KEY SUCCESS FACTORS AND FIRM CAPABILITIES

Having defined the playing field for each new multimedia industry segment, the next task is to understand the key success factors for each segment, and how today's players are positioned for the future. A review of the starting positions of players in each of today's three vertical industries indicates that some segments will be more competitive than others (figure 4-1).

- *Content* is provided by myriad players in many distinct businesses. In the area of video/interactive offerings, the media/entertainment industry has a clear advantage.

- *Packaging* is divided among the three industries, with no dominant player. As a result, computer software companies, cable and television programmers, current information service providers of telephone and on-line networks, as well as numerous new entrants, probably including the telephone companies themselves, will end up competing for control of the packaging function; indeed, they are already encroaching on each other's arenas (e.g., Sega moving into cable and computer games).[30]

- *Transmission* is the domain of wireline and wireless telephone companies. Their only threat is the possible use of cable as second local loops.

- *Manipulation* will have two very different competitive spheres. The information highway software subsegment will be a battleground for the computer and telecommunications industries; although traditional manipulation software and processing are likely to remain computer industry functions, the exact form of processing (file server versus workstation, for example), and its location (on or off the network) is more debatable.

- The *terminal* market is almost equally divided among the telephone, television, and personal computing industries, suggesting that the "set-top box" universal terminal market is up for grabs.[31]

## Content

Content is the easiest segment to address because it will remain closest to its current form (when "form" refers to production rather than distribution). While the multimedia revolution will overthrow existing distribution advantages (such as retail outlets or mail-order expertise), key success factors in each of the discrete content businesses will remain those that lead to the production of the highest-quality content at reasonable prices. In entertainment, the most creative content producers will be as successful as they are today—although since content will have to be created for more than one medium (i.e., film or television), new modes of creativity will be required. In news gathering, winners will be those entities that provide the desired coverage most cost-effectively. Therefore, winners will be firms that today excel at providing their particular content; their returns will remain high but will vary widely.

**Hypothesis (11):** Success in individual content markets will depend on quality and the cost of producing content, not on current distribution strength.

Content providers will not, in our view, have much of a struggle with packagers tempted to use their own scope economies to produce lower-quality content and force it on consumers they control. We believe that consumers will allow high-quality, independent content providers to survive and prosper, and no superpackager will emerge as a bottleneck distribution monopolist. Although this implies that content suppliers need not integrate forward, there are strategic reasons why packagers and transmission firms will want preferential access to high-quality, recognizable content. Thus content providers will be approached by other industry players to form alliances. They will be in the driver's seat, and should agree to participate only if they are offered substantial rewards over and above those of continuing independent operation.

**Hypothesis (12):** Quality content providers will be able to earn above-normal profits because of their value to packagers and transmission companies as alliance partners.

## Packaging

Key success factors for packagers center on customer ownership and appropriate vertical scope. Owning customers is difficult for packagers that are intrinsically intermediaries between content providers and customers. Moreover, packagers must work through other intermediaries that have direct customer contacts, the transmission companies. Thus, to be profitable, packagers must first actively develop unique packages that override the reputations of content providers and the direct customer contacts of transmission companies. This will be difficult, but not impossible, to achieve. For example, MTV successfully plays this role today, in spite of attempts by record companies to create their own music network.[32]

The MTV example demonstrates two other critical determinants of customer ownership—first-mover advantages and brand name. When, for example, Sony must decide whether to switch from MTV to a new music network, it must recognize the distribution breadth and cost advantage that MTV possesses. In particular, in businesses that exhibit huge economies of scale, the first mover able to secure wide market access is quickly able to build a cost structure that is difficult for others to replicate.

The first mover also usually establishes an attractive brand name that strengthens its customer ownership. When consumers are choosing to source their multimedia needs from ATT, the local LEC, the local cable company, or an entrepreneurial start-up, the fact that their brand preference hierarchy probably matches this order will have a major impact (see table 4-4).

The fourth determinant of customer ownership will be a packager's technological capability. This might seem an unusual requirement for success in what is essentially a creative role, but given the enormous technological uncertainty surrounding the evolution of the multimedia industry, understanding and exploiting the limits of technological feasibility will be critical in the short term. In the early years of interactive television, for example, technology will determine the number of choices available to viewers for interactive responses. Designing wonderful game shows that allow viewers to answer Yes or No will quickly become a redundant skill as interactivity extends to a much broader range of data interchange. Staying at the forefront creatively will require a deep understanding not only of customers' needs but also, and more important, of the technical capabilities and limitations of the information superhighway.

---

**Hypothesis (13):** Success in packaging will depend primarily on customer ownership, which in turn will come from creativity, early-mover advantages, brand name, and technological know-how.

---

Vertical scope—that is, the degree of integration (backward into content and forward into transmission)—will also be a key determinant of packagers' success, although the appropriate scope will vary over time. Early in the industry life cycle, broader scope in both directions will be more important. To exploit first-mover advantage, a packager will need access to the best content in order to assure customers that their new service offers the most desirable product. This does not require ownership of content, but it does suggest that packager contracts or alliances with content providers will be critical.

TABLE 4-4

## Major U.S. Interactive Multimedia Trials

| Company —Allies | Location | Objectives | | | Number of Participants | Services Offered |
|---|---|---|---|---|---|---|
| | | REGULATORY | TECHNICAL | MARKET | | |
| Time Warner —USW, AT&T, Toshiba, Sci. Atl. | Orlando, FL | | • | • | 4,000 | VOD, HS, VG, TV, E, PCS, NOD |
| US WEST | Omaha, NE | • | • | • | 375 technical/ 9,000 market | VOD, HS, VG, E, I |
| PacBell | Milpitas, CA | • | • | • | 1,000 | HS, VG, E, I |
| Cox | Omaha, NE | | • | • | 5 technical/ 2,000 market | VOD, HS, VG, TV, E |
| Bell Atlantic | Northern Virginia | • | • | • | 300 technical/ 2,000 market | VOD, HS, VG, E, I |
| Viacom/ AT&T | Castro Valley, CA | | • | • | Up to 1,000 | VOD, HS, VG, TV |
| GTE/AT&T | Manassas, VA | | • | | 1,000 | HS, VG, E, I |
| CellularVision/ Bell Atlantic | Brooklyn, NY | | • | | — | WV |

Services:  VOD — Video on Demand          HS — Home Shopping       VG — Video Games
TV — Interactive Program Guide     E — Education            PCS — Personal Comm. Services
NOD — News on Demand               I — Information Services   WV — Wireless Video Services

Initially, packagers will also have to extend their scope forward into transmission because network hardware and software will be inextricably linked to developing effective packages—but here contracts will not be enough, at least in the early days. Packagers will need to work closely with network providers to understand the technological limitations of a network and, if possible, to help establish network parameters. Due to the inherent degree of uncertainty, such working relationships cannot be arranged contractually before standards are established.[33]

In the early years, of course, many packagers will be content or transmission companies, so at least one link will already be internalized. Later, when standards are established and uncertainty is reduced, it will be possible to negotiate traditional contractual arrangements to capture the value of any remaining linkages between packaging and content or transmission, so these businesses will start to unbundle.

**Hypothesis (14):** Successful packagers will develop alliances with quality content providers and transmission companies in the short term.

These arguments apply particularly to firms striving to become broad-scope superpackagers. Clearly, these players will require enormous resources, as well as first-mover advantages, to win—suggesting that winners will most likely emerge from among the first entrants. On the other hand, it will always be intrinsically easier to enter fragmented, specialist packager areas. Any entrepreneur, entering at almost any time, has the potential to become a viable niche packager.

**Hypothesis (15):** The importance of first-mover advantages to content providers and consumers suggests that broad-scope superpackagers will emerge from the current active participants.

## Transmission

Two sets of key success factors exist in the transmission segment: one for local loops and one for long-distance transmission.

*Local Loops.* Provided, as seems to be the case, that a set of competitors does not achieve an overwhelming investment cost advantage, success in local loops will be based on the fact that this is primarily a customer-service business. Although strategic pricing may still produce differentially higher utilization, it will be customer-service strengths in provisioning, repair, billing, and brand name that determine success. The relative strengths and weaknesses of the four types of potential multimedia transmission players—LECs, IXCs, cable, and wireless companies—are summarized below.

**Hypothesis (16):** Unless substantial investment cost differentials among various participants in the local service business can be achieved, companies with efficient customer service capabilities, notably LECs, will be successful.

Due to regulatory pressures during the 1980s, LECs are not only very strong in most aspects of customer service, but also increasingly efficient in operations. This positions them very well for success in multimedia transmission. However, LECs lack any entertainment capability for early entry into the broader multimedia market. Unlike telephony, where price can be an important entry tactic, cable entry will probably require differentiated content to encourage customer switching. To acquire content, LECs will most likely form alliances with quality content providers or packagers (for example, the Disney deal with three LECs[34] and the aborted Bell Atlantic/TCI merger[35]). The strategic need for such an alliance will diminish as market presence is established and market contracts for content replace more formally structured alliances.

Today, IXCs have strengths in sophisticated network management, brand name, and strategic pricing. On the other hand, they generically suffer from having no local loop infrastructure (and therefore weak customer links). Their most logical market entry, beyond wireless and a limited presence through CAPs, is to resell LEC or cable facilities, which necessarily puts them at somewhat of a disadvantage. Additionally, they lack entertainment experience. And finally, ATT, in particular, because it outsources its billing, currently lacks of direct customer contact, which will be vital for success in local markets.

Cable companies are very poorly positioned: they have the worst customer service and brand reputation of any likely competitor; they lack switching or sophisticated network management capabilities; and they have not experienced the regulatory pressure to reduce costs and enhance service that has strengthened LECs. They have access to entertainment content now, but are likely to consolidate in the future so as to offer broad distribution to content providers in order to counter the anticipated telephone companies' alliances in content.[36] In addition, to generate telephony volume, they will probably have to partner with telephone companies, most likely an out-of-territory LEC (e.g., the aborted Bell Atlantic/TCI merger), or, if permitted, an IXC. Clearly, such alliances would bring cable companies valuable capabilities in switching and network service management.

**Hypothesis (17):** Telephony companies wishing to provide broadband service in local areas will form alliances with content providers and become packagers of quality content. Cable companies will consolidate to offer broad distribution to content providers and will seek telephony alliances to access switching capabilities.

Wireless service—whether cellular or PCS—will be seen as a complement to, rather than a substitute for, wireline communications for five to eight years. Price differentials, limitations on data transmission, and the current lack of national coverage of wireless networks will slow their penetration into broad-based domestic markets, temporarily limiting wireless to high-volume telephone users. Wireless players will need to form alliances to offer the national coverage that is key to penetrating business markets. As the market broadens, the ability to market nationwide will create superior brand awareness and reduce marketing costs, thus attracting domestic customers and strengthening the advantage of nationwide wireless providers. This is the logic behind the current alliance activity in the wireless industry (such as Nextel's acquisition binge[37] and the alliance of Bell Atlantic and NYNEX).

**Hypothesis (18):** Successful wireless companies will offer nationwide service. Mergers and alliances will lead to nationwide wireless networks.

*Long-Distance Transmission.* Long-distance transmission networks face the problem of retaining customer control. In principle, the transmission function is a wholesale commodity that, with recent advances in network quality, is essentially transparent to customers. Therefore, we might reasonably expect to see long-distance companies disintermediated by players that control customers, whether the provider of service is the local loop (whatever form that takes) or the content packager that customers desire. In this scenario, LECs, for example, would become resellers of long-distance minutes and would use simple, low-cost routing algorithms and their enormous bargaining power to make the long-distance business a very unprofitable, cost-driven one (because the marginal cost of capacity is so low).

Long-distance companies could prevent this outcome either by maintaining current artificial barriers to the resale of their product by regulators or (notably ATT) by leveraging current brand name strengths into those other two businesses that do provide customer contact. But even if ATT is able to become a packager or a local access provider with control of its customers, the long-distance transmission component of its business would still be best treated as a stand-alone entity for which the key to success would be low cost.

Thus, whichever way the long-distance market plays out, the key to success in long-distance transmission will be low-cost service provision. This presents a transition problem to existing long-distance companies that must retain customers as they move into local loops or packaging businesses while simultaneously learning to dramatically cut costs of basic network operations.

**Hypothesis (19):** The key to success in long-distance transmission will be the low-cost provision of commodity products. IXCs are likely to form alliances with participants in other businesses to enter more structurally attractive markets—notably packaging and manipulation.

## Manipulation

As manipulation separates into three very different segments—traditional manipulation software, information highway software, and processing/storage hardware—different key success factors will emerge in each.

*Traditional Manipulation Software.* Success in traditional manipulation software will probably depend on the same things it does today, and therefore we expect the same kinds of players to win. The only change will be the decreasing frequency of start-ups' establishing new standards within an application. The value of an installed customer base will provide incumbents with major advantages and allow them to gradually extend their scope to related markets.

**Hypothesis (20):** In operating systems, tools, and applications software, market incumbents will increasingly dominate.

*Information Highway Software.* The experience of the software industry suggests that success in information highway software (including telecommunication and computer wholesale applications, and middleware) will derive from prowess in setting standards, which in turn will come from technological capability, alliance-building skills, and first-mover advantages.

Since so many industry observers are wondering about Microsoft's future role, it is critical to distinguish between retail and wholesale applications. Retail applications, such as the consumer GUI, are the traditional domain of Microsoft, which understands the consumer/computer interface and consumer needs extremely well. A very different environment, where Microsoft has traditionally had no presence or poor success, is that of wholesale, computer/computer interface applications. While it is reasonable to expect Microsoft to continue to perform well in the former, its success in the latter is more questionable because of the two very different technological requirements.

The technological requirements of this new kind of software are so various—involving interactivity, connectivity, real time, and digital switching—that neither the computer industry nor the telecommunications industry has an overwhelming advantage. Today, the computer industry is focused on interactivity, in terms of the human/machine interface, and complex manipulation, and is only beginning to offer real-time products, most of which are relatively simple (e.g., LAN software, low-level protocols). On the other hand, the telecommunications industry (notably IXCs) is producing a stream of real-time applications involving computer/computer interfaces (e.g., data filtering and amplification, call following, caller signaling). IXCs could have the capability and credibility to develop and establish nationwide, real-time standards that will garner the lion's share of network intelligence residing in complex wholesale applications using "smart" servers with "dumb" terminals, such as those needed to run the PCS business. For these applications, it is unlikely that PCSs, for example, will replicate much of the customer billing and account verification services that telephone companies already provide, so they will be outsourced.[38] Competition among telephone companies will then be in terms of price, system reliability, and the fundamental design and ease of use of wholesale applications services offered to packagers. A second example of this kind of application is the SS7 protocol, in which competitive differentiation will come not from simply switching original information around the superhighway, but from improved processing of "information about the information" that travels in parallel with that basic information. In general, we might call these "open AIN" businesses that treat intelligent networks as platforms, much like DOS, but in this case for network applications.

Such applications hold the best hope for long-distance transmission companies to build profitable market positions. To achieve this, however, they will have to acquire some of the skills of a manipulation company. Accordingly, we expect to see numerous alliances where computer and software companies use their database manipulation skills to complement the switching capabilities of transmission companies.

Such alliances would also benefit computer companies. The computer industry is working to develop smart servers that act as centralized data manipulators, an outcome that Oracle and IBM, for example, would prefer. But industry participants must move closer to transmission and software businesses if they are to escape the commoditization of the basic processing and storage businesses.

It is only in a scenario in which a relatively dumb network server is complemented by smart terminals that Microsoft has a clear advantage. Microsoft wants to keep intelligence at the lowest possible level, with minimal network interactions, so that it can be the major player in manipulation. Accordingly, it is today pushing products like Tiger, a PC-based file server system.

Given the technological uncertainty, product offerings for video on demand, global positioning satellites, home shopping, and similar services will proliferate for a considerable period of time, and multiple proprietary and differentiated wholesale application packages will be developed. However, in the long run one may expect standardized offerings (if not true standards) to emerge for such applications—and one of these types of players will predominate, with revenue distributed accordingly.

**Hypothesis (21):** Competition in manipulation will occur between applications at the telecommunication, computer, and terminal levels, but there will be no clear winner for a long time.

Because these applications involve the activities of terminals, transmission, manipulation, and packagers, and their inherent profit potentials, they are currently the focus of much intercompany alliance activity, such as that of Intel, Microsoft, and General Instruments.[39] Some of this activity is mergers and acquisitions, some is joint ventures, and some is more in the nature of prime contractor relationships. While we cannot hope to predict which companies will win, or even the form of the standards that will eventually emerge, we can suggest that there will probably be important first-mover advantages in the standard-setting competition.[40] If an LEC, for example, establishes a successful standard in its interactive test market (table 4-4 lists such tests), it will be hard to dislodge because of the huge complementary investments in switching, network infrastructure, set-top boxes, and other items involved. Switching costs from a standard central architecture to the entire network architecture will be very high, so participating in a standard that receives early acceptance will be critical to competitive success.

**Hypothesis (22):** Manipulation standards will be important sources of profits. Early movers that combine terminals, transmission, manipulation, and packaging capabilities will be in an advantageous position.

*Processing/Storage Hardware.* In processing, key success factors will increasingly relate to the low-cost provision of commodity products. Differentiation may come from unique components, such as microprocessors, but computer storage and processing hardware boxes will continue toward commoditization. Even currently differentiated products (such as video servers) will rapidly become commodities. Thus computer companies will have to continue to lower costs, and improve service and software products, if they are to survive (at least at the consumer end of the multimedia business). In their place, suppliers of differentiated components, such as displays and integrated circuts (ICs), will capture the value from the hardware business, leaving computer companies as assemblers.

**Hypothesis (23):** Successful processing companies will increasingly become low-cost providers of commodity boxes. Profits from hardware will continue to be captured by differentiated component suppliers.

## Terminals

Competitors with the appropriate sets of resources and capabilities to succeed in the terminal market are likely to have recognized two important features of that market. First, it will be a high-volume consumer market. The ubiquitous nature of the terminal and its potential combination of telephone, television, video game player, personal computer, and videocassette player suggest a likely household penetration rate of over 100 percent, generating a U.S. domestic market of at least ten million units per annum and worldwide annual sales of over fifty million units per annum.[41]

The second aspect of the terminal market is that it is unlikely to be homogeneous, because horizontal and vertical differentiation in a market of that size is inevitable. Consumers will be differentiated from commercial and industrial users; and their demands for portable and fixed-base, large- and small-screen displays, combination and single-use units, for example, will also be highly differentiated. It is, in fact, quite unlikely that a single terminal will become the ubiquitous household unit, because individual preferences, needs, and incomes differ too widely to justify such broad-based commonality.

The keys to success in such markets will echo those in the current consumer electronics market. Indeed, the growing importance of assembly costs and management of distribution channels is pushing the personal computing industry in that direction. Consumer electronics and telephone equipment manufacturers are already overlapping.

In the terminal business, high-volume manufacturing (primarily assembly) and product design and innovation capabilities, established brand names, and distribution channels will, therefore, become the most crucial to success. These factors favor the emergence of companies that serve mass markets, surrounded by specialists that focus on either niche markets (e.g., Bang and Olufsen's unique Scandinavian design in the consumer electronics market) or supply unique components (e.g., Sharp's dominance in LCD screens). Indeed, it will probably be consumer electronics companies that dominate the terminal market. Hardened to intense competition through successive waves of new product innovation, they have developed the capabilities needed to succeed in terminals by diversifying into the increasingly low-technology computer assembly business.

**Hypothesis (24):** Consumer electronics firms with product design and innovation capabilities, high-volume assembly, and consumer marketing and distribution will be likely winners in terminals markets. Specialists will continue to occupy the many niches in consumer markets.

The history of content providers being acquired by terminal companies (for example, Sony's purchase of Columbia) will be a short-lived phenomenon. After Matsushita prevailed in the VCR standards battle because Sony failed to win over content providers to its standard,[42] Sony decided to become an important content provider in order to influence future terminal standards, such as for digital audiotape versus minidisk. However, the importance of content in terminal standards will disappear when content is distributed via digital networks, with standards set thereon. Thus the link between content and terminal companies will be abolished, and Sony's, Philips's (Polygram Records), and Matsushita's content ventures will be spun off as independent businesses or sold to transmission or packager companies that value them higher. The important lesson from this experience is that attempts to fight the horizontal reconfiguration of the industry will fail. Trying to connect software content and terminal hardware in a unique vertical format will not succeed. For similar reasons, if Sega and Nintendo try to sustain video games as stand-alone vertical industries, they are likely to be overwhelmed by the multimedia juggernaut.

**Hypothesis (25):** Attempts by terminal companies to rebuild discrete vertical industries with unique technologies will fail.

Table 4-5 summarizes the key success factors by industry segment.

## IMPLICATIONS AND CONCLUSIONS

Recognizing that the three previously defined discrete vertical industries will be reconfiguring into five horizontal segments, we have a powerful framework for analyzing the future structure of the multimedia industry, the strategies and competitive advantages of individual players, and the wisdom of various kinds of alliances. In general, this framework suggests the following broad conclusions for players operating in each element.

- *Content* companies, such as Disney, face excellent prospects. Quality content providers now have the opportunity to enter into some very attractive alliances on favorable terms. Disney is doing just that in its deals with three LECs.

- *Packagers* face perhaps the greatest challenges and opportunities, because this segment is the most novel and companies are approaching it from different directions. These players need to make many alliances and to be prepared for big wins and big failures as the industry evolves.

TABLE 4-5

KEY SUCCESS FACTORS BY INDUSTRY SEGMENT

| Value Structure (Typical players) | Key Success Factors |
|---|---|
| Content | Cost/quality, independent of distribution |
| Packaging | Customer control<br>• Creativity<br>• High quality content<br>• Brand name<br>• Early mover<br>Technological acumen<br>Vertical scope<br>• Content and transmission alliances |
| Transmission | Cost/quality of customer service and provisioning<br>National coverage, interoperability, and branding<br>Broadband service capabilities |
| Manipulation | |
|   Traditional software | Incumbents |
|   Information highway software | Standards setting, technological prowess, and alliance skills<br>Manipulation and transmission skills |
|   Processing hardware | Low-cost assembly<br>• Specialized components, capture profit |
| Terminals | High-volume assembly<br>Product design and innovation<br>Consumer marketing and distribution |

- *LECs* will need to work simultaneously on upgrading their broadband network capabilities and building volume to fill that capacity. Given the prospective excess capacity in local loops, LECs need to make very targeted facility investments. They are in a good position to build volume by developing vibrant roles as packagers through careful alliances (e.g., the Ovitz and Disney deals).

- *IXCs* face a similar challenge. They, too, must be careful about maintaining utilization of their long-distance capacity, and they also have bright prospects in other horizontal segments (specifically, information highway software). To do this, they must be prepared to confront and/or co-opt software companies, particularly Microsoft, Oracle, and the like. ATT's strategy seems to confirm these conclusions.

- *Computer companies* need to recognize the limited future of their processing hardware and decide whether to move upstream into transmission connectivity or remain in more stand-alone applications.

- *Terminal producers* have the opportunity to shape consumer preferences for a multiplicity of new products.

## Alliances

Earlier we developed a number of hypotheses concerning the locus and rationale for alliances that are generally supported by the data (see table 4-6). Proceeding up the functional chain, we observed that content providers are likely to be the focus of considerable alliance activity as packagers and transmission companies try to lock up quality content to differentiate consumer offerings (hypotheses 10, 14, and 17). The most prolific source of alliances is, indeed, in the content sector, reflecting the current value of content to a broad range of participants in other industry sectors. The fact that content and terminal providers account for the least alliance activity (only 5 of 165 deals) supports our contention that alliances to establish terminal standards have been rendered moot by the multimedia standard-setting game.

Packagers should be involved in content alliances to differentiate product offerings, and with transmission companies to incorporate technological knowledge of network capabilities into their more creative function (hypothesis 12). Indeed, we find that more than half of packagers' deal activity is with content and transmission providers.

Transmission companies should be involved in alliances with each other. Wireless companies need to build nationwide networks (hypothesis 15); cable companies need to develop national distribution scale to counteract the potential entry of LECs (hypothesis 14), and to acquire switching capabilities through alliances with telephony companies (hypothesis 16). Thus, the fact that 80 percent of alliances are within the network sector comes as no surprise. The remaining alliances should be scattered all over the map as transmission companies try to acquire the capabilities needed to establish wholesale package standards (hypotheses 18 and 19), and to leverage their size and market awareness into fundamentally more attractive businesses (hypothesis 16). In terms of alliance activity outside the sector, these firms are the most active and evenly distributed.

Manipulation and terminal providers (hardware and software companies in the data) are attractive partners to transmission providers and

TABLE 4-6

ALLIANCE ACTIVITY

|  |  | Target | | | | | |
|---|---|---|---|---|---|---|---|
|  |  | PACKAGING | CONTENT | NETWORKS | SOFTWARE | HARDWARE | TOTAL |
| Initiator | PACKAGING | 36 | 17 | 5 | 6 | 9 | 73 |
|  | CONTENT | 10 | 137 | 7 | 6 | 5 | 165 |
|  | NETWORKS | 11 | 13 | 116 | 6 | 8 | 154 |
|  | SOFTWARE | 0 | 4 | 3 | 8 | 3 | 18 |
|  | HARDWARE | 7 | 3 | 5 | 36 | 47 | 98 |
|  | TOTAL | 64 | 174 | 136 | 62 | 72 | 508 |

packagers seeking assistance in developing standards (hypotheses 18 and 19). They are thus much more often the targets than the initiators of partnerships.

Manipulation/transmission alliances, such as ATT's acquisition of NCR, have yet to arise in great numbers, but we expect to see more of this activity soon.

The alliance activities observed in these functions are at least partially explained by the premise of our analysis that firms are entering into alliances to acquire capabilities that they currently lack, but that they believe to be essential to their success.

## Summary

Industry convergence has inspired a great deal of radical reorganization in many corporations, but many of those moves cannot be explained by our framework. Rather, they seem to be driven by mimetic diversification (i.e., "It's all right for me to do this because my competitor just did it"), or naive heuristics (e.g., "This business must be worth investing in because it will be the Microsoft of the future"), or the pure seductive power and glamour of Hollywood.

Clearly, there is enormous uncertainty about the future evolution of the affected industries. But this should not hinder our attempts to think in more structured ways about the future. The payoff of even a little knowledge at this stage is large enough to justify the investment, and we believe that the framework laid out in this paper will enable companies to do this.

## NOTES

1. Anthony G. Oettinger, "Telling Ripe from Hype in Multimedia," Incidental Paper, Harvard University Center for Information Policy Research, July 1994.

2. Gary Hamel and C. K. Prahalad, *Competing for the Future* (Boston: Harvard Business School Press, 1994).

3. Richard P. Simon and Barry A. Kaplan, "Communacopia: A Digital Communication Bounty," Goldman Sachs Investment Research, July 1992; John Hagel III and Thomas R. Eisenmann, "Navigating the Multimedia Landscape," *The McKinsey Quarterly* 3 (1994): 39–55.

4. Michael E. Porter, *Competitive Strategy* (New York: Free Press, 1980).

5. B. Wernerfelt, "A Resource-Based View of the Firm," *Strategic Management Journal* 5 (1984): 171–180; J. B. Barney, "Firm Resources and Sustained Competitive Advantage," *Journal of Management* 17 (1991): 99–120; M. A. Peteraf, "The Cornerstones of Competitive Advantage: A Resource-Based View," *Strategic Management Journal* 14 (1993): 179–191.

6. Stephen P. Bradley and Jerry A. Hausman, eds., *Future Competition in Telecommunications* (Boston: Harvard Business School Press, 1989); Joseph Baylock, Stephen P. Bradley, and Eric K. Clemons, "Enhanced Communications Services: An Analysis of AT&T's Competitive Position," in *Future Competition in Telecommunications,* Stephen P. Bradley and Jerry A. Hausman, eds. (Boston: Harvard Business School Press, 1989); Stephen P. Bradley, Jerry A. Hausman, and Richard L. Nolan, *Globalization, Technology, and Competition: The Fusion of Computers and Telecommunications in the 1990s* (Boston: Harvard Business School Press, 1993); Stephen P. Bradley, "The Role of IT Networking in Sustaining Competitive Advantage," in *Globalization, Technology, and Competition: The Fusion of Computers and Telecommunications in the 1990s,* Stephen P. Bradley, Jerry A. Hausman, and Richard L. Nolan, eds. (Boston: Harvard Business School Press, 1993); David J. Collis, "The Evolution of Firm Boundaries: The Case of the Baby Bells," Division of Research Working Paper 93-064, Harvard Business School, January 1993; "Rating the RHCs," *Telephony* 221 (December 16, 1991), 26–29; P. William Bane, Ronald M. Serrano, and Debra McMahon, "LECs Must Learn the Marketing Game," *Telephony* 223 (August 31, 1992), 22–24; "Telco Reduces OSP Trouble Reports: No News Is Good News," *Telephone Engineer and Management,* April 1, 1993; Joao Baptista and Jerome Moitry, "PCS: An Exercise in Marketing Skills," paper presented to IIRC PCS Conference, Paris, January 1995; Joao Baptista, Mitch Goldstein, and Peter Clark, "Can the European Operators Compete," in *International Telecommunications Update 1995/96,* Paul Chambers, ed. (London: Kensington Publications, 1995); P. William Bane, J. P. A. Baptista, J. Estin, and M. P. Goldstein, "International Carriers: Benchmarking Performance," *Telecommunications* (Americas ed.), February 1995, 21–23, 54.

7. Michael Fahey, "From Local to Global: Surveying the Fiber Landscape," *Telecommunications* (Americas ed.), November 1993, 33–38.

8. Kathy Rebello, "Your Digital Future," *Business Week*, September 7, 1992, 56–60, 64.

9. Charles F. Mason, "Iridium Forges Ahead with Its Grand PCN Plan," *Telephony*, November 1, 1993, 28–34.

10. Nielsen Media Research, *1992–1993 Report on Television* (1993), 8.

11. Ronald Grover, "Ovitz: How Many Fields Can the King of Hollywood Conquer?" *Business Week* (industrial/technology ed.), August 9, 1993, 50–55.

12. John Hagel III and William J. Lansing, "Who Owns the Customer," *The McKinsey Quarterly* 4 (1994): 63–76.

13. Mercer Management Consulting, "Future Policy for *Telecommunications* Infrastructure and CATV Networks: A Path Toward Infrastructure Liberalisation" (December 1994).

14. Catherine Arnst, "Phone Frenzy: Is There Anyone Who Doesn't Want to Be a Telecom Player?" *Business Week*, February 20, 1995, 92–97.

15. However, it is difficult to imagine the United States and Europe going in such different directions without one suffering in the end.

16. Joanie Wexler, "AT&T/McCaw Merger Could Lower Prices, Spur Innovation," *Network World*, September 26, 1994, 10–11.

17. Bruce DeMaeyer, "PCS Auctions: Ready or Not, Here They Come," *America's Network*, November 1, 1994, 34–35.

18. P. William Bane, Dekkers L. Davidson, and Ronald E. Grant, "The Making of Wireless Competition," *PCIA Journal*, June 1994, 16.

19. Naoyuki Koike, "Cable Television and Telephone Companies: Towards Residential Broadband Communications Services in the United States and Japan," Harvard University, Program on Information Resources Policy, 1990.

20. "Multimedia in Britain: Down the Line," *The Economist*, November 26, 1994, 76.

21. Mercer Management Consulting, 96, 98.

22. Peter W. Huber, *The Geodesic Network: 1987 Report on Competition in the Telephone Industry* (Washington, D.C.: U.S. Department of Justice, 1987), and "The Technological Imperative for Competition," in *Future Competition in Telecommunications*, Stephen P. Bradley and Jerry A. Hausman, eds. (Boston: Harvard Business School Press, 1989).

23. Company confidential information.

24. David Rohde, "CAPs Invade the Suburbs," *Network World*, October 4, 1993, 33.

25. Mark Landler, "Baby Bells Advance in Long Distance," *The New York Times*, April 29, 1995, sec. 1, p. 35.

26. Peter W. Huber, Michael K. Kellogg, and John Thorne, *The Geodesic Network II: 1993 Report on Competition in the Telephone Industry* (Washington, D.C.: The Geodesic Company, 1992).

27. "International Prices Tumble at ICA Meeting," *Communications News*, July 1993, 32.

28. As a horizontal tool that can potentially be used in all applications interfaces, the GUI can clearly be an enormous source of revenue.

29. Richard Ross, "Managing Distributed Computing," *Information Systems Management*, Summer 1994, 41–50.

30. Mark Berniker, "Sega Channel Readies for Debut," *Broadcasting & Cable*, June 20, 1994, 40.

31. Andrew Kupfer, "Set-Top Box Wars," *Fortune*, August 22, 1994, 110–118.

32. Mark Landler, "Will MTV Have to Share the Stage?" *Business Week* (industrial/technology ed.), p. 38.

33. Joseph Farrell and Garth Saloner, "Standardization, Compatibility, and Innovation," *Rand Journal of Economics* 16 (Spring, 1985): 70–83.

34. Larry Armstrong, "The Baby Bells Go Hollywood," *Business Week*, August 29, 1994, 34–35.

35. Ian Scales, "Irreconcilable Differences?" *Communications International*, December 1994, 4–7.

36. Larry J. Yokell, "Cable TV Moves into Telecom Markets," *Business Communications Review*, November 1994, 43–48.

37. Patrick Flanagan, "National Wireless Picture Getting Murkier," *Telecommunications* (Americas ed.), November 1994, 15–16.

38. Vince Vittore, "Buildout Could Bring a Bloodbath," *America's Network*, December 1, 1994, 40–41.

39. Jennifer Edstrom, "Hardware's Stake in Convergence," *Computer Reseller News*, November 14, 1994, SS27–SS30.

40. Michael Katz and Carl Shapiro, "Network Externalities, Competition, and Compatibility," *American Economic Review* 75 (June 1987): 424–440.

41. *Computer Industry Forecasts*, Second Quarter 1995.

42. Michael A. Cusumano, "Strategic Maneuvering and Mass-Market Dynamics: The Triumph of VHS over Beta," *Business History Review*, Spring 1992, 51–94.

CHAPTER 5

# WHAT DOES INDUSTRY CONVERGENCE MEAN?

Shane Greenstein

Tarun Khanna

## INTRODUCTION

The Allegheny River forms in Pennsylvania, loops into western New York, and then flows southward into Pennsylvania. The Monongahela River forms in West Virginia and flows northward into Pennsylvania. At the very center of Pittsburgh, these two major waterways converge and become the Ohio River. Until they converge, geographers and everyone who uses them can distinguish them; where they converge, there is neither one nor the other but only a new thing: the Ohio River.

Industries that have been distinct historically, even as recently as a decade ago, converge in an analogous way. However, at the boundaries where formerly separate industries come together in a new industry, economic ambiguities arise. Ambiguity at economic boundaries is a sign of

*Earlier versions of this paper were presented at the Harvard Business School Colloquium on Colliding Worlds, the Strategic Alliances and Interconnection Conference, sponsored by the International Telecommunications Society, Colorado, January 1995, and the Information Economy Conference at the University of Michigan, March 1995. We wish to acknowledge the input of participants at these conferences, and also of Tim Bresnahan, Garth Saloner, and David Yoffie. Shane Greenstein wishes to acknowledge partial funding from the Computer Industry Project at Stanford University and NSF IRI-92-09321. He also acknowledges the hospitality of the Center for Economic Policy Research at Stanford University. Tarun Khanna acknowledges support from the Division of Research at the Harvard Business School.

vitality in capitalist economies and has been a feature of the U.S. economy for some time. But, recent or not, convergence in evolving industries deeply affects the activities of the firms involved.

Ames and Rosenberg, describing the birth, evolution, and development of industries on the frontiers of technology at the turn of the century, introduced the concept of technological convergence.[1] This refers to the fact that a few broadly similar processes of production (e.g., using lathes and drills) were being introduced into a large number of industries (e.g., bicycles and automobiles). The same technical process gradually diffuses into a wide range of industries.

Addressing similar issues, Bresnahan and Trajtenberg use the related concept of general-purpose technologies to refer to technological systems that enhance the productivity of many industries. Rail transport, the steam engine, and machine tools are general-purpose technologies that, according to Bresnahan and Trajtenberg, have driven growth and market evolution in the twentieth century by diffusing into almost every industry with which we are familiar.[2]

The traditional literature on the evolution of industries has tended to look for industry life cycles and dominant designs.[3] Here, the emphasis is on the evolutionary pattern of an industry and how its development influenced that industry's growth, almost as though such patterns were preordained. Other authors have studied how the activities of individual firms influence the development of their industry.[4] However, when they discuss how and why firms change their activities, they focus on activities only within the relatively well-defined boundaries of the given industry rather than on what happens at the boundaries between industries.

We study the ways in which the boundaries between industries shrink or even dissolve to accommodate growth. In particular, neither the communications industry nor the computer industry can be understood unless we recognize that the boundaries between them are very fluid.

Our concern in this paper is with how the boundaries between industries evolve, especially those between computers and communications. Accordingly, we shall distinguish between two kinds of convergence, two different ways that the boundaries between the markets for computer products and the markets for communications products are dissolving. It is a given among professional observers that these two industries are converging. Our hope is that the analytic framework we offer will clarify what that means in a wide variety of examples.

The first four sections develop our analytical framework: first, we define the kinds of convergence; second, we consider the locus of convergence; third, we identify some economic effects of the different kinds of convergence; and fourth, we consider the motives for competitive and cooperative behavior that the kinds of convergence provide. The fifth section explores the usefulness of this framework by applying it to analyze one segment of the multimedia landscape: the evolving relationships between phone and cable companies. Last, there is a brief summary section.


## THE KINDS OF CONVERGENCE

We suggest that there are two primary kinds of convergence: convergence in substitutes and convergence in complements.


### Convergence in Substitutes

Two products converge in substitutes when users consider either product interchangeable with the other. Convergence in substitutes occurs when different firms develop products with features that become increasingly similar to the features of certain other products. It also occurs when firms develop standard bundles of components: common arrangements of components for performing a particular set of functions, as when a firm sees a keyboard, monitor, and central processing unit (CPU) as a complete system.

Think of the product (e.g, a word-processing software program) as being used in a variety of tasks: writing reports, developing bibliographies, and composing correspondence. These different tasks use different features of the product to different extents. Each user can therefore use the product for one, two, or all of these tasks. Thus, when a firm changes certain features of a familiar product, those developments might have very different effects on different users and/or on different tasks. In time, products that become more and more similar will be viewed by users as being increasingly substitutable for one another. Users buy one or another complete system because they consider that any one of the systems can do what any one of the others can do.

So there are two ways that products converge in substitutes (can be used interchangeably). First, a given set of users might be willing to use the two products as substitutes in an increasing number of tasks. And second, an increasing number of users might begin to think of the products as substitutes in a given set of tasks. Products that are becoming increasingly substitutable can, but do not have to, follow the same technical trajectory to achieve greater substitutability. More frequently, the products are unrelated at one time, but develop their increased substitutability over time, as the history of computing platforms shows.

Until the late 1970s, the mainframe and minicomputer industries were distinct. Mainframes and minicomputers were sold to different customers and served different purposes. Roughly speaking, mainframes were for commercial general-purpose use and for sophisticated mathematical computations. Minicomputers were for controlling repetitive processes and were dedicated to single tasks. Technical innovations in the mid-1970s blurred these distinctions, allowing minicomputers to perform multiple tasks simultaneously. Thus, manufacturers of mainframes and minicomputers could increasingly compete with one another for users of powerful, large-system computers. In this way, markets that were less related in the 1970s were increasingly brought into contact in the early 1980s.[5]

## Convergence in Complements

Two products converge in complements when the products work better together than separately or when they work better together now than they worked together formerly. Convergence in complements occurs when different firms develop products or subsystems within a standard bundle that can increasingly work together to form a larger system. The output from the system can potentially be greater than the sum of the parts, that is, each component raises the marginal product of the others. This happens when the components together perform a new function that neither can do alone (e.g., an alarm and a timer together form an alarm clock). As with convergence in substitutes, there are two ways in which products converge in complements (can accomplish more together than separately). First, a given set of users can find that two products work better together for a larger set of tasks. Second, an increasing number of users can find that two products are complementary for their specific purposes.

As with convergence in substitutes, the products are often unrelated at one time and then converge in complements (develop complementarity) over time. The first PCs were used in the late 1970s by hobbyists in the home.[6] Apart from the hobbyists, PCs were first employed as essentially intelligent terminals in large business applications, that is, as complements to the existing mainframes. They were used for very simple programming tasks and for very minor processing before the main computations were sent back to the mainframe or the minicomputer.[7] Thus, there was little overlap in the tasks performed by PCs and those performed by more powerful computers.

The first users of the PC—engineers, hobbyists, or professional computer personnel with some training—had some complementary assets in place that allowed them to reap the benefits of the PCs. They had either a mainframe or supermini computers. These early users were later out-numbered by less technically sophisticated generalists. PCs evolved to be used for three major applications in the early-to-mid-1980s: word proces-sors, databases, and spreadsheets. From the mid-to-late 1980s, PCs were being used for more general-purpose and business applications.

Another example of convergence in complements is the compara-tively recent development of on-line databases. These products employ both advanced on-line transaction computing technology (e.g., hardware architecture and software) and data compression methods for telecom-munications. The combination of two new technologies delivers a quasi-automated service that did not even exist in the 1960s.

## Levels of Analysis and the Kinds of Convergence

Having distinguished between convergence in substitutes (interchange-ability) and convergence in complements (use in concert), we now point out that, depending on the level at which a computing system or a com-munications system is analyzed, a particular instance of convergence may be construed as being of either kind. It may be interpreted as a conver-gence in substitutes at one level of analysis and, equally appropriately, as a convergence in complements at a different level.

An operating system (e.g., DOS) may be a complement to a particu-lar hardware platform (e.g., a 486 Intel chip). It may also separately be a complement to another hardware platform (e.g., a Pentium chip). However, at the level of the system (the operating system plus the hard-ware platform), the different combinations of operating system and plat-form are substitutes for each other. A change that enhances the complementarity of the relationship between the operating system and either the 486-based computer or the Pentium-based computer may also enhance the extent to which the two systems are viewed as substitutes for each other.

Examples of a similar flavor abound. Local area network (LAN) com-munication protocols developed the ability to attach PCs using either the DOS or the Apple operating system. At the level of the individual operat-ing system and the LAN, PCs using either DOS or System 7.5 converge in complements: each is able to raise the other's marginal products. However, at the level of the overall system (LAN plus operating system), there is a convergence in substitutes: the DOS operating system attached to a LAN is now seen as equivalent (in more respects than before) to an Apple operating system attached to a LAN. Thus, a convergence in complements at the level of the components is analogous to a convergence in substitutes at the level of the system.

Now reconsider the evolving relationship between PCs and minicomputers and mainframes. Ironically, though the PC was a complement to larger platforms in the early years, it has now become a substitute for those platforms for many uses. Shifts in the user base, combined with a rapid rate of continuing technical development in mainframes and PCs, have brought large and small platforms into competition for a variety of uses.[8] PCs today are diverse enough to compete for the same users that previously had small minicomputers or workstations. Many tasks, for which one would use only more powerful computers several years ago, are now performed equally well by PCs. Even more dramatic is the coming competition with large platforms. The promise of client/server technology—linking PCs together—now offers a substitute for large mainframe platforms.

Think of an ensemble of tasks that have to be performed (e.g., accessing, updating, reading large databases). At a point in time, the mainframe is unambiguously better for some tasks, the minicomputer for other tasks, and the PC for others, while they are considered equally suitable for the remaining tasks. Thus, at the level of the individual task, the mainframe and minicomputer are often substitutes. However, at the level of the ensemble of tasks, the mainframe and the minicomputer and the PC are appropriately seen as complements. In time to come, we can expect that technological evolution will render the PC and the minicomputer and the mainframe substitutable for one another for an increasing number of tasks. At the level of the individual task, then, PCs and minicomputers and mainframes will have converged in substitutes. At the level of the system, there is also potentially a change in the degree to which mainframes and minicomputers will be seen as complements. For example, mainframes are better suited for organizationwide, centrally managed large databases, while minis are better suited for departmental computing. Thus a convergence in substitutes at the level of the components may be analogous to a convergence in complements at the level of the system, the mirror image of the situation for the PCs and the LAN.

These examples illustrate how the boundaries between otherwise distinct markets shifted in a short period of time. These shifts reflected changing relationships of substitution and complementarity between hardware and software. Mainframes and minicomputers, traditionally used for distinct purposes, became substitutable for a wider variety of tasks. PCs and more powerful machines, initially used very much as complementary machines, evolved into substitutes for one another for a variety of tasks.

## Other Examples of Convergence

Two other examples of markets with shifting boundaries will display the usefulness of our distinction between convergence in substitutes and convergence in complements: the video game industry and customer-owned communication technologies.

*The Video Game Industry.* Historically, video game firms were not viewed as being in the same arena with computer and communication firms. A video game was a device that featured crude, cartoonlike animation and responded to a simple system of controls. Momentous changes in technology, in both hardware and software, made this industry a powerful illustration of the shifting relationships between firms competing in hitherto distinct industries. On the software side, video games provide content to companies eager to find more material to transmit to the homes of TV watchers. Whereas historically there was no meaningful relationship between cable companies and video game firms, today firms in each industry have assets that are useful to the other. The cable companies get content, and the video game companies can use the cable infrastructure to distribute their product more widely. In 1994, Time Warner and Telecommunications, Inc. (TCI) announced that they would test-market the Sega Channel (a Japanese cable company that transmits only video games) in the United States.[9] Subscribers who bought or rented special hardware would be able to download video games from the cable system.

Software developments also have brought video game firms into contact with the film and computer industries. Both the film and video game industries benefit from technological developments in visual effects, inspired at least in part by work being done at computer companies.[10] Silicon Graphics and the Industrial Light and Magic Unit of Lucasfilm are creating the Joint Environment for Digital Imaging (JEDI). Video games have begun to move away from their crude animation and are now using actual footage from films rich in special effects, like *Jurassic Park*. Both films and games are using computer-generated backgrounds and even what industry observers call synthespians (synthetic actors).[11] Thus, not only do we see increasing convergence in complements between the film and computer industry, on the one hand, but films and video games appear to be headed in the direction of sharing a number of features that are increasingly becoming substitutes for one another.

On the hardware side of the video game industry, Sega hopes to use the hardware required to play its own games as the hardware necessary to operate interactive cable TV systems in the future. The competition to develop set-top boxes that will endow televisions with intelligence of sorts has attracted at least two additional classes of firms: providers of operating systems and semiconductor producers. Using the hardware as a computer of sorts is not far-fetched. In Japan, such hardware forms the basis of the Nintendo Network. With Nintendo's 1988 launch of the Family Computer Communications Network System, users of its Famicom (Family Computer) video game system could use a modem to transform a cartridge into a terminal through which to access on-line services.[12]

***Customer-Owned Communication Technologies.*** There is also a shifting relationship between computers and the infrastructure of the public telephone companies. Local-area networks (LANs) and wide-area networks (WANs) have always had to work together with the public telephone network to some extent. However, the boundaries between the customer's equipment and that of the local telephone company are no longer clear. This trend has antecedents in changing FCC policies, growth of markets that can equip customer premises, and the evolution of network technology. While it is difficult to identify a single catalytic event, the choices today contrast sharply with those of the 1960s when AT&T dominated all facets of the telecommunications industry.[13]

Today's large users have the option of designing their own network to suit their communication/computing needs and the idiosyncratic features of their organization. They can also determine the points at which they interconnect with the public network, not to mention where/how they connect with their own computing networks. To an increasing extent, a large organization may substitute out of one network owned by a public utility into another network (customer-owned or leased from a third party for some services). Thus, there is a convergence in substitutes between components of the network. At the same time, users' choices of where to place the boundaries between networks depend on the relative technological capabilities inherent in the networks, and on their ability to manage the interface between the networks—not a trivial task. Users must ensure that their local networks and the public network work together (whether on an ISDN line or using simple modem technology), and that the new complementarity remains reliable (possibly with a second line from a competitor that provides access on the local loop). These combinations of networks lead to many new services, a phenomenon that may be thought of as a convergence of complements at the system level.

Currently, internal buses in computers work much faster than does the telephone network, effectively decoupling computers from the network. However, the advent of broadband networks will likely reverse the current relationships between network speeds and computer speeds. It will then be feasible to conceive of a firm as part of a seamless network of computers. In fact, with complete digitization, some have suggested that the entire public switched network could effectively be a large processor.[14] The set of tasks uniquely suited to computer networks within a firm and the tasks suited only to the public network will change, as will the set of tasks that the two networks can perform equally well.

## CONVERGENCE ALONG THE VALUE CHAIN

While convergence of any sort is ultimately brought about by the actions of a collection of firms, we adopt the perspective that an individual firm can take the converging environment as given. From that perspective, we need to understand which of a firm's activities are affected by each kind of convergence. To help us understand firms' interactions with a converging environment, we rely on an analytical construct called the *value chain*.[15] This conceptual model construes a firm as a bundle of activities that collectively produce value for the end user. Broadly, we can think of the value chain as being divided into three stages: procurement, production, and distribution. Firms interact with each other in the converging environment at different points along the value chain. Convergence might occur in the production stage of the value chain. Customers may perceive a product (e.g., Dell's design of PC hardware) as becoming increasingly substitutable for another particular firm's product (e.g., IBM's design of PC hardware) or as increasingly complementary, as when customers increasingly used Dell's PCs in tandem with IBM's mainframes without difficult changes in their network. We can say, then, that Dell's PCs and IBM's PCs converge in substitutes at the production stage, and that Dell's PCs and IBM's mainframes converge in complements at the production stage.

Products can also converge at the procurement (preproduction) stage. Two products converge in substitutes at the procurement stage when, for instance, one input becomes interchangeable with another input, perhaps from a supplier who previously had limited geographic distribution or a restricted customer base due to government regulation (e.g., cable firms or local telephone firms). Two products may also converge in complements at the procurement stage when, for example, products are sold together as a bundled unit (e.g., suites of shrink-wrapped software applications).

Instances of convergence in substitutes and/or complements also occur in the distribution stage of a firm's value chain. A firm might decide to alter the distribution of its product. A convergence in substitutes at the distribution stage occurs as the firm increasingly distributes its product through a different, hitherto distinct, channel. Alternatively, the firm could increasingly use its usual distribution channel to distribute some hitherto unrelated product. In this case, a convergence in complements at the distribution stage has occurred. Either type of change would affect a firm's ability and willingness to continue using its old method of distribution. Of course, a firm could decide to alter its ways of distributing its product for reasons that have little to do with convergence in the distribution stage. For example, a convergence in substitutes or complements at the production stage might cause the firm to alter its use of existing distribution channels.

One example of convergence in complements in the distribution stage is provided by products that integrate data, voice, and video. New technologies for transmitting and compressing data now make it possible to transmit data, voice, and video in the same fashion (by digitizing them). Because these data streams can be manipulated easily, and because of the increasing bandwidth, it is possible to cater to individual tastes for video, voice, and data much more exactly. These firms are obviously reevaluating their traditional ways of transmitting their products as they find that a number of alternative distribution channels are beginning to look more substitutable for one another.

Convergence at one position in a value chain may well cause convergence in another position. Firms making products that serve identical functions (substitutes) or that are used in concert (complements) by a significant part of the customer base are more likely to use similar distribution channels for these products than for unrelated products. In this case, a convergence in substitutes or complements at the production stage of the value chain could well precipitate a convergence at the distribution stage. However, convergence in the distribution stage could also occur independently.

At first glance, there may seem to be a fourth stage at which products converge in the value chain: the stage at which barriers between distinct kinds of customers dissolve. If we were to speak carelessly here, we might be tempted to say that customer bases converge. But in fact that is simply another way of saying that the products are converging in substitutes or in complements at any stage of the value chain. Firms would not develop products that are interchangeable (converge in substitutes at the production stage) unless they had very good reason for believing that more and more customers would buy them interchangeably. Firms would not distribute their products in channels distinct from their usual channels (convergence in substitutes at the distribution stage) unless they believed that more and more customers wanted to buy those products in the new channel. Nor would firms develop products that work better together than separately (converge in complements at the production stage) unless they had good reason to believe that more customers wanted to use, and would therefore buy, the newly combined products. Nor, finally, would firms distribute their products in two or more channels or distribute two different products in the same channel (convergence in complements at the distribution stage) unless they knew or hoped that more and more customers were buying them in all these channels.

We might even be tempted to say that the enlargement of the customer base is a natural consequence of dissolving barriers between formerly distinct kinds of customers. But this manner of speaking, too, is merely another way of talking about the kinds of convergence at any of the stages. Firms would not develop products that are interchangeable unless they had good reason to believe that developing those products would cause more and more customers to buy them. (Readers can make out the parallel arguments for the kinds of convergence at each of the stages.)

Consider the case of TVs and PCs. PCs are unambiguously better suited for some tasks (for example, tasks involving keyboard input), but there is an increasing range of situations where the two devices are more interchangeable than they were before.[16] PCs are acquiring better video capabilities, and TVs are increasingly becoming more than just dumb receptacles for an incoming video/audio signal. Suppose that TV firms and PC firms were both selling separately to the same customer group (e.g., technically sophisticated home users). While these customers originally thought of the TV and PC as serving distinct purposes, they might begin to think of them as substitutes for one another. Suppose there is a second group of customers (e.g., beginning home users) that buys only a TV or a PC, but not both. Now that PCs and TVs are substitutes, customers in the second group are no longer content to restrict themselves to the manufacturers of TVs or of PCs; instead, they investigate the range of firms that provide both TVs and PCs. Customers of the PC firms now become customers of the TV firms as well, and vice versa. A convergence in substitutes has enlarged. But that merely says that when products are interchangeable, more and more people buy them interchangeably. Convergence of either kind at any stage is in fact the process of removing barriers between formerly distinct kinds of customers.

We might think of one kind of barrier as artificial: barriers that are set by public policy. Regulatory barriers provide captive customers to certain firms. When those artificial barriers are lowered or removed, formerly captive customers are free to buy from other firms. Here, convergence in complements and/or substitutes somewhere along a firm's value chain cannot enlarge the customer base until the artificial barriers between customers are lowered or removed.

The slow melting of monopoly restrictions in providing regulated cable and telephone services is leading to new service, which makes it the obvious example. Fluidity at the boundaries occurs throughout the telecommunications industry because the FCC and state regulators intervene in many aspects of telephone and cable. In addition, the history of antitrust problems leaves a legacy of restraint agreements, such as the Modified Final Judgment, the restrictions of which also are eroding with time.

## SOME ECONOMIC CONSEQUENCES OF CONVERGENCE

Despite the fact that the different kinds of convergence often occur in tandem, discussing them separately allows us to distinguish clearly between their very different economic effects, particularly the effects on market concentration.

Consider convergence in substitutes at the production stage. As products become increasingly substitutable for each other, more firms begin to occupy the same market. The TV and PC markets, for example, are now populated by firms that were formerly active in only one or the other market. Thus, there is a clear decline in market concentration in each of the formerly distinct TV and PC markets. Virtually every example of convergence in substitutes (that we know of) results in widening technical opportunities, enlarging the potential points of entry to a market and increasing its competitiveness. The form of this expansion will differ across markets, however. It can take the form of racing to extend the functionality of products.[17] It can also be a combination of extending and filling in the product space, which usually coincides with reduction in price/performance.[18] In either case, the set of products available to consumers expands, as does the functionality associated with those products.

Changes in market concentration that accompany convergence in complements at the production stage make a wholly different set of considerations relevant. Definitions at market boundaries are often unclear in this situation because the markets themselves are still taking shape. The products await development of new components and of system integration tools, and the standardization of interfaces. Convergence in complements is a situation rife with technical uncertainty, since incremental technical change usually arrives slowly, from many sources, and with many failures before commercial success is widely realized.[19] Moreover, the rate and direction of technical change depend on whether standards are fixed and known. We observe rapid rates of technical change if technically complementary products are easy to produce, as when standards are easy to adopt. We observe slower improvements if technical standards are not well defined and raise so much uncertainty that no one can easily design new components.

Furthermore, the ownership of property rights to the technologies that enable components to work together raises critical issues for the long-term development of market structure. If technical standards are open, in the sense that nonproprietary technical standards exist and are widely used, then the industry is likely to become competitive as new vendors of components enter (e.g., PC component manufacturing). The locus of competition will be at the component level, as opposed to the system level. This is the pattern of the PC industry, where multiple specialist firms compete to provide different components for systems (e.g., disk drives, monitors, coprocessors of various kinds, software add-ons, etc.). Buyers wanting to customize these components for their own needs can purchase all of them not only from the provider of the overall PC product but also from independent component manufacturers.[20]

If, on the other hand, technical standards are closed, in the sense that a single firm owns proprietary rights to widely adopted standards, then market evolution depends on the strategies of the owner of the standard. The owner of technology may choose to limit entry into complementary component markets because exclusive knowledge of the technology can be used to maintain competitive advantage (IBM used this strategy to enhance its dominance in the markets for peripherals for mainframes). The owner of the technology may also provide and support a complete integrated system. This strategy may make the owner resist outsourcing any part of the system (this is the traditional model for large computer manufacturers).

Proprietary owners also may license out their technology liberally, inducing makers of subcomponents to support their standard. Such vendors have decided to make their revenue in only a few choice parts of the value chain. Owners of a technology also may intentionally design their products without proprietary features, effectively inviting entry into subcomponent markets.[21] We can also say that the strategy of the owner depends on market structure, potential competitors' reactions, legal restrictions, and many other factors. Therefore, where proprietary standards are important, it is especially difficult to predict dynamic market behavior associated with convergence in complements.

Convergence in substitutes at the distribution stage also changes market concentration. On the one hand, more firms now use the same distribution channel. For a given capacity of this channel, the price per unit of capacity rises. One possible outcome could be a shakeout among firms that had used the channel, now that they face higher distribution costs. The leaving of some would increase market concentration. On the other hand, the fact that more firms, which used a different channel in the past, now use a common channel implies that the costs of distribution have fallen for them (otherwise, they would be less likely to switch to the new channel). One can imagine a greater number of firms in equilibrium in this industry, with a corresponding fall in market concentration.

Convergence in complements could also occur at the distribution stage. Complementary technological developments might result in an increase in the capacity of the distribution channel. If there is excess capacity, one can imagine that the costs of distribution to all users would fall (by an amount that depends on the distribution of property rights among the owners of the channel capacity). Equilibrium concentration might then be lower.

## COOPERATION, COMPETITION, AND THE KINDS OF CONVERGENCE

Depending on the nature and location of convergence, incentives for cooperation and competition will differ. Some kinds of convergence afford greater motives for competition, while others favor cooperation. In discussing the implications of various kinds of convergence for a particular firm, we adopt the perspective that the firm is not vertically integrated into its procurement or distribution stages.

We group motives for cooperation into two broad categories. First are the resource-based explanations. Within this category, firms cooperate to (a) benefit from diverse knowledge bases, (b) access financial resources, or (c) access tangible nonfinancial assets. They may also cooperate to find use for existing infrastructure. The second category includes more dynamic explanations for cooperation. Firms cooperate to influence the way a particular standard emerges. They may form alliances, or they may invest in organizations that develop standards, or they may arrive at de facto cooperation on standards as a result of implicit agreements.[22]

Consider convergence in substitutes at the production stage. Since firms are pitted against relatively unfamiliar rivals, this kind of convergence is most likely to lead to increased competition. There are no resource-sharing incentives to cooperate.

All the action here is on the competitive front, and thus vendors may be easily blindsided. Any incentives to cooperate, if they exist, have to do with collusive arrangements designed to protect the value of existing resources in an industry filling up with new players. There are also incentives to (partially or fully) vertically integrate in order to control scarce distribution capacity or to access scarce production resources. Consider, for example, the following scenario: Product A now has functionality that brings it into competition with product B. Firm B is vertically integrated in distribution, firm A is not. Firm A will now have incentives to integrate distribution of product A to match product B, particularly if consumers are more familiar with purchasing product B in one location where A is not usually found. Similarly, if production of both A and B relies on scarce productive resources, there are incentives for firms to backward-integrate to control this resource.

Convergence in substitutes represents one of the most celebrated aspects of creative destruction: the unanticipated invention of entirely new ways of achieving a product of economic value. We wish to echo an observation often made by economists of industry evolution: it is generally in society's interest to keep open channels for developing and commercializing new ideas that threaten established products and ways of doing business. Since no firm likes to find itself in such an uncertain environment, all firms have incentives to cooperate in order to discourage (or slow down) rates of change.

With convergence in complements at the production stage, resource-based motives for cooperation abound, as firms seek to combine their assets in mutually advantageous ways that were hitherto impossible. Firms' knowledge assets are likely to change in value as component functionality expands. Therefore, firms scramble to enhance the value of sub-components that may contribute to a greater system. However, this is easier said than done. It requires close monitoring of technical developments and changes, and, by its nature, is very speculative.

Among dynamic reasons for cooperation, the clearest is the need to influence the shape of future standards, either to gain proprietary rights over them or to prevent rivals from doing so. Firms also may turn to cooperative mechanisms in an attempt to prevent being blindsided, a situation that arises if a firm does not perceive the utility of a potential complement and is preempted by a faster rival. Firms turn to alliances with potential component manufacturers to resolve these uncertainties. These alliances, as well as standards development organizations, provide forums for transmitting information and for coordinating decision-making on the design of complementary components.

On the competitive side of convergence in complements, there is room for a new kind of competitor. There is typically a large market opportunity for system integrators because of the considerable added value associated with making products work together (e.g., LAN system integrators today). Incentives to vertically integrate exist, but for different reasons than those in convergence in substitutes. Here, the motive is to control access to a scarce product that might be used with one's own product.

The public policy concerns connected with convergence in complements center on two related issues. Since property rights or standards may play a large role, convergence in complements gives rise to exclusionary behavior when competitors form an alliance. Second, alliances and organizations that develop standards can play a very healthy role when there are dynamic reasons for cooperation. Government policy should encourage the healthy aspects of cooperation while preventing the exclusionary aspects. As illustrated by the recent interaction between Microsoft and the Department of Justice, such trade-offs are likely to be a concern of public policy for some time to come.

The overall effect of convergence in substitutes and/or complements at the distribution stage is to raise or to lower the capacity of the distribution channel relative to the number of firms seeking access to it. Thus, with convergence in substitutes, firms that had hitherto used distinct channels now find it possible to use the same channel, potentially creating a scarcity of channel capacity. However, if there is an accompanying increase in channel capacity owing to convergence in complements, there may be a resultant surplus of channel capacity. In either case, there is room for cooperation between firms operating at different stages of the value chain, with the relative bargaining power of the firms and their channel providers varying according to the extent to which convergence has created channel scarcity/surplus.

Following removal of regulatory barriers, the situation may take on the characteristics either of convergence in substitutes or of convergence in complements. In general, removing regulatory barriers forces incumbent firms to evaluate their core assets. They may invest heavily in these assets to combat new substitutes, or they may be compelled to enter into alliances designed to protect these core assets. One additional implication favoring collusion between firms deserves mention. Theoretical work and empirical analyses specific to the airline industry have established that as firms face each other in multiple markets, the threat of retaliation against a firm initiating aggressive competitive tactics is magnified, leading to a reduction in such behavior.[23] As regulatory barriers dissolve and firms begin to face each other in multiple markets, the prospect of retaliation may blunt the effect of increased competition.

Several implications result from this analysis:

- Not all types of convergence increase incentives for cooperation. For example, convergence in substitutes usually decreases them.

- Many kinds of cooperation have little to do with convergence, but many motives for cooperating are misunderstood without understanding convergence.

- Competitive blindsiding is likelier because of convergence in substitutes. Firms may also be blindsided by convergence in complements if new functionality results and has broad appeal.

- Convergence in complements gives rise to exclusionary behavior when competing firms form an alliance and exclude one or more other competitors. Otherwise, cooperation among firms should be encouraged in markets undergoing this type of change.

- Government has two opportunities to change the rate and direction of convergence. First, it can influence the removal of regulatory barriers. The recent redefinitions of restrictions on the lines of business of local telephone exchanges is an obvious example. Second, government may or may not influence the use of alliances and mergers.

## APPLYING THE FRAMEWORK

To explore the usefulness of our analytic framework, we have chosen to apply it to an open question of great importance: how the various pieces of the much-heralded information superhighway will end up relating to each other. First, we sketch out a simplified map[24] of a cross section of the superhighway, then we use our distinctions between the kinds of convergence to examine the collaborative agreements being signed between telephone and cable companies. We especially try to make sense of some of the newsworthy strategic and policy implications that arise from these cooperative agreements.

## Information Superhighway: Sketch of a Cross Section

There are three types of actors in this cross section. At one end of a chain of events are the content producers (Hollywood studios, retailers, video game producers, educational software producers). In the middle, this content is distributed through AT&T's nationwide long-distance network or some other medium. We call this segment transmission stage interaction (TSI), referring principally to the interaction between the telephone and cable companies and the computer network providers. Finally, there is the reception stage interaction (RSI): the competition and cooperation going on between firms that try to create ways to help the end user navigate through the influx of data. How are these firms organized, and what will they sell?

At the content-producing end, firms such as AT&T and others propose to act as clearinghouses for these data by building networks of digital storage devices around the country that will store and update all the content. While it is not yet clear what information will make up most of the content in the commercially successful networks of the future, most of the incipient experiments include such things as new services, airline and entertainment schedules for local areas, government statistics, online search networks such as Nexus and Lexus, E-mail bulletin boards, and any digital information that a consumer might want to download from the World Wide Web: books, pictures, musical performances, movies, even an exercise video.

In the middle, TSI is concerned with the common agenda of transmitting information to the end user. Historically, cable companies have transmitted video, phone companies have transmitted voice (and data through modems), and computing network providers and system integrators have found ways to attach their networks to existing telephone networks. However, three classes of technological developments (data manipulation and compression techniques from the computer industry, developments in fiber optics, and advances in digital switching technology) have made it technically feasible for cable and telephone companies to transmit all kinds of data, blurring the technological distinction between a network/system integrator and a telecommunications/cable firm. Only government restrictions continue to preserve traditional separation between these products.

At the far end, variations on the appliances that will be used in navigating the information highway are available: personal digital assistants

(PDAs) such as Apple's Newton, newfangled digital TVs, videophones, variations on video game players, and personal computer software. It is not yet obvious which of these devices will dominate, whether one or many will dominate different types of activities, or whether any of them will acquire commercially profitable extra capabilities.

What makes these developments so unpredictable is that it is not clear how they will all fit together in delivering a final product. From the consumer's standpoint, there is still little more than confusion, interrupted by the introduction of an occasional new product or toy with benefits that are exaggerated and a use that is not quite as easy as indicated. From the vendor's viewpoint, speculation and betting run high because design and operation decisions at one stage have consequences for design and operation decisions at other stages. Moreover, even though there are few customers today, decisions today may influence the direction of technical change for years, freezing out the slow movers. Whoever wins TSI will have a big say in the hardware device that wins RSI.[25] Thus, it is no surprise that computer companies involved in RSI have begun to form alliances with players involved in TSI, and vice versa: each wants to influence the other.

## Collaborative Agreements and the Kinds of Convergence

The collaborative agreements that phone and cable companies are currently signing with one another can easily be understood in light of the motives provided by the kinds of convergence we have distinguished. First, convergence in substitutes at the production stage has already occurred. There is no longer any meaningful technological distinction between each firm's ability to carry voice and data transmissions.[26] Moreover, the lowering of regulatory barriers opens up opportunities for both types of firms. Phone companies want to benefit from the experience that cable companies have with accessing home users, while cable companies, desiring to introduce interactivity to film-watching, are increasingly interested in the experience of phone companies with switching technologies. Thus, each each type of firm's knowledge assets can potentially be utilized more effectively in concert with the other type of firm's knowledge assets, a case of convergence in complements at the production stage.

Second, there is also convergence in substitutes in the distribution stage. Phone companies want to collaborate with cable companies. This convergence arises from the fact that both voice and video can now be transmitted using the same distribution channel. Currently, local phone companies receive 90 percent of their profits from wired phone service.

Because they realize that people are switching to wireless communication, their partnership with cable companies is at least partially motivated by the hope of keeping their land lines humming with all kinds of interactive services.

A third reason for the collaboration has to do with getting around regulatory barriers. Historical regulatory regimes have forbidden phone companies from operating in each other's geographic territories. However, local Regional Bell Operating Companies (RBOCs), through their alliances with cable companies that have subscribers all over the country, can access rival phone companies' territories as well. Thus, their cooperation is an indirect way around the restrictions on customer base overlap placed by the regulatory framework.

Of course, this is a simplification of the particular set of reasons that might underlie a given collaborative agreement between a phone company and a cable company. Currently, there appear to be at least two approaches to collaboration taken by cable companies.[27] The degree to which a particular kind of convergence is important varies according to the approach. One approach is exemplified by Time Warner, which has allied itself with an RBOC (US West) and has chosen to stay away from wireless telephony. Instead, it focuses on developing selected telephone markets, an approach at least partially influenced by the heavy concentration of its cable subscribers. US West provides technical expertise and funds to help Time Warner upgrade its cable wires for local phone service. The second approach is exemplified by cable companies, such as TCI, that are betting on wireless. Thus the long-distance phone company Sprint, along with TCI and other cable companies, is trying to develop nationwide cable, local, long-distance, and wireless services.

Some crucial public policy issues underlie this situation. First, it is hard to imagine that a free hand for cooperative agreements between phone companies and cable companies is the appropriate policy. Part of the motivation of the participants in cooperative agreements is to protect the value of existing infrastructure, as when all firms try to stave off the competitive consequences of convergence in substitutes. If that occurs at the expense of slowing a general move away from wireline and toward wireless communication, probably the end users and society as a whole will suffer the consequences. We are certainly not the only observers to note this. However, efforts to delay the onset of convergence in substitutes is one of the main policy dangers here.

Second, the emergence of technical standards in one of or both TSI and RSI raises a public policy question. Our framework has an implication for this debate. Cooperation among firms developing technical standards should receive flexible antitrust treatment when there is no danger of exclusionary behavior. For example, cooperative cross-licensing arrangements between close technologies should be encouraged by the FCC and related government bodies, particularly in the absence of well-defined standards.

However, our framework identifies the key policy conflict in this environment. There is a public interest in fostering cooperation that leads to development of new standards for the purpose of developing new products—the more convergence in complements, the greater the technological advances we are likely to see. However, it is not uncommon for new products to embody proprietary technologies that discourage cooperation between firms. On the one hand, proprietary standards enhance the returns to new technology and the likelihood of new product development. On the other hand, they delay the convergence in complements that leads to greater cooperation from different RSI and TSI vendors. We think that this conflict is endemic to convergence on the information superhighway and that government actions, either good or bad, can alter the outcome of this conflict. Unlike some of the more polemic trade press (about government policies in converging industries), our analysis shows why there is no simple solution: either much intervention or none at all. Sometimes government intervention, principally by the FCC or Justice Department, will be justified solely on theoretical economic grounds and sometimes not; the economic merits of this intervention must be weighed in a case-by-case basis.

Finally, it appears that barriers between customer bases will inevitably dissolve. Artificial restraints on this eventuality will merely succeed in delaying its realization, because firms will continue to expend valuable resources to find ways around the restraints. We see few public policy reasons for this delay except, perhaps, to foster the development of standards for interconnection at local telephone exchanges. Aside from this one issue, most of this goal was enhanced by FCC-mandated standards in the customer-premises equipment market several decades ago, and there seems to be little scope for similar action by the FCC today.[28]

## SUMMARY

This essay identifies two distinct types of convergence—convergence in substitutes and convergence in complements—and stresses the importance of appreciating where, in the chain of activities of a firm, the convergence occurs. In explicitly focusing attention on the different ways in which industry boundaries may be fluid, we move away from the traditional focus of studying evolution within well-defined boundaries. We have tried to clarify when these different kinds of convergence might occur together, and have argued that, despite this, the analytical distinctions are important inasmuch as they help us identify very different economic effects. In particular, firms' incentives for cooperation and competition differ quite extensively, depending on the nature and location of convergence.

Throughout, we are concerned primarily with firms' responses to convergence of different various kinds and, peripherally, with policy implications that influence those responses. While we have focused on understanding firms' reactions to different kinds of convergence, the influence of firms' actions on the nature and location of convergence deserves much more attention, as does the issue of how individual firms shape the boundaries of their industries.

---

## NOTES

1. See Edward Ames and Nathan Rosenberg, "Technological Change in the Machine Tool Industry, 1840–1910," in Nathan Rosenberg, ed., *Perspectives on Technology* (Cambridge: Cambridge University Press, 1977).

2. Timothy Bresnahan, and Manuel Trajtenberg, "General Purpose Technologies: Engines of Growth?" *Journal of Econometrics* 65 (January 1995): 63–108.

3. See, for example, W. J. Abernathy and James M. Utterback, "Patterns of Innovation in Technology," *Technology Review* 80, no. 7 (1978): 40–47; Kim B. Clark, "The Interaction of Design Hierarchies and Market Concepts in Technological Evolution," *Research Policy,* 14, no. 5 (1995): 235–251.

4. See S. Klepper and E. Graddy, "The Evolution of New Industries and the Determinants of Market Structure," *Rand Journal of Economics* (Spring; 1995): Marco Iansiti and Tarun Khanna, "Technological Evolution, System Architecture, and the Obsolescence of Firm Capabilities," *Industrial and Corporate Change,* 2 (1995); and Tarun Khanna "Racing Behaviour: Technological Evolution in the High-End Computing Industry," *Research Policy* 24, no.6 (1995): 933–958).

5. See Timothy Bresnahan and Shane Greenstein, "Technological Competition and the Structure of the Computer Industry," CEPR Discussion Paper no. 315, Stanford University, June 1992, for further analysis.

6. Paul L. Robertson and Richard N. Langlois, "Modularity, Innovation, and the Firm: The Case of Audio Components," in Frederic M. Scherer and Mark Perlman, eds., *Entrepreneurship, Technological Innovation, and Economic*

*Growth: Studies in the Schumpeterian Tradition* (Ann Arbor: University of Michigan Press, 1992).

7. Andrew L. Friedman and Dominic S. Cornford, *Computer Systems Development: History, Organization and Implementation* (New York: John Wiley and Sons, 1989).

8. See Iansiti and Khanna; and Bresnahan and Greenstein.

9. *Wall Street Journal,* March 15, 1994.

10. Salomon Brothers report, Global Equity Research Division, "Interactive Multimedia: When Worlds Converge," 1994.

11. See, for example, "Hollywood Scuffle," *Business Week,* December 12, 1994.

12. As of 1991, 130,000 users subscribed to its home shopping, banking, rail and air reservations, and stock brokerage services. A. Brandenburger, M. Burnett, and J. Kou, "Power Play: Nintendo in 8-Bit Video Games," Harvard Business School Case, 1995.

13. Eli Noam, "From the Network of Networks to the System of Systems, an End of History in Telecommunications Regulation?" *Regulation,* November 1993, 26–33; and Robert W. Crandall, *After the Breakup: U.S. Telecommunications in a More Competitive Era* (Washington, D.C.: Brookings Institution, 1991).

14. "The Future Surveyed," *The Economist,* Anniversary issue, 1993.

15. Michael Porter, *Competitive Advantage: Creating and Sustaining Superior Performance* (New York: Free Press, 1985).

16. Some of Packard Bell's multimedia computers come equipped with cable-ready TV, answering machine, fax, stereo radio, and CD-ROM drive (*Business Week,* January 9, 1995).

17. Tarun Khanna, "Racing Behavior: Technological Evolution in the High-End Computing Industry," *Research Policy* 24, no.6 (1995): 933–958.

18. Manuel Trajtenberg, *Economic Analysis of Product Innovation: The Case of CT Scanners* (Cambridge, Mass.: Harvard University Press, 1990).

19. Nathan Rosenberg, "Uncertainty and Technological Change," in Ralph Landau, Tim Taylor, and Gavin Wright, eds., *The Mosaic of Economic Growth,* (Stanford, Calif.: Stanford University Press, 1996).

20. See Robertson and Langlois.

21. For examples, see Paul A. David and Shane M. Greenstein, "The Economics of Compatibility Standards: An Introduction to Recent Research," *Economics of Innovation and New Technology* 1 (1990): 3–41; and Shane, M. Greenstein, "Invisible Hands and Visible Advisors: An Economic Evaluation of Network Standardization," *Journal of the American Society for Information Science* 43, no.8 (1992): 538–549.

22. William Lehr, "Standardization: Understanding the Process," *Journal of the American Society for Information Science* 43, no.8 (1992): 550–555.

23. See Douglas Bernheim and Michael Whinston, "Multimarket Contact and Collusive Behavior," *Rand Journal of Economics* 21 (1990), for theoretical work; and W. Evans and I. Kessides, "Living by the 'Golden Rule': Multimarket Contact in the U.S. Airline Industry," *Quarterly Journal of Economics* (1994): 341-366 for empirical analyses.

24. For another overview of the landscape, see Hagel and Eisenmann (1994).

25. Julio Rotemberg and Garth Saloner, "Interfirm Cooperation and Collaboration," in Michael Scott Morton, ed., *Information Technology and Organizational Transformation* (New York: Oxford University Press, 1992), provides a strategic analysis of these concerns.

26. For example, see Noam.

27. See, for example, "Now, Time Warner Is a Phone Company," *Business Week,* November 21, 1994.

28. See Crandall.


# REFERENCES

Abernathy, W. J., and James M. Utterback. "Patterns of Innovation in Technology." *Technology Review* 80, no. 7 (1978): 40–47.

Ames, Edward, and Nathan Rosenberg. "Technological Change in the Machine Tool Industry, 1840–1910." In Nathan Rosenberg, ed., *Perspectives on Technology.* Cambridge: Cambridge University Press, 1977.

Bernheim, Douglas, and Michael Whinston. "Multimarket Contact and Collusive Behavior." *Rand Journal of Economics* 21 (1990).

Besen, Stanley M., and Garth Saloner. "Compatibility Standards and the Market for Telecommunications Services." In R. W. Crandall and K. Flamm, eds., *Changing the Rules: Technological Change, International Competition and Regulation in Telecommunications.* Washington, D.C.: Brookings Institution, 1988.

Brandenburger, A., M. Burnett, and J. Kou. "Power Play: Nintendo in 8-Bit Video Games." Harvard Business School case, 1995.

Bresnahan, Timothy, and Shane Greenstein. "Technological Competition and the Structure of the Computer Industry." CEPR Discussion Paper no. 315. Stanford University, June 1992.

Bresnahan, Timothy, and Shane Greenstein. "The Competitive Crash in Large Scale Commercial Computing." In Ralph Landau, Tim Taylor, and Gavin Wright, eds., *The Mosaic of Growth.* Stanford, Calif.: Stanford University Press, 1996.

Bresnahan, Timothy, and Manuel Trajtenberg. "General Purpose Technologies: Engines of Growth?" *Journal of Econometrics* 65 (January 1995): 63–108.

Clark, Kim B. "The Interaction of Design Hierarchies and Market Concepts in Technological Evolution." *Research Policy* 14, no.5 (1995): 235–251.

Cockburn, Iain, and Rebecca Henderson. "Racing to Invest? The Dynamics of Competition in Ethical Drug Discovery." *Journal of Economics & Management Strategy* 3, no.3 (1995).

Crandall, Robert W. *After the Breakup: US Telecommunications in a More Competitive Era.* Washington, D.C.: Brookings Institution, 1991.

David, Paul A., and Shane M. Greenstein. "The Economics of Compatibility Standards: An Introduction to Recent Research." *Economics of Innovation and New Technology* 1 (1990): 3–41.

Evans, W., and I. Kessides. "Living by the 'Golden Rule': Multimarket Contact in the U.S. Airline Industry." *Quarterly Journal of Economics* (1994): 341–366.

Friedman, Andrew L., and Dominic S. Cornford. *Computer Systems Development: History, Organization and Implementation.* New York: John Wiley and Sons, 1989.

Greenstein, Shane M. "Invisible Hands and Visible Advisors: An Economic Evaluation of Network Standardization." *Journal of the American Society for Information Science* 43, no. 8 (1992): 538–549.

Hagel, John, and Thomas Eisenmann. "Navigating the Multimedia Landscape." *The McKinsey Quarterly,* no. 3 (1993): 39–56.

Hammer, Michael, and James Champy. *Reengineering the Corporation.* New York: Harper Business, 1993.

Iansiti, Marco, and Tarun Khanna. "Technological Evolution, System Architecture, and the Obsolescence of Firm Capabilities." *Industrial and Corporate Change* 2 (1995).

Khanna, Tarun. "Racing Behavior: Technological Evolution in the High-End Computing Industry." *Research Policy* 24, no.6 (1995): 933–958.

Klepper, S., and E. Graddy. "The Evolution of New Industries and the Determinants of Market Structure." *Rand Journal of Economics,* Spring 1990: 27–44.

Lehr, William. "Standardization: Understanding the Process." *Journal of the American Society for Information Science* 43, no.8 (1992): 550–555.

Noam, Eli. "From the Network of Networks to the System of Systems: An End of History in Telecommunications Regulation?" *Regulation,* November 1993: 26–33.

Porter, Michael. *Competitive Advantage: Creating and Sustaining Superior Performance.* New York: Free Press, 1985.

Robertson, Paul L., and Richard N. Langlois. "Modularity, Innovation, and the Firm: The Case of Audio Components." In Frederic M. Scherer and Mark

Perlman, eds., *Entrepreneurship, Technological Innovation, and Economic Growth: Studies in the Schumpeterian Tradition*. Ann Arbor: University of Michigan Press, 1992.

Rosenberg, Nathan. "Uncertainty and Technological Change." In Ralph Landau, Tim Taylor, and Gavin Wright, eds., *The Mosaic of Economic Growth*. Stanford, Calif.: Stanford University Press, 1996.

Rotemberg, Julio, and Garth Saloner. "Interfirm Cooperation and Collaboration." In Michael Scott Morton, ed., *Information Technology and Organizational Transformation*. New York: Oxford University Press, 1992.

Salomon Brothers report, Global Equity Research Division, "Interactive Multimedia: When Worlds Converge," 1994.

Trajtenberg, Manuel. *Economic Analysis of Product Innovation: The Case of CT Scanners*. Cambridge, Mass.: Harvard University Press, 1990.

CHAPTER 6

# CREATING VALUE AND SETTING STANDARDS

*The Lessons of Consumer Electronics*
*for Personal Digital Assistants*

Anita M. McGahan
Leslie L. Vadasz
David B. Yoffie

One might describe the late 1970s and early 1980s as the decade of consumer electronics, and the mid-1980s through the mid-1990s as the decade of the personal computer. During this period, the PC emerged as the dominant technology device at work, at school, and in the home. While the PC has been widely recognized as a business and educational tool, it is not as well appreciated as an entertainment and communication device. This perception is bound to change. By 1994, more than 40 percent of the personal computers sold in the United States were purchased for home use.

In the 1980s, the same technologies that made possible advances in processing power were also applied to achieve greater portability and lower cost of manufacture. The first manifestations of this effort were the electronic organizers that have flooded the market since the mid-1980s. Sharp's Wizard and Casio's Boss are perhaps the best-known products in this class, but Hewlett-Packard and many others have sought to bring some of the rudimentary functions of the personal computer into the

*We are grateful to Greg Keller for research assistance, and to the Division of Research of the Harvard Business School for financial support.

realm of handheld devices. These lightweight gadgets carry low prices (usually around $300), require relatively modest computing resources, and boast long battery lives, but have limited compatibility with PCs and limited input capabilities (tiny keyboards and pens).

While computing technology drove the business and consumer markets through the early 1990s, opportunities in communications technology raised new challenges. Local area networks, pagers, cellular phones, and the development of infrastructure for accessing data through landline wireless networks have created a new frontier for makers of computers, consumer electronics products, and even telephones. A new market is emerging for portable, lightweight products that perform sophisticated computing functions, interface with the installed base of computers, and access data through various communications networks anytime and anywhere. Buyers are demanding that these devices be manufactured and delivered to the customer cheaply. The generation of products designed to meet this demand offers significant improvements over electronic organizers and have been called by many names, including personal digital assistants (PDAs), personal communicators, and mobile companions. Many analysts agree that these handheld devices will complement the personal computer as a key technology device for both business and personal use.

Despite the new features and convenience promised by the current generation of these products (here dubbed PDAs), market acceptance has been disappointing. Through the mid-1990s, users have been reluctant to purchase PDAs because of high prices and immature technology. Much of the performance pledged by the pioneering firms, particularly Apple Computer and AT&T, has not yet materialized. Handwriting recognition is poor, little application software is available, and communications capability is limited and expensive. PDAs may yet catch on, but there are several missing ingredients. One prerequisite for mass acceptance is a ubiquitous wireless network with a wide range of complementary services. Features that can make PDAs irresistible will be the delivery of services and functions—along with powerful messaging and communicating capability—wherever and whenever a user wants.[1]

If the PDA is to become another mass product like the TV, PC, or cellular phone, buyers must also perceive the emergence of a standard that guarantees compatibility both across devices and with forthcoming releases of software. Emergence of a standard will attract software developers with the promise of access to large numbers of prospective customers.

The interaction of these two effects—the availability of complementary services and the establishment of a standardized interface between hardware and software—will generate the momentum required for PDAs to deliver real consumer value. Of course, standards are also necessary to allow communication with the installed base of computers, fax machines, and other related products. To date, standards have not been developed for PDAs. In the same way that the lack of a dominant standard impeded rapid adoption of new technologies in consumer electronics and early personal computers, a multiplicity of standards in PDAs will impede rapid market acceptance.

Although the first generation of PDAs has clearly failed, new generations may eventually become as commonplace as the TV or the PC. This paper argues that firms working on the new generations of PDAs can learn from the triumphs and failures of previous efforts in consumer electronics over the past fifty years. The broadest lessons from consumer electronics can be summarized in two propositions. First, to achieve mass penetration, PDAs will have to offer compelling value in combination with complementary services like wireless communications and on-line services. Second, once PDA manufacturers have defined a product of compelling value, they must develop standards. When both of these conditions are met, customers may perceive that PDAs offer greater value than existing products like portable PCs and electronic organizers.

The conditions required for PDAs to generate complementarities and to establish standards are integrally related. Manufacturers of PDAs, like makers of other consumer electronic products, must confront the reality of network effects: PDAs will become increasingly valuable when other users adopt the product. Network effects are important to market development for several reasons. First, the variety and range of available software will increase with the number of users. This response has been endemic in consumer electronics. Recording companies offered a greater variety of titles on compact discs as sales of hardware grew, for example. Similarly, software that enhances the utility of the PDA will grow as the user base expands. Just as the greater variety of CD titles induced additional buyers to purchase the CD hardware, so more software will induce greater purchases of PDAs. The diffusion of network effects among PDA users will also corroborate the value generated through interaction with complementary services and systems.

Network effects are important for a second reason: the costs of learning to use a PDA will decline as usage increases. By the late 1980s, new users of personal computers typically relied on coworkers and extensive information in the press for advice on adopting the technology.

Finally, network effects will drive down the cost of distribution and service through growing competition and higher volumes. For example, as televisions became popular in the 1950s and 1960s, an ancillary service industry emerged that lowered maintenance costs and encouraged additional adoption.

To explore these themes, this paper is divided into three sections. In the first section, we briefly describe the history of PDAs, with a particular focus on Apple and AT&T—the pioneers of the concept. We will focus on their visions for the products, their divergent strategies for creating compelling value in connection with established products, and their approaches to creating standards. Although no single optimal strategy dominates all others in the market for PDAs, we believe that the strategies adopted by the pioneers did not fully reflect available information about the prospects for market development. In particular, their approaches were not fully informed by the experiences of consumer electronics firms. In the second section of the paper, we explore the successes and failures in defining products and developing standards in several consumer electronics industries over the last fifty years. The analysis examines efforts to develop new product categories in FM radio, 8-track cassettes and audiocassettes, video recorders, videodiscs, and compact discs. In the third section of the paper we derive some generalizations about the role of several important variables, including first-mover advantages, open versus proprietary strategies, and the significance of backward compatibility for market acceptance. Finally, we draw conclusions about the future for creating value and standards in PDAs.

## DEVELOPMENT AND EVOLUTION OF PDAS

The original idea for the PDA came from two distinct trajectories: wireless communication devices, such as cellular phones, and personal computers. Visionaries in both industries saw the possibility of making cellular phones smarter and computers pocket-sized. As with many new product categories, the companies that have introduced PDAs began with a dream and a wish—a dream for the next new hit product that would take the market by storm and a wish to be the standard-bearer, the RCA of radio, the Sony of CD players, the Microsoft of operating systems. More than a year after the initial introduction of PDAs, companies were still dreaming and wishing. By the end of 1994, the largest entrants into the market included Apple, AT&T, Tandy, Casio, Sharp, Motorola, and IBM and Bell South. Despite the fact that none of the available products had a compelling feature set, and clearly no standard has yet emerged, industry analysts estimated that roughly one hundred thousand units were shipped in 1993, and that shipments would more than double in 1994 and double again in 1995.[2]

The early pioneers of the PDA were Sharp and Casio, the companies that introduced the electronic organizer in the 1980s. Little more than calculators and electronic appointment books that included calendars, schedules, and address directories, these products were sold in niche markets, often to business executives, for approximately $300. By the early 1990s, companies were introducing a new generation of more powerful electronic organizers. Hewlett-Packard, for example, introduced its 95-LX, which included a built-in Lotus 1-2-3 spreadsheet; and Psion and Poqet PC offered products with powerful text editing features. But even these new electronic organizers had serious limitations, including difficult data entry functions, poor connectivity features, and limited compatibility with the installed base of personal computers. Despite the fact that hundreds of thousands of these products were sold over the years, electronic organizers were often perceived as little more than "electronic toys." Widespread anticipation of a mass market in this category did not emerge until Apple Computer CEO John Sculley raised expectations for the PDA in 1992.

## The Computer Trajectory: Apple's Newton

The term PDA was coined by John Sculley at the Las Vegas Consumer Electronics Show in January 1992. Sculley's original idea was to call the device a "personal communicator," but the acronym "PC" was already taken.[3] Like the first radio, the first black-and-white TV, and the first consumer videocassette recorders, Apple's concept for the PDA was to break new ground; to move beyond the personal computer to take advantage of the merging of telecommunications, computing, and data content. Apple's promise was exciting: it would offer a handheld wireless device that would interpret common human (rather than esoteric computer) commands; link personal files, addresses, and lists; convert handwriting into digital type; and communicate easily via phone, fax, or modem to the rest of the world through landlines or cellular connections. Sculley's message was to create compelling value to the typical consumer and make the PDA the next great consumer product.

Starting around 1987, Apple's Advanced Technology Group began to explore the feasibility of a device that would be an order of magnitude less expensive than a computer ($300 vs. $3,000 at the time), small, and mobile. The original product concepts ranged from a pocket fax machine to the first digital consumer electronic gadget. Within Apple's laboratories, there were two parallel efforts along these lines in the late 1980s: the first was primarily a software effort to facilitate wireless communications; the second, originally under Jean Louis Gassée, was an integrated hardware–software project focused on building an expensive (about $8,000), high-powered, portable device. Although the two technologies were distinct, they were highly complementary.

Nonetheless, in the spring of 1990, Apple made two sequential decisions that led it in opposite directions. The first was to spin off the software project in newly created General Magic. Apple—under financial pressure at the time—retained a financial interest in the partnership, but the spin-off reduced its cash drain and gave General Magic more credibility in creating independent telecommunications standards. Then, about three months later, Sculley decided to keep the Newton project, but only if it met several conditions: the product could not be another computer—it would not have a keyboard, lots of memory, or a hard disk. In addition, it would have to be "cheap"—less than $1,500. In other words, the Newton would break new ground.

The vehicle for breaking new ground emerged in the fall of 1991, when there appeared to be great enthusiasm in the industry for pen-based computing. Start-up companies like EO and GO were raising significant amounts of venture capital to make the power of computing accessible, through pen input, to the millions of people scared of a keyboard. Sculley's desire to capture this enthusiasm led him to two moves that he later said would "haunt the Newton forever." First, in announcing the Newton and introducing the category of PDA, Sculley described the market for all converging technologies as an untapped *$3.5 trillion* market. He was quoted by the press as seeing a $3.5 trillion market for products like PDAs. Sculley thus stimulated imitation more than a year before the product would be available. Second, the announcement of Newton at the Consumer Electronics Show led to the assumption that it would be a mass consumer product, even though management had not yet decided on Newton's ultimate positioning. Moreover, the product was hyped as a notepad, with handwriting recognition as the key feature. Despite the original concept of a personal communicator with artificial intelligence and fax and phone capabilities, handwriting became the defining characteristic. In essence, as we will see later in the discussions of the videodisc, digital tape, and other consumer products, the Newton had been overpositioned.

When the Newton ultimately hit the market, it was late and performed badly compared with the expectations set by Sculley. Under great pressure to get a product to the market by the summer of 1993, Apple failed to deliver many of the feature sets it promised. The handwriting recognition, while better than virtually any other product on the market, still suffered from unacceptably low quality for the average user. Furthermore, a driving force behind the PDA was the integration of communications into a computing device; the first Newton, however, had limited communications capabilities that came at an unacceptably high premium for an already overpriced product.

The initial problems with the Newton created a new industry term, the "dreaded Newton effect."[4] According to one industry analyst, "the Newton couldn't possibly live up to the hype Apple put out about it. Consumers felt betrayed."[5] Microsoft's Chairman William H. Gates was quoted as saying the Newton may have "set the category back a couple of years."[6] In essence, the Newton was little more, and some even argued a little less, than an expensive electronic organizer.

Although Apple's early efforts to produce a consumer product of compelling value had clearly failed, an argument could be made that Sculley created enthusiasm for the category, which generated interest among software developers; that interest in turn, could help Apple build demand and create a standard. Apple's management understood that creating a standard was critical for Newton's ultimate success. An abundance of software and services was necessary to drive demand, and making Newton a dominant standard was one of the keys to generating such software and services.

Although Apple had been the prototypical closed computer company in the 1980s and early 1990s, Sculley's vision for Newton was different from the start: Apple *wanted* to create a *relatively* "open" standard. Rather than own all aspects of the hardware and software environment, as it did for the Apple II and the Macintosh, Sculley's strategy underlying the Newton was to license all of the key component technologies and get a royalty slice of each layer. The core of the strategy was that Apple would define the hardware and operating system standards, but allow licensees, with limitations, to sell virtually identical compatible products head-to-head against the Newton (figure 6-1).

Figure 6-1 shows Apple's standard-setting strategy. At the bottom of the chain, Apple codesigned the microprocessor (the ARM chip) and supporting chips (ASICs) with a British company, but would make them widely available. ARM would have multiple manufacturers, such as Texas Instruments, Sharp, VLSI Technology, GEC Plessy, and Cirrus Logic, to ensure competitive pricing and supply. Next, Apple would develop the Newton operating system and hardware design, then license both to *selected competitors*. Sharp Corporation of Japan would manufacture the

FIGURE 6-1

APPLE'S STANDARD-SETTING STRATEGY

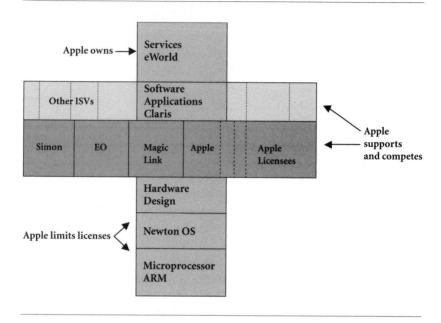

first product and be among Apple's first licensees. Other licensees included Motorola and Siemens, followed by Toshiba and Matsushita. (One year after the Newton's introduction, only Sharp had introduced a Newton-like product, with fifteen thousand units shipped in its first year; Siemens and Motorola produced complementary products that relied on Newton technology.) Apple would also develop applications and developer kits, which it would license and sell to independent software vendors. The only part of the food chain Apple would own outright was eWorld, Apple's proprietary on-line services. Newton and Macintosh users would subscribe directly, and the Newton would ultimately connect to eWorld through various channels, including wireless connections such as Skytel.

A second thrust of Apple's strategy was to create links with the installed base of computers. For the Newton or any PDA to be a mass-marketed product, Apple would need to ensure its ability to interact with other devices that handled relevant information. First-generation products had limited capacity to communicate with PCs using Windows, but were somewhat easier to connect to Macintoshes. As a result, it was not surprising that the vast majority of early adopters of the Newton were Macintosh users. Yet for the Newton strategy to work, Apple had to go beyond its current installed base.

Another part of Apple's strategy was to disseminate pieces of the technology around the world to create the infrastructure and platform for future development. For example, part of the agreement with Siemens was to integrate Newton technology with Siemens's Rolm PBX switches.[7] Apple also planned to work jointly with Toshiba on next-generation data processors for advanced telecommunications functions for the Newton; and Apple extensively supported independent software vendors. By June 1994, Apple claimed that more than three thousand developers were working on applications for the Newton; only half were Macintosh developers, and 15 percent were developers for Microsoft's Windows. Despite the slow start, many analysts remained optimistic. Pointing out that the Macintosh took two generations before it took off, one noted: "It will take two or three iterations before these things are any good, [t]he grandson of Newton will be a great product."[8]

Leveraging the great anticipation, Apple sold 50,000 units in the first month, but the number dropped to 7,500 over the next four months. By July 1994, only ninety thousand had been sold.[9] Subsequently, Apple introduced new versions of the Newton with better handwriting recognition, more built-in communication functions, lower prices, and longer battery life. However, without extensive communications capability that connected to services with real consumer value, the product remained a fancy electronic organizer. In the summer of 1994, Apple repositioned the existing product, with some success, as a handheld computer for mobile professionals, such as sales reps who want to keep track of data. Apple's CFO noted, "We always knew that there'd be business users for the Newton. But our marketing message and approach at the launch was wrong."[10] In the first quarter of 1995, Apple began to ship the second Newton model, the MessagePad 120. The basic price was under $700. In addition to the pen input, it had an optional keyboard and accepted a PC card for either memory expansion or fax/modem capability. The communication capabilities began to offer some of the features originally promised, including wireless connections to eWorld, ARDIS, NewtonMail, and AT&T messaging. Despite these improvements, Apple continued to suffer from two key problems: its initial positioning, which created expectations of value that still had not been fully met, and its inability to generate momentum around a standard.

## The Communications Trajectory: AT&T's EO

While Apple delivered a computing device that would eventually offer communications, AT&T sought to give a communications device the power of a computer. AT&T's thrust into this market came in mid-1993 when EO, a small Silicon Valley start-up in which AT&T was a major investor, introduced the personal communicator, the EO 440 and the EO 880. In 1994, EO announced major layoffs and a redirection in its strategy, including the discontinuation of further development of its personal communicators.

What were the factors leading to these events? The origin of EO goes back to the formation of GO Corporation in 1987. This venture-backed company was formed to develop a new, innovative operating system, which among its features included a pen-based input interface. In order to demonstrate the capabilities of the new operating environment, GO also developed a prototype tablet with a 16-bit microprocessor (Intel 286) and a liquid crystal screen for both output and pen-based input.

Along the way, AT&T became one of the corporate investors in GO. In 1991, EO was founded by former GO employees with AT&T, venture capital, and other corporate investments. By mid-1993, AT&T had a majority stake and the EO personal communicators were launched. Unlike the Newton, which was originally targeted to the mass market, the EO was aimed at corporate customers. Given AT&T's core business, it was not surprising that the products were rich in communication features. Both land-line and wireless capabilities were included. The products could do voice, data, and fax communication. They included speakers and voice recording. All this was supported by the GO operating system, running on AT&T's 32-bit microprocessor (the AT&T Hobbit), and a fair amount of memory, including a hard disk. Expansion capability was supported through PCMCIA slot(s). All these capabilities required some compromise: the size of these machines was quite large (from 10.8 by 7.1 by 0.9 inches to 13 by 9 by 1.1 inches), and they weighed from 2.2 to 4.1 pounds, which meant they were not pocket-sized. Furthermore, battery life was about four hours, a relatively short time for mobile corporate users. And the costs were considerable: the cheapest, stripped-down model was over $1,500, and the top of the line approached $4,000.

The machine received both praise and criticism. Although it had advanced communications features, some problems were not satisfied by ease of use. One could attribute much of the criticism to typical first-generation issues, which resulted in added hurdles to acceptability. Hand-writing recognition was—as for all products in the current generation of machines—a real annoyance. Although the initial focus was on corporate purchases, the machine lacked compatibility with personal computers used by most corporations. For noncomputer users, the machine, although advertised as having many easy-to-use capabilities, was still quite complex. Since the new machine used a new operating environment, there were few applications available. Furthermore, if vertical applications were the target, such applications required additional software development, which in turn required more investment in time and work. Of all the capabilities that existed in the marketplace, the only complementary assets that the machines could utilize immediately were the telephone and cellular infrastructures. In sum, the products did not offer a compelling enough value at the price. During 1993, an estimated four thousand units were shipped,[11] making it difficult for AT&T to justify the ongoing investment. By the summer of 1994, AT&T announced that no further EO products would be shipped, leading to the collapse of EO as an ongoing enterprise.

Like Apple, AT&T had originally sought to create a new standard around its architecture (see figure 6-2). Whereas Apple's standard was built around the hardware design for Newton and the operating system, AT&T tried to build a standard around the Hobbit microprocessor.

FIGURE 6-2

AT&T's MODEL FOR EO

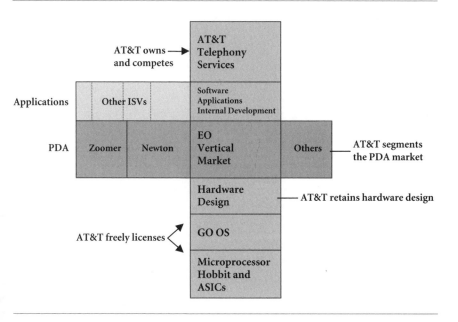

Through 1992 and 1993, it was aggressively promoting the Hobbit as the ideal low-powered, but fast, reduced instruction set computer (RISC) processor for the PDA market. In fact, Apple's earlier work on handheld computers was based on a predecessor of the Hobbit architecture.[12] One advantage of Hobbit as a standard setter over Apple's ARM architecture was that it was an open-market chip set available from AT&T. Furthermore, the GO operating system was available as an open-market product. Customers wanting to use the ARM architecture had access only to the CPU core, and had to develop their own chip sets for their systems. (Apple promised to make their chip sets and Newton operating system available to a limited number of partners.) AT&T, on the other hand, designed a family of Hobbit chips, which included the CPU and a number of support chips. AT&T was offering these as complete solutions, which did not require customers to develop their own chip set. With both the GO operating system and the Hobbit chip set available on the open market, one could have conceived of compatible products from a number of companies. However, by the time of EO's demise, no large company had announced plans to offer an EO-compatible product, and certainly none based on these technologies were available on the market.

The lack of momentum behind EO and Hobbit, as well as Newton and ARM, created a problem of scale for both companies. With limited volumes being shipped, the cost associated with developing and supporting these chip families became difficult. New generations of chip architecture require larger and larger investments. Unless Apple and its partners generated larger volumes to amortize the high fixed costs, Apple's semiconductor partners, as well as Apple and its licensees, would have to subsidize the ongoing development of ARM and the related chip sets. The problem for Hobbit was even more severe, since there was no stream of products that could support the ongoing development.

## The Forthcoming Battle for the PDAs

The slippage by Apple and the first-round failure by AT&T created a potential vacuum in the market for PDAs. In the second half of 1994, several firms, including Motorola, Sony, Casio, and a joint venture of IBM and Bell South,[13] introduced new products to occupy this vacuum. In addition, General Magic, the Apple spin-off, developed two key technologies that were filling some of the gaps. General Magic's MagiCap and Telescript were included in Motorola's and Sony's PDAs as well as AT&T's messaging services. Even original electronic organizers started to look like PDAs: for instance, in late 1994, Sharp introduced the Zaurus, a one-pound device with pen and keyboard input that offered a repertoire of communication and service options. As electronic organizers became smarter and more communicative, and PDAs proliferated and matured with greater funtionality, the line between these products began to blur.

All of these firms had to answer three big questions: (1) How should they define the PDA product to create a compelling value proposition that large numbers of consumers would desire? (2) A closely related question —which trajectory would offer the greater reward, the computer trajectory with an emphasis of tying to the installed base of PCs or Macs, or the telecommunications trajectory of adding functionality to the cellular phone? (3) Would standards be necessary for PDAs' widespread adoption, and how would those standards develop? The initial failures in the PDA market did not spell its ultimate doom. As we will see in the next section, false starts have been fairly common in similar industries. It is also uncertain whether Apple and AT&T can emerge as winners in the PDA market. AT&T has exited, at least temporarily. And Apple, having overpositioned the initial product, still faces the classic Catch-22 for businesses with network externalities: without more Newtons and Newton-compatible hardware in the hands of consumers, software and services will not develop; but software and services will not develop until more Newtons are in the hands of users. Nonetheless, Apple has persevered, continuing to upgrade, promote, and refine the product positioning. In addition, recognizing the need for greater openness, Apple helped establish an eighteen-company PDA Industry Association, with the charter to conduct research and education, and to create standards.[14]

Although Apple made significant progress with the Newton since its introduction, many of its competitive advantages in PDAs were dissipated by its initial entry strategy. Real first-mover advantages have historically gone to companies that defined the categories, created the brand, and built an installed base of hardware with complementary assets (software and services). By 1994, most of those potential advantages had disappeared for the pioneer.

## LESSONS FROM CONSUMER ELECTRONICS

Many of the problems faced by Apple and AT&T reflect issues confronted by consumer electronics firms at the inception of market development for many products that later became blockbusters, and some that eventually failed. This section reviews the history of early market development in major consumer electronics industries, with attention to complementarities with established products and to the emergence of technological standards. The cases highlight the tension between adoption of hardware (i.e., radios, TVs, compact disc players) and software (e.g., broadcast programming, music recordings). In each case, the resolution of this tension had important implications for the widespread adoption of the technology.

## The Thirty-Year Struggle to Establish FM Radio[15]

In 1919, the Westinghouse Corporation founded the modern broadcast industry by establishing the first AM radio station to offer regular programming. The company soon replicated its formula for programming in other cities. Thomas S. W. Lewis, a historian of the industry, notes that "Westinghouse's plan was simple: create a demand for the equipment and then listeners will purchase the [company's] sets."[16] Westinghouse immediately faced competition in broadcasting from a newly formed company called the Radio Corporation of America (RCA). RCA was formed by General Electric, Westinghouse's principal competitor in the manufacture of electric equipment, with assets recently acquired from the Marconi Wireless Telegraph Company, a pioneer in broadcast technology. Although Marconi had been a pioneer in introducing the telegraph, it had not adapted the technology for broadcasting radio programs.

RCA held the rights to Marconi's original patents on radio technology and to General Electric's patents on equipment for transmitting radio signals. In the early 1920s, RCA made several agreements that solidified its advantages. First, it acquired a transmission patent from AT&T in 1920 in exchange for 10.3 percent of RCA ownership. The second agreement emerged after representatives from Westinghouse and RCA met to discuss the resolution of conflicts over their patents. The two firms agreed that RCA would obtain Westinghouse's transmitting stations and rights to several of Westinghouse's patents on receiver technology. RCA would subcontract 40 percent of its orders for transmitting and receiving equipment to Westinghouse. Westinghouse also obtained 20.6 percent ownership of RCA. With these agreements, two major firms with experience in complementary technologies came to control virtually all of the broadcast programming and equipment markets.

For several years, the two firms pursued strategies for widely disseminating the standardized AM radio sets at the same time that they promoted broadcast programming. In 1928, intervention by the Federal Trade Commission, which charged RCA with anticompetitive practices, led to a related 1932 settlement in which GE and Westinghouse relinquished their ownership of RCA and discontinued their manufacture of radio sets for two and a half years. The agreement did nothing to weaken RCA's strength in broadcast programming, and gave the firm a window of opportunity to increase its presence in the manufacture of radio equipment.

In 1933, Edwin Howard Armstrong, an established inventor of radio equipment, presented his old friend David Sarnoff, president of RCA, with a new opportunity. Armstrong had previously sold some of his AM radio patents to RCA, and had agreed to give RCA rights of first refusal on succeeding inventions. Armstrong's frequency-modulation technology, or FM radio, marked a significant improvement over AM radio in the quality of the transmission. The improvement was so great that it would eventually make possible the creation of regional networks through transmission of signals between stations.

From David Sarnoff's perspective, the disadvantages were twofold. First, FM radio would make RCA's existing investments in AM transmitting stations, as well as its customers' investments in AM receivers, obsolete. Annual radio sales by U.S. manufacturers had increased from 100,000 in 1922 to 3.8 million in 1933, worth $230 million at retail.[17] Annual billings for advertisements by American radio stations had grown from $4.8 million in 1927 to $57 million in 1933.[18] Although precise information on RCA's shares in these industries is not available, its Annual Reports from the period indicated 1933 revenues of $62 million, largely from products related to AM radio. In 1939, about $60 million of the firm's $110 million in revenues was attributable to manufactured products, including AM radio receivers and transmitters. RCA's wholly owned broadcast affiliates, the National Broadcasting Company (NBC) and the American Broadcasting Company (ABC), sold $45 million in advertisements in 1939.[19] The second disadvantage of FM, from Sarnoff's perspective, was that it would compete for consumers' resources with the impending introduction of television.

Between 1933 and 1937, Sarnoff asked Armstrong to perform tests and institute improvements in his FM technology. In 1937, Armstrong decided Sarnoff was stalling, and licensed the technology to General Electric. Several FM stations began to broadcast programs with transmitters manufactured by General Electric. In 1940, Armstrong speculated that FM would be more popular than AM in five years.

He was wrong. Four significant developments effectively blocked the dissemination of FM radio. First, RCA introduced television at the 1939 World's Fair in New York. The new product was promoted as the successor to radio. Second, Sarnoff and others at RCA convinced the Federal Communications Commission (FCC) to change the allocation of frequencies on the radio spectrum to accommodate television broadcasts. With a single decision in 1944, the entire existing infrastructure for FM radio became useless.[20] Third, consumers' incentives to purchase FM radios decreased when the FCC allowed the simultaneous broadcast of programs over both AM and FM channels.[21] Finally, the Columbia Broadcasting System, a competitor of RCA in AM programming, succeeding in convincing the FCC to limit FM stations in broadcasting to more than one local market. The stated rationale for the rule was to protect stations from remotely based competitors, but its effect was to quell the resurgence of FM technology.

Between the mid-1940s and the early 1960s, only a few FM radio stations operated in the United States. What delayed the introduction of FM radio? First, FM offered no significant complementarities with existing technologies. Firms that had invested in AM technology would have to replace their equipment, and consumers would have to purchase new receivers. The FCC's decision to allow simultaneous broadcast diluted the advantages of owning both AM and FM receivers. Finally, the FCC's decision to limit the range of FM broadcasts restricted the opportunity to achieve large-scale benefits through the simultaneous dissemination of software (i.e., broadcasting programs) and hardware (i.e., receivers). Thus, the decision essentially quelled the benefits of standardization.

## Color Television[22]

David Sarnoff and RCA were responsible for the widespread commercialization of television in the United States. Robert Sobel, an RCA historian, states that Sarnoff made public statements describing television as early as 1924.[23] Despite Sarnoff's forecasts, RCA did not unveil its first black-and-white television receiver to the public until 1939.

RCA delayed the introduction of its black-and-white television to avoid competition with AM radio and to allow it to obtain access to critical patents on equipment manufacture.[24] During the 1930s, television sets were built by amateurs to receive signals broadcast by NBC and CBS from New York. In 1938, a small firm run by entrepreneur Allen DuMont attempted to introduce a commercially produced television; he failed when NBC suspended the broadcast of television programs to counteract the threat.[25] Upon the introduction of RCA's set in 1939, NBC resumed broadcasting and expanded its programming schedule to include sports events and movies. By the end of the year, seventeen American companies sold television sets.

A landmark FCC decision in the mid-1940s changed the stakes in dissemination of black-and-white technology by opening the spectrum to accommodate a wider range of programs. In 1944, the FCC established new rules on the allocation of the radio spectrum to dedicate UHF for television broadcast, and to block FM broadcasts on the VHF bands that had been shared by FM and black-and-white television. CBS had lobbied for access to UHF to test color broadcasts.

The FCC's decision sparked competition to establish an installed base of television sets and to obtain programming revenue. RCA and NBC became champions of VHF-compatible technology. One reason that RCA promoted the VHF standard was that its existing manufacturing facilities and products had been designed to produce hardware that would receive only VHF broadcasts. Another was that the VHF band accommodated only twelve channels over which broadcasting could occur. UHF accommodated seventy channels. The possibilities for establishing a dominant position on VHF appeared to be much greater.[26] To promote acceptance of its products, RCA lowered its prices and licensed the technology for manufacturing television sets to competitors. Sobel estimated that RCA's share of the market for television sets dropped from 100 percent in 1946 to 12 percent in 1950.[27] Over the same period, the number of receivers sold by American manufacturers increased from 10,000 annually to 7.5 million annually; prices dropped from an average of $500 to $360.[28]

The establishment of a standard for color television followed a path that eventually became strikingly similar to the one that had emerged in black-and-white. In 1948, the newly appointed chairman of the FCC, Wayne Coy, began an investigation of the appropriate standards for color television. Approvals of new broadcast licenses were suspended until completion of the investigation. In 1949, the FCC approved broadcasts of color programs over UHF channels, to begin in 1950. The decision clearly favored CBS: NBC would have to make significant capital expenditures to convert its transmission equipment to UHF. In addition, the success of UHF would attract new broadcasters away from VHF, and could potentially make existing black-and-white VHF television sets obsolete.

Sarnoff and RCA resisted UHF through an industry association called the National Television Systems Committee (NTSC). Members of the group agreed not to build UHF sets and not to broadcast on UHF channels. RCA also initiated a lawsuit to stall the introduction of color broadcasts by CBS on UHF channels. During the delay, RCA continued research into broadcast technology that would allow transmission of color programs on VHF bands that could be received by existing black-and-white television sets. Sarnoff was hoping for a technical solution that would create complementarity between black-and-white and color television by allowing black-and-white viewers to benefit from the additional programming that would be introduced for color receivers.

In 1951, RCA's lawsuit was settled in favor of CBS. Prior to its resolution, CBS had acquired the manufacturing assets of a small producer of televisions with the intention of producing the sets necessary to stimulate demand for its color broadcasting. RCA and the other members of the NTSC then turned to another avenue to limit the threat from color. An NTSC boycott effectively guaranteed that no other major manufacturer would offer televisions to receive CBS's color broadcasts. CBS did introduce its television sets a few days after the Supreme Court's decision, but failed to sell them in volume. Four months later, its television sets were withdrawn from the market.[29] Without multiple hardware producers building to the same standard, and without a broad set of complementarities with existing products, CBS's system faltered.

At about the same time as the CBS introduction, RCA achieved a breakthrough in the development of a color broadcast technology that would allow existing black-and-white television sets built for the VHF standard to receive color signals. RCA promoted the system under the aegis of the NTSC. Even CBS acknowledged the new system's viability. In December 1953, the FCC adopted RCA's "tricolor" system as the VHF color standard. Although several manufacturers offered VHF color televisions in 1954, sales were disappointing. Between 1954 and 1959, annual sales of color televisions in the United States were no greater than one hundred thousand units per year. Besides high prices, the major impediments to widespread adoption were the lack of color programming and the relatively poor quality of color television sets. The 1955 review in *Consumer Reports* recommended that consumers wait for the next generation of color televisions before making purchases. It noted that color reception tended to fade with use, and that color sets did not reproduce black-and-white broadcasts with the same clarity as black-and-white televisions.[30]

In the late 1950s and early 1960s, both the broadcast networks and independent stations gradually increased color programming, and manufacturers improved the quality of television receivers. Although the improvements were gradual, the year 1960 marked a turning point in the sale of television sets. Between 1960 and 1965, annual sales of color televisions in the United States increased from 120,000 units to 2.7 million units.[31] This increase was accompanied by a dramatic increase in sales of black-and-white sets: in 1965, 8.4 million black-and-white TVs were sold, up from 5.7 million in 1960. Unit sales of black-and-white sets had decreased before 1960 from a peak of 7.7 million in 1955.[32] By 1965, prices of color sets had dropped only marginally from their introduction levels, and the market was dominated by the industry's first mover, RCA. By one estimate, RCA held a 42 percent share of the market for color televisions in 1965.[33]

## Cassette Tapes

The first tape recorders had been developed in Germany during the 1930s. Following the end of World War II, manufacturers in Germany, Britain, and the United States improved quality and began to market reel-to-reel tape recorders to radio stations and record companies.[34] As the industry developed in the 1950s, reel-to-reel products became popular among a small pool of classical music fans.

The first major breakthrough in consumer adoption of cassette tape came in 1963, when George Eash and Earl Muntz adapted existing 4-track cartridge tape systems for use in automobiles. Tape cartridges had been available for many years for business dictation and other uses, but had not become widespread for reproduction of music because their quality was too low. Eash and Muntz's adaptation was viable partly because the sound of a moving car masked many of the flaws in reproduction.

Shortly after Eash and Muntz introduced their 4-track system, Lear Jet promoted a different car system based on a similar concept that used 8-track cartridges. The Lear Jet system effectively lengthened playing time by recording on both sides of the tape: 8-tracks offered eighty minutes of programming, whereas the 4-track system offered only forty minutes. To encourage adoption of its system, Lear Jet struck an agreement with RCA to make available RCA's library of music titles on 8-track tapes. The agreement, which assured a supply of software that would be compatible with Lear's hardware standard, marked a turning point for the new format. The 8-track obtained hegemony over 4-track when Lear Jet won a contract with Ford to offer the system as an option on its 1965 automobiles.

In the mid-1960s, record companies actively encouraged widespread adoption of 8-track players. The systems were viewed as complements to long-playing records (LPs) because they offered a different combination of features: greater convenience but at the cost of quality in reproduction. The 8-track posed no direct threat to sales of LPs because they did not have recording capability. Consumers who wanted to play popular music on 8-tracks had no option but to purchase prerecorded tapes.

At the same time 8-tracks became popular in the United States, a different system became popular in Europe. Philips of the Netherlands had developed a small, dual-track cassette designed for business dictation. Although the system had recording capability, the quality of reproduction was not comparable with that of 8-tracks, and cartridges were incompatible with existing 8-track players. Nonetheless, the system became popular among teenagers in Britain for taping rock-and-roll music. Philips began to promote its cassette system for audio entertainment in the United States in 1966.

Philips faced two important challenges as it entered the U.S. market. First, Lear Jet had a lead of several years with the incompatible 8-track. Second, Philips had to contend with resistance to its format from record companies, which viewed the Philips cassette as a threat to the LP. Cassettes were perceived as a greater threat to LPs than 8-tracks because of their recording capability. Philips promoted sales of cassette machines by waiving all licensing fees to manufacturers. As a result, several chose to convert their production capacity from 8-tracks to the new cassette technology.[35] With the decision to license, Philips pursued a strategy that essentially forced record companies—the firms that controlled software —to issue product on the new standard because dissemination of hardware was so great.

Between 1965 and 1970, markets for 8-tracks and cassettes grew simultaneously. Automobile manufacturers continued to offer 8-tracks as options on new cars, and cassette systems became popular for home use, including the recording of radio broadcasts and LPs.[36] Through the late 1960s, sales of LPs also grew significantly. RCA and CBS, leaders in the publication of music on LPs, began to issue new releases on cassettes in 1969. Their move was interpreted as an endorsement of the new format.[37] By 1971, the sales volume of prerecorded cassettes reached ninety-six million, about 25 percent of 8-track volume.

During the late 1960s and 1970s, two major improvements in the quality of the cassette system contributed to its growth. First, TDK Electronics, a tape manufacturer, improved the quality of the tape itself. In 1969, the TDK SD line was marketed as the first high-fidelity cassette, and in 1971, TDK introduced chromium cassette tape, an improvement that allowed greater accuracy in reproduction of high-frequency recordings. TDK's advances initiated a continuing series of improvements in the quality of tape produced by specialized manufacturers in the 1970s.

The second major improvement in the cassette system was the Dolby system. Dolby was fundamentally an improvement in the method of recording, and therefore principally affected the hardware required for the tape system. Although a system called Dolby A was used in commercial applications in the 1960s, it did not become available on players for consumer use. In the 1970s, a different system, called Dolby B, became widely available.

The Dolby system and improvements in the quality of tape fueled the popularity of home recording of LPs for use in portable cassette decks and automobile systems. This popularity in turn created demand for frequency modulators and other ancillary hardware that allowed users to improve the quality of their recordings. Record companies attempted to stem home recording by offering prerecorded tapes that were designed for use in car stereos, systems that typically incorporated smaller speakers than those in the home. The effect of this effort was to reduce the quality of prerecorded cassette tapes, a development that inadvertently further encouraged home recording. A 1970 review in the *New York Times* noted that "a person owning a good cassette deck and premium tape can make better cassettes from records and FM than he can buy."[38]

In 1973, American consumers spent $76 million on prerecorded cassette tapes and $385 million on prerecorded 8-track tapes. They spent another $100 million on blank cassette tapes, which sold at about one-third the price of prerecorded tapes. The 8-track remained popular among older consumers who had invested in a library of cassettes for use in their automobiles. The cassette was associated with younger consumers, particularly teenagers, who had time to make home recordings and used the tapes in their homes.

The gradual shift toward the predominance of the cassette was driven by hardware: it occurred with increases in the sales of cassette decks over 8-track decks. By 1974, American consumers had bought fifteen million new tape decks for home use, about two-thirds of which were cassette decks and one-third were 8-track decks. In the same year, about five million new tape decks were sold for use in automobiles. Although 8-tracks were probably still more popular for automotive use, the automotive segment had been dwarfed by the home segment. Cassette decks had become more popular than 8-track decks.[39]

By the end of the 1970s, additional developments in the recording industry and the audio equipment industry sealed the fate of the 8-track, even though sales of 8-track tapes continued to outpace sales of prerecorded cassette tapes through the decade. Aggregate sales of prerecorded music on all formats—LPs, 8-tracks, and cassettes—grew less quickly after 1978 as the baby boom generation matured. As the recording industry increased prices on prerecorded music in all formats, in order to maintain revenue and compensate for home recording, consumers' preferences for home recording intensified. This development favored the cassette system over the 8-track system.

In 1979, Sony's introduction of the Walkman led to such a profusion of cassette hardware that the end of the 8-track became inevitable. The Walkman exploited a feature other than the recordability of the cassette: its small size. By 1983, sales of *prerecorded* cassette tapes reached $1.8 billion, exceeding those of both 8-tracks and LPs. Sales of blank tapes remained strong at $300 million. Analysts attributed the relative increase in sales of prerecorded cassettes to the fact that the Walkman and other new portable cassette players were not designed for recording, a fact consistent with the view that record companies may not have resisted cassettes to the same extent once the Walkman was popularized.

## Videocassette Recorders[40]

The first commercially available devices for recording television broadcasts were introduced in 1956 by the Ampex Corporation, a small research firm, at prices of about $50,000. By 1961, about nine hundred of the systems had been sold to schools, airlines (for in-flight movies), and other businesses that used the equipment in specialized applications. In the early 1960s, Ampex traded some of its patent rights to RCA and to Sony in exchange for access to the technologies for manufacturing televisions and transistors. Through the 1960s, none of these firms developed a video recorder that was widely adopted for home use. Video recorders remained specialty products used by institutions.

By 1971, Sony had developed a prototype for a home video recorder called the U-Matic. Tapes for the U-Matic were housed in self-contained cassettes instead of on reels. The new packaging made the product considerably easier to use. In 1970, representatives of Sony met with counterparts at JVC and Matsushita, two other Japanese firms known to have invested in the development of videocassette recorders for home use. In 1971, each of the three firms introduced products that conformed to the same standard, an adaptation of Sony's U-Matic design. Nonetheless, sales of the U-Matic were disappointing. Observers cited high prices and the unwieldiness of both the U-Matic machines and the tapes as reasons for slow adoption of the product. Consumers also may not have attached great value to the products because they were not viewed as strongly complementary to existing television systems. Unlike audio entertainment, viewers apparently preferred to watch their favorite shows at their scheduled times. Sony, JVC, and Matsushita terminated their joint development arrangements but sustained an agreement to exchange patent rights.

By 1974, Sony had developed a new videocassette recorder that it called Betamax or Beta to distinguish it from the earlier generation of U-Matic. Beta represented a substantial improvement: the tape was narrower and packaged in a smaller cassette, and the VCR player was smaller and cheaper to produce. In a 1992 paper, Cusumano, Mylonadis, and Rosenbloom indicate that Sony intended to attract JVC and Matsushita to the standard, but waited until after it had refined its design and committed to manufacture. The rationale was that commitments to manufacturing capacity would force the firm to avoid compromises in product design; a contingent of managers at Sony blamed collaboration on development for the failure of the U-Matic.

JVC and Matsushita rejected Sony's Beta standard. They had lost money on the U-Matic, and recognized that Sony's early commitment would allow it to bring manufacturing capacity onstream six to twelve months before any other company. Managers at JVC also conjectured that Sony's design was flawed in several ways. Sony had achieved miniaturization of the cassette tapes partly by limiting recording length to one hour. JVC's newest prototype, dubbed VHS (for Video Home System), was simpler to manufacture and accepted tapes that allowed two hours of recording.

Sony introduced its Betamax players and cassettes in the summer of 1975 to great fanfare. The product soon become more popular among consumers than the U-Matic. Sony marketed the $1,300 Betamax with the message that consumers could use it to tape their favorite television shows onto blank cassettes, then watch the shows when convenient; analysts estimate that twenty thousand units were sold in 1975 and 150,000 in 1976.[41]

In October 1976, seventeen months after the introduction of Betamax, JVC introduced the first VHS recorder. Hardware that conformed to the VHS standard was soon introduced by Matsushita and several other European and Japanese manufacturers that purchased the recorders from JVC under original equipment manufacturer (OEM) agreements. Blank tapes for both the Beta and VHS standards were available from hardware manufacturers.

Cusumano, Mylonadis, and Rosenbloom identify several major advantages that allowed VHS to supersede Beta as the predominant standard in VCRs:

- *Superior Distribution.* The proliferation of companies selling hardware on the VHS standard led to advantages in shelf space. In addition, Matsushita secured a critical contract in the U.S. market to provide RCA with VHS players on an OEM basis.

- *More Features and Better Marketing.* Competition among adherents to the VHS standard led to promotion of the product with concepts other than deferred viewing of a particular program (the principal Sony marketing message). Competition also led to the introduction of special features on VHS.

- *Efficient Manufacturing.* Matsushita and JVC jointly designed subsequent versions of VHS products with the lowest possible manufacturing costs. Competition among VHS adherents also led to increases in manufacturing capacity.

The proliferation of prerecorded movies did not occur until the mid-1980s, after VHS had displaced Beta as the leading standard for VCRs. By that time, makers of prerecorded cassettes were attracted to production of titles for the VHS standard because the installed base of VHS players was larger than that of Beta players. The original video software conceived by both Sony and JVC was the blank tape, but the software that popularized the products was the prerecorded movie.

## Videodisc Players[42]

In the mid-1960s, manufacturers of audio and video equipment considered opportunities to develop a successor generation of products to the color television. Market surveys showed consumer interest in a video playback device analogous to the audio LP. The main advantage of the product was that it would give the user greater control of the time of viewing. In her account of the videodisc, Margaret Graham reports that at least ten incompatible systems were introduced in the late 1960s and early 1970s.[43]

In the spring of 1970, a joint venture called Teldec, between the recording companies Telefunken and Decca Records, introduced a videodisc player based on a needle that read grooves off a plastic disc. The system was confined to black-and-white reproduction of images and was limited to five minutes of playing time. It had no recording capability. It was scheduled for introduction in late 1972, with players available for $250 and half-hour prerecorded programs for $6.50.[44]

During the 1960s, RCA, the world's leading seller of color televisions, engaged in several simultaneous development efforts related to videodiscs and videotape, including an analog disc playback system, an analog tape-recording system, and a laser-tape playback system. In the early 1970s, financial pressure forced RCA to specialize its development strategy. The reception of Telfunken and Decca's videodisc led RCA to renew its efforts to develop and introduce an analog disc playback system. The firm diminished its commitment to development of tape-based systems. RCA planned to unveil its videodisc in 1975; executives expected that lag would give RCA the time necessary to design a technically superior and less expensive player.

In 1973, Philips surprised the industry by demonstrating a proprietary videodisc system that was clearly superior to those of its competitors. Graham reports that "[RCA researchers] came away from a new Philips demonstration at the Berlin Radio and Television show in 1973 convinced that the Philips system was superior in both features and performance. Moreover, Philips announced plans to market its product simultaneously in Europe and the United States in 1975."[45] To encourage acceptance of its players, Philips entered an agreement with MCA, an entertainment company, to make movies available on discs designed for the system.[46]

Philips's successes led RCA's staff to change plans. RCA announced that a proprietary system would be launched late in 1976 with features that were competitive with those of Philips.[47] In 1975 and 1976, RCA attempted to curtail the advantage that Philips would obtain if it were to introduce its product on time by offering favorable licensing terms on hardware to Japanese manufacturers. RCA was rebuffed. Delays and modifications had led to compromises in design, and many of the Japanese companies had committed to new videotape technologies. RCA also pursued agreements that would let it expand the software available for its system.

Prior to the introduction of either system, Philips and RCA competed to attract users to their proprietary standards. The battle, chronicled in cover stories by both *Business Week* and *Forbes* in 1975 and 1976, occurred at a time when the prices of videodisc systems were significantly lower than those of videotape systems.[48] Distinct strategies emerged as the two producers tried to distinguish their systems. Philips emphasized the technical superiority of its system, while RCA claimed that efficiency in production would make its players less expensive in the long run.

Competition between the two standards led both entertainment companies and consumers to delay investment in the technology. Entertainment companies resisted printing their movies on videodiscs for either type of player because they did not want to be locked out if the other type should become the sole standard in the long run. Consumers also waited for a shakeout. They did not want to invest in videodisc players until a broad library of software became available, and until they received assurances that it would continue to be available. The press reported unexpectedly high manufacturing costs at both RCA and Philips.

In July 1977, RCA announced that it would discontinue efforts to ramp up production of videodiscs but would redouble development efforts. Researchers soon invented a machine that allowed higher-quality reproduction on a "machine that was one-half the size of its predecessor and contained one-third as many parts."[49] Discs for the system held two hours of programming, twice as much as the previous version. The system was not compatible with either Philips's system or the previous RCA system.

Philips finally introduced its system through its Magnavox subsidiary in December 1978. Videodisc players sold at retail for about $700, comparable with prices for the newest generation of videotape recorders targeted at the mass market. RCA's player was introduced in March 1981, at $499. From the consumer's perspective, the advantage of videodisc players over videotape recorders was the broader library of titles available on the medium. Like audio, the industry had adopted a model in which the discs, a playback-only medium, would become the principal vehicle for prerecorded programming. Tapes would become the medium for transferring programs through time.

By 1978 and 1979, MCA, still committed to the Philips standard, was frustrated with delays in the manufacture and distribution of hardware. Early in 1980, it negotiated an agreement with Japan's Pioneer Electronics Corporation to begin production of videodisc players on the Philips standard.[50] Shortly after Pioneer began to promote the Philips standard, RCA began advertising and distributing of its incompatible system. Consumers were not interested. Videodiscs suffered from continuing confusion about standards, increasing competition from videotape, and a reputation for poor reliability.

RCA withdrew its videodisc from the market in 1984, a year in which it sold 550,000 systems. In that same year, sales of videotape recorders reached forty million. Several sets of circumstances contributed to the failure of the videodisc. Production delays, design flaws, and the emergence of the videotape recorder had major, direct effects on the medium. Neither RCA nor Philips created a groundswell of interest among software vendors to produce discs for its standard. Several other, more subtle problems also stemmed acceptance. RCA and Philips engaged in competition on technological features that ultimately led both firms to ignore simpler, lower-cost formats that might have led to earlier introduction and acceptance.[51] Media coverage of the products raised consumers' expectations about features and delivery times. When the systems were late and did not reliably incorporate the features, consumers were disappointed.

# Compact Discs[52]

In the late 1970s, Philips recognized that its videodiscs would not generate a significant volume of sales, and looked for opportunities to apply its optical imaging expertise in other markets. One of the obvious candidates was consumer audio electronics.

Optical imaging in the reproduction of digitized audio signals had two principal advantages over the existing LP and cassette tape formats: first, it offered greater accuracy in reproduction, especially of high frequencies; and second, the discs themselves were more durable. Although the compact disc did not offer recording capability, it did incorporate several features that made LPs more attractive than cassette tapes, especially to listeners of classical music. These features included the ability to search and move between tracks easily, and clarity in reproduction of both high and low frequencies. Philips's executives reported that although classical music listeners were likely to flock to the CD, popular music listeners would probably be slow to accept the format. Fans of popular music, the larger of the segments by a factor of six, had demonstrated a preference for recording over reproduction accuracy by abandoning their LPs in favor of the cassette tape.[53]

In the late 1970s, Philips recognized that Sony and several other manufacturers were developing optical imaging technologies for the audio market. Recent experiences in videodiscs, videotape, and cassette tape led Philips to approach Sony about a preproduction agreement on a standard. Both Philips and Sony had interests in major record companies. Philips owned 50 percent of Polygram (the German electronics company Siemens owned the remaining 50 percent), and would soon obtain full ownership. Sony was affiliated with CBS Records through a joint venture. Two other companies—Telefunken and JVC—had demonstrated prototypes of audio disc technologies on standards different from those under development by Philips and Sony.

By 1981, Philips and Sony had agreed on a standard for the audio CD, and had convinced over fifty equipment manufacturers and recording companies to produce players and discs for the system. When the system was introduced in Europe, the United States, and Japan in 1982 and 1983, no competing format attracted attention. JVC and Telefunken never introduced a competing standard.

Developments in videodiscs and videotapes led Philips and Sony to encourage widespread manufacture of CD players by competing electronics firms in order to establish their standard. Licensing fees were judged to be quite low by most firms in the industry. Polygram and CBS Records offered a broad range of classical and jazz programs to complement the players. Competition among hardware manufacturers drove down prices relatively quickly. The nature of the technology and manufacturing process meant that the players offered by different electronics companies were quite similar. Initially priced at $900–$1,200, players became available for $600 by the end of 1984.[54]

By the middle of 1986, consumers and reviewers complained that too few popular titles were available on CDs, despite their $14–$18 price tags. As record companies ramped up production, consumers began to replace their inventories of LPs and prerecorded cassettes with titles on compact discs.[55] Record companies embraced the new format because it promised to displace home recording, a phenomenon that had cut significantly into sales of LPs. Demand for a wider variety of titles led equipment manufacturers to design portable and car players, further fueling demand for discs. The widespread adoption of compact discs surprised almost all industry analysts. By 1985, sales of CD players in the United States exceeded one million, significantly greater than sales of videocassette recorders at the same point in that industry's development.

In a 1993 article, a senior executive at Sony reflected on the rationale for cutting prices on CD players soon after their introduction: "Our goal was to shrink the period of market growth to three years instead of the five or six years it would usually take."[56] The firm's objective was to bolster sales of discs and of specialized equipment, including its portable Discman and car players. Sony also sold CD components to other equipment manufacturers.

The impending development of digital cassette tape created a complementary incentive for both Philips and Sony to encourage prompt adoption of the CD. As early as 1985, the firms recognized that the next generation in audio products would be a recordable digitized medium having a quality of reproduction comparable with that of the CD. Digitized tapes were forecast for introduction in the early 1990s. There was a short window of opportunity for establishing the CD; failure would subject the technology to the problems that had plagued the videodisc.

## LESSONS FOR PDAS FROM CONSUMER ELECTRONICS

These short histories in consumer electronics illustrate the problems and issues of building demand and setting standards. Common solutions to these problems include strategic alliances and the impact of reputation and recent experience on strategic behavior. (In chapter 9 of this volume,

Benjamin Gomes-Casseres and Dorothy Leonard-Barton address these issues in the market for PDAs.)

The most relevant lessons in these cases with respect to complementarities and standardization fall into three categories. First, in most consumer industries where there are network externalities, separate and independent hardware and software industries must develop to generate buyer value. These industries cannot develop independently without common acceptance of technological standards. Second, first-mover advantages have been powerful in the history of consumer electronic products, but when the market develops slowly or when the speed of imitation increases significantly, first movers often lose their advantage. Finally, backward compatibility—that is, compatibility with the installed base of related products—facilitates and hastens market acceptance.

## Creating Value and Setting Standards: From Integration to Separation of Hardware and Software

In each market we have studied, two defining features made standardization a critical issue. The first is that buyers obtain value through combined use of both hardware and software. In some situations, hardware and software are integrally bundled into a single package. In others, hardware and software are offered by different vendors and evolve as separate industries. In general, hardware took the form of a durable good that was purchased relatively infrequently and was used as a vehicle that allowed the user to obtain access to software. Software and other complementary assets, in turn, were purchased and consumed relatively frequently, but had no value for users without hardware. In this context, software includes cassette tapes, compact discs, and broadcast media, as well as applications that run on a desktop computer. Hardware includes cassette decks, radios, televisions, and PCs.

In several industries, early entrants bundled hardware and software into a single package, usually with a proprietary or semiproprietary standard. In every case, early entrants had significant interests in returns on both hardware and software. Early manufacturers of radios and televisions, for example, were also broadcasters; early sponsors of the compact disc, Sony and Philips, were owners of music companies that would sell CDs; Apple and AT&T (partly through EO) were selling PDAs and related hardware (the Hobbit microprocessor) and software (Newton OS, Newton applications, and services). While some early entrants in consumer electronics continued to participate in markets for both hardware and software, massive demand did not build until separate hardware and software industries emerged. Large numbers of consumers apparently refused to make commitments to hardware until they were guaranteed a competitively priced supply of software.

On one level, this might be surprising. There are obvious advantages to vertical and horizontal integration from the firm's perspective, especially in greater control over product design and in a "razor and blade" approach to profitability. Nevertheless, acceptance in the mass market invariably occurred only after the development of separate hardware and software industries. In the broadcast industries—radio and color television—this separation was mandated through federal intervention. In cassette tapes, videocassette recorders, and compact discs, separate industries evolved because the firms that had introduced the technologies explicitly promoted their independent development to enhance acceptance of their products. One explanation is that competition to establish a standard forces the adoption of a technically efficient interface. In most cases, fully integrated companies specialized in the production of either hardware or software as the mass market evolved.

The development of separate industries and vertical disintegration is less surprising if one assumes that rational buyers consider the prices and features of both hardware and software in their calculation of the value. *Network effects* are important to this calculation. A network effect arises when the value of the hardware and software to each user increases when others also use the products. Network effects were important in all of our cases: radios and TVs became more valuable to consumers as hardware disseminated and demand for broadcast programming exploded; 8-track cassettes and audiocassettes became more valuable as the installed base grew and created demand for more prerecorded music; mass-market demand for prerecorded videotapes occurred after patterns of consumer adoption favored the VHS hardware standard; and the videodisc failed, at least in part, because the installed base of prerecorded software did not materialize in a timely fashion.

The existence of network effects creates enormous pressure on first movers to disseminate hardware in order to facilitate acceptance. Buyers, as we have seen, often resisted the purchase of hardware until a clear standard emerged and they were guaranteed availability of software and of complementary services at competitive prices. The critical locus for standards was the interface between hardware and software; consumers accepted hardware and software that varied widely in quality and other attributes as long as it was compatible with the standard. This behavior created the same paradox confronted by Apple, AT&T, and others in the

PDA market: hardware providers attempt to retain control of profitable software sales, and therefore resist endorsing an open architecture; but in the absence of a common open architecture, producers forestall the bandwagon effect necessary to create a vibrant software market.

Agreement on a single standard is an alternative to the simultaneous promotion of incompatible, proprietary hardware. The problem of a nonproprietary standard for the innovating firm is that it invites profit-dissipating competitive *imitation* with the intention of enhancing network effects among buyers. In most circumstances, a firm cannot successfully attract other companies to its standard if it withholds knowledge about componentry in an attempt to retain an advantage over rivals. The royalty on components must be low enough, and the licensing agreement sufficiently comprehensive, to make the agreement attractive to other firms.

Firms that sponsor a nonproprietary standard therefore cannot expect to earn extraordinary profits on basic hardware over the long run. In many cases, the innovating firms hope to appropriate above-average returns either in the short run, before imitation occurs, or in sales of complementary software. If consumers ultimately become committed to a hardware platform (the razor), the innovating firm may lock consumers into an annuity stream of complementary assets or software (the blade). This approach may be most effective if it is implemented while competitors subscribe to incompatible proprietary standards, and therefore exclude themselves from access to early-mover advantages in the markets that ultimately become the standard for the industry. Other firms may accept an innovator's invitation to license a nonproprietary technology in the hope of obtaining an efficiency or differentiation advantage in the hardware itself, or simply of taking advantage of high, short-run growth.

The tension of solving the network problem while limiting imitation plagued all of the pioneers in consumer electronics and likely will remain a critical issue in the PDA market for several years to come. In consumer electronics, the tension has sometimes been resolved through a waiting game; in some markets, buyers eventually begin to purchase hardware and software on proprietary standards because the value offered through the combination is too great to resist even at high prices. This outcome is unlikely in PDAs if they continue to offer no greater value for consumers than electronic organizers do. In this case, network effects and standards will be irrelevant; PDAs will be nothing more than a niche market with a multitude of stand-alone products.

If PDAs are to deliver the value originally promised by Apple—wireless communications, and an array of software applications and services available to the mass market—then standards will be necessary in the long run. Apple explicitly recognized the need for setting standards in its approach to the PDA market,[57] and its strategy of selective licensing to create a limited number of competitors was part of an effort to resolve the need for volume without too much imitation. The problem with this approach is that it may fall prey to a trap that Sony fell into with VCRs; Sony might have restricted competition while it had a technological lead in VCRs by limiting the licensees for the Beta format, but a limited number of competitors meant a limited installed base relative to VHS and, ultimately, the collapse of the format.

## First-Mover Advantages

One of the most striking features of standardization in consumer electronics is the frequency with which early entrants capture and retain leadership in their industries. Westinghouse's and RCA's commitments to radio in the 1920s secured them leading positions for over forty years. RCA's and NBC's early interests in television gave them advantages that persisted through the 1970s (for RCA) and the 1980s (for NBC). Similarly, Philips's and Sony's early commitments to compact disc technology led to their dominance in that industry.

A close inspection of first movers' approaches reveals subtle dynamics. Theory suggests that first movers have a window of opportunity during which they may be protected from significant competition. During this period, they experience relatively less pressure from imitators and therefore have greater opportunities to implement a razor-and-blade strategy. Under these conditions, we would expect first movers to sell both hardware and software (at least at initial stages), and to subsidize either hardware or software, if necessary, to build an installed base.

This dynamic occurred in every case noted above, as well as several others in which the first mover later ceded market share to followers. Consider, for example, CBS's ill-fated entry into the production of color televisions. This entry was designed to enhance demand for CBS broadcasts over UHF channels. CBS acquired a television manufacturer in order to guarantee a supply of the hardware necessary to play its software (i.e., to receive its broadcasts). Similarly, Sony sold blank videocassette tape as a complement to Betamax recorders. In another example, Westinghouse's rationale for the first radio stations in the 1920s was that "listeners will purchase the [company's] sets." This logic also seems to drive Apple's strategy in PDAs; by moving first, by establishing the category, and by selling the Newton operating system, Apple hopes to obtain sales of "blades" in the form of software applications available from its software subsidiary, Claris, and in the form of services available through eWorld.

The consumer electronics cases also reveal that the power of first movers may be greatest in new categories with few incumbent players. Imitation was relatively slow in cases such as radio and 8-track cassettes, where there were few competitors and substantial uncertainty about market demand. In most of the other cases, however, the first movers were challenged quickly. In color television and videocassette recorders, for example, the first mover was displaced within a few years when a group of competitors allied to sponsor incompatible alternatives. Less than two years elapsed before RCA and Matsushita successfully launched aggressive promotions of alternative platforms in TVs and VCRs.

The cassette tape industry provides a distinctive example of a situation in which the second mover did not attract allies to its standard, and in which the migration to the new technology required a long period of time. Philips's audiocassette standard was promoted in the American market shortly after Lear Jet's 8-track was introduced. By the time of the promotion, RCA had pledged to make its titles available on the 8-track, and Ford had made 8-track players an option on its new automobiles. Although the Philips audiocassette system eventually had features superior to the 8-track (e.g., recordability with comparable quality), it did not displace the 8-track as the dominant standard for more than a decade.

The history of first-mover advantages in consumer electronics may also be suggestive for the future of PDAs. Apple, despite its early weakness, is clearly the first mover. The company has defined the category—to date—and leads in the currently relevant technology, including handwriting recognition, small form features, and ease of use. Yet Apple's first-mover advantage is by no means secure; it has not built a large enough installed base or created a strong enough product offering to ensure that alternative architectures or imitative products could not overtake the Newton. This problem may have been exacerbated by the stimulation of interest in the concept a full year in advance of the Newton's introduction.

## Backward Compatibility

A third theme that emerges from this research is the importance of backward compatibility—that is, hardware compatibility with the installed base of related software products (which were adopted in connection with a previous generation of technology). Backward compatibility is a special type of complementarity.

In consumer electronics products and in PDAs, consumers and sometimes manufacturers impeded growth for fear of making their prior investments in software libraries obsolete. For example, RCA slowed adoption of FM radio partly because of concern over the implications for AM broadcasting; David Sarnoff also recognized that consumers would not react favorably if their black-and-white RCA televisions did not receive monochrome versions of new color programming (i.e., if UHF became the standard for color broadcasting). One risk of incompatibility was that consumers would buy neither color televisions nor new black-and-white televisions. Aggregate demand for all products was at stake. Similarly, the slow adoption of audiocassettes after the introduction of 8-track was partly a function of consumers' recent investments in libraries of 8-track tapes.

PDAs have a special problem in building market acceptance that is analogous to the original creation of AM radio and black-and-white television broadcasting. PDAs will not deliver great value until consumers collectively invest in complementary assets, especially a sophisticated telecommunication network. The creation of highly valued on-line services by independent vendors will also prove critical to the adoption of PDAs. The collective nature of the investment may slow development of this resource, and hence of the market for PDAs. Moreover, just as color TV was easier to sell because it retained compatibility with black-and-white broadcasts, the utility of the PDA would be enhanced by strong linkages to the installed base of personal computers, Macintoshes, and paging devices. Yet unlike the manufacturers of radios and TVs, which had direct control over broadcast firms, and therefore could develop necessary programming, existing PDA manufacturers must make their products compatible with software sold by other firms. Furthermore, PDAs will not drive adoption of the telecommunication network—cellular phones and pagers will. PDAs are also unlikely to drive the primary demand for relevant on-line services—PCs and Macs will do that.


## CONCLUSION

PDAs are likely to become a relatively high-volume market in the future, but massive acceptance will not occur until the products deliver substantially greater value to buyers than existing products do. Delivery of this value will depend on the evolution of the markets for both PDA hardware and software. Incentives for investment in these markets will be driven by the presence of complementary systems like wireless telecommunications, as well as by the adoption of standards within the PDA industry. Standardization in turn will affect the availability of complementary technology. The history of consumer electronics suggests that the first movers in these markets will achieve a sustained competitive advantage if they offer an open architecture, promote widespread adoption of complementary infrastructure, and ensure compatibility with the installed base of PC and Macintosh software.

## NOTES

1. *Wall Street Journal*, February 11, 1994, p. R6.

2. BIS Strategic Decisions projected sales of PDAs to grow to 269,000 in 1994, 507,000 in 1995, and 1.8 million in 1997; Forrester Research estimated that slightly less than 100,000 would be sold in 1993, slightly more would be sold in 1994, and more than a half million in 1995. Estimates were reported in *PC Week*, February 28, 1994, and *Business Week*, July 11, 1994, respectively.

3. Interview with John Sculley, April 1994.

4. Charles McCoy, "Gadfly or Guru? Andy Seybold—Newsletter Writer, Consultant, Evangelist—Is Helping to Shape the Wireless Industry; Who Is This Guy, Anyway?" *Wall Street Journal*, February 11, 1994, p. R18.

5. Ibid.

6. *Wall Street Journal*, February 11, 1994, p. R6.

7. Securities Data Company, Comprehensive Summary Report, 1994.

8. Quotes by Kimball Brown, the chief analyst for mobile computing for Dataquest, and Andrew Seybold, publisher of a mobile-computing newsletter in *Wall Street Journal*, February 2, 1994, p. B1.

9. "Newton: Will What Fell Down Go Up?" *Business Week Online*, July 11, 1994.

10. Quoting Joseph Graziano, *PC Week*, August 22, 1994, p. 49.

11. *PC Week*, February 28, 1994, p. 25.

12. Doug Menuez, *Defying Gravity* (Portland, Oreg.: Dynagraphics, Inc., 1993).

13. The introduction of Simon, the IBM and Bell South product was reported in *PC Week*, August 22, 1994, p. 45. Simon was an $895 cellular phone with a screen, GUI, pager, fax, and E-mail capabilities. Motorola's Envoy was a more expensive PDA aimed at AT&T's original target: vertical business markets. Sony also introduced the Magic Link personal communicator, which promoted General Magic's software. Compaq's plans were reported in *The Economist*, July 2, 1994, p. 60. However, in the fall of 1994, Compaq's products were on hold. After some initial excitement generated by Sculley, Compaq shelved plans for an early introduction of its PDA until possibly 1996, because

of its belief that the market for PDA was still too immature. *PC Week,* August 22, 1994, p. 45.

14. "PDA Makers Form Industry Alliance," *PC Week,* January 23, 1995, p. 41.

15. This section draws principally on Thomas S. W. Lewis, *Empire of the Air: The Men Who Make Radio* (New York: HarperCollins, 1991). Also see Peter Fisher, "The Diffusion of Systems Products: The Case of FM Radio," Harvard University working paper, October 1993.

16. Lewis, 153.

17. "Retail Radio Sales in the United States, 1922–1939," *Broadcasting: 1940 Yearbook,* p. 14.

18. "Estimated Radio Gross Billings," *Broadcasting: 1948 Yearbook,* p. 16.

19. RCA Annual Report, 1940 and 1941; "National Networks' Gross Monthly Time Sales," *Broadcasting: 1940 Yearbook,* 12. ABC was owned by RCA until 1941, when it was divested to meet requirements of the FCC.

20. Ibid., 303.

21. Stanley M. Besen, "AM vs. FM: The Battle of the Bands," *Industrial and Corporate Change* 1, no.2 (1992): 375–396, citing Don V. Erickson, *Armstrong's Fight for FM Broadcasting* (Tuscaloosa: University of Alabama Press, 1973), p. 82.

22. This section draws on Robert Sobel, *RCA* (New York: Stein and Day, 1986).

23. Sobel, 124.

24. Ibid., 126–127.

25. Ibid., 127.

26. Ibid., 152–153.

27. Ibid., 151, citing *Electronic Industries* (January 30, 1963), p. 101.

28. Ibid.

29. Sobel, 162.

30. "The New RCA Color Receiver," *Consumer Reports,* November 1955, p. 528.

31. Sobel, 166, citing Skinner and Rogers, *Manufacturing Policy in the Electronics Industry,* p. 60.

32. Ibid.

33. "Color TV Set Makers Turn Sales Volumes Up," *Business Week,* January 23, 1965, p. 144.

34. "Miles of Tape," *The Economist,* July 26, 1958, p. 270.

35. "Music Maker for the Masses," *Business Week*, February 24, 1968, p. 109.

36. Chapple and Garofalo, p. 95.

37. "RCA, CBS Plan Cassette Recordings, Giving a Major Boost to the Young Medium," *Wall Street Journal,* March 4, 1969, p. 9.

38. Donal Henahan, "The Lowly Cassette Comes of Age," *New York Times,* March 15, 1970, p. 34.

39. Recording Industry Association of America; Paula Dranov, *Inside Music Publishing: The Record Industry.*

40. This section draws on Michael A. Cusumano, Yiorgos Mylonadis, and Richard S. Rosenbloom, "Strategic Maneuvering and Mass-Market Dynamics: The Triumph of VHS over Beta," *Business History Review,* Spring 1992, pp. 51–92; James Lardner, *Fast Forward: Hollywood, the Japanese, and the Onslaught of the VCR* (New York: Norton, 1987); P. Raganath Nayak, and John M. Ketteringham, *Breakthroughs* (New York: Rawson Associates, 1986); and Ralinda Young, The World VCR Industry (Boston: Harvard Business School Publishing, 1987).

41. See Cusumano, Mylonadis, and Rosenbloom.

42. The primary source for this section is Margaret B. W. Graham, *RCA and the VideoDisc: The Business of Research* (Cambridge: Cambridge University Press, 1986).

43. Ibid., 22.

44. Although scheduled for 1972, the system was not introduced until later. In the early 1970s, videodisc systems were significantly less expensive than videotape systems. The U-Matic videotape player introduced by Sony in 1971 sold for $2,500.

45. Graham, 161.

46. *Wall Street Journal,* September 24, 1974, p. 36.

47. Graham, 162.

48. "Videodiscs: The Expensive Race to be First," *Business Week,* September 15, 1975, p. 58, reported videodisc player prices of $400 to $500 and videotape player prices of about $1,300. Movie-length programs, available in their entirety on Philips's and RCA's systems, were available for $10 to $15 apiece.

49. Graham, 204.

50. Ibid., 40.

51. Graham describes this phenomenon in terms of both firms' interest in cutting-edge technology.

52. See A. M. McGahan, "The Incentive Not to Invest: Capacity Commitments in the Compact Disc Introduction," in Richard S. Rosenbloom and Robert A. Burgelman, eds., *Research on Technological Innovation, Management and Policy,* vol. 5 (Greenwich, Conn.: JAI Press, 1993).

53. See A. M. McGahan, "Philips Compact Disc Introduction (A)," Case no. 792-035 (Boston: Harvard Business School Publishing, 1992).

54. Len Feldman, "Bye-bye LP Hello, CD?," *Popular Science,* November 1983, p. 158.

55. Jack Egan, "The Stunning Success of CDs," *U.S. News & World Report,* February 23, 1987, p. 41.

56. Takashi Shibata, "Sony's Successful Strategy for Compact Discs," *Long Range Planning,* August 1993, p. 20.

57. Interview with John Sculley.

CHAPTER 7

# LARGE FIRMS' DEMAND FOR COMPUTER PRODUCTS AND SERVICES

*Competing Market Models,*
*Inertia, and Enabling Strategic Change*

Timothy F. Bresnahan
Garth Saloner

## INTRODUCTION

The organization of the value chain in the computer industry is undergoing profound change. The nature of this change is depicted in two contrasting market models. In the vertical market model, large, vertically integrated vendors of proprietary systems, working hand in glove with selected partners, provide most of the functions in the value chain. In the horizontal market model, there are distinct suppliers at each stage of the value chain. They provide components conforming to standardized interfaces that users then combine into systems.[1]

The vertical market model, inspired in large part by the success of the IBM coordination strategy in selling System/360 and its descendants, was used in designing and selling large computer systems for solving large business problems in large organizations. A lead vendor, such as IBM, DEC, Burroughs, or Wang, designed mainframe or minicomputer system architectures. Those architectures involved a wide variety of components

*The authors are affiliated with the Department of Economics and the Graduate School of Business, Stanford University, respectively. We thank participants at Stanford's Computer Industry Forum and at the Colliding Worlds Conference for helpful comments, and the Sloan Foundation for funding of the Stanford Computer Industry Project.

based on many hardware, software, and communications technologies. The lead vendor provided or obtained technical progress in all of these.[2] In user companies, professionalized and centralized management information systems (MIS) groups managing the "glass house" procured computer systems and organized their use.

The horizontal market model was most successful in the personal computer market, where specialized, focused, vendors produced components to standardized interfaces. End users could combine distinct components to suit their tastes, much as they could do with stereo components.[3] Buyers of these systems in large enterprises were individuals, dispersed throughout the firm, who used them for personal productivity applications. System and software choices were largely decentralized and managed by the individual, group, or department.[4]

The two models served very different purposes in parallel markets. Thus they coexisted, supplying distinct information technology needs inside the same large customer companies. Increasingly, however, these market models are in a head-on crash. Dramatic advances in networking technology mean that small systems can be linked together—which, combined with their growing power, means that client/server architectures are competitors for the same applications that were once the exclusive domain of the mainframe.[5] This is the competitive crash in large-scale computing. The lessons of this technical and economic convergence are important in their own right and may apply more broadly to the themes and industries covered in this volume.

There are two distinct drivers behind the competitive crash. One is purely technological; client/server architectures and mainframe architectures have very different technical characteristics of power, ease of use, flexibility, and so on. The other driver combines the changing business model of the computer firm and the move to the horizontal market model. These two drivers are so closely linked that many industry participants increasingly refer to the vertical and horizontal market models as the "old" and the "new," respectively.[6] The widely held view that the new model will triumph over the old has two corresponding parts, the superiority of the new market model and the technological superiority of its products.

Economic theory tells us how to compare the relative productive efficiency of the vertical and horizontal market models.[7] In the vertical model, a lead vendor produces an entire system or works hand in glove with partners to design and produce a system. The lead vendor solves the problem of coordinating the myriad components that must interoperate in a system. However, the price that is paid for this explicit coordination is a small number of producers (often only one) of each component. In the extreme, where a single, vertically integrated firm produces the entire system, it is the sole producer of each component. It is exceedingly unlikely that any single firm is the best worldwide producer of every component. While there is competition among lead vendors, that competition occurs at the level of the entire system. The "winner" of that competition is the one that is best overall, not the best at every component. (A metaphor sometimes invoked to describe this phenomenon is "An eighteen wheeler travels only as fast as the slowest wheel.")

In the horizontal market model, in contrast, the coordination among components is achieved by the standardized interfaces themselves. Competition occurs at the component level, so that the "winner" in each component is the best worldwide producer of that component. This leaves end users free to put together a system from among the best components possible; thus they are able to construct the system that best serves their needs from the best components available.[8] That, at least, is the theory.

Hopes and expectations for client/server are so high partly because of a correspondence between the new technology and the new market model. Though client/server applies to companywide or divisionwide computing, it offers potential advantages to the information end user. The advantages that are touted here include the greater ease of use of small systems clients, broader access to critical company data, faster response to business units' queries, closer to real-time response to customer needs and wants, and lower MIS staff and capital budget requirements. The mission of specialist vendor companies is to support different parts of the using organization. Personal computer hardware and software vendors, for example, have developed great expertise in providing low-cost ease of use in single-user systems. In the new market model, these vendors also provide to the clients. Other technical requirements, such as powerful server hardware and software, or networking products, can be provided separately. Buyers will have wide choice in each technology. Thus, the market incentives facing vendors are both powerful and focused. Each vendor will have a specific body of customer needs to fill, and the market will reward the best producers in each segment.

The end result is predicted to be a market for companywide computing that is as successful as the personal computer market. For sellers, revenue and profitability growth will resemble those in personal computers in the 1980s.

For large buyers, technical progress and responsiveness to user needs will be dramatically increased. Their response will also be dramatic as companywide uses of IT quickly grow more productive and valuable. The strategic use of IT—led by strategic downsizing to client/server architectures—will explode.

A movement from a vertical to a horizontal market model therefore has profound implications for the organization of the industry supplying information technology, for competition among vendors, and for the ultimate success and failure of those competitors. It is therefore important to obtain as clear a picture as possible of whether and how rapidly such a change might take place. That is the primary objective of this study.

That issue can only be partially addressed by focusing on the supply side. The rate of technological change can inform us about the speed with which the positive vision of the horizontal market model will become feasible. This is a vision put forward by technologists who say the industry has left the "bad, old" world of proprietary systems, dinosaur-like large, integrated sellers, and hard-to-use mainframes for a "good, new" world of open systems, fleet-footed, focused organizations, and easy-to-use small systems.

However, the supply side can *only* inform us about technological feasibility. New information technologies enable successful adoption in customer companies. They do not compel it. To go beyond feasibility, the new technology must be adopted. Buyers must be convinced by the technologists' vision and willing to embrace it. Adoption, far from being a passive act, is a complex technical change activity. When a new market model accompanies new information technologies, these considerations are redoubled. Buyers need to assess not only how well the new products serve their technical needs, but also how well the new market model serves their business needs. Many technologists and journalists will tell you that this transition is well under way. After a slow start, the adoption of client/server architectures has taken off, and the transformation of companywide computing cannot be far behind.[9] They have in mind the usual S-shaped diffusion curve for a new technology. Now past the initial difficult pioneering applications, we are ready to go on to the steep part of the S with many high-payoff applications.

We disagree. Very serious challenges remain before the horizontal market model effectively serves information technology buyers' needs. Our findings arise from an analysis of buyers. The horizontal market model assigns an unprecedented degree of power to buyers, and as a result they will determine the pace and direction of the transition. To learn about the pace and direction of the shift in market models, we conducted an interview study of IT-using enterprises in fourteen vertical markets.

We found much to suggest that the technical and market visions of the horizontal model will *someday* be very important. Where we saw strategic adoption of client/server technology by user companies, it was impressive. And in those few and difficult success stories, much of the rosy picture of the technical possibilities offered by new IT was correct. However, the idealized technological description of the horizontal market model has not yet been realized. There is a significant gap between technologists' thinking and users' thinking. Buyers of information technology have always had difficulty realizing the apparent promises of technical advance.[10] At this moment, with its promised vision of new technical possibilities and new market organization, the gap between expectations and realizations is at a peak.

For buyers, in contrast with stereo components that can be easily strung together with copper wire, the task of mapping available technology into solutions for the end user is complex. There is a gap between technology and use. This gap always existed to some extent in the vertical model, but the absence of a lead vendor to provide the coordination exacerbates the problem. Among sellers, interface standards between component layers do not yet exist. Perhaps most important, the challenge that the end-user organization faces is not simply to find the right technology for the problem at hand, but a much more complicated problem of adapting the organization so that it can be combined with information technology to provide increased productivity and competitive advantage. Successful adoption of the new technology requires organizational change by the end users that is ill defined, risky, and very difficult to undertake. The problems have little to do with the ability of the vendors to generate new technology, or the right technology. Instead, the bottleneck is the using enterprises' difficulty in adopting the technology and effecting organizational change to take full advantage of it. This leaves a commercialization gap that existing market models fill only partly.

We conjecture that this situation is not unique to the particular transformation we study. Much of IT consists of general-purpose technologies, calling for complex complementary investment in application.[11] The slow, textured diffusion process we document may be the normal state of affairs.

In the following section we briefly describe the scope of the study and the methodology employed. In the third section, we introduce the standard diffusion model as a useful conceptual tool for thinking about the movement from the vertical to the horizontal market model, and briefly explain why that model fails to capture the complexity of this transition. The failure of the simple model leads us to delve more deeply into the factors that are driving the transition and those that are holding it back. These factors are explored in the fourth section. The third and fourth sections together report eight findings about the current state of demand for computer systems in large organizations. In the following two sections, we draw the main conclusions and implications. The fifth section focuses on conclusions that illuminate the making and selling of information technology. We discuss what we see as the major impediments to success of the market model now being used in IT and the strategic marketing model being used in a variety of IT firms. In this section, we are attempting to help bridge the vision gap between sellers and buyers of IT. In the sixth section, we examine the future for the users, focusing on the problems and prospects for true strategic downsizing. The seventh section concludes.

## SCOPE AND METHODOLOGY

Demand is most readily gauged at the time when substitution of one product or technology for another is under consideration. The movement from the vertical to the horizontal market model is not easily described as a change from one specific technology to another, however. First, it is still early in the development of client/server technology. Neither standards for interfaces between market layers nor dominant designs within market layers have yet emerged. Second, the horizontal model permits much user choice, and there is a wide variety of different technologies among which to choose.

There are some broad trends, however. The movement generally is from large, proprietary mainframes (or minicomputers) to alternatives. Sometimes the change is to a smaller, more efficient, stand-alone workstation. Most commonly, however, the change is toward networked smaller computers in a client/server model. Almost always the change has put the computing power on, or closer to, the end user's desk. Computing power is being dispersed through the organization and away from the mainframe. It involves more open hardware and software.

We did not want to get hung up on the issue of precisely what technology end users were moving toward. Since we had the benefit of an interview format, we were able to be somewhat expansive in our characterization of the alternatives to the mainframe. Sometimes our interviewees spoke about "downsizing" (or "rightsizing"), sometimes about decentralization, sometimes about distributed computing (although this technically has a somewhat different connotation), and sometimes about adopting client/server architectures. In what follows, we refer to this generally as "client/server technology" for simplicity, because this is the closest current label for the phenomenon represented by the movement to the horizontal market model.

We focused our attention on decisions by users to move an existing application off a mainframe and onto a client/server network, or the decision of whether to put a new application onto the existing mainframe or onto a client/server network.[12] Therefore, the natural starting point for our inquiries within end-user organizations was the senior data processing managers in the "glass house." However, it obviously is important also to obtain the perspectives of end users of MIS services and of senior executives whose role it is to plan the overall IT strategy of the company. Thus our study extended to them as well.

We conducted the study by carrying out on-site and telephone interviews with multiple respondents in each firm in fourteen different vertical markets, using semistructured interviews. To do this, we enlisted the help of sixteen Stanford Graduate School of Business MBA students and a doctoral student during the first half of 1993. The vertical markets covered and the number of companies interviewed are shown in table 7-1. Over one hundred interviews were conducted at more than seventy-five companies.

TABLE 7-1

SCOPE OF THE INTERVIEWS

| Vertical Market | Firms Interviewed | Total Interviews |
|---|---|---|
| Automotive R&D | 5 | 7 |
| Banking | 4 | 7 |
| Consulting | 7 | 7 |
| Government | 7 | 10 |
| High Technology | 5 | 8 |
| Higher Education | 7 | 16 |
| Hospitals | 6 | 6 |
| Insurance | 3 | 6 |
| Investment Banking | 5 | 10 |
| Oil Exploration | 9 | 13 |
| Pharmaceuticals | 7 | 8 |
| Retail/Wholesale | 5 | 6 |
| Telecommunications | 5 | 6 |
| Trucking | 4 | 7 |

Although our interview format was open ended and unstructured, there were several things we did plan and attempt to control. Within each vertical market, we made an effort to find both leading adopters and firms that had not yet attempted the transition. At each site, we attempted to gain a profile of the technologies used in the "before" era, and the respondents' vision of the business justification for investment in IT systems in their company. We also sought information about the attractions of and barriers to client/server technology. While many respondents viewed the information about their company's specific situation as sensitive, they were comfortable with our use of the information without the company's name. Finally, our findings and conclusions are not based just on counting heads among the interview respondents. To be sure, the frequency of a response matters, but so do its intensity and how carefully it has been considered.

## THE LAY OF THE LAND

In this section we briefly lay out our major findings of fact about the transition. No attempt is made in this section or the next to draw broad conclusions from, or to synthesize, these findings. Those tasks are left to the fifth section.

A movement from an established technology to a newer technology typically diffuses through the population of potential adopters over time. It is useful to contrast our observation of the adoption of client/server with the standard diffusion model. That model posits that there is a distribution of the benefits to end users from adopting a new technology. A typical distribution of benefits might be as in figure 7-1. As suggested by the figure, the distribution of benefits to end users is often bell-shaped, with a small number of firms for whom the benefits of adopting a given technology are very high, but with the majority of firms falling between the extremes. When the new technology first becomes available, only those for whom the benefits are very high are likely to adopt. As the costs, risks, or other impediments to adopting the new technology fall, the benefits exceed the costs for more and more firms, so that the rate of adoption picks up. If the benefits of adopting a new technology have the bell shape illustrated in figure 7-1, the rate of diffusion will have the familiar S-shape depicted in figure 7-2. We shall see that in the present instance, the standard diffusion model is half right. It is right in that the bell-shaped distribution of adoption probabilities holds. It is wrong in the prediction that there will soon be a takeoff to rapid adoption of strategic

FIGURE 7-1

DISTRIBUTION OF BENEFITS TO END USERS

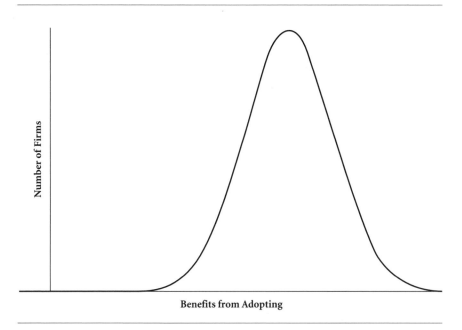

Benefits from Adopting

client/server architecture applications. We first examine the half-right part, then the half-wrong part.

**Finding 1:** Seen from enough distance, the standard diffusion model provides a description of the transition to client/server.

In particular, if one is prepared to ignore some important complexities, the bell-shaped distribution of values and of adoption likelihoods holds. There is a small group of high-benefit users; these are very likely to be early adopters. There is another small group of very low-benefit, low-likelihood potential users. In between, there is a large group of users with intermediate values and likelihoods. While it masks some significant complexity among buyers, a depiction of three different kinds of buyers illustrates this point.

There is a set of buyers who have been aggressively changing the way they do their computing toward machines that are physically separated

FIGURE 7-2

## THE S-SHAPE DIFFUSION CURVE

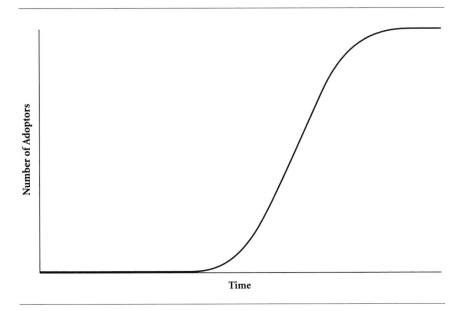

Number of Adoptors

Time

(and sometimes logically separated) from the mainframe. These are buyers with number-crunching, intensive applications, such as oil exploration sites and investment banks. For these applications, the superior price performance of stand-alone workstations and the ease of using these machines for number-crunching, intensive applications have become compelling.

At one oil exploration site we were told of the years of conflict with MIS over the $6 million per year in charges it was required to bear for the Cray supercomputer. When discussions between the "center" and the geographically separate oil exploration group reached an impasse, MIS reportedly said, "If you don't like it, pull the plug." So the site did, and within a few months was able to obtain superior functionality from workstations that required a one-time purchase costing $700,000. Another company told us how it was able to relegate the mainframe to a server and deploy workstations for the number-crunching, at a cost saving of $500,000 per year.

For these users the driver is MIPS (millions of instructions per second) arbitrage, using the much more cost-effective processing power of smaller machines, and represents the final stages of a decades-old trend.

Numerically intensive computing has long been moving off general-purpose mainframe computers, first to minicomputers and more recently to workstations.

At the other extreme were those firms that clearly were not considering a fundamental change in strategy in the near future. These were mainly firms with very large transactions-processing requirements, such as banks. These buyers believe that despite very rapid technical progress in networked small systems, they are still constrained by the maximum feasible task that networked small systems can undertake. For example, one banker told us, "I clear twenty million checks a day. I will never leave mainframes." Buyers in this category tend, in interviews, to be somewhat disinterested in the details of client/server technology.

Eliminating the above two groups from the set leaves the bulk of the firms in the market. Most are attracted by the promises in the rosy picture of client/server and the new market model, and thus are considering strategic change in the information technology infrastructure associated with companywide applications. However, many of these buyers are unwilling to make a leap into the brave new world that is the technologists' vision of the new order; rather cautiously, they are running small-scale "experiments" with client/server and adopting it slowly and incrementally.

The third group is clearly much larger than the first two, showing the correctness of the bell-shaped distribution of values.[13]

Does it follow from the existence of the bell-shaped distribution of user benefits that we have moved out of the flat part of the S-curve and are poised for takeoff in the steeper part of the curve? Through the lens of the standard diffusion model, the fairly large amount of downsizing by users of the first type might lead one to this conclusion. Such a view is consistent with much of the hype about client/server in the trade press. Throughout 1992 and 1993, the trade press consistently reported that downsizing to client/server had completed its initial, small phase, and was predicted to take off into rapid market growth. In late 1993 and early 1994, the same trade press began to report that the takeoff was actually under way, and that a very substantial number of formerly mainframe applications were in the process of migration.[14] While we agree with the facts behind this journalistic analysis, we disagree with the conclusion.

**Finding 2:** The adoption process for client/server technology is considerably more textured than the standard diffusion model predicts.

The above description of those users "sure to change" is disconcerting for the standard diffusion view. These are not the users with the highest propensity to adopt an enterprise strategy of moving to client/server. Rather, they are end users in large organizations for whom downsizing solutions are excellent partial solutions for their particular specialized needs. The new technology is compelling for them, and diffusion has swept rapidly through their population. It is a mistake, however, necessarily to think of them as the beginning of the true wave of companywide adoption toward the technological vision held by the proponents of the horizontal market model. If all the horizontal market model and client/server did was complete the multidecade progression of number-crunching applications off mainframes onto smaller platforms, they would not be very important.

The standard diffusion model fails to describe adoption of client/server technology in large enterprises because of a key maintained assumption of that model that does not hold in this setting. That is the assumption that pioneer and mass-market adopters are doing the same or similar things technologically. In fact, the adoption of client/server is not always coupled with strategic changes in IT use and applications. Sometimes the close coupling is there. We saw, for example, really innovative cost and billing control systems in competitively threatened hospitals. Changing the hospital into a business and giving it a business IT infrastructure were closely linked.

But we also saw downsizing for much different motives and in different forms. Downsizing can happen idiosyncratically at the group or department level to make an end run around the "glass house." "Renegades" abound that, frustrated with the slowness of MIS to respond to their ad hoc queries, have decided to install systems of their own that will provide them with the access to business data they need in a timely manner.[15] Our oil exploration interviewees were in this category. They are qualitatively different from the strategically repositioned hospital.

Other different phenomena include MIS shops that do "aerosol downsizing" with the primary goal of being seen to downsize.[16] Examples include simple change on the client—keeping a mainframe application but replacing the proprietary end-user terminals with personal computer clients offering the same functions. Examples also include simple change on the server—porting a legacy application to an open systems platform without altering it at all. While these "aerosol downsizing" migrations provide some value, they are not the same as the strategic, high-payoff vision of the possibilities of client/server.

Some adopters we spoke to were in large, but relatively young, organizations. These are interesting firms to look at because their computing needs are similar to those of other large organizations, but their switching costs are lower because they tend not to be locked in to proprietary legacy systems of the old model. These firms had disproportionately adopted client/server as their overall computing model. The growth of this kind of application is driven by the rate of creation of new firms in the economy, not by the rate of diffusion of client/server across an existing stock.

This variety—different kinds of adopters are using the technology in fundamentally different ways—may leave the S-shaped diffusion curve as a good ex post rationalization of the spread of client/server. But it means that using the S-curve as a forecasting device is a terrible mistake.

To sum up, most of the firms where we conducted interviews had done some adoption of client/server technology, but very few had committed to a strategy of moving away from the centralized, mainframe-based model.[17] Consequently, a distinction must be drawn between those companies that have done some adoption of client/server technology and those that have decided to adopt a strategy of moving away from the mainframe toward this newer computing model.

---

**Finding 3:** Relatively few buyers have committed to a strategy of moving away from mainframes toward dispersed models of computing, such as client/server.

---

This is not to say that there will not be diffusion of this technology. Quite to the contrary, it simply suggests that in terms of deliberate, strategic adoption, the diffusion process is still in the lower tail of the S-shaped diffusion curve. Indeed, most of the buyers think that they will eventually move in this direction. To see what will happen in the future, however, it is important to distinguish between superficially similar technical choices that involve radically different business goals.

The fundamental question is whether the large enterprise trade-off between the "old" and the "new" is qualitatively like that for the users in the first group above, who have already switched, and merely quantitatively different. The answer to this is a resounding "no." The cost-benefit trade-off for those who have already adopted hinged for the most part on the question of MIPS arbitrage. The cost of computing power provided by newer workstations is significantly lower compared with the cost on a mainframe. For number-crunching applications, this drives the decision. This is most decidedly not the trade-off that is being made by the chief information officer (CIO) for the enterprise as a whole.

The problem that the CIO faces is not primarily one of cost, but of how to exploit information technology to increase productivity or provide competitive advantage. The horizontal market model is not yet up to this challenge, and there is a significant difference in the perceptions of suppliers and buyers with respect to the relative merits of the horizontal model. There are three main deficiencies in the current status of the horizontal market model that we discuss in more detail in the fifth section but will preview here.

The idealized technological description of the horizontal market model has not yet been realized. Sellers do not yet behave as the model says they do. Buyers find that they cannot just plug and play. This is partly a technological problem. But it is also a problem that the transition itself involves complex technical and business change inside the user's organization. In the transition that is resulting from the competitive crash described above, and still smarting from bets they placed that locked them into now defunct or declining mainframe vendors, buyers are reluctant to place big bets.

To flesh out this view, we turn in the following section to a more detailed description of what our interviewees told us about the attractions of, and barriers to, adopting client/server technology. For the purposes of the next two sections, we drop the number-crunching applications of the unrepresentative early adopters. Instead, we focus on the needs and problems of mainstream business use in large organizations.

## ATTRACTION OF, AND BARRIERS TO, ADOPTION OF CLIENT/SERVER

We begin with a description of the main attractions to client/server technology.

**Finding 4:** The main attractions to client/server technology (more important reasons listed first) are superior applications development environment; MIS backlog/ad hoc queries; end-user ease of use; lower training costs; distributed functionality; new applications/uses; cheap MIPS.

The above factors are listed roughly in order of importance, with factors of roughly equivalent importance listed together. At the top of the list are two elements that reflect end users' frustration with the responsiveness of MIS to their needs for information. Better information can be used to make the end user's job easier or to make important business decisions, rather than simply for routine processing of large data sets. Our interviews suggested that a good measure of the likelihood that there would be a movement away from the mainframe in an organization was the number of file cabinet drawers of ad hoc queries that had been received, but not processed, by MIS. Related to this is the fact that the desktop computing environment is superior for applications development, so that centralized or department-level MIS is able to be more responsive to the ad hoc queries in that environment.

The superior applications development environment is particularly important in settings where speed is part of the firm's competitive advantage. Financial institutions that are competing by creating new financial instruments need to be able to develop applications rapidly, and the superior applications development environment of the smaller systems wins out. One MIS manager in a pharmaceutical company, talking with us and a large internal customer, said, "We compete on time as much as on price and quality these days." One business unit manager in a financial service company talked about changing MIS's development cycle to more closely match product life cycles in the markets she competes in. Thus, one reason to move forward to client/server is a view that the existing MIS backlog is having a real, negative impact on the business side of the company.

The next categories of factors are important for some of our later conclusions. Dispersed systems are valued in large part because they can be used to restructure the way the firm does business, and to get information to the people who need it when they need it. But for IT to become pervasive within an organization, it must be easy to use and easy to learn how to use. The old mainframe environments are at a big disadvantage vis-à-vis alternatives in this regard.

Significantly lower in importance is the desire of users to be empowered to manipulate data in centralized databases from geographically dispersed locations. That is not to say, of course, that these users do not want the ability to have manipulations performed on data that are useful to them in making business decisions (which, as discussed above, they do care about deeply), it is just that they do not seem to have a strong desire to have that functionality distributed to their site. The issue is timely access to data, not control over it. Frequently, these motives lead to a partially downsized solution in which an operations database remains on the mainframe, but a for-analysis copy is regularly sent to the client/server system. Thus, paychecks may still be written using a mainframe employment database, like human resource managers (HRM) in different units benchmark with the analytical copy. Another example has analytical copies of key financial data used for cost-control studies. Our interviewees told us the point was to use an easy interface to get data resources into the hands of more noncomputing professionals and managers.

One of the unknowns (at least to us) going into this study was how much of the attraction to client/server technology was a result of new applications that were available only on this technology. Somewhat surprisingly, this did not emerge as a major consideration. For the most part, the applications that we found users performing, or considering performing, on the new systems were the same ones they had been performing on older systems. In many cases, these same applications were being carried out in different ways or by different people; in that case, it was usually due to the superior applications environment rather than because the new system enabled a brand-new application. This situation will surely change with time.

At the bottom of the list of attractions is cheaper processing power. If there is a single lesson to be learned about the attractions of the new systems (and, indeed, as we shall see shortly, about the barriers), it is that it is not about cost savings. The fraction of total costs that is accounted for by the costs of processing power is small. (Exceptions are the number-crunching, intensive applications referred to above.) Moreover, most of the clients in client/server systems are idle or not intensively used much of the time, making simplistic MIPS arbitrage arguments uncompelling. Our average interview subject thought that the cost comparison between mainframes and client/server over the whole life cycle was "roughly a wash," in the words of an MIS director in a transportation company. There was some disagreement about this average cost estimate, with those few who expected big cost savings unsurprisingly more likely to move forward.

There is a corollary to the cheaper-MIPS point that is true, however. Many different users expect that client/server applications will be more scalable. Server capacity may be added in smaller incremental lumps than were possible with mainframes. This might permit IT costs to be brought into closer connection with business-unit needs. Similarly, if clients are truly independent, they may be added or upgraded. Thus the cost advantage of client/server may be more flexible, not cheaper, MIPS.

**Finding 5:** The main barriers to client/server technology (more important reasons listed first) are adequate legacy applications; unsettled standards; inadequate network management tools; ignorant business managers; long transition time; FUD, MIS fiefdoms; concerns about data integrity; transition costs.

As with most tales of slow adoption of a new technology, inertial forces loom large. In this case, the largest inertial force is that established organizations have legacy systems that, although not perfect by any means, are performing adequately. Existing systems with their imperfections are highly respected because, despite their clumsiness, inelegant code, and opaque user interfaces, they work. Users are all too aware of the costs of changing to systems that hold the promise (but no proof) of superior performance but the attendant risks of failure.

A second barrier, somewhat below the first in importance, is the uncertainty about what exactly to switch to. A wide variety of client/server standards is not yet in place. For example, the operating system standards battles are far from settled on either client or server. Buyers are reluctant to commit too quickly to a system that time will prove was the losing standard.

At roughly the same level of importance is a technological impediment, dissatisfaction with existing network management tools. For example, version control for applications on ten thousand geographically dispersed clients is not something that firms feel they can realistically maintain with existing network management tools.

Business manager ignorance, FUD (fear, uncertainty, and doubt), and MIS fiefdoms are interrelated. The people who have the most to gain from the move to new systems are the business managers who want access to data for business management purposes. However, these are typically not the people in the organization with technological expertise. The people with that expertise typically reside within MIS. Some of them see a movement to a dispersed computing environment as a diminution of their power and control. The people who have the desire to change are imperfectly informed about whether change is feasible and cost-effective, and those who have that information can be biased against change.[18]

Another technical consideration that arose frequently in our interviews, although typically not as a decisive factor, was concern about data integrity. This arose in a variety of situations. First, system management tools are not as well developed for networked systems as they are for mainframes, so that risks of losing data from a system malfunction are higher. For many applications, waiting for the technical shortcomings to be resolved is the best strategy. Second, and more important, once data access is dispersed through an organization, control of data is harder. It is difficult to undertake a full transition to the new computing model in which there is only a single companywide representation of data. To the extent that partial downsizing solutions are adequate, such as having end users query copies of company data, users can work around this barrier.

Perhaps most interestingly, "money"—this time in the form of dollar transition costs—is at the bottom of the list again. The decision about whether to switch to newer systems is simply not about money. This is not to say that users in the organizations we interviewed were not facing increasing scrutiny of IT expenditures—they were. It is also not to say that the transition costs were considered to be small—they were not. Several firms in the process of transition told us painful stories about the extent to which they had underestimated the transition costs and the difficulty of transition. (Users complained, for example, of the "hidden costs" of training end users, maintaining software in networked environments, and lost productivity during a lengthy transition.) The dollar costs and benefits as measured by cheaper, smaller machines, versus the costs of replacement, are not what is driving the decision in most of the firms we spoke to.

Rather, if we interpret findings 4 and 5 as a whole, the issue is one of IT systems' functionality when integrated into the using organization. The struggle we uncovered is between the very strong desire among users for information systems that are well integrated with their processes of doing business and capable of producing quick access to data that is useful for business decision-making, on the one hand, and legacy systems that work, are reliable, and easy to manage, on the other. Those who are pushing for change inside the organization are not looking to save costs; they are looking to use IT for competitive advantage and to improve organizational performance.

While the above remarks generalize across users, the users we interviewed clearly differed in the specifics of what they thought client/server might do. Interestingly, there was considerably more difference across user industries than within each industry. Indeed, remarkably similar stories were told within each vertical market. As our students reported, it seemed to them that each industry had the same consultant selling each of the firms in the industry the same story.

The differences across users are summarized in the following three findings.

**Finding 6:** One important determinant of differences in strategic adoption behavior is the relative importance of "backbone" applications versus "information for decision-making."

In the firms we interviewed, uses could typically be categorized as (1) back office applications (payroll, accounting, etc.); (2) "backbone applications" (transaction processing in banks, logistics in distribution, etc.)— applications that are "mission critical" and must function successfully for the day-to-day operation of the business; and (3) information for decision-making (ad hoc queries).

The back office applications were, to all intents and purposes, irrelevant to the decision to switch to strategic client/server systems. However, where there is a large and significant "backbone," there is also typically a powerful MIS group that controls the IT function in the organization and that is typically slower to embrace newer, decentralized technologies. Typical examples of industries in this category are banking and insurance. This is not to say that we did not find companies in these industries moving aggressively toward client/server. In fact, we did. However, they were fairly rare, and in these cases the changes were being driven by forward-looking MIS managers who were bucking the industry trend.

In contrast, organizations where business end users have power (hospitals, consulting firms, educational institutions, etc.) tended to be moving the most rapidly, demonstrating the power of users who want information to increase productivity or aid in decision-making in those organizations to get it. This category goes beyond traditional "decision support" applications on large systems. It includes delivering information in a timely way to company and division policy makers, as well as such applications as real-time support of customer service and other operations.

**Finding 7:** The degree of pressure from the competitive environment is another important determinant of differences in strategic adoption behavior.

Firms in environments where the competitive use of information is increasingly becoming viewed as a source of competitive advantage are likely to be the quickest to adopt the new technology. Examples include hospitals facing changes in third-party billing procedures and increased competition from "niche" players; telecommunications companies where billing is a source of competitive advantage (MCI's Friends and Family plan, for example); trucking, where deregulation has led to an increase in competition; and pharmaceuticals, where changes in health policy and the desire for time compression in drug approval are factors.

An intensely competitive environment shifts power in the organization toward those who favor radical change. Thus the transition is more likely to occur in organizations recently shocked by competition. Modern competitive environments move quickly, and the support for rapid action provided by many strategic client/server applications is particularly valuable in competitive environments. These increases in speed can be measured in minutes or in days, depending on the application. Knowing where all shipments on all trucks are in real time can be valuable in scheduling. If a marketing representative can tap those data, it provides instant information for customers about shipment status. On a longer time frame, reasonably quick access to cost data can support an informed competitive pricing response within days rather than at the end of a quarter. In both cases, the key competitive advantage comes from having time-valuable information when you need it.

**Finding 8:** The presence of a "champion" for the new technology is a major determinant of adoption behavior.

In some of the industries we examined, virtually identical firms divide between being at the cutting edge (or, more likely, the "bleeding edge") of technology adoption and being laggards. Upon closer inspection, in the firm that was moving aggressively, there was often a single individual who had decided to champion the move. Typically these are those rare individuals who understand both the technological possibilities that new technologies offer, and what the organization's business needs are.

Some forward-looking organizations have sought an outsider to play this role. The shortage of people with first-rate technical knowledge combined with specific business vision appears to be one bottleneck in the broader diffusion of strategic client/server.

## IMPLICATIONS OF THE FINDINGS FOR THE HORIZONTAL MARKET MODEL

The above eight findings paint a picture of the current marketplace that has some very familiar features. Put together, however, those features imply that the usual mental map of appropriate supplier behavior and organization held by many people is seriously off. In this section, we consider the implications of our findings for the organization of vendor companies and for the industrial organization of IT industries.

End users' complaints about the vertical market model are well known and certainly are not contradicted by our findings.

**Conclusion One:** Buyers are dissatisfied with the vertical market model.

For almost two decades, buying organizations have had the same fundamental problems with the vertical market model. Technical change in large proprietary systems, though sustained and at times rapid, has done little to alleviate these problems. The difficulty of using mainframe systems is the background to these complaints. Because they are so difficult to use, control of computing resources has had to be centralized and professionalized. This leads to the very difficult problem of user relations. In-house technologists and line business managers must jointly determine the feasibility and desirability of new IT initiatives. Yet these two groups are staffed very differently and it is quite difficult to achieve communication between them. Friedman and Cornford call this the "problem of user relations" and argue (1) that it is a major bottleneck for successful technical progress in IT applications and (2) that a long series of reorganizations of the role of MIS has failed to alleviate it.[19] We doubt that they would analyze the recent reorganization initiative associated with the CIO title any differently. Similarly, many initiatives in large-systems computing and in software design methodologies for large projects were announced as being the solution to exactly this problem.

The vertical market model was very effective at providing incremental technical progress for its main customers, MIS. The same mainframes got more powerful and also cheaper in a price/performance sense. Yet the vertical model did not take full advantage of the emerging new technologies to provide broad ease of use throughout companies. The emergence of the minicomputer, and especially the personal computer and workstation market segments, induced some rumblings about the vertical market model on the part of users. Surely some of that ease of use could be deployed in the development of large systems or in giving broad end-user access to large systems. In the 1980s, microprocessor-based computing became the cutting edge of the IT business overall, but in a way not integrated into companywide systems. The rumblings were underscored by demonstration effects. MIS began to question whether it was being given the best possible technical support under the vertical model. Second, business end users became familiar with small-systems business computing. They began to ask why companywide applications were not as accessible and usable as the ones on their own desktops.

These problems were crystallized when the changing competitive environment in the IT business itself began to reveal disadvantages of the business model of the vertically integrated vendor firm. Because of the importance of technological coordination in their product strategies, these traditional firms had slow and deliberate product development strategies. Newer, specialized firms tended to move very quickly on product development and on key product features decisions. The decision to port a vertically integrated vendor's software products to environments other than its own computer systems could be painfully slow, for example. A frequent complaint about vertically integrated vendors in this era is that they had lost touch with customers' rapidly moving needs.

Even the best customers of the vertically integrated firms began to see them as backward-looking and defensive. The vendors' decision processes were seen not only as slow but also as excessively focused on selling their own proprietary technology. Buyers could see that they would be made better off using some of the vendor's product lines differently. For example, in the new world a legacy application running on proprietary mainframe hardware and software might be efficiently run on the same software but on more open hardware. Vendors, in the initial phases of the transition, were slow to let buyers make that kind of change. As a result, even now buyers are very suspicious of vertically integrated vendors' motives. This is a strategic disadvantage for the systems integration lines of business that have emerged within some of those vendors, as buyers wonder whether the integrator will be biased toward the parent company's technology.

These disadvantages of the vertically integrated vendor model were visible in the product markets and in the stock markets. Our interviewees were very aware of them. However, we found that the technologists' view that the horizontal market model is on the verge of correcting these failings is not shared by end users. Buyers and suppliers are on different pages of the book. Or perhaps in different books.

**Conclusion Two:** Buyers are dissatisfied with the horizontal market model.

As previewed in the third section, there are various reasons that the horizontal market model is not yet living up to the promise held out by technologists. The first of these has to do with technological problems exacerbated by competitive forces on the supply side that we discuss a little later.

**Conclusion Three:** The horizontal market model is not yet in place.

The rosy vision of the horizontal market model is at its most complete in the personal computer market but is incomplete even there, and is less and less complete as one moves toward larger and more complex systems. Interface standards are fuzzy at best, and as a consequence the "plug and play" promise of the horizontal world has not been fulfilled. Rather than being freed from dependence on any vendor's proprietary technology, buyers still fear being held hostage to bets they place today.

Almost all client/server products and services are sold as "open" and are complacent with objective industrywide standards. Yet everyone in the industry knows that some standards are particularly favorable to the technologies of some companies. As a result, there are flash points of disagreement over which of several competing standards to follow. Examples include the interface between operating systems on the desktop and network operating systems. Users who tilt toward Microsoft and against Novell will make dozens of specific decisions about the way desktop applications interact with each other, interact with the operating system, and use remote data. Detailed decisions about programming, interprogram communications, the right applications programming interface (API), and so on will be wired deeply into the code of applications written now and into the human capital of the company's IT professionals. These decisions will be quite different from those made by users that tilt the other way. It is unlikely that changing back will be costless if one interface vision or the other is a marketplace failure and the products are badly supported in the future.

We do not mean to single out the companies just named as being particularly involved in interface uncertainty. The current situation is full of these examples, with competing desktop operating systems (DOS/Windows vs. OS/2 or DR/DOS) interfacing with competing network operating systems (Netware vs. the integrated portions of Windows' descendants) and telecommunications protocols (ATM vs. FDDI, Ethernet vs. Token Ring) being only the most visible. The boundary between the application on the client and the database software on the server is not clear, either. Nor is the extent to which "middleware" products and access standards make it easy to change databases on the server while preserving user access programs on the client or vice versa. Nor is the extent to which the newly somewhat more portable software products of the old vertically integrated companies will be truly open.

In each of these areas, all vendors say that they will support all important technologies in adjacent layers. Their products are open in the sense that they plan to build links to all other important products. Yet buyers know that vendors prioritize the connections that they make to other firms' products, because the strategy of universal interconnect is very expensive to develop. The products in the other layers have their own idiosyncrasies, and connecting to all of them in a high-performance way can be quite difficult. It is completely sensible to expect that some interconnections will be difficult or that they will become easy only after a long wait.

As a result, "open" does not mean that everything works easily with everything else. An "open" strategy means a wide variety of things in a wide variety of different contexts. Just as the Eskimos needed multiple words for "snow," so IT professionals now need a wide variety of words for "open." The romantic picture of open systems and the new market model is less a hard reality than technologists' wish-fulfillment exercise. There are so many things technologists would like to be true: that everything should "plug and play"; that only technical excellence should matter for commercial success; that marketing should not matter; that everyone should behave altruistically in standards committees and in the de facto standard-setting process; that great fortunes made in IT reveal the best technologists from a level playing field. Although it is a very encouraging prescription for behavior, this romantic picture is sadly lacking as a description.

**Conclusion Four:** There is a fundamental problem in commercialization of technology, that is, there is a significant "gap" between available technology and buyers' ability to deploy that technology to solve their business problems.

The technological shortcomings of the horizontal market model may be resolved soon. However, the strength of the horizontal market model is also a potential weakness. While the presence of standardized interfaces would permit vendors to specialize in individual components of the value chain, the explicit coordination of the vertical market model is lacking. The technologists' vision is that end users simply "put the pieces together" themselves. There are serious impediments to doing this, however. Strategic client/server applications involve nontrivial technical progress in their design and implementation. Choosing among the wide variety of available products, even if they were perfectly interoperable, would involve a careful assessment of desired features and performance. Performance and capacity planning is a difficult exercise with well-understood components like mainframes, and much more so in client/server environments. Thus, the tasks of running downsized applications still have a considerable MIS-like component.

One problem is that traditional MIS is deep in expertise for dealing with the mainframe environment and less well positioned to provide leadership for changes using client/server technology. Compounding this problem is the fact that in terms of relative power within the user organization, traditional MIS may not gain from change. Quite to the contrary, the newer systems bring with them decentralization of control and empowerment of end users. An additional liability for MIS is that an element of the new vision is the use of dispersed computing to solve end users' business problems. The traditional focus of MIS on the "glass house" and centralized computing problems has not endowed them with an in-depth understanding of the increased productivity and competitive advantage-producing opportunities that new systems might enable. Business end users who possess this knowledge are even less knowledgeable about what the latest technology can provide than are MIS.

We do not, however, want to leave the impression that we found MIS to be indifferent to the changing needs of end users or to the changing climate within organizations. Quite to the contrary, we found that for the most part MIS had discovered, or were on the verge of discovering, their internal customers, and many "glass houses" were attempting to change rapidly. They were not, however, well positioned to do so. Many were frustrated at the difficulty of making changes. The partial downsizing and aerosol downsizing applications we described above are a rational response to this frustration.

Independent of the problem of staying abreast of the rapid rate of technological change is the problem that the task of "putting the pieces together" is complex and, given that the adoption of new systems occurs frequently across companies but infrequently within a single company, is a function that is increasingly likely to be outsourced.

Outsourcing solutions to closing the gap present their own problems. Paramount among these is the fact that existing vendor–buyer relationships are badly structured for this. Specialist providers of workstations, networking infrastructure, databases, and so on have developed business strategy models that are designed to exploit the economies of specializing in their narrow band within their horizontal layer. Such vendors are poorly positioned to provide integrated solutions to buyers. In addition to this problem is the fact that there is a misalignment of incentives between buyers and sellers: buyers are more sure that vendors will profit from the investment in new technology than that they themselves will profit from any purported new capabilities the new technology will give them.

The above conclusions combine to explain another important phenomenon on the supply side.

**Conclusion Five:** There is an emerging convergence of the marketing models of a wide range of vendors.

A wide variety of vendors with very different underlying strengths and sources of competitive advantage are now using quite similar marketing models, all stressing client/server technology as a solution to the business end users' need for dispersed information useful in business decision-making. Very similar marketing presentations are made by vendors of database technology, systems integrators, vendors selling operating systems and applications platforms on the client computer, and so on. This convergence leads to an important failure of the horizontal market model.

Whereas the horizontal market model would encourage specialization, the desire to position products as critical to business solutions offers different incentives. Some vendors vertically integrate into adjacent layers. ("Vertical integration" has sufficiently negative connotations and is never used for this phenomenon, which is instead called offering functionality or convenience to customers.) Another common arrangement is tight vertical links between firms in adjacent layers. Sometimes these are cooperative technology exchanges in which the products are designed to interact intelligently with one another's specific features. Other collaborations are more of a cross-marketing type. A more downstream firm can sell access to its customer base to a more upstream collaborator with a variety of bundling arrangements. The reasons for this backward and forward integration vary somewhat. The two primary reasons are (1) to take advantage of the fuzziness in interface standardization, in an attempt to create a de facto standard around the vendor's technology; and (2) to use explicit coordination by a lead vendor, mimicking to some extent the old solution of the vertical market model, rather than force end users to struggle with compatibility problems.

The reasons for and effects on productivity of these contrasting motives are quite different. In the case of the first, we are seeing competition for the rents that are created by the practical imperfections in the horizontal market model. Much of the effect of this competition is to slow the realization of the vision of the horizontal market model, and to create and distribute rents for and among vendors at the expense of users and, probably, of overall social efficiency.

In the case of the second motivation, we are seeing an example of the principle that the market abhors a gap between technology and its use. Vendors are responding to a genuine user need—that for coordination among distinct lines of technical progress to solve business problems. In the bad old days, this function was well performed by the marketing departments of the vertically integrated vendors. They could feed back information about users to technologists and encourage the simultaneous development of the necessary future technologies in a way that would interact. This coordination task is still valuable and now typically must cross vendor firm boundaries.

It is our conjecture that the second, likely more positive, motivation is more important, depending on where in the value chain the vendor is situated. More downstream firms are more likely to have this motivation, while more infrastructural products are likely to be characterized by the first motivation. The dramatic increase in systems integration, systems management outsourcing, consulting, and related services is an indication of the size of the commercialization challenge.

It is difficult to believe that these new commercialization services offer a complete solution to the gap. Each does offer either consulting services for the transition to the client/server world, or software products that embody elements of client/server solutions, or both. Yet this type of firm, by its very nature, does not have the strong feedback loops to the development of new technology that existed inside the old fully vertically integrated model.

There is another reason to think these commercialization specialists will not complete the horizontal market model. Part of the business logic of these firms arises from building knowledge about solutions at one user's site and reusing that knowledge in other users' sites. This economizes on the very considerable costs of solving the business problem the first time. Since business problems tend to arise in particular businesses, this motivation leads to the emergence of vertical market "practices" or lines of business.

Two powerful forces limit the deployment of this business logic. Competition is a major motivation for strategic use of client/server technology. Yet a leading user company in a highly competitive environment has no incentive to share—through an intermediary—the knowledge underlying its strategic change. Quite the contrary. Second, adopting companies are suspicious that they might be sold a "cookie-cutter" solution, not one that fits their specific needs. Either to gain competitive advantage or to ensure appropriate fit, many companies will choose to limit use of the new commercialization or outsourcing services, and instead maintain strong in-house development capability.

## THE FUTURE OF LARGE COMPUTER SYSTEMS

So far we have described the technological reasons that the horizontal market model is not yet in place and the commercialization gap is implicit in the horizontal model. We now turn back to users, and consider the main implications for the future pattern of adoption of new information technologies.

**Conclusion Six:** Successful adoption of the horizontal market model involves organizational change on the part of user companies. That is, successful deployment of client/sever technology often requires fundamental change in the way the firm is organized and carries out business. This goes beyond business process reengineering to what we call "enabling strategic change."

Adoption of new information technology is easiest when it simply involves the automation of existing processes. When information technology is used to create competitive advantage, however, it will typically involve a change in the way business processes are performed and, if it is large enough in scope, in the way the firm is organized.

As examples, consider some of the competitively motivated strategic downsizing implementations we discussed above. We will discuss hospitals, then telephone companies.

Start with a hospital considering the adoption of client/server technology. Hospitals face a number of problems that they would like the new technology to address. All of these problems have been brought into sharp relief by today's more competitive environment for health-care supply. For example, hospitals can ill afford the payables problems that arise when third-party insurers reject bills. They would very much like to have on-line eligibility checking, automated verification of the coverage of policies, and so on. This is a difficult set of management problems because it involves changing the way nonmedical personnel influence health-care decisions. Another problem involves deciding how to price in the changing competitive environment. Large insurers and even large employers demand complex special terms. Niche competitors, such as walk-in clinics, are getting very good at taking away profitable business. It is a key challenge in meeting these outside forces to figure out what the hospital's products cost. Yet most hospital systems are not "product" related. Thus, there is more to building a decent costing model than capturing the data in existing systems and repackaging it. There may be a need to fundamentally rethink the way that individual therapeutic activities are bundled into "products" and the products are sold. It doesn't help that health-care professionals typically do not think in terms of products.

Another example from the same industry involves the automatic storage and retrieval of patient information. The payoff for this is potentially enormous, because a good deal of very expensive employees' time is spent learning about patients. There is good reason to believe that a combination of paper recall systems and patient interviews leads to incomplete information for therapeutic decision-making. An automated and portable patient information system, however, would call for large changes in how physicians think about their work and their relationships to patients. It is not a systems integration problem to have an effective version of such a system; it is a problem in the fundamental reorganization of health-care delivery organizations.

The telephone example tells us something about what motivates breakthrough changes in business behavior. Having a product that cuts across many customers, like MCI's Friends and Family, or across the many sites of a business customer, permits new marketing initiatives. The role of IT is to enable the shipping of products this complex; a product is basically a bill from an IT perspective. Another potential role of IT is to support decision-making to define new products. What control over their telephone costs would business competitors prefer, and what kinds of discounts would be net-revenue-maximizing in the household long-distance business? Perhaps more important than the motivation, the telephone examples tell us something about the likely decision-making process for large IT-enabled changes in business behavior.

Consider two distinct lines leading to a major decision, each of which involves both new technical capability in a firm's IT and a new marketing capability. In the first line of thought, the MIS people in the company begin to describe, in the broad general terms of our introduction, the capabilities of client/server architectures. In one of their frequent meetings, the technologists convince company marketers that this means there is now a possibility to completely remake the business with a whole new concept of the customer and the customer's relationship to the company.

In the second decision-making process, a marketing manager driven by competition comes up with a new model of the relationship with the customer, perhaps because a competitor company is already implementing that model. The manager is told that MIS can begin to produce an inferior version of the bill that is the operational core of the new marketing system in about eighteen months, and that thereafter alterations in the form of the bill will take only four to six months when MIS is not backlogged. The MIS people volunteer that it may be possible to achieve these changes faster by using client/server architectures.

The second decision-making process strikes us as much more likely to occur in practice. The realization that new technology and the new business goal are complementary is forced upon the company. Thinking through what is needed to reach the new business goal reveals that IT capability is a bottleneck. In the first train of thought, the same realization involves "pushing on a rope."

The distinction matters. Organizational change of this kind is difficult and risky. It involves changing the roles of many employees, not simply retraining existing employees in a new technology. The roles of many marketing employees, as well as the role of the marketing department, change in the "new bill" example. Very important decisions that employees may have thought were the defining parts of their jobs may be removed from them, and automated or handed over to other departments. Also threatening to autonomy is the possibility that workers may be much more closely second-guessed when they leave an electronic trail of their decisions.

It is little surprise that much attention is being placed on mini-downsizing along with the rationalization or "reengineering" of very specific business practices. Further, the rhetoric of the reengineering movement, with its emphasis on complete abandonment of existing capabilities, is easy to understand.[20] Both relate to the ease with which some specific, clearly broken business practice can be completely redesigned and reimplemented. The problem of keeping the working parts of a complex organization while changing the parts that are less functional is not so straightforward.

**Conclusion Seven:** Since organizational reengineering is complex, difficult, and slow, so, too, will be widespread diffusion of truly strategic adoption of the horizontal market model.

## CONCLUSIONS

There is a new computing model emerging with both intelligent use of new technologies in user organizations and a new, horizontal market model for the information technology industry itself. Realization of the full gains of the new computing model has both huge promise and huge problems. The few truly impressive examples of strategic use of the new model in adopting companies convince us of the promise. The competitive advantage that is achieved by successful strategic use of the new model is breathtaking. This is because it is right for the competitive environment of today. It offers more than the promise of pure cost reduction (though there are some savings to be had) because of the opportunity for dramatically improved speed and responsiveness to customers and to changing conditions.

If strategic use of these models diffuses widely, there is a real possibility for a productivity revolution in lower-management and middle-management white-collar work. Other converging technologies, such as those associated with the information superhighway, are closely associated with other (buying and selling) white-collar work. Taken together, these areas are a very large fraction of contemporary employment, enough that the implications for the well-being of the whole economy, not just the individual companies adopting, could be enormous. This revolution could transform office work as much as farm mechanization transformed field work and mass production transformed factory work.

Yet the process of transition to the new model is very difficult. The three workplace revolutions could be mid-nineteenth century for agriculture, early twentieth century for manufacturing, and well into the twenty-first century for administration. The main blockages at this time are not technological. The pure technologists have largely done, or are now doing, their job. Instead, the primary blockage is in the shortage of business ideas and the will to put those ideas in place in the using organization. It takes a good deal of will and a great idea, for the transition is wrenching and risky. The diffusion of the new computing model is slow because of these difficulties. It is our intention to continue to study this transition, because we think that its promise could be realized faster if its true nature were better understood by adopting companies.

A second blockage is that the new computer industry market model has yet to emerge. The horizontal market model remains more of a hope than a reality for supplying to companywide applications. At the moment, we have an almost horizontal model that delivers far less than the full promise of the fully horizontal model. It does not yet offer a satisfactory replacement for the old vertical market model's main advantage, effective coordination mechanisms for developments in different technologies. Without clearly defined interface standards and market boundaries, it is still far from the well-performing perfect competition of economic theory. Buyers are strongly motivated to turn to intermediaries, such as systems integrators, for relief from these problems; yet intermediaries are an incomplete solution. These problems, although they occur in supplying companies, are not primarily technical in nature. They relate to the industrial organization that will optimize over (1) the rate of genuinely useful technical progress and (2) the trust of potential users in the solutions that vendors offer and in vendors' motives. We think that the issue of what company and industry structure will yield these outcomes is a first-order research problem for us.

## NOTES

1. An industry participant's early take on the change from the vertical to the horizontal model is Grove [1990].

2. The situation in minicomputers was never completely centralized, because many firms were quite independent of DEC. After the "unbundling" of systems hardware and software by IBM in the late 1960s, alternative sources of supply for many mainframe components (including the computer itself) grew in importance. We think that the representation in the "vertical" model is valuable despite these exceptions. It is notable that both defenders of the efficiency effects of the lead role of the central vendor—such as Franklin M. Fisher, John J. McGowan and Joen E. Greenwood, *Folded, Spindled, and*

*Mutilated: Economic Analysis and U.S. v. IBM* (Cambridge, Mass.: MIT Press, 1983)—and writers who thought it provided excess market power—such as Gerald W. Brock, *The U.S. Computer Industry* (Cambridge, Mass.: Ballinger, 1975)—agree that there was centralized responsibility for the direction of technical progress under this system.

3. Once again, the exceptions do not disprove the main point. The representation applies most truly to the PC-compatible market, once known as the IBM-PC compatible market. In the Apple Macintosh world, there has been tight bundling between systems software and hardware, and Apple continues to play something of a lead vendor role in enforcing standard interfaces.

4. This has led to a rather romantic view of the users of personal computers as "liberated" from centralized MIS. Once again, there are exceptions. Some companies have always maintained internal procurement standards, leading to a somewhat more centralized "buyer." The "customer" is still correctly characterized in text, however. The recent importance of local-area and wide-area networking has led to a growth in centralization of procurement. This is an important trend to which we shall return.

5. Or superminicomputers. The important movement is away from large, proprietary systems sold by large, integrated companies. We will use "mainframe" to cover any system used like one, intending to catch the movement away from DEC superminis as well as IBM or Unisys mainframes.

6. Charles H. Ferguson, and Charles Morris, *Computer Wars* (New York: Times Books, 1993), summarizes much of this discussion of a break point in the history of the industry.

7. See Joseph Farrell, Hunter K. Monroe, and Garth Saloner, "Systems Competition Versus Component Competition: Order Statistics, Interface Standards, and Open Systems," July 1994 (mimeo), for a model along these lines.

8. The corresponding weakness of the horizontal model is the difficulty of coordination. This may lead to very considerable wasted effort if competing standards-setting efforts arise. It may also be an opportunity for some vendors to abuse the de facto standard setting process. See Stanley M. Besen, and Garth Saloner, "Compatibility Standards and the Market for Telecommunications Services," in R.W. Crandall and K. Flamm, eds., *Changing the Rules: Technological Change, International Competition and Regulation in Telecommunications* (Washington, D.C.: Brookings Institution, 1988).

9. See note 15.

10. Andrew L. Friedman and Dominic S. Cornford, *Computer Systems Development: History, Organization and Implementation* (New York: John Wiley and Sons, 1989), devotes several chapters to the history.

11. Timothy F. Bresnahan and Manuel Trajtenberg "General Purpose Technologies: 'Engines of Growth'?," *Journal of Econometrics.*

12. In the early phases of the diffusion of client/server, actual replacements were comparatively rare. But many projects in this period were designed and planned to be full mainframe replacements, even if that is not how they worked out in the end.

13. This kind of quantitative conclusion must of course be tentative in any study based on interview evidence from a smallish sample of user companies. It is buttressed by the systematic statistical work of Timothy F. Bresnahan and Shane Greenstein, "The Competitive Crash in Large-Scale Commercial Computing," in Ralph Landau and Gavin Wright, eds., *Growth and Development: The Economics of the 21st Century* (Stanford, Calif: Stanford University Press 1994).

14. See Johanna Ambrosio, "Client/Server Costs More Than Expected," *Computerworld,* October 18, 1993, p. 28; Andres Boughton, "Power Play," *Computerworld,* November 22, 1993, pp. 97–102; John Kador, "Downsizing Is Ready for Prime Time Midrange Systems," *Computerworld,* May 12, 1992, pp. 50–51; Judy Larocque, "Client/Server Trends," *IEEE Spectrum,* April 1994, pp. 48–50; "Full Speed Ahead to Client/Server," *Midrange Systems,* March 25, 1994, pp. 1–2; and Charles Babcock, "Survival in Risky Business," *Computerworld,* May 9, 1994, p. 6.

15. This also leads to technical problems with the standard diffusion model that can be easily repaired within the standard framework. For example, client/server decision-making is diffused widely through the organization and there are many "adoption dates." The adoption is not an "all or nothing" event, taking place at a single point in time. These problems have been solved by standard diffusion modelers—for example, Anthony A. Romeo, "Interindustry and Interfirm Differences in the Rate of Diffusion of an Innovation," *Review of Economics and Statistics* 57, no.3 (August 1975): pp. 311–319.

16. Many frustrated MIS interviewees in the "middle group" of companies emphasized the importance of being seen to act.

17. Moreover, even those who had shifted significantly toward client/server technology had kept, and intended to keep, their mainframe installations, at least as servers.

18. The frequency of this kind of remark was surprising, given the more common finding that MIS has little power in organizations. See Henry C. Lucas "Organizational Power and the Information Services Department," *Communications of the ACM* 27, no.1 (January 1984): pp. 58–65. We conjecture that the power of MIS is larger in times of radical systems-capability change.

19. See Friedman and Cornford.

20. See Michael Hammer and James Champy, *Reengineering the Corporation* (New York: Harper Business, 1993).

# REFERENCES

Ambrosio, Johanna. "Client/Server Costs More Than Expected." *Computerworld*, October 18, 1993, p. 28.

Babcock, Charles. "Survival in Risky Business." *Computerworld*, May 9, 1994, p. 6.

Besen, Stanley M., and Garth Saloner. "Compatibility Standards and the Market for Telecommunications Services." In R.W. Crandall and K. Flamm, eds., *Changing the Rules: Technological Change, International Competition and Regulation in Telecommunications.* Washington, D.C.: Brookings Institution, 1988.

Boughton, Andres. "Power Play." *Computerworld*, November 22, 1993, pp. 97–102.

Bresnahan, Timothy F., and Shane Greenstein. "The Competitive Crash in Large-Scale Commercial Computing," In Ralph Landau and Gavin Wright, eds., *Growth and Development: The Economics of the 21st Century.* Stanford, Calif.: Stanford University Press 1994.

Bresnahan, Timothy F., and Manuel Trajtenberg. "General Purpose Technologies: 'Engines of Growth'?" *Journal of Econometrics.*

Brock, Gerald W. *The U.S. Computer Industry.* Cambridge, Mass.: Ballinger, 1975.

Caldwell, Bruce. "Client/Server Report: Looking Beyond the Costs." *Information Week*, January 3, 1994, pp. 51–56.

Farrell, Joseph, Hunter K. Monroe, and Garth Saloner. "Systems Competition Versus Component Competition: Order Statistics, Interface Standards, and Open Systems." July 1994. Mimeo.

Ferguson, Charles H., and Charles Morris. *Computer Wars.* New York: Times Books, 1993.

Fisher, Franklin M., John J. McGowan, and Joen E. Greenwood. *Folded, Spindled, and Mutilated: Economic Analysis and U.S. v. IBM.* Cambridge, Mass.: MIT Press, 1983.

Friedman, Andrew L., and Dominic S. Cornford. *Computer Systems Development: History, Organization and Implementation.* New York: John Wiley and Sons, 1989.

"Full Speed Ahead to Client/Server." Midrange Systems, March 25, 1994, pp. 1–2.

Hammer, Michael, and James Champy. *Reengineering the Corporation.* New York: Harper Business, 1993.

Kador, John. "Downsizing Is Ready for Prime Time Midrange Systems." *Computerworld*, May 12, 1992, pp. 50–51.

Larocque, Judy. "Client/Server Trends." *IEEE Spectrum*, April 1994, pp. 48–50.

Lucas, Henry C. "Organizational Power and The Information Services Department." *Communications of the ACM* 27, no.1 (January 1984): 58–65.

Mansfield, Edwin. "Industrial Research and Development: Characteristics, Costs, and Diffusion of Results." *American Economic Review* 59, no.2 (May 1969): pp. 65–71.

Rogers, Everett M. *The Diffusion of Innovations.* New York: The Free Press, 1983.

Romeo, Anthony A. "Interindustry and Interfirm Differences in the Rate of Diffusion of an Innovation." *Review of Economics and Statistics* 57, no.3 (August 1975): pp. 311–319.

Stoneman, Paul. *The Economic Analysis of Technological Change.* New York: Oxford University Press, 1988.

# CHAPTER 8

# PATENT SCOPE AND EMERGING INDUSTRIES

## Biotechnology, Software, and Beyond

Josh Lerner

Robert P. Merges

## INTRODUCTION

The convergence of technologies discussed in this volume will affect the structure of the computer hardware and software and communications industries in complex ways. Public policies can do much to facilitate or hinder the restructuring of these industries in response to their changing technological opportunities. In this paper, we consider one policy mechanism—the strength of intellectual property protection—and how it affects the evolution of industry structure. A heightened awareness of this relationship may help us tailor patent policy to influence the development of these converging industries.

Lending importance to this issue is the growing importance of intellectual property protection, particularly patents, at the frontiers of computers and communications. The breadth of two U.S. patent awards in this area have sparked controversy. Optical Data Company's Patent

*The authors are affiliated with Harvard Business School and University of California at Berkeley School of Law (Boalt Hall), respectively. We thank Jesse Reyes of Venture Economics for access to data; the Division of Research at Harvard Business School for financial support; and participants in the Colliding Worlds preconference and conference—especially David Yoffie and Ashish Arora—for helpful comments.

#5,173,051, "Curriculum planning and publishing method," was denounced by rivals as a "patent on the Socratic method."[1] Patent #5,241,671, "Multimedia search system using a plurality of entry path means which indicate interrelatedness of information," inspired Compton's NewMedia to demand royalties from virtually the entire multimedia industry. While the U.S. Patent and Trademark Office has agreed to reexamine both patents, these developments have stimulated discussion about how intellectual property should be protected in emerging industries. These conversations have also been fueled by the controversies surrounding the Graphics Interchange Format, the technology underlying the compression of graphic images on the Internet and many on-line services, which has been the subject of well-publicized patent disputes between Stac and Microsoft and between Unisys and software developers offering services through CompuServe.[2] While the importance of intellectual property protection is indisputable, a rich dialogue between lawyers and economists about these issues, such as has characterized the antitrust and tax areas, has yet to emerge.

In this paper, we argue that awarding broad patents in emerging industries makes considerable sense. Since the pioneering work of Coase, it has been recognized that clearly defined property rights lower transaction costs.[3] Many studies have documented that these rights lead to less socially wasteful litigation and increase the willingness of investors to commit capital to projects. For example, recent empirical work shows that replacing the informal quasi-property rights of squatters with clear ownership has numerous beneficial results. For instance, more secure, formal property rights lead to a greater willingness to exchange and consolidate property holdings, and increase both owners' and outside investors' willingness to invest in the land.[4]

More recently, it has been argued that *broader* property rights lower transaction costs as well. For instance, Arora claims that increasing patent scope allows licensors to transfer more informal "know-how" along with the patent rights.[5] The wider scope of the patent gives the licensor greater legal recourse against an opportunistic licensee. Lending support to this claim is the observation that when intellectual property rights are very narrow, few licensing transactions occur. For instance, trade secrets offer exceedingly narrow intellectual property protection, protecting only against misappropriation: "The acquisition of a trade secret by a person who knows or has reason to know that the trade secret was acquired by improper means."[6] Thus, a firm cannot sue a rival that discovers its trade secret independently or through "reverse engineering" (the disassembly of a device to discover how it works). This is unlike patent protection, which allows the awardee to prosecute others who infringe, regardless of the source of the infringers' ideas. Pooley notes that very few "naked" trade secret licenses are observed, suggesting that the information covered only through this very narrow property right is difficult to transfer in an arm's-length exchange.[7] Similar evidence is found in Sullivan's interviews and surveys of licensing practices among computer hardware manufacturers in Silicon Valley.[8] He found that among the most important factors considered by firms in deciding whether to license a technology was the breadth of protection that the licensor can offer the licensee as part of the license.

The lowering of transaction costs that apparently accompanies strengthened intellectual property rights should reduce the costs of licensing transactions. This may make it easier for small firms specializing in research and development to exist as independent entities. (These firms may have several advantages that allow them to be more effective environments for the pursuit of innovations than large firms; for instance, because outcomes can be measured more exactly, incentives that are more linked to performance can be offered.) Because the commercialization of products is likely to entail substantial economies of scale and scope, small research-intensive organizations are unlikely to be able to successfully commercialize many of their innovations alone. Strong intellectual property rights may allow these small firms to efficiently license technologies to large firms that can market these products. By contrast, if intellectual property rights are weak, the licensees may incur steep transaction costs, and will be less likely to receive an acceptable return on their investment in R&D. If this is the case, most innovative activity will take place within larger firms, at the expense of the considerable advantages associated with entrepreneurial ventures.

We do not argue, however, that lower licensing costs due to stronger intellectual property rights will necessarily lead to all innovations' being pursued in independent firms. There are many strategic reasons for some innovations to be pursued in the same firms that ultimately market products. But if an industry structure with numerous smaller firms makes sense, then broader intellectual property rights may make such a structure feasible.[9]

Despite our general enthusiasm for this argument, we note that the link between patent scope and industry structure is limited in some important ways. To begin, broader patents will not make much of a difference when firms cannot successfully protect their key assets through intellectual property protection. If patent protection is ineffective, and no alternative legal mechanism serves as a viable substitute, strengthening patents will have no effect.

Second, policymakers' ability to influence patent scope diminishes over time. As a technology matures, and as the body of technical literature and products flourishes, patents become narrower. This growing body of "prior art" limits the sweep of patent claims, making broad patents increasingly rare. For example, generally speaking, only radically new chemical structures, such as buckminsterfullerene, can receive broad patents; otherwise, the mature chemical industry fights bitterly to obtain relatively narrow claims over the increasingly well-understood classes of existing chemicals. The many "dosage form" patents in the pharmaceutical industry are a good example of this. As a consequence, policy makers cannot influence patent scope in an industry to the same degree in all stages of that industry's development, and policy options in the infant industry stage—when technologies are still emerging and converging—are most important.

After developing this argument, we examine the biotechnology and software industries. We measure how the breadth of patent protection has evolved in these industries over time. Using a proxy for the scope of patent protection based on the International Patent Classification (IPC) scheme, we show that in both cases the patent system awarded broad rights in the early growth phase of the industry's technology. The data show that over time, however, the breadth of protection has narrowed considerably. We present corroborating evidence from practitioner accounts. We argue that, given the advantages of having at least some small firms in these industries, this pattern of patent protection makes policy sense.

## INDUSTRY EVOLUTION AND PATENT SCOPE

One way to view industry structures is that they fall along a spectrum. At one extreme is an industry with a single giant firm; at the other is one where a multitude of small firms inhabit each business segment. Each extreme has its strengths and weaknesses.

In an industry with one firm (or only a few firms), economies of scale and scope can be realized. In addition, the costs of transactions within the firm are likely to be lower than those between firms, which are more likely to require extensive negotiations and to be prone to opportunistic behavior. But the large firm may also face problems. Bureaucratization is likely to lead to slow or ineffective decision-making. Shirking or self-dealing by managers may be prevalent and difficult to detect. While an industry dominated by small firms is unlikely to achieve the same economies in production and is likely to face problems in contracting, the problems associated with size will be less severe.

It is difficult to say in advance what industry structure will be ideal. The optimal place along the spectrum is likely to vary with the underlying technology and the nature of the market. But we can consider how the presence of weak or strong intellectual property rights will affect the evolution of industries. If the ideal industry is dominated by a few large firms, the system of intellectual property protection is unlikely to impede its evolution to this form. But the nature of protection will have a major effect on the feasibility of an industry dominated by small firms. Several studies have suggested that strong intellectual property rights allow firms to effectively undertake collaborative or licensing arrangements.[10] And, as mentioned, strong intellectual property rights limit the potential for opportunistic behavior by contracting parties, and may allow the greater transfer of informal know-how. With weak intellectual property rights, the costs of entering into technological licensing agreements may be impossibly large.

Thus, the optimal structure for very dynamic industries is hard to predict in advance. Policy makers should strive to provide maximum flexibility, in order for the optimal form to emerge. Allowing broad property rights early in the industry—along with an antitrust environment that does not limit joint ventures or acquisitions—may facilitate this discovery process.

At the same time, we wish to emphasize that broad patents may impose social costs as well. Gilbert and Shapiro and Klemperer argue that because monopolies impose social costs, in many cases it is better to award narrow but lengthy patents.[11] Merges and Nelson document a number of cases where excessively broad patents were awarded early in the history of a technology, and some of them seem to have slowed the development of the relevant industry.[12] Examples include the Selden automobile patent and some early biotechnology patents. While *excessively* broad patents such as these are difficult to defend, there is room to argue that where the requirements of patentability have been met, policy makers confronting a new industry or technology should consider awarding relatively broad patents early on. As discussed earlier, this will have the effect of encouraging a more diverse set of organizational forms to develop in the industry.

Thus, one pattern that may be observed is a narrowing of patent protection over time. In the early stages of an industry, when the ideal structure is not clear, broad patent awards may make sense. As the role of small firms becomes less important with industry maturation and consolidation, narrowing of the breadth of patent protection may make sense. As discussed above, the narrowing of patent scope may also reflect a natural evolution, driven by the increasing amount of "prior art."

## PATENTING IN BIOTECHNOLOGY AND SOFTWARE

This section provides a brief introduction to the evolution of patenting in the biotechnology and software industries. We will not attempt to do justice to the complex legal and policy questions concerning patents in these areas, but will highlight a few points of commonality and difference.[13]

Both biotechnology and software have posed challenges to the existing notions of patentability. To be entitled to utility patent protection (the most common form of U.S. grant), an innovation must satisfy three criteria. Under 35 U.S.C. 101–103 and 112, it must be

- A process, machine, manufacture, or composition of matter

- New, useful, and nonobvious

- Disclosed in sufficient detail that a skilled person could build and operate it.

The scope of patentable subject matter has traditionally not included fundamental scientific discoveries. A frequently invoked rationale for this omission is that many scientists care little for monetary rewards, and would have pursued the discoveries in any case. Consequently, to grant patent awards for purely scientific discoveries would be socially wasteful.

Patents on compositions containing living organisms have been issued since an award to Louis Pasteur in 1870. These include awards for yeast compositions to be used in brewing and for sterility tests containing spores. Prior to the 1980s, however, the U.S. Patent and Trademark Office (USPTO) had a policy of not issuing grants on plants and animals created by technology. They argued that these organisms were "products of nature" and not a process, machine, manufacture, or composition of matter. This policy changed after the 1980 Supreme Court decision in the *Diamond* v. *Chakrabarty* case.[14] After Chakrabarty's patent application for oil-eating bacteria was rejected by the USPTO, the decision was appealed. In a 5–4 decision, the Supreme Court ruled that the discovery was patentable as either a manufacture or a composition of matter.

The decision greatly enhanced the ability of biotechnology firms to raise capital from private and public investors. Virtually all new biotechnology firms relied heavily on patent protection. This reliance on patents has been necessitated by the high degree of mobility among research personnel and the long lag times between patenting and commercialization, which have rendered traditional mechanisms for protecting intellectual property (such as trade secrecy and learning-curve economies) ineffective.

Patents continue to be important in biotechnology, but they are imperfect mechanisms for protecting intellectual property. As opposed to the pharmaceutical industry, which has traditionally resolved patent disputes through cross-licensing agreements, over 125 suits have been filed involving new biotechnology firms.[15] These have engendered a complex and occasionally contradictory body of case law. A second problem has been posed by the lengthy delays from time of application to award for many biotechnology grants. These delays have been attributed in large part to the USPTO's slow response in adding patent examiners to its biotechnology office, and to the eagerness with which private firms have hired away these examiners.

The USPTO has been equally reluctant to allow the patenting of software. The issue was initially examined in 1966 by the President's Commission on the Patent System, which concluded that the lack of an effective classification scheme and the already large volume of programs made patenting impossible.[16] The commission recommended that software continue to be protected by copyright instead.

The ability of the software industry to receive protection from copyrights is a substantial difference from the situation in the biotechnology industry. Particularly since the 1980 amendments to the Copyright Act of 1976, software firms have been able to receive automatic seventy-five-year protection for their work. This protection, however, is extended only to the expression of the ideas, not to the ideas themselves. Ongoing litigation is exploring to what extent copyright protection prohibits works that are substantially similar.

As in the case of biotechnology, the USPTO's willingness to grant patents for software has increased in response to a series of Supreme Court decisions. In its initial two decisions in this arena, *Gottschalk* v. *Benson* and *Parker* v. *Flook,* the court upheld USPTO's refusal to issue patents to software programs on the grounds that "basic tools of scientific and technological work" were unpatentable.[17] The 1981 decision in *Diamond* v. *Diehr* ushered in an important change.[18] This decision held that a patent for a rubber-curing process that incorporated a computer program was patentable as an industrial process. The decision, however, left ambiguous the extent to which programs can be patented, and was initially viewed as a narrow decision.[19] While the Supreme Court has not revisited the issue subsequently, the Court of Appeals for the Federal Circuit (since 1982, the centralized appellate court for all intellectual property cases) has generally taken a positive view of the patentability of software.[20] Software firms have responded by filing a large number of applications, and the USPTO has been increasingly willing to issue awards. Substantial divisions still exist within the software industry as to the advisability of patent protection and its likely impact on the industry.

## EMPIRICAL ANALYSIS

### Developing the Sample

Identifying biotechnology and software patents is difficult. First, these patents tend to be assigned to a variety of subclasses, often mixed in with other awards. Second, the analysis below will employ a proxy for patent breadth based on the International Patent Classification (IPC). If we used the patent classification scheme to identify awards, the analysis would likely be biased.

We thus defined biotechnology and software awards as those granted to firms specializing in these fields. We realized that consequently we were examining only a fraction of awards. Many biotechnology awards have been made to universities and major pharmaceutical companies, and many software awards to integrated computer hardware and software manufacturers, such as IBM. There seems little reason to expect, however, that the pattern of breadth in patent awards to dedicated firms should differ from that in awards to established concerns.

We identified biotechnology and software firms by using two sources. In both cases, we used the records of Venture Economics to identify venture-backed firms. Venture Economics, a unit of Securities Data Company, compiles information from institutional venture investors. We included those firms in the classes 4000, "Biotechnology," and 2700, "Software." Many software firms—with small product development costs and modest working capital needs—do not, however, receive venture financing. We supplemented the list of software firms with active and research companies in Compustat whose primary industry assignment is (or was) in classes 7371, "Computer Programming Services"; 7372, "Prepackaged Software"; and 7373, "Computer Integrated Systems Design."[21] This search led to the identification of 350 biotechnology and 248 software firms.

We identified patents assigned to these firms by using a CD-ROM database prepared by the USPTO.[22] This listed awards to both publicly and privately held firms. We included awards to these firms' subsidiaries, joint ventures, and R&D limited partnerships. We identified name changes, joint ventures, subsidiaries, and R&D limited partnerships from a variety of reference sources.[23] We obtained information on the classification of each patent, as well as its award date, by using BRS Information Technologies' PATDATA database.[24] These searches generated a total of 1,661 biotechnology awards and 245 software patents. Table 8-1 summarizes the top five recipients of patents in these two samples.

## Developing a Proxy for Patent Scope

The best way to measure patent scope might be through subjective assessments.[25] With the help of molecular biologists and lawyers, we could assess the breadth of claims in each patent. Firms do indeed hire lawyers to undertake such analyses before acquisitions, licensing agreements, and other transactions. An analysis of a single patent often takes several weeks. Such an effort did not appear to be a practical way to develop a sample of sufficient size for an empirical analysis. Instead, we employed a proxy for patent scope: the number of subclasses into which the USPTO assigns the patent.

TABLE 8-1

REPRESENTATION OF FIRMS IN THE BIOTECHNOLOGY AND SOFTWARE
PATENT SAMPLES

**Panel A: Biotechnology Firms, 1981–1992**

| FIRMS | NUMBER OF PATENTS |
| --- | --- |
| Cetus Corporation | 211 |
| Genentech | 148 |
| Genetics Institute | 53 |
| NeoRx Corporation | 45 |
| Chiron Corporation | 43 |
| Total, all firms | 1,661 |

**Panel B: Software Firms, 1986–1993**

| FIRMS | NUMBER OF PATENTS |
| --- | --- |
| Microsoft Corporation | 31 |
| Adobe Systems | 11 |
| Bachman Information Systems | 9 |
| Bolt, Beranek and Newman | 9 |
| BMC Software | 8 |
| Total, all firms | 245 |

NOTE: The table indicates the number of awards to the five most-frequently represented firms in the sample, as well as in the sample as a whole.

Patent classifications are determined through a careful process.[26] A supervising primary examiner reviews the incoming patent applications, then assigns each to one of the over one hundred thousand U.S. patent subclasses. This classification determines which examining group reviews the application. A patent examiner in the assigned group then evaluates the proposed patent. To assess the novelty of the application, the examiner searches previous patents issued in the original and related subclasses, as well as various other databases. At the time of award, the patent examiner assigns the patent to one or more U.S. patent subclasses. The examiner has a strong incentive to classify these patents carefully, because the classifications are used in searches of the prior state of the art. To ensure the accuracy of the classification and to maintain consistency across examining groups, an official known as a "post classifier" reviews the classification of all issuing patents.

At the same time that the examiner assigns the patent to U.S. patent subclasses, he also assigns it to one or more IPC subclasses. The IPC system had its origin in the Council of Europe's 1954 European Convention on the International Classification of Patents for Invention. The classification system has been managed by an international (rather than a purely European) agency since 1969. Since that year, U.S. patents have been classified according to both the U.S. and IPC schemes.[27]

The IPC and U.S. classification schemes differ in three respects. First, the quality of the classification schemes differs. The World Intellectual Property Organization carefully guards the integrity of the IPC classification scheme through periodic reviews. While the USPTO goes to considerable pains to ensure that patents are placed in the proper subclasses, it devotes limited attention to the *arrangement* of the U.S. subclasses: the U.S. classification has not had a systematic overhaul since 1872.[28] The power to introduce subclasses lies with the patent examiners, who can develop and locate "informal" subclasses with little review.[29] Second, the principles that motivate the two classification schemes differ. The USPTO stated shortly after it began reporting IPC classifications: "It is well recognized that the two systems are conceptually different; the U.S. system being based primarily on structure and function while the International Classification is primarily industry and profession oriented."[30] Thus, the IPC scheme reflects the economic importance of new inventions, as opposed to the technical focus of the U.S. scheme. Finally, the first four levels of the IPC classifications are nested. This is in contrast with the U.S. system, where 435/40 is a subset of 435/39, which is in turn a subclass of 435/34, but 435/41 is not a subclass of any of these.[31]

Because of these features, we employed the IPC classification as a proxy for patent scope. We counted the number of IPC classes to which patent examiners assigned each patent. We used only the first four digits. For example, we counted a patent assigned to classes C12M 1/12, C12N 1/14, and C12N 9/60 as falling into two classes, C12M and C12N.

Lerner validates this proxy as a measure of patent scope in four ways, using the sample of biotechnology patents described above.[32] His first assessment of the economic significance of the scope proxy examines citations in later patents. Patent examiners delineate the extent of a patent award by citations to previous patents, which describe the prior art. Citations are the legal equivalent of property boundary markers, showing where the claim touches upon preexisting ones. Applicants have a duty of disclosure to reveal related patents. In fact, the enforceability of the patent depends on the forthrightness with which applicants cite the prior art. Furthermore, patent examiners review and supplement these citations. In a study of CT scanners, Trajtenberg shows that the number of subsequent citations reflects the economic importance of a patent.[33] Lerner analyzes the impact of patent scope on citations through a regression analysis. He shows that, evaluated at the mean of the independent variables, an increase of one standard deviation in the proxy for the scope of a patent increases the expected number of citations per year by 11 percent.

Lerner's second test examines whether the patent has been the subject of litigation. Often the USPTO awards patents that appear to overlap. These disputes are usually resolved through negotiations. Often the conflicting parties sign a cross-licensing agreement, under which each party licenses its patent to the other. The alternative approach to resolving these disputes, litigation, is costly and time-consuming. Because of these significant costs, models in the law-and-economics literature suggest that firms should litigate only economically important patents. In a regression analysis, broader patents are significantly more likely to have been litigated. At the mean of the independent variables, an increase of one standard deviation in patent scope increases the probability of litigation by 41 percent.

A more qualitative validation of this proxy for patent scope relies on the judgments of twelve intellectual property attorneys specializing in biotechnology. Lerner conducted a telephone survey of three law professors, four corporate officers, and five lawyers in private practice. He asked each to name the most economically important patents awarded to independent biotechnology firms, excluding precedent-setting patents whose economic importance was relatively minor. (An example is the

Chakrabarty patent, the case used to establish that living, man-made organisms were patentable.) The patents identified by survey respondents were classified into significantly more four-digit IPC classes than the other patents awarded to new biotechnology firms.

Finally, Lerner examined the valuations placed on firms during the venture capital investment process. Venture capitalists typically invest in privately held firms, often in high-technology industries. In each financing round, the venture capitalists and the entrepreneur negotiate a valuation of the firm. Because these firms have few assets other than their intellectual property, if a relationship between intellectual property and valuation exists, this is a natural place to observe it. Using a sample of 535 financing rounds at 173 venture-backed biotechnology start-ups, Lerner shows that patent scope has an economically and statistically significant impact on the valuation of those firms. An increase of one standard deviation in average patent scope at the mean of the independent variables translates into a 21 percent increase in firm value.

Table 8-2 summarizes the distribution of the proxy for patent scope, the number of four-digit IPC classes, in all patents in the sample.

## EMPIRICAL ANALYSIS

We examined whether the scope of patents awarded has changed over the period in several ways. Table 8-3 presents the mean number of four-digit IPC classes, as well as the number of patents awarded to firms in the sample, for several periods. In both the biotechnology and the software awards, there appears to have been a narrowing of scope. The mean number of IPC classes of the biotechnology awards is about 0.18 lower after 1988; the breadth of software patents also appears to fall steadily.

We tested the significance of these patterns in two ways. First, we examined whether the mean number of IPC classes differs in these periods through $t$-tests and an $F$-test. We also employed a nonparametric Wilcoxon test, which compares the median number of classes. While we believe that a patent assigned to two four-digit IPC subclasses is on average broader than an award assigned to only one, we are unsure whether it is twice as broad. Through the use of a median test, we did not impose any such restrictive assumptions.

Table 8-4 reports the $p$-values from tests of the null hypothesis that the number of four-digit IPC classes in these periods does not differ. In each case, the null hypothesis is rejected at conventional confidence levels. In the case of the biotechnology patents, the equality of means and

TABLE 8-2

SCOPE OF AWARDS TO BIOTECHNOLOGY AND SOFTWARE FIRMS

| | Number of Patents Awarded to Sample Firms | |
|---|---|---|
| NUMBER OF IPC CLASSES | BIOTECHNOLOGY | SOFTWARE |
| 1 | 832 | 154 |
| 2 | 552 | 66 |
| 3 | 223 | 12 |
| 4 | 45 | 13 |
| 5 | 3 | 0 |

NOTE: The table indicates the number of four-digit IPC classes of the patents awarded to these firms.

TABLE 8-3

SCOPE OF AWARDS TO BIOTECHNOLOGY AND SOFTWARE FIRMS, OVER TIME

Panel A: Biotechnology Firms

| | MEAN IPC CLASSES | NUMBER OF PATENTS |
|---|---|---|
| 1981-1988 | 1.81 | 556 |
| 1989-1992 | 1.63 | 1105 |

Panel B: Software Firms

| | MEAN IPC CLASSES | NUMBER OF PATENTS |
|---|---|---|
| 1986-1987 | 1.82 | 38 |
| 1988-1992 | 1.55 | 141 |
| 1993 | 1.30 | 66 |

NOTE: The table indicates, for several periods, the mean number of four-digit IPC classes of the patents awarded to these firms.

medians are both rejected at the 1 percent level of confidence. In the software case, where sample sizes are smaller, the level of statistical confidence is not as great, but in all cases the null hypothesis is rejected at the 5 percent confidence level.

We then examined this pattern in a regression analysis. We used as the dependent variable the number of four-digit IPC classes into which the patent is classified. The independent variable is the date of the patent award expressed as a continuous variable (e.g., an award on July 1, 1992,

TABLE 8-4

TESTS OF EQUALITY OF SCOPE OF AWARDS TO FIRMS
IN THE BIOTECHNOLOGY AND SOFTWARE SAMPLES

Panel A: Biotechnology Firms

| | P-VALUE, TEST OF EQUALITY OF… | |
| --- | --- | --- |
| | MEAN IPC CLASSES | MEDIAN IPC CLASSES |
| 1981–1988 v. 1989–1992 | 0.000 | 0.001 |

Panel B: Software Firms

| | P-VALUE, TEST OF EQUALITY OF… | |
| --- | --- | --- |
| | MEAN IPC CLASSES | MEDIAN IPC CLASSES |
| 1986–1987 v. 1988–1993 | 0.017 | 0.017 |
| 1986–1992 v. 1993 | 0.009 | 0.016 |
| 1986–1987 v. 1988–1992 v. 1993* | 0.007 | — |

NOTE: The table indicates, for each period, the *p*-value from *t*-tests and non-parametric Wilcoxon tests that the mean number of four-digit IPC classes of the patents awarded to these firms are the same in each period.
*p*-value is from an *F*-test of the joint hypothesis of no difference across the three periods.

is coded as 1992.5). Reflecting our concerns about the interpretation of the dependent variable, we employed an ordered logit regression (see table 8-5). This specification treats a patent assigned to three IPC classes as broader than an award in two classes, but does not assume that the former is 50 percent broader.[34]

In both cases, the independent variable measuring the award date was significant at the 1 percent confidence level. One way to assess the magnitude of the coefficient is to examine the effect of a one-year change on the predicted number of subclasses. In the case of the biotechnology patents, the predicted fraction of patents assigned to more than one four-digit subclass in January 1989 was 50.6 percent; in January 1990, it was 49.3 percent. Among software patents, the predicted fraction of patents assigned to more than one four-digit subclass in January 1989 was 43.9 percent; in January 1990, it was 39.3 percent.

One concern with this analysis is that it may reflect unobserved factors. In particular, the composition of technologies being patented may have changed. Some technologies may be inherently broad and cost-cutting; others may be narrower. It would not be surprising if researchers initially pursued the most important technologies. This could lead to a

TABLE 8-5

ORDERED LOGIT REGRESSION OF SCOPE OF AWARDS TO FIRMS
IN THE BIOTECHNOLOGY AND SOFTWARE SAMPLES, OVER TIME

| Independent Variables | Biotechnology | Software |
|---|---|---|
| Award date | -0.05 [0.02] | -0.14 [0.05] |
| Constant 1 | -102.76 [40.74] | -287.14 [108.41] |
| Constant 2 | -101.14 [40.74] | -285.46 [108.39] |
| Constant 3 | -99.24 [40.74] | -284.75 [108.79] |
| Constant 4 | -96.45 [40.74] | |
| Log likelihood | -1806.57 | -228.88 |
| $x^2$-statistic | 6.36 | 7.11 |
| $p$-Value | 0.012 | 0.008 |
| Number of Observations | 1,661 | 245 |

NOTE: Each patent awarded in the sample period is used as observations. The number of four-digit IPC classes of the patents awarded to these firms is the dependent variable. The independent variables include the award date (with July 1, 1992 expressed as 1992.5, etc.) and several constants. Standard errors in brackets.

narrowing of patent awards over time, without any policy shift by the USPTO.

To address this concern, we reran the regressions. We added dummy variables for the most frequent nine-digit U.S. classifications into which these patents had their primary assignment. (We alternatively employed dummies for the most frequent twenty, thirty, and forty classifications.) Even after this correction for the changing technological mixture of awards, the coefficients of the independent variable measuring the date of the patent application remained significantly negative at the 1 percent confidence level.

## ADDITIONAL EVIDENCE

The evidence presented above can be corroborated by practitioner accounts suggesting that the scope of patent awards in biotechnology and (less clearly) software has been narrowing over time. This section reviews this evidence.

Many observers believe that biotechnology patent awards in the early and middle 1980s were very broad. In 1988, for instance, Edward Lentz (at the time associate patent counsel at SmithKlein Beckman) noted: "Claims to biotechnology inventions seem uncommonly broad in comparison to typical chemical cases and, therefore, seem especially vulnerable to attack under [U.S. patent legislation]. One can speculate as to the reasons for this. Postulated reasons range from the inherent imprecisions of the biological sciences to, in some cases, overreaching and/or naïveté."

Conversations with patent attorneys suggest that the scope of biotechnology awards has narrowed significantly since 1988. In several awards, the USPTO has taken a narrow view of the allowable breadth of patent awards. In the case upheld by the U.S. Court of Appeals for the Federal Circuit as *In re Wright,* the USPTO limited a 1983 patent application for "a process to produce a live non-pathogenic vaccine for a pathogenic RNA virus" to cover only the vaccine that confers immunity in chickens to the Prague avian sarcoma virus.[35] It is also illustrative to compare the abstracts of the two transgenic mouse patents that have been awarded to Philip Leder's laboratory at Harvard University. Patent #4,736,866, "Transgenic non-human mammals," awarded in April 1988, read: "A transgenic non-human eukaryotic animal whose germ cells and somatic cells contain an activated oncogene sequence introduced into the animal, or an ancestor of the animal, at an embryonic stage." Patent #5,175,383, "Animal model for benign prostatic disease," awarded in December 1992, was far more narrowly constructed: "A male transgenic mouse containing germ cells and somatic cells which contain a recombinant gene which is a vertebrate gene in the int-2/FGF family which is capable of promoting benign prostatic hyperplasia or hypertrophy in said transgenic mouse, said gene being introduced into the mouse, or an ancestor of the mouse, at an embryonic stage." One of the few public discussions of the change by a USPTO employee is Kushan;[36] Yang and Hamilton is an account in the popular business press.[37]

The evidence on software is more ambiguous. The USPTO has been repeatedly criticized for its overly broad awards.[38] Some evidence suggests that the USPTO is responding to these changes. One example is the greater willingness by the USPTO to reexamine awards that are perceived as too broad, such as those to Optical Data Corporation and Compton's NewMedia discussed in the introduction. More generally, the Software Patent Institute—a nonprofit organization established by Apple Computer, Microsoft, IBM, Lotus, and several other firms—has compiled a collection of software manuals and programs going back to the 1960s. The USPTO has begun to search this database prior to granting patent awards.[39]

Other practitioners, however, feel that these changes may have arisen as much by accident as by design. Discussions suggest that in the examination groups responsible for these technologies, the USPTO has responded to the influx of patent applications by hiring additional examiners with specialized academic training. Reflecting either their greater knowledge of the subject matter or their academic training, these examiners may be inclined to take a more narrow view of what constitutes an allowable patent claim.

## CONCLUSIONS

In this paper, we examined the evolution of the scope of patent awards over time. We developed a rationale for why the scope of awards should be broad in an industry's formative years, when the ideal industry structure is uncertain. Our argument was predicated on the suggestion that broader intellectual property awards will make it less costly to license innovations. If discoveries can be effectively licensed with a minimum of expense, then smaller firms specializing in research—which may have other important advantages—may be economically viable. If not, the high transactions costs associated with licensing awards may result in such organizations' being unable to earn an attractive return on their investment in research and development.

We noted several important qualifications to our argument. First, it is not clear that an industry that receives broad intellectual property grants will actually include many smaller firms. Rather, broad patent grants will add such an industrial structure to the set of possible structures. Second, we noted that patent scope will naturally narrow over time, as the "prior art" in the field builds up. This is a policy that can be more effectively implemented while the industry is still young and key technologies are still emerging. Finally, we acknowledged that inconsistently broad patent awards may have socially harmful consequences.

We then examined patents awarded to biotechnology and software firms. We employed as a proxy for patent scope the number of four-digit IPC classes to which each award was assigned. We showed that in both cases, there appears to have been a significant narrowing in the breadth of patent protection over time. We suggested that our explanation provides one interpretation for the patterns.

This paper suggests several avenues for future research. We will briefly mention two of these. First, the considerable differences in the scope of patent protection across countries provide a way to examine the impact of patent protection on industry evolution and firm behavior. European nations, for instance, differ in their willingness to recognize broad biotechnology patents. Have these differences affected the mixture of firms in these countries, or the strategic behavior of the firms that have appeared? A second opportunity is suggested by the large number of technology licensing agreements among U.S. firms in these industries. (Many of these are publicly disclosed in filings with the U.S. Securities and Exchange Commission.) How has the changing breadth of intellectual property protection in recent years documented above affected the types of contracts that these firms have entered into? Have the payments between parties shifted in response to these changes? Has the use of restrictive covenants evolved? A better understanding of these patterns would shed light on the impact of the breadth of patent protection in converging industries, and help the tailoring of patent policy to encourage the industries' rapid development.

More generally, top management of technology-intensive firms must pay attention to intellectual property policy, and play a leadership role in shaping policy in this arena. This is one of the crucial mechanisms through which the federal government affects the evolution of innovative industries, particularly ones where technologies are rapidly converging. It is far too important to be left in the hands of those who stand to benefit from a complex, arcane system.

## NOTES

1. G. Bisson, "Patent Questions Plague Industry," *MacWeek* 8 (February 14, 1994): 32.

2. See P. H. Lewis, "Software Companies Upset by Demands for Royalties," *New York Times*, January 5, 1995, p. C1. Bruising patent battles are anticipated over the ownership of the MPEG-2 image compression technology, which is expected to be critical in high-definition television and many advanced multimedia applications. M. Voorhees, "New Video Technology Faces Mega-Licensing Woes: MPEG II May Be Open, but It's Also Highly Proprietary—CableLabs Tries to Create Voluntary Patent Pool." *Information Law Alert*, February 10, 1995.

3. R. Coase, "The Problem of Social Cost," *Journal of Law and Economics* 30 (1960): 1–44.

4. D. Feeny, "The Development of Property Rights in Land: A Comparative Study," in Robert H. Bates, ed., *Toward a Political Economy of Development* (Berkeley: University of California Press, 1988); and B. Mueller, L. Alston, G. Libecap, and R. Schneider, "Land, Property Rights, and Privatization in Brazil," *Quarterly Review of Economics and Finance* 34 (1994): 261–280.

5. A. Arora, "Licensing Tacit Knowledge: Intellectual Property Rights and the

Market for Know-How," Working Paper 91-35 (rev.), Heinz School of Public Policy and Management, Carnegie-Mellon University, 1992.

6. R. M. Milgrim, *Milgrim on Trade Secrets* (New York: Matthew Bender, 1993).

7. J. Pooley, *Trade Secrets: A Guide to Protecting Proprietary Business Information* (New York: American Management Association, 1989).

8. P. H. Sullivan, "A Preliminary Survey of Royalty Rate-Setting Practices in the U.S. Computer Hardware Industry," Consortium on Competitiveness and Cooperation Working Paper 93-17, 1993.

9. An alternative rationale for broad patent awards for pioneering technologies, based on *ex ante* incentives to innovate, is presented in H. F. Chang, "Patent Scope, Antitrust Policy, and Cumulative Innovation," *Rand Journal of Economics* 26 (1995): 34–57.

10. D.J. Teece, "Technology Transfer by Multinational Firms: The Resource Cost of Transferring Technological Know-How," *Economic Journal* 87 (1977): 242–261; R. E. Caves, H. Crookell, and J. P. Killing, "The Imperfect Market for Technology Licenses," *Oxford Bulletin of Economics and Statistics* 45 (1983): 249–268; and Arora.

11. R. J. Gilbert and C. Shapiro, "Optimal Patent Length and Breadth," *Rand Journal of Economics* 21 (1990): 106–112; and P. Klemperer, "How Broad Should the Scope of Patent Protection Be?" *Rand Journal of Economics* 21 (1990): 113–130.

12. R. P. Merges and R. R. Nelson, "On the Complex Economics of Patent Scope," *Columbia Law Review* 90 (1990): 839–916.

13. For overviews, see U.S. Office of Technology Assessment, *New Developments in Biotechnology: Patenting Life*, pt. 5, Series on New Developments in Biotechnology (Washington, D.C.: U.S. Government Printing Office, 1989); U.S. Office of Technology Assessment, *Finding a Balance: Computer Software, Intellectual Property and the Challenge of Technological Change* (Washington, D.C.: U.S. Government Printing Office, 1992); and R. P. Merges, *Patent Law and Policy* (Charlottesville, Va.: Michie, 1992).

14. 571 F.2d 40, 197 U.S.P.Q. 72 (Cust. & Pat. App. 1978), cert. dismissed, 439 U.S. 801, 99 S.Ct. 44 (U.S. 1978), reconsideration, 596 F.2d 952, 201 U.S.P.Q. 352 (Cust. & Pat. App. 1979), cert. granted, 444 U.S. 924, 100 S.Ct. 261 (U.S. Cust. & Pat. App. 1979), vacated as to Bergy, 444 U.S. 1028, 100 S.Ct. 696 (U.S. Cust. & Pat. App. 1980), aff'd 447 U.S. 303, 100 S.Ct. 2204, 206 U.S.P.Q. 193 (U.S. 1980).

15. J. Lerner, "Patenting in the Shadow of Competitors," *Journal of Law and Economics* 38 (1995): 563–545.

16. Because the contents of these programs were unknown to the USPTO, the commission felt that examiners could not accurately assess the "prior art" (the level of previous knowledge in the industry).

17. For *Gottschalk* v *Benson*, see 441 F.2d 682, 169 U.S.P.Q. (BNA) 548 (Cust. & Pat. App. 1971), cert. granted, 405 U.S. 915, 172 U.S.P.Q. (BNA) 577 (U.S. 1972), 409 U.S. 63, 175 U.S.P.Q. (BNA) 673 (U.S. 1972); for *Parker* v *Flook*, see 559 F.2d 21, 195 U.S.P.Q. (BNA) 9 (Cust. & Pat. App. 1977), 437 U.S. 584, 198 U.S.P.Q. (BNA) 193 (U.S. 1978); for the quote, see *Gottschalk* v *Benson*, 409 U.S. at 67.

18. 602 F.2d 982, 203 U.S.P.Q. (BNA) 44 (Cust. & Pat. App. 1979), 450 U.S. 175, 209 U.S.P.Q. (BNA) 1 (U.S. 1981).

19. P. Samuelson, "Benson Revisited: The Case Against Patent Protection for Algorithms and Other Computer Program-Related Inventions," *Emory Law Journal* 39 (1990): 1025–1154.

20. See, for instance, *In re Alappat*, 33 F.3d 1526, 31 U.S.P.Q.2d 1545 (Fed. Cir. 1994) (en banc); *In re Iwahashi*, 888 F.2d 1370, 12 U.S.P.Q.2d (BNA) 1908 (Fed. Cir. 1989).

21. To be included in Compustat, a firm must have made a public filing with the U.S. Securities and Exchange Commission. Neither of these data sources captures the many private software firms that have not received financing from institutional or public sources. Our goal, however, is to create a representative sample of firms whose technological focus is on software.

22. U.S. Department of Commerce, Patent and Trademark Office, Office of Patent Depository Library Programs (USPTO/OPDLP), *CASSIS/BIB User's Guide*, (Washington, D.C.: USPTO/OPDLP, 1990); and USPTO/OPDLP, "ASSIST Disk Notes" (Washington, D.C.: USPTO/OPDLP, 1991), unpublished documentation.

23. Especially from Corporate Technology Information Services, *Corporate Technology Directory* (Woburn, Mass.: Corporate Technology Information Services, 1993 and earlier years); North Carolina Biotechnology Center, Biotechnology Information Division (NCBC), *North Carolina Biotechnology Center Documentation for Actions Database* (Research Triangle Park, N.C.: NCBC, 1990); NCBC *North Carolina Biotechnology Center Documentation for Companies Database* (Research Triangle Park, N.C.: NCBC, 1990); National Register Publishing Company, *Directory of Corporate Affiliations* (Wilmette, Ill.: National Register Publishing Co., 1992); *BioScan: The Worldwide Biotech Industry Reporting Service* (Phoenix, Ariz.: Oryx Press, 1992); and Predicasts, Inc., *Predicasts F&S Index of Corporate Change* (Cleveland: Predicasts, 1992).

24. A related question is the period over which to examine the patents. In a few cases, there are very early awards to these firms. These are almost invariably cases where a firm changed its technological focus over time—for instance a firm that shifted from computer hardware manufacturing to software. In the case of biotechnology, we employ all awards after 1980, the year of the seminal *Diamond* v *Chakrabarty* decision. In software there is no single clear-cut

decision that opened the floodgates for patenting. Instead, we note that in the sample, the pace of patenting of these firms is trivial prior to 1986. This observation is corroborated by the more general patterns documented by J. T. Soma and B. F. Smith, "Software Trends: Who's Getting How Many of What? 1978 to 1987," *Journal of the Patent and Trademark Office Society* 71 (1989): 415–432. We consequently used this as our first year. The biotechnology sample was collected through September 1992; the software sample, through December 1993.

25. This discussion is based on J. Lerner, "The Importance of Patent Scope: An Empirical Examination," *Rand Journal of Economics* 25 (1994): 319–333.

26. This discussion is based on USPTO, *Finding a Balance.*

27. World Intellectual Property Organization (WIPO), *General Information on the Third Edition of the International Patent Classification* (Geneva: WIPO, 1981).

28. U.S. Department of Commerce, Patent Office, *Development and Use of Patent Classification Systems* (Washington, D.C.: U.S. Government Printing Office, 1966).

29. U.S. Department of Commerce, Patent and Trademark Office (USPTO), *Examiner Handbook on the Use of the U.S. Patent Classification System* (Washington, D.C.: U.S. Government Printing Office, 1984).

30. USPTO, *Manual of Patent Examining Procedure,* 3rd ed., 30th rev., (Washington, D.C.: U.S. Government Printing Office, 1971).

31. USPTO, *Manual of Classification* (Washington, D.C.: U.S. Government Printing Office, 1993).

32. Lerner, "The Importance of Patent Scope."

33. M. Trajtenberg, "A Penny for Your Quotes: Patent Citations and the Value of Inventions," *Rand Journal of Economics* 21 (1990): 172–187.

34. The results are also robust to the use of an ordinary least-squares specification, which does make this assumption.

35. 999 F.2d 1557, 27 U.S.P.Q.2d (BNA) 1510 (Fed. Cir. 1993).

36. J. P. Kushan, "Protein Patents and the Doctrine of Equivalents: Limits on the Expansion of Patent Rights," *High Technology Law Journal* 6 (1991): 109–148.

37. C. Y. Yang and J. O. Hamilton, "Are the Patent Police Ganging up on Biotech?" *Business Week,* June 13, 1994, 84–85.

38. An example is "PTO Hears from Silicon Valley on Patent Protection for Software," *Patent, Trademark and Copyright Journal* 47 (1994): 307.

39. G. Smith, "Lines Drawn in Patent Battle: Multimedia Firms Banding Together to Fight Compton's," *San Francisco Examiner,* November 28, 1993, p. E-1; and R. L. Cook, "Software Industry Anticipates a Flood of Patent Litigation," *National Law Journal* 16 (January 24, 1994): S2–S4.

## REFERENCES

Arora, A. "Licensing Tacit Knowledge: Intellectual Property Rights and the Market for Know-How." Working Paper 91-35 (rev.), Heinz School of Public Policy and Management, Carnegie-Mellon University, 1992.

*BioScan: The Worldwide Biotech Industry Reporting Service.* Phoenix, Ariz.: Oryx Press, 1992.

Bisson, G. "Patent Questions Plague Industry." *MacWeek* 8 (February 14, 1994): 32.

BRS Information Technologies. "PATDATA." McLean, Va: BRS Information Technologies, 1986. Unpublished documentation.

Caves, R. E., H. Crookell, and J. P. Killing. "The Imperfect Market for Technology Licenses." *Oxford Bulletin of Economics and Statistics* 45 (1983): 249–268.

Chang, H. F. "Patent Scope, Antitrust Policy, and Cumulative Innovation." *Rand Journal of Economics* 26 (1995): 34–57.

Coase, R. "The Problem of Social Cost." *Journal of Law and Economics* 3 (1960): 1–44.

Cook, R. L. "Software Industry Anticipates a Flood of Patent Litigation." *National Law Journal* 16 (January 24, 1994): S2–S4.

Corporate Technology Information Services. *Corporate Technology Directory.* Woburn, Mass.: Corporate Technology Information Services, 1993 and earlier years.

Feeny, D. "The Development of Property Rights in Land: A Comparative Study." In Robert H. Bates, ed., *Toward a Political Economy of Development.* Berkeley: University of California Press, 1988.

Gilbert, R. J., and C. Shapiro, "Optimal Patent Length and Breadth." *Rand Journal of Economics* 21 (1990): 106–112.

Klemperer, P. "How Broad Should the Scope of Patent Protection Be?" *Rand Journal of Economics* 21 (1990): 113–130.

Kushan, J. P. "Protein Patents and the Doctrine of Equivalents: Limits on the Expansion of Patent Rights." *High Technology Law Journal* 6 (1991): 109–148.

Lentz, E. T. "Adequacy of Disclosure of Biotechnology Inventions." *AIPLA Quarterly Journal* 16 (1988): 314–338.

Lerner, J. "The Importance of Patent Scope: An Empirical Examination." *Rand Journal of Economics* 25 (1994): 319-333.

Lerner, J. "Patenting in the Shadow of Competitors." *Journal of Law and Economics* 38 (1995): 563–595.

Lewis, P. H. "Software Companies Upset by Demands for Royalties." *New York Times,* January 5, 1995, p. C1.

Mansfield, E. "R&D and Innovation: Some Empirical Findings." In Z. Griliches, ed., *R&D, Patents and Productivity.* Chicago: University of Chicago Press, 1984.

Merges, R. P. *Patent Law and Policy.* Charlottesville, Va.: Michie, 1992.

Merges, R. P. and R. R. Nelson, "On the Complex Economics of Patent Scope." *Columbia Law Review* 90 (1990): 839–916.

Milgrim, R. M. *Milgrim on Trade Secrets.* New York: Matthew Bender, 1993.

Mueller, B., L. Alston, G. Libecap, and R. Schneider. "Land, Property Rights, and Privatization in Brazil." *Quarterly Review of Economics and Finance* 34 (1994): 261–280.

National Register Publishing Company. *Directory of Corporate Affiliations.* Wilmette, Ill.: National Register Publishing Co., 1992.

North Carolina Biotechnology Center, Biotechnology Information Division (NCBC). *North Carolina Biotechnology Center Documentation for Actions Database.* Research Triangle Park, N.C.: NCBC, 1990.

NCBC. *North Carolina Biotechnology Center Documentation for Companies Database.* Research Triangle Park, N.C.: NCBC, 1990.

Pooley, J. *Trade Secrets: A Guide to Protecting Proprietary Business Information.* New York: American Management Association, 1989.

Predicasts, Inc. *Predicasts F&S Index of Corporate Change.* Cleveland: Predicasts, 1992.

"PTO Hears from Silicon Valley on Patent Protection for Software." *Patent, Trademark and Copyright Journal* 47 (1994): 307.

Samuelson, P. "Benson Revisited: The Case Against Patent Protection for Algorithms and Other Computer Program-Related Inventions." *Emory Law Journal* 39 (1990): 1025–1154.

Smith, G. "Lines Drawn in Patent Battle: Multimedia Firms Banding Together to Fight Compton's." *San Francisco Examiner,* November 28, 1993, p. E-1.

Soma, J. T., and Smith, B. F. "Software Trends: Who's Getting How Many of What? 1978 to 1987." *Journal of the Patent and Trademark Office Society* 71 (1989): 415–432.

Sullivan, P. H. "A Preliminary Survey of Royalty Rate-Setting Practices in the U.S. Computer Hardware Industry." Consortium on Competitiveness and Cooperation Working Paper 93-17, 1993.

Teece, D. J. "Technology Transfer by Multinational Firms: The Resource Cost of Transferring Technological Know-How." *Economic Journal* 87 (1977): 242–261.

Trajtenberg, M. "A Penny for Your Quotes: Patent Citations and the Value of Inventions." *Rand Journal of Economics* 21 (1990): 172–187.

U.S. Department of Commerce, Patent Office (USPO). *Development and Use of Patent Classification Systems.* Washington, D.C.: U.S. Government Printing Office, 1966.

U.S. Department of Commerce, Patent and Trademark Office (USPTO). *Manual of Patent Examining Procedure.* 3rd ed., 30th rev., Washington, D.C.: U.S. Government Printing Office, 1971.

USPTO. *Examiner Handbook on the Use of the U.S. Patent Classification System.* Washington, D.C.: U.S. Government Printing Office, 1984.

USPTO. *Manual of Patent Examining Procedure.* 5th ed., 14th rev., Washington, D.C.: U.S. Government Printing Office, 1992.

USPTO. *Manual of Classification.* Washington, D.C.: U.S. Government Printing Office, 1993.

U.S. Department of Commerce, Patent and Trademark Office, Office of Patent Depository Library Programs (USPTO/OPDLP). *CASSIS/BIB User's Guide.* Washington, D.C.: USPTO/OPDLP, 1990.

USPTO/OPDLP. "ASSIST Disk Notes." Washington, D.C.: USPTO/OPDLP, 1991. Unpublished documentation.

U.S. Office of Technology Assessment. *New Developments in Biotechnology: Patenting Life.* Part 5, Series on New Developments in Biotechnology. Washington, D.C.: U.S. Government Printing Office, 1989.

U.S. Office of Technology Assessment. *Finding a Balance: Computer Software, Intellectual Property and the Challenge of Technological Change.* Washington, D.C.: U.S. Government Printing Office, 1992.

Voorhees, M. "New Video Technology Faces Mega-Licensing Woes: MPEG II May Be Open, but It's Also Highly Proprietary—CableLabs Tries to Create Voluntary Patent Pool." *Information Law Alert,* February 10, 1995.

World Intellectual Property Organization (WIPO). *General Information on the Third Edition of the International Patent Classification.* Geneva: WIPO, 1981.

Yang, C. Y., and J. O. Hamilton. "Are the Patent Police Ganging up on Biotech?" *Business Week,* June 13, 1994, 84–85.

CHAPTER 9

# ALLIANCE CLUSTERS
# IN MULTIMEDIA
*Safety Net or Entanglement?*

Benjamin Gomes-Casseres
Dorothy Leonard-Barton

PDAs are defined as highly portable, easy-to-use computing and communication devices aimed at the mass market.[1]

The ideal PDA enables a user to take notes, keep a calendar, schedule
appointments, and send and receive data (text, voice, video), fax and e-mail
messages. It also gives users access to on-line services.[2]

## INTRODUCTION

Personal digital assistants (PDAs) burst onto the market in the early
1990s, as a result of the fusion of technologies from at least four industries—computer hardware, computer software, telecommunications, and
consumer electronics. Technology fusion can occur within the bounds
of a single corporation, when companies have "added one technology
to another and [come] up with a solution greater than the sum of its parts

*The authors gratefully acknowledge the research assistance of Marilyn Matis, Sarah Tabler, Dimos
Arhodidis, and the research support of the Harvard Business School's Division of Research.

—in technology fusion, one plus one equals three."[3] However, technology fusion increasingly occurs *across* corporate boundaries.[4] As Robert Gussin of Johnson & Johnson noted, "Technology has become so sophisticated, broad, and expensive that even the largest companies can't afford to do it all themselves."[5]

Indeed, though companies from the four industries participated in the PDA business, each had limited in-house capabilities to enter the PDA market. Depending on the industry of origin, shown in figure 9-1, they were strong in one aspect of the emerging PDA business but lacked other aspects. As a result, they used interfirm alliances to combine the technology elements needed to develop, manufacture, and sell PDAs.

This product development strategy has become common for multimedia products, as well as for many other information-based products. The study of the PDA market is thus instructive because it foreshadows product development practices in emerging markets for information-based products.

Three characteristics of the PDA market are often found in these emerging markets: (1) a convergence of technologies; (2) uncertainty in customer demand; and (3) pressures to bring products to market quickly. We will discuss the convergence of industries in great detail in the next section. Uncertainty of customer demand, the second characteristic, is observed in both product and process technologies. This uncertainty stems from the newness of the business, as well as from the fact that the product represents a merging of capabilities from different existing industry segments. Uncertainty and convergence compound each other, so that while would-be PDA producers knew they had to combine technology and components from different industries, they did not know the precise mix of ingredients needed for a successful product. Finally, most PDA producers thought that there were advantages to being first to market with an innovative product. An early introduction, they thought, would boost their recognition and image; more important, it might help them set technical standards that would sustain their market position as the industry matured.

Taken together, these characteristics meant that firms were driven to conduct product experiments under severe time pressure. Since the features and markets of a successful PDA were unknown, all the firms had to experiment with different product designs and features. These experiments, as we shall see, took place in different "laboratories"—some were done on the technical drawing boards inside the firms, and others were done in the marketplace. Also, as more and more firms entered with their own experiments, each was able to learn from the successes and failures

FIGURE 9-1

ENTRANTS BY PRIOR INDUSTRY

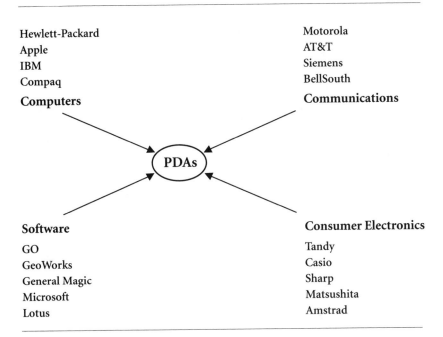

| | |
|---|---|
| Hewlett-Packard | Motorola |
| Apple | AT&T |
| IBM | Siemens |
| Compaq | BellSouth |
| **Computers** | **Communications** |

| | |
|---|---|
| **Software** | **Consumer Electronics** |
| GO | Tandy |
| GeoWorks | Casio |
| General Magic | Sharp |
| Microsoft | Matsushita |
| Lotus | Amstrad |

of the others. The ecology of the PDA population itself, therefore, constituted a grand laboratory for experimentation with product features.

This experimentation drove the evolution of PDA designs. For example, customer feedback—one of the outputs from the market experiments—drove individual firms to modify their PDA offerings from one generation to the next. At the same time, as firms observed the results of others' experiments, they introduced PDAs with different sets of features, leading to shifts in the population of PDA features available in the market. We call this process *market experimentation,* to emphasize that the product evolved in response to market pressures and feedback.[6] Experimenting in the market was not unique to the PDA business, as is shown by the early history of video recorders, personal computers, computer software, and many other products.

With PDAs, however, market experimentation went hand in hand with another process: the proliferation of *alliance groups,* sets of firms linked to each other through collaborative arrangements. These groups enabled firms to combine quickly the capabilities and components from different industries. In keeping with the evolution of product offerings, the PDA alliance groups changed over time, as firms learned new capabilities and as market feedback suggested the need for new partnerships. This role of alliance groups is related to that in RISC processors, VCRs, automobiles, and airlines,[7] but the process of market experimentation in PDAs compounded the instability of the groups.

Market experimentation and alliance formation were thus intricately intertwined. The firms in this industry, after all, were searching for both the right market approach and the right set of capabilities. To find out what customers demanded and to establish their market position, they experimented. To find and gain access to the capabilities needed to supply this demand, they sought alliances. Figure 9-2 shows how the rise of alliances went hand in hand with the introduction of PDA products. In examining the history of these products in the rest of this paper, we will focus on the roles of market experimentation and alliance clusters.

## THE CONTEXT: NEW PRODUCTS FOR NEW MARKETS

Studying an emerging industry at its inception is rather like observing tornadoes and trying to predict their behavior. Velocity, rate of maturation, and even the path likely to be followed are difficult to anticipate. Companies creating new markets must define their products under conditions of extreme uncertainty. Figure 9-3 schematically presents the two factors influencing the degree of uncertainty inherent in new product definitions in general: the maturity of the technological design underlying the product line and the degree of alignment between the proposed product line and the current customer base. Variance along these two dimensions determines the level and types of uncertainty that new product developers face, and consequently the types of information needed and available.

### Technological Maturity

Translating science into technology and the subsequent embedding of that technology into products follows a kind of life cycle. When science is first being harnessed to practical purposes of work or play, and the proposed product is completely novel to the world, the developer's primary concern is Can I make it work? Can I invent solutions to the problems intervening between understanding the technology's potential and realizing it in a commercially viable product or service? (See top of vertical axis in figure 9-3.) Once technical feasibility is proven at some level of benefit

FIGURE 9-2

PRODUCT INTRODUCTIONS AND ALLLIANCES IN PDAS

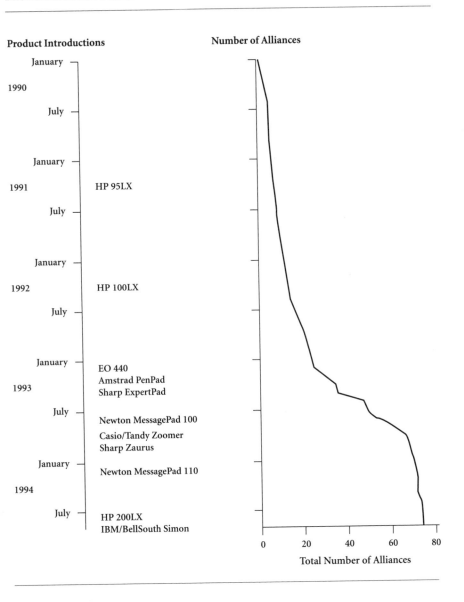

for customers, the challenge is always to produce the next generation, or the next leap in performance. However, while one team of developers focuses on that innovation, usually another simultaneously seeks enhancements and refinements to the basic design embodied in the first

FIGURE 9-3

TECHNOLOGY AND MARKET FACTORS SHAPING THE NEW PRODUCT
DEFINITION SITUATION

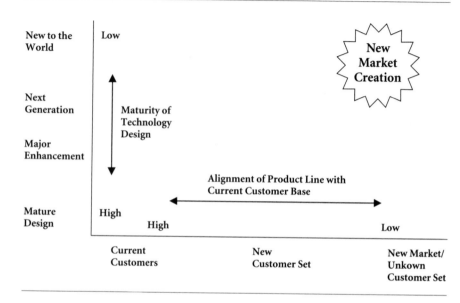

line of products. Therefore, redesigns emerge with increasing frequency as one moves down the axis toward mature design, where "new and improved" usually entails a change that is more cosmetic than fundamental. That is, at the bottom of this vertical axis, when the technology is quite mature, the development question has become What minimal technological innovation will maintain or improve our status?

## Market Alignment

Figure 9-3 also indicates the degree to which the proposed product aligns with the desires and needs of the current customer base. Assuming that a product's performance in the market is satisfactory enough to warrant further investment, reasonably simple product enhancements for current customers can be highly profitable. The left-hand side of the axis is therefore likely to be the easier to manage. The major question guiding the import of knowledge from the market is What features do our current customers need and want in our product line? At this side of the axis, customers are known quite well. Channels of information from the market are well established and sources are clearly identified.

The concomitant observation is that market uncertainty increases as one moves to the right, climaxing in the frontiers of new market creation, where new product developers cannot even be certain that they have identified the correct set of users as they undertake design. At this side of the axis, the major questions facing new product development often are Who will benefit from using this technology? Who is the customer?

All of the PDA producers discussed in this paper operated in the region at the extreme right-hand upper corner of the figure, where new, often unproven technologies interact with the need to identify, profile, and understand a new set of customers. Even within this range of high uncertainty, however, there was still variance among company strategies, as the more detailed look at this quadrant provided by figure 9-4 illustrates. Some companies chose to design at the cutting edge of technology and simultaneously to seek an entirely new set of customers, thus hitting the extremes of both types of uncertainty. Others took a (relatively) more conservative approach, integrating proven technical components into the new product configuration and seeking new customers—but at the fringes of their established customer base. As we will see, even such conservatives have not necessarily served the market that they initially targeted, and therefore their strategies evolved. In essence, the companies' initial strategies for market creation differed. The positioning of their initial products reflected interesting choices of partners and assumptions about their customers.

## ALLIANCE GROUPS AND PRODUCT DEVELOPMENT

From the start, competition in the PDA field was not among individual firms but among groups or clusters of allied firms. All the PDAs studied here were developed in a collaboration involving two or more firms. The number of alliances in each of the competing clusters varied from over twenty in Apple's group to four in Amstrad's. In every cluster, each member contributed specific capabilities and fulfilled specific functions in the cycle of product development and launch. As a result, the design of each group and the effectiveness of collaboration among group members helped to shape the product offerings and the competitive advantage of the group.

FIGURE 9-4

PDA DESIGN CHOICES: TECHNOLOGY AND MARKET INNOVATION

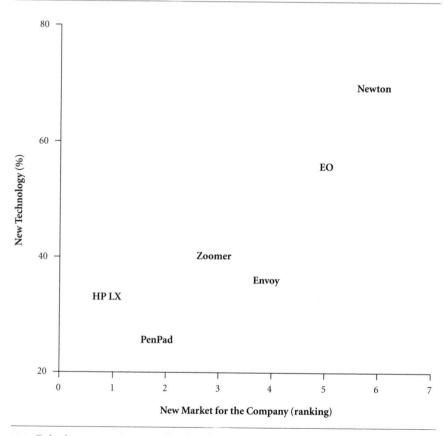

NOTE: Technology newness is percent of product features that are new technology. Market newness ranking indicates degree to which the targeted market was new to the company (high ranking) or consisted of existing customer sets (low ranking).

## Collective Competition

Collective competition is not unique to PDAs. It is found in other information technology fields, such as in reduced instruction-set computing (RISC), as well as in other complex industries, such as automobiles and international airline services. In each instance, the companies cluster together because none has all the pieces of the puzzle or the scale of operations needed to compete effectively. The degree to which the group as a whole is effective in competition against other groups depends on variables such as the following:

- The size of the group, which affects the scale of operations and the degree of market penetration

- The composition of the group, which determines the mix of capabilities available to it

- The structure of the group, which affects whether members work together smoothly or engage in destructive intragroup competition

- The governance of the group, that is, the way the group manages its internal affairs to maximize the benefits of collaboration

- The growth pattern of the group, that is, whether expansion is orderly and purposeful or chaotic and unmanaged.[8]

These variables also affected competition in the PDA field, though in somewhat different ways than in more mature industries. In the rest of this section, we shall explore how alliance groups affected the process of product development in PDAs.

## Innovation and Dependence on Allies

As a general rule, firms in the PDA market used alliances when they lacked capabilities they thought they needed to enter the field. Because the PDA business arose out of the convergence of various technologies and markets, none of the potential entrants had a complete set of capabilities. Still, not every company needed or chose to rely on alliances to the same extent. Some had more internal capabilities than others, and even those that lacked certain capabilities sometimes chose to develop them rather than rely on partners.

The firms' choices regarding whether to use alliances involved a trade-off between innovation and dependence. This tradeoff is evident in figure 9-5, which plots each firm's degree of dependence on external allies against the proportion of new technology in its product offering. The data on which this chart is based are shown in table 9-1. Apple, for example, relied the least on external sources for its technology, and produced the most innovative PDA on the market. Hewlett-Packard and Amstrad were at the other extreme—high dependence on allies, and less innovative products.[9]

The aggregate data as well as our case studies suggest that alliances were frequently used to gain access to the existing technology of partners. This enabled the allies to enter the market quickly and with less technological risk than if either were to develop a brand new technology. As

FIGURE 9-5

## PDA PRODUCT DEVELOPMENT STRATEGIES: INNOVATION VERSUS DEPENDENCE

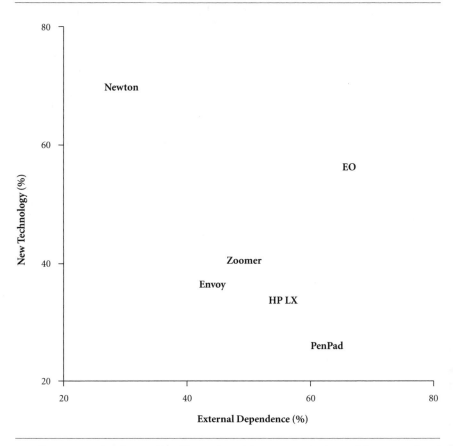

NOTE: Percentages are based on number of features in total that are new technology and that are contributed by partners.

a result, a high reliance on partners was correlated with a technologically conservative product. When Hewlett-Packard (HP) and Lotus collaborated on the 95LX, for example, each contributed tried-and-true technologies and skills. Lotus had the dominant spreadsheet on the market and a lot of experience with DOS-based software. HP was the market leader in high-end calculators and had a burgeoning business in small form-factor computers. Furthermore, these partners used Microsoft's well-established MS-DOS operating system and Intel's standard 8086 microprocessor. Of course, these allies had to collaborate extensively to make all these pieces of the puzzle fit together, but

TABLE 9-1

FEATURES OF PDAS BY NEWNESS AND SOURCE

| Product Features | Newton | PenPad | Zoomer | EO880 | HP100 | Envoy |
|---|---|---|---|---|---|---|
| **INTERFACE** | | | | | | |
| Pen | ● | □ | ● | ● | | ■ |
| Cursive | ● | | | | | |
| Block | ● | □ | ● | ● | | |
| Keyboard | | | | □ | ■ | □ |
| **CHIPS** | | | | | | |
| CPU | ● | □ | □ | ○ | □ | ■ |
| **FORM FACTOR** | | | | | | |
| Palmtop miniaturization | ● | ○ | ■ | | ■ | ● |
| Desktop capability | | | | | □ | ● |
| **SOFTWARE** | | | | | | |
| Operating system | ● | ■ | □ | ○ | □ | ○ |
| Application software | □ ■ | ● ■ | ● ■ | ● | ● ■ | ○ |
| **COMMUNICATIONS** | | | | | | |
| Phone line-compatible | | | | □ | | □ |
| Infrared link | ○ | | ○ | | ● | ○ |
| Paging radio | | | □ | | □ | ■ |
| Cellular phone | | | | □ | | |
| Fax/data modem | □ | □ | □ | □ | | ■ |
| Two-way wireless | | | | | | ■ |

○  External, new tech.
□  External, old tech.
●  Internal, new tech.
■  Internal, old tech.

they were not inventing major new pieces. The product was developed and launched in about sixteen months, which executives at HP and Lotus consider was a short time to market.

At the other extreme, firms that aimed to introduce radically new technology frequently relied more on internal development efforts. Apple is the best example of this model. Most of the features of the Newton MessagePad were new to the market, and Apple's previous experience was only loosely related to the work behind the Newton. Even though Apple and Sharp collaborated in the design of the product, most of the new technologies came from inside Apple. The development of the first MessagePad took longer than that of the 95LX, but it is hard to say by how much. Apple first invested in ARM—supplier of Newton's CPU—in November 1990, almost three years before the Newton was launched.

Apple thus aimed for a more innovative product than did HP, but it also accepted more technological risk. The HP LX series was immediately well accepted by the market, and sold almost 390,000 units in three years. In 1994, independent analysts still rated it the most useful PDA on the market.[10] The Newton MessagePad, on the other hand, was acclaimed for its radical innovations, but the product was at best experimental. While eighty-five thousand units were sold in the first six months after introduction, these sales fell far short of Apple's expectations. In effect, Apple's strategy of radical innovation forced it to do more experimentation in the market than HP.

Apple hoped that its slower and riskier approach would yield a PDA technology that was more valuable in the market and was more appropriable than jointly developed or off-the-shelf technologies. This reasoning suggests that alliances may be good for sharing existing technology but poor at developing new proprietary technologies.

## The Growth and Composition of PDA Alliance Clusters

While there were differences in the degree to which the PDA companies relied on alliances, the uses to which they put their alliances tended to be similar. As in other fields, firms in PDAs used alliances for three purposes: (1) to learn or develop new technologies; (2) to gain access to components and services; and (3) to position themselves in the market.[11]

In the first case, the firms used *learning alliances* to transfer knowledge, share innovation, and build experience. In principle, therefore, a PDA firm with experience in the consumer electronics business can use an alliance with a computer software firm to learn about software development. These alliances thus lead to a true merging of the "convergent" capabilities. In the second type of alliance—*supply alliances*—the partners do not internalize one another's capabilities, and no such merging occurs. The hypothetical PDA firm, for example, would continue to rely on the software developed and provided by its partner. The alliances facilitate transactions for components and, perhaps, the design of compatible technologies. *Positioning alliances* are part of a marketing strategy, not of product development and manufacture, as is the case with the first two types. In this third type of strategy, the firm uses relationships to reach specific markets or to promote its standard.

The PDA firms used each type of alliance, and they did so systematically during the process of developing and launching their products. As a result, the growth of the alliance clusters followed a common pattern, which is depicted in figure 9-6.

FIGURE 9-6

## GROWTH OF ALLIANCE CLUSTERS DURING PRODUCT DEVELOPMENT (AVERAGE FOR SIX PDAs)

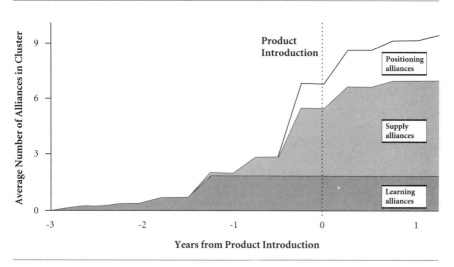

NOTE: Average of data for Newton, EO, HP LX, PenPad, Zoomer, and Sharp.

Each of the PDA entrants began with one or two learning alliances; on average, these were formed a little over a year before the product was launched. These learning alliances helped shape the basic design of the product and accounted for most of the new technology developed. In the year or so before product introduction, the companies lined up suppliers for critical components and services. On average, each of the clusters examined here contained about five such supply alliances by the time the product was being sold. Finally, just before product introduction, and for some time after that, the companies lined up partners to help them penetrate vertical markets, sell abroad, and spread their standards. The clusters varied greatly in the representation of positioning alliances, with Apple having the most and HP having none.

The systematic distribution of alliances over the PDA development cycle stemmed from a complex relationship between product development and collaboration. At some times during the cycle, the alliances were outcomes of preceding product design decisions; at other times, the design decisions were the outcome of earlier alliance choices. Alliances, in other words, were both causes and effects in the product development process.

*Learning Alliances to Shape the Product.* It is easy to see how product design choices lead to alliances when the firm lacks a capability to implement the chosen design. Because all PDAs combined technologies and markets from different industries, all new entrants needed alliances to fill gaps in their capabilities.

It is less obvious how alliances influence product designs, but the data in table 9-2 provide evidence of this type of effect. Each of the six PDAs listed there was developed by a pair or triad of companies—the early learning alliances in the product development cycle. And, in each case, the specific skills and visions of this small set of allies shaped product design decisions. Apple, as we saw, relied much on its internal software capabilities; but its hardware alliances with ARM and Sharp helped shape the Newton. The MessagePad used ARM's chip and Sharp's miniaturization hardware. Similarly, EO combined GO's operating system, some telecommunication technology, and a microprocessor from AT&T, and the vision and miniaturization expertise of the Active Book Company. The HP LX series, as we saw, embodied at its core the technologies of HP and Lotus, the pair of companies that linked up early in a learning alliance. The same is true for Amstrad and Eden's PenPad, Casio and Tandy's Zoomer, and IBM and BellSouth's Simon.

The companies in the initial pair or triad developing each product always came from different industries. However, the precise combination of industries varied—Apple and Sharp combined computers and consumer electronics, HP and Lotus combined computer hardware and software, IBM and BellSouth combined computer and telecommunications, and so on. This variation affected the design of the initial PDA products. Thus, the Newton was stronger in computing than the EO and the Simon, the 95LX was strong in calculating functions, and the PenPad and Zoomer were designed from the start to be mass-market products. The variation in PDA products on the market in 1994, therefore, stemmed not only from variety among the entering firms but also from variety among the combinations of early allies.

*Supply Alliances to Assemble Capabilities.* The starting points of the PDA clusters thus differed from each other. Over time, however, the clusters came to look more and more alike, as each expanded to encompass a similar pool of capabilities. This growing similarity in the combined capabilities of the groups was achieved through the use of supply alliances after the initial designs of the products had been established. The most important of these supply alliances are listed in table 9-3.

TABLE 9-2

LEARNING ALLIANCES THAT SHAPED FIRST-GENERATION PRODUCT DESIGNS

| Product | Alliance | Result |
|---|---|---|
| NEWTON MESSAGEPAD 100 | • Apple and ARM<br>• Apple and Sharp | PDA built around ARM's chip that used Apple's operating system and handwriting recognition, and Sharp's miniaturization, manufacturing, and LCD capabilities. Also, Sharp is developing a series of PDAs building on Apple designs. |
| EO 440 | • ATT and GO<br>• ATT and Active Book Company | PDA built around AT&T's Hobbit chip that used GO's operating system and ABC's capabilities in computer design. AT&T's influence created a PDA strong in communication features. |
| 95LX | • HP and Lotus<br>• HP and Intel | PDA that looked like HP calculators, with a built-in 1-2-3 spreadsheet, and based on MS-DOS and Intel chip standards. It emphasized compatibility with PCs. |
| PENPAD | • Amstrad and Eden | PDA designed for the mass consumer market, but with Amstrad's proprietary architecture. |
| ZOOMER | • Casio and Tandy | Another PDA designed for the mass consumer market, with strong organizing and calculator functions. |
| SIMON | • IBM and BellSouth | PDA designed for advanced cellular-telephone users. |

The new wave of supply alliances complemented the internal capabilities of the initial set of companies that designed the product. Thus, while HP and Lotus had software, hardware design, and manufacturing capabilities in-house, they went to Intel for chips, to Motorola for communication technology, to Microsoft (and later to Intuit) for more software, and to RadioMail for communication services. Each of the other groups had a similar mix of capabilities, embedded either in the original designers or in their allies. All groups had to have software capabilities, manufacturing, and chips; most also had communication and information services as part of the pool.

TABLE 9-3

SUPPLY ALLIANCES THAT FILLED GAPS IN INTERNAL CAPABILITIES OF LEAD FIRMS

**Newton MessagePad Series**

| INTERNAL CAPABILITIES | of Apple<br>of Sharp | Software<br>Manufacture, H/W design |
|---|---|---|
| ALLIANCES | GEC-Plessey Semiconductors<br>Ameritech, BellSouth, and US West<br>America Online<br>Pen Magic, Money | Chip supply<br>Communication services<br>Information services<br>Financial services |

**EO Series**

| INTERNAL CAPABILITIES | of AT&T | Communication services, chips |
|---|---|---|
| ALLIANCES | GO, Pensoft, others<br>Matsushita<br>Lexis<br>RadioMail | Software<br>Manufacture<br>Information services<br>Communication services |

**LX Series**

| INTERNAL CAPABILITIES | of HP<br>of Lotus | Manufacture, H/W design<br>Software |
|---|---|---|
| ALLIANCES | Intel<br>Motorola<br>Microsoft, Intuit<br>RadioMail | Chip supply<br>Communication features<br>Software<br>Communication services |

**PenPad**

| INTERNAL CAPABILITIES | of Amstrad<br>of Eden | Marketing<br>Software, H/W design |
|---|---|---|
| ALLIANCES | Chinese firm<br>Dancall | Manufacturing<br>Communication services |

**Zoomer**

| INTERNAL CAPABILITIES | of Casio and Tandy | Marketing, H/W design |
|---|---|---|
| ALLIANCES | GeoWorks, Intuit, Palm<br>AST<br>America Online<br>CompuServe | Software<br>Manufacturing<br>Information services<br>Information services |

TABLE 9-3 continued

SUPPLY ALLIANCES THAT FILLED GAPS IN INTERNAL CAPABILITIES OF LEAD FIRMS

**Sharp PDAs**

| INTERNAL CAPABILITIES | of Sharp | Manufacture, H/W design |
|---|---|---|
| ALLIANCES | Apple | Software |
| | GeoWorks, Palm, Oracle | Software |
| | AT&T | Communication features |
| | Motorola | Communication features |

**Simon**

| INTERNAL CAPABILITIES | of IBM | H/W design, chips, software |
|---|---|---|
| | of BellSouth | Communication services |
| ALLIANCES | Mitsubishi | Manufacture |

*Positioning Alliances to Market the Product.* The alliance clusters in PDAs differed substantially in one respect—the number of positioning alliances in the group. EO, PenPad, Zoomer, and Sharp each had one major positioning alliance, whereas Apple had eleven, as shown in table 9-4. This points partly to a difference among the firms in ambition and competitive strategy. From the beginning, Apple strove to make parts of the Newton into an industry standard, from which it hoped to earn royalties.[12] It also signed on six licensees and four distribution partners in vertical or foreign markets. None of the other firms attempted such a strategy.[13]

One reason why Apple was alone in promoting its technology through alliances lay in the design and alliance choices it had made early on. As noted above, Apple aimed for a radically new technology and did most of the work internally. Other firms shared the responsibility for developing their PDA and were more conservative in technology choices. As a result, Apple had something of value to license and promote, whereas the others did not.

Lotus and HP represent the other extreme in design and alliance choices. In fact, Lotus originally thought that it could license out the design for a PDA with built-in spreadsheet and collect royalties, much as Apple aimed to do with Newton. However, Lotus was not willing to invest in the initial development of the technology: HP funded all of Lotus's work on the LX and paid a substantial royalty for use of Lotus's 1-2-3 in

TABLE 9-4

Positioning Alliances That Helped Market the Products

| Product | Alliance | Market |
|---|---|---|
| NEWTON MESSAGEPAD SERIES | Sharp, Motorola, SNI, Cirrus, Matsushita, LSI<br>Retailers<br>Deutsche Telekom, Alcatel, British Telecom<br>Harris | Licensees<br>Mass market<br>Foreign markets<br>Vertical markets |
| EO SERIES | Olivetti | Foreign markets |
| LX SERIES | (No positioning alliances) | |
| PENPAD | Scottsdale | Foreign markets |
| ZOOMER | AST | Licensee |
| SHARP PDAs | Priority Management | Vertical markets |

the product. As a result, Lotus became accustomed to receiving a stream of cash from HP. Promoting the technology as an industry standard would have required breaking the relationship with HP, which wanted to keep the technology proprietary. Lotus's dependence on HP's business— and HP's lack of control over all the pieces of the technology—barred both companies from pursuing a standards strategy.

The cases of Apple and HP/Lotus represent the polar cases along a continuum. The general lesson is this: The more innovative and self-reliant a company is, the more technology it will have to offer to marketing allies. Consequently, the firms that use fewer learning and supply alliances early in the product development cycle might be expected to use more positioning alliances later on.

EO is a puzzling exception to this rule. By most of our measures, the product was reasonably innovative and, in the end at least, AT&T controlled most of the inputs. Still, the product was not well promoted and AT&T formed only one major positioning alliance (with Olivetti). Several conditions may have contributed to this outcome. First, EO's champions were not AT&T managers but outside entrepreneurs. Second, key pieces of the EO technology—such as the GO operating system and the PenSoft pen interface—were recent acquisitions of AT&T. Third, the one piece of the product that was clearly AT&T's—the Hobbit microprocessor—did not receive sufficient corporate backing to survive in the long run. Perhaps because of the patchwork of interests involved, therefore, AT&T

did not invest enough in maintaining the product or in promoting it to potential partners. Still, even as they were liquidating the company, EO's managers were hopeful that the technology could be licensed to an outside company.

**Strategic Limitation.** Considered in their totalities, the alliance clusters of the PDA players looked remarkably similar. This "matching" phenomenon, in which each set of firms matches the capabilities of the others, is a frequent feature of collective competition. One curious consequence of this phenomenon is imitative alliance behavior among rivals. Even when they are not sure which capabilities they will need—as was the case in PDAs—rivals will tend to match each other's alliance moves so as not to be left "without a dance partner." Because usually only a limited number of firms can supply certain capabilities, it is important to ally with them early, even when the firm is not sure these capabilities will be needed. It is far worse, this reasoning goes, for the cluster to be left with an incomplete set of capabilities later on.

This type of strategic rivalry around partnerships was one reason for the surge of alliances in PDAs in 1993 (see figure 9-2). Some of these alliances were intended to preempt a competitor rather than to supply a critical component. Intel's alliance with VLSI that aimed to develop a chip set for PDAs, for example, was partly motivated by a desire to preempt Intel's archrival, AMD, from acquiring VLSI. When the threat of an AMD acquisition faded—and the first generation of PDAs failed—Intel broke off the alliance.[14]

Other PDA alliances were less readily explained as preemptive moves, but were still strategic in nature. Some companies allied themselves with several competing partners. Sharp licensed Apple's Newton operating system as well as GeoWorks's GEO; AT&T supported both GO's operating system and General Magic's Magic Cap; and Apple allied itself with three telecommunication services providers. In each case, these companies were creating a portfolio of options through these overlapping alliances. The fear, always, was of being left without an alliance with a firm that later proved to have a key service or component.

The high degree of uncertainty and the future importance of standards in PDAs thus lies behind many of the links between alliance clusters shown in figure 9-7. The alliance clusters in PDAs were particularly "blurry" at their boundaries, unlike, for example, the clusters in the RISC field. The companies that tended to span the boundaries between alliance clusters (i.e., that belonged to more than one cluster) tended to be those offering a broad service—such as BellSouth, America On-Line, and

RadioMail—or those with the potential of becoming a standard in PDAs —such as General Magic, GeoWorks, or Intel. It is not yet clear what the result of this blurriness of the groups will be, but we speculate that it tends to make the composition of the groups more unstable, and the commitment of members to each other less deep, than they otherwise would be.

## FROM MARKET IDENTIFICATION TO MARKET EXPERIMENTATION

As noted earlier, PDA producers operated toward the extremes of two kinds of uncertainty, technological and market; the degree of each was largely a matter of managerial choice, since the market was undefined. The companies that assumed their customers were keyboard-phobic were forced by that assumption to decide among several technologies of varying maturity.[15] To record a user's handwriting only, rather than translating it into ASCII text, "digital ink" is adequate. In this application, the handwriting is stored as an image that can be retrieved and read by the user. Much more technically difficult is actual handwriting recognition, which was judged by some experts to be only about 70 percent reliable.[16] The difficulty in handwriting recognition is its weakness not only in interpreting some pretty sloppy writing but also in matching the scribbles to a known word. Tandy/Casio's Zoomer, EO's 440/880, and Apple's MessagePad all supported handwriting recognition, but only the MessagePad interprets cursive. When it does so, it relies on dictionary-based recognition, which means that the system makes wild guesses if it doesn't have the word in its 10,000-word vocabulary. The immaturity of handwriting recognition has profoundly affected the desirability of this function and the viability of appealing to a mass market. Therefore, technology uncertainty has interacted with identification of market.

### Market Identification

The greatest difficulty in creating a new market is determining the target set of users. Many radically new products go through the expensive, frustrating process of coevolving with customers' understanding, as technical potential gradually is shaped to meet identified needs. Figure 9-8 illustrates an array of research tools that can be used to extract information from the market to guide new product definition. When customers are known well and the product category is familiar, surveys, focus

FIGURE 9-7

ALLIANCE GROUPS IN PDAS

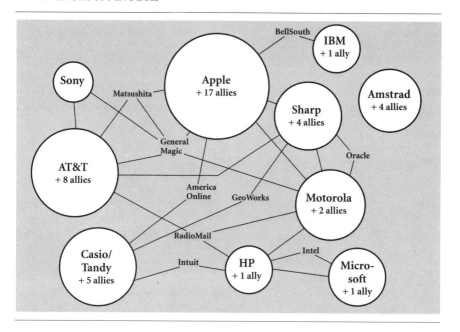

groups, and lead-user polls can provide very detailed information about their preferences.[17] Because the customers can refer to a known product, they can answer most questions about their preferences, and their responses are reasonably reliable guides to new product development. For instance, drivers know what they like and do not like in cars and can be quite articulate in expressing preferences. Consumers can be queried about everything from the obvious preferences in size and cost to such subtleties as engine sound, tightness of steering, and ability to "feel" the road. Despite the tremendous sophistication of such interviewing techniques, however, they can uncover only those needs and desires about which the informants are aware and that they can articulate.

When technologies are reasonably well understood, but developers are seeking new customer sets, empathic design is an applicable tool.[18] Empathic design is the creation of products or services based on a deep, (i.e., empathic) understanding of unarticulated user needs. This understanding is developed through *actual observed behavior* of potential users, as opposed to espoused behavior, self-reported behavior, or opinions. Empathic understanding, moreover, is almost always obtained through *direct interaction* between the product developers (engineers, designers)

FIGURE 9-8

MARKET RESEARCH TOOLS

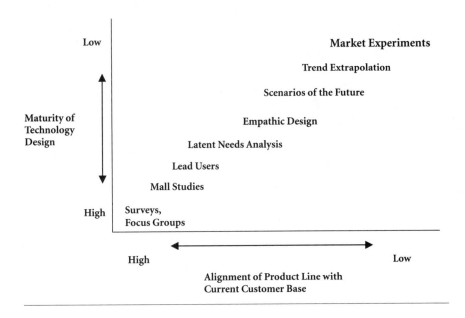

and the potential product users.[19] In designing the MessagePad, Apple managers approached this technique by hiring a cultural anthropologist to observe people and note their use of such readily available tools as Post-it Notes.[20]

However, at the extreme right-hand side of figure 9-8, product developers cannot be certain of observing the right group of people until they ascertain who will in fact have use for the new product category. Therefore the market research tools most applicable at this extreme are various forms of prediction or market experimentation. That is, either developers attempt to foresee the future through the intuition of industry experts or an extrapolation of current social, political, or technological trends, or else they must experiment in the market. The expectation that there would be a mass market of keyboard-phobic users for PDAs[21] has been driven in part by a simple extrapolation of general trends toward more portable computers and telephones—the evident desire to access information anywhere, anytime. However, the problem with such extrapolations is that the point of convergence is quite vague. Who are the users whose needs are greatest for such portability? What kinds of applications will they need? How much are they willing to pay for a product that meets those needs? As discussed later in some detail, all the PDA producers missed a specific market target to some degree, and none found trend extrapolation particularly prescient.

## Initial Product Designs

Market experimentation is generally necessary for two reasons: first, the developers are uncertain about the target market, and second, users have no idea of what the technology can do, and therefore cannot guide product definition. Dialogue with users is bounded by their experience. If potential users are to make useful suggestions, some referent product must already exist in the market. If no such exact referent exists, potential users try to understand a new product concept by drawing analogies to current products. Initially, they will mentally lump the new product concept with items familiar to them; researchers have long known that "an individual will behave toward a new thing in a manner that is similar to the way he behaves toward other things he sees the new thing as similar to."[22] The only way to wean users away from misleading analogies is to have a prototype to which they can react.[23] Obviously, the closer that prototype is to the real product, the more realistic is the feedback provided. Because existing products are potentially misleading analogies for PDAs, the PDA producers have been forced to conduct extensive market experimentation.[24] We will discuss the different experimentation strategies that they have taken in the "Market Experimentation" section. First, however, let us consider how the companies arrived at an initial product definition, given that they had no existing market research to guide them beyond general desires for more communication, faster, anywhere.

Three forces appear to have driven the initial product definition of PDAs: (1) the vision of the early champions; (2) the product analogy suggested by the home industry of the most powerful founding alliance partner; (3) the existing core capabilities (market and technology) of the original alliance partners. The second two are related, of course, but not identical.

The concept of a personal digital assistant is usually attributed to John Sculley of Apple, since he was by far the most vocal and visible salesman for the idea: "Newton will be seen as the defining technology of the digital age . . . a focal point for the coming convergence of . . . computers, communications and consumer electronics."[25] The complete vision for the MessagePad was of course both more (in the sense of additional detail) and less (in terms of delivery) than this vision implies. However, the original Newton team had quite strong ideas about the concept. As the marketing director, Michael Tchao, explained it to John Sculley, the Newton would "capture, organize, and communicate ideas and data. Something that would work the way people do. No keyboards or commands. No technical training required. It would be an electronic, digitized piece of note paper that could be scribbled on and that would be smart enough to interpret the meaning of the scribbles."[26] The initial champion for EO was Herman Hauser, prolific founder of companies, whose British start-up, the Active Book Company, "built the world's first single-chip notebook computer using the ARM as the microprocessor and integrating everything onto that single chip."[27] The Hewlett-Packard 95-100LX actually started as the brainchild of Lotus's general manager of portable products, Leon Navickas. These early champions profoundly influenced the starting point for the PDAs.

However, as discussed in greater detail in the previous section, the initial alliances had an even greater impact. Some of the PDA producers themselves were at first uncertain about the correct analogy. Is a PDA an information processor (a computer? a calculator?)? Is it an electronic "day-timer," one of the small leather date books and personal calendars that so many professionals carry? Is it a communication device—a sort of telephone—but also like a computer with a modem? The analogy chosen tends to be influenced by existing capabilities of alliance partners. Steve Sakoman, the director of the Newton development division, revealed the preconceptions guiding the Newton team even as he was stating that they were starting from ground zero: "The idea was to see if the personal computer could be rethought without carrying around a lot of baggage."[28] EO designated its PDA as a "communications-intensive device"[29] because "AT&T wants traffic on its network. The way to get traffic is to get people to use these devices."[30] HP's PDA was more of a supercalculator, as one would expect from the company's history. Amstrad's PenPad was a fancy electronic toy because that was where Amstrad's market was perceived to be. As Amstrad's director of international marketing, David Hennell, put it, the firm was looking for a "mass market avalanche" to create the "almost impulse purchase."[31]

These forces determined the starting point for each company's PDA. It is still too early in the history of this emerging product category to trace exactly how successive generations will differ as the market voices preferences and desires. Only a few of the companies have launched more than one model. However, some future product plans are known, and there is some evidence available to suggest that the major players are pursuing quite varied market experimentation strategies.

## Market Experimentation

At least three quite different market experimentation strategies can be deduced from the evidence so far: Darwinian selection, market morphing, and vicarious experimentation. Each of the three is described below, and each is shown schematically in figure 9-9 as a separate vertical panel. Over time (which is represented on the vertical axis for the whole figure), companies tried out products that were variously positioned along a given design feature (represented by the arrow at the top of each of the three panels). This horizontal axis could measure any number of design features or functions, such as the degree of portability, the type of operating system, the richness of communication capability. As figure 9-9 suggests, each company tried out products varying along one or more design dimensions, sometimes experimenting sequentially and sometimes virtually simultaneously. None of the three strategies is quite the same as traditional market testing, in which a product is launched in a limited geographic region before it is rolled out across the nation or the globe.[32]

***Darwinian Selection.*** Darwinian selection involves placing different versions of a product on the market simultaneously, for a test of the survival of the fittest. The Japanese are well known for the kind of "product churning" to which such market experimentation leads—that is, turning out dozens of possible versions of a product to home in on the one preferred by most customers. About a thousand new soft drinks are brought out annually in Japan; almost all of them fail within a year.[33] Sony has tried out numerous models of its Walkman, many of which never made it past an initial test run of a few thousand units. An example was a Walkman built into the bottom of a tote bag for teenagers. (It didn't sell.)

In the PDA market, Sharp continued to market a number of different versions of its Zaurus pocket organizer in Japan in the same years (1993–1994) during which it brought out both the Expert Pad and the Easy Pad in the United States (see table 9-5). The developers are not always certain of how features will be used. For example, asked why the Zaurus, which is sold only in Japan, included the option of an English interface, developers explained that many Japanese speak English. The unspoken assumption was that customers would therefore *want* an English interface at times. Sharp developers may make such assumptions because of past experience with customers' finding unanticipated uses for a product. For instance, when Sharp first brought out a machine with two CD players, observers questioned why anyone would want two; no suggestions for use were included with the product. However, teenagers had

FIGURE 9-9

THREE DIFFERENT MARKET EXPERIMENTATION STRATEGIES

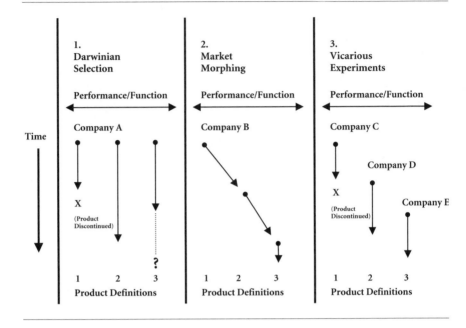

the answer: create your own music tapes by mixing tracks from two CDs. Within a few months, Sanyo and JVC followed suit, bringing out their own two-CD machines.[34]

Sharp is also hedging its bets on PDA operating systems. Its Expert Pad uses Newton architecture from Apple, and the company intends to bring out another product using that same architecture—but not in partnership with Apple. The Zaurus line of products uses Sharp's own operating system; its PT9000 is based on GeoWorks's GEOS (operating system). When (some would say "if") Microsoft's Winpad becomes available, Sharp plans a product based on that as well.

The essential assumption underlying Darwinian selection seems to be that it is preferable to make many trials of various potential standards than to make one big bet. Darwinian selection is a heavily market-driven strategy; companies following it are positioning themselves to be ready to produce a stream of products based on whatever standard emerges. They are therefore less concerned with shaping and influencing the market than some of the next set of companies to be considered, which follow a market-morphing strategy.

TABLE 9-5

## SHARP PRODUCT TIMELINE

|  | 1987 | 1988 | 1992 | 1993 | 1994 | 1995 |
|---|---|---|---|---|---|---|
| EXPORT PRODUCTS |  | OZ7000 (US) IQ7000 (non-US, non-Japanese) | OZ9000 | OZ9500 Expert Pad | Easy Pad (PT9000 in Japanese) |  |

|  | 1987 | 1988 | 1992 | 1993 | 1994 | 1995 |
|---|---|---|---|---|---|---|
| DOMESTIC PRODUCTS | PA7000 |  | PVF1 (Y120K) | PI3000 Zaurus (Y65K) | PI4000/FX (Zaurus; Y75K/91K) | Galileo |

*Market Morphing.* "Market morphing" refers to the iterative process through which companies design and redesign successive generations of products in a deliberately experimental process to identify a commercially acceptable product definition. As EO president and CEO Bob Evans observed, "If you hit it right and succeed with the first product, it's wonderful, but you need the customer experience."[35] Because the market is so immature, no one is certain who will use the PDA and how it will be used. Therefore, each company chooses a starting point, and then the product concept is "morphed" toward one that will exactly match the needs of the individuals who are emerging as the logical set of users.

Companies differ on their starting points in terms of closeness to existing product categories and in the speed of the morphing process. Apple, EO, and, to a lesser degree, Amstrad started with the viewpoint that they were creating a whole new product category and were conscious of each other's progress in defining the market. As John Sculley observed in 1990, "The real market value for the industry shifted from people who built computers to people who built the technology"; he developed a corporate strategy that aimed to "strengthen our relationships with telecommunications companies, to move more into services, and in fact, to expand the whole value chain, eventually bringing in hundreds of companies, each participating in some different way." Ultimately, he hoped to move Apple away from the "'desktop' metaphor, in which computers are used primarily for spreadsheets and word processing, and toward a 'conversation' metaphor, in which there would be greater interaction among users."[36] The quotes in table 9-6 present examples of managers' and industry experts' impressions about the market targeted for some of the initial product launches. Managers at Apple and EO were especially conscious that they would have to educate the consuming public about how the devices worked and could be used, since no one had a PDA. Unfortunately for Apple, the MessagePad was unable to live up to the hype of the promotion and Newton became the butt of jokes.

Hewlett-Packard's 95LX and 100LX models started at a more modest point—or at least with a more precisely defined market (see table 9-6). The assumption was that current users of HP's higher-priced calculators were the logical target, and that this traditional market would be expanded by the inclusion of Lotus's popular 1-2-3 spreadsheet. The 95LX and 100LX were expected, as an advertisement declared, to be the "Road-warrior's weapon of choice." Similarly, Casio and Tandy aimed at a market not far removed from their traditional ones; their machines were elaborate versions of personal organizers (like Sharp's Zaurus and Wizard lines).

Whatever the starting point, managers in these companies assumed that market feedback was necessary to guide further development. However, unlike Sharp, the companies following a market-morphing strategy essentially bet on one initial product concept and design, and assumed they would gradually both create a need for their design and home in on the exact features desired by their customers. EO managers reported that they expected from the beginning that they would have to iterate a few times to get it right. That expectation was dashed in early 1994 when AT&T set a cap on spending, essentially cutting off further development funds. EO managers felt they had "learned what the customer really wanted" just as the company was shutting down.[37] EO's first product, the 440 and 880 (which were essentially the same, except that the 880 had a faster CPU, a larger screen, and more memory), was targeted at a general audience of mobile communicators. "We look at the communications orientation of PDAs as opposed to the computer/organizer orientation," explained an AT&T vice president and general manager of personal communications.[38] However, that communications orientation was very broadly defined. The EO was initially targeted at a very general class of users who were pictured as "calling up an article on a national politician's speech, watching video highlights of a football match, scribbling a note and faxing it to your office, calling up your bank account, TV schedules and a hundred other services."[39]

Even before the 440/880 was launched, managers realized the product was off the mark and was "not a market-maker."[40] A severe limitation on the changes that could be made was that a whole line of products had

TABLE 9-6

## PDA TARGETED MARKET SEGMENTS

| Product | Which Market(s) Targeted | Comments |
|---|---|---|
| **APPLE** | | |
| Newton MessagePad 100 Newton Message Pad 110 | Mass consumer<br><br>Business people<br>Vertical markets (e.g., Sales, Education, Medical) | APPLE ADVERTISING CAMPAIGNS<br>October 1993   Mass consumer with business leanings<br>March 1994   Business person<br>August 1994   Mobile salesperson<br>PRESS REVIEWS<br>"The Birth of a Platform: Launch of Apple's Newton is a Watershed Event"<br>"It's *the* coolest electronic toy of the year."<br>The "Ferrari" Effect—Won Gold Medal for Design in Business and Industrial Products<br>"[T]he Newton is not a home appliance."<br>"After a disastrous debut as a consumer product, the Newton is at last finding success as a strategic platform in vertical markets."<br>"The Newton is winning friends among doctors." |
| **AMSTRAD** | | |
| PenPad | New to computers<br>More comfortable with a pen | "True consumer mass market"<br>"Everyone can write"<br>"PenPad is #1 Selling PDA in Europe today" |
| **HEWLETT-PACKARD** | | |
| 95LX 100KX 200LX | Mobile business executives<br>Salespeople<br>Vertical market (e.g., insurance claims reps.) | HP ADVERTISING CAMPAIGN<br>October 1993   "The Road Warrior's Weapon of Choice"<br>PRESS REVIEWS<br>"Remains the unquestionable powerhouse of PDAs."<br>"Clearly defines the best there is in PDA spreadsheets."<br>"May be the most popular way for executives on the go to keep up with their electronic mail." |
| **MOTOROLA** | | |
| Envoy | Business market, particularly mobile users<br>Slogan: "No wire, No limits"<br>Multi-tiered distribution approach | "Price will limit it to business users; user interface better matched to consumer market."<br>"[Envoy has] . . . slick software and painless communications—a device such as this could have broad appeal."<br>"Envoy is also the first of the second-generation personal communicators that analysts expect to sell better than [first-generation PDAs by Apple, Tandy and Casio.]" |

been envisioned from the beginning of the company, and engineers were at work on the next product, code-named Loki, long before the 440/880 was brought out. Loki 1 was all the way to a development viability test #3 model—that is, a fully functioning model—by the spring of 1994 and was scheduled for launch in December 1994, to be shipped in volume by February 1995. Its successor, Loki 2, was scheduled to be launched in July 1995, and shipped in volume by September 1995. As this schedule suggests, EO was driven by the perceived necessity to iterate product versions quickly. Therefore the company had invested tremendous engineering resources in product development before it received market feedback on the 440/880.

What EO came to realize was that it should be targeting as its market the upper 20 percent of cellular phone users, professionals spending more than $1,000 yearly on wireless communication. Such individuals, it found through focus group interviews and one-on-one explorations of need, regarded the telephone as an essential productivity tool. They were not particularly price-sensitive and usually purchased top-of-the-line equipment. With this now clearly defined market in mind, the EO designers no longer were interested in the functionality offered by Telescript, an object-oriented communications language that was used to develop intelligent agent software routines. It became clear that EO didn't need this alliance for future products. It was able to focus in on the product concept of a highly communication-centered piece of equipment that supported all the activities of professionals conducting business while in their cars. Such individuals needed not only easy storage and retrieval of telephone numbers but also a way to make notes about needed follow-ups, to access voice mail readily, and to schedule meetings.

The other first movers in the PDA market also received market feedback that caused them to change their product definition. Amstrad managers, accustomed to assembling electronic products such as compact disc players for the consumer market, assumed that they were producing another electronic gizmo that would appeal to a mass audience. Again, market feedback from initial sales clearly indicated that this was a mistaken target. The general public was disinterested. Instead, Amstrad realized that its market would be "mobile business people," and its second generation is being developed with this different market in mind.[41]

Apple's original MessagePad was not communication-centered, a fact for which the market penalized the company, and Apple managers have admitted that they wished they had designed more communications into the original product concept. Apple sells an optional networking kit so that users can download information into their Macintoshes or PCs. But the infrared beaming capabilities—that enable Newton users to send messages to one another—have limited use.[42]

Hewlett-Packard similarly experienced surprises from the market, albeit less dramatic ones. HP teamed up with Lotus to deliver the 95LX and 100LX, but the company's original assumption was that the spreadsheet was much more important to its customers than the personal organizing facility. The market informed it otherwise; customers greatly appreciated the organizer functions.[43]

In all these cases, the product concepts have become both more focused and differently focused as the developers have received market feedback. EO, Amstrad, and Apple initially took more risk by aiming quite vaguely at a general market. HP's starting point was much more precise: an existing set of customers. However, its product was not exactly on target either. Given the inability of companies to identify their user population, it is not surprising that a third set of companies is doing its experimentation vicariously, that is, letting the pioneers shape the market and figure out who wants what in the way of a PDA.

***Vicarious Experimentation.*** Either deliberately or by default, IBM, Motorola, and Compaq are pursuing a "follower" strategy in market entry. Given the delays in product launch announced by all three companies, it is a reasonable assumption that they are learning from observing the sources of the arrows in the backs of their pioneering colleagues. IBM showed a portable cellular phone with a touchpad screen (looking a lot like Simon) as early as 1992 at the Fall Comdex industry show. Representatives of the company were quoted then as believing that communications-based applications would drive the PDA market; however, they also confirmed that they had several different prototype PDAs under development.[44] The advent of Simon has been delayed; it seems to be positioned between the communication-centered PDAs such as EO's 440/880 and Motorola's Envoy, on the one hand, and the computation- and organizing-centered PDAs such as HP's, Casio/Tandy's, and Psion's, on the other.

These companies are assuming that getting it right is more important than getting something out soon. (Certainly IBM proved this to be a viable strategy in the personal computer market.) One of the problems these companies may avoid, depending on how soon they are able to determine their own target market with some precision, is relying upon the reactions of early adopters for guidance in product development. As numerous studies of the diffusion of innovations have shown, the first 1 to 3 percent of the eventual user population who adopt an innovation tend to be poor predictors of the motives and desires of the rest of the user population.[45] These "innovators" adopt innovations for highly idiosyncratic reasons that are usually not representative of the rest of the population. The great puzzle is figuring out when the adoption curve has absorbed this tiny percent and moved on to encompass the next 10–15 percent of people, the "early adopters," who are better predictors of future purchase motives. Estimates of the eventual market size for PDAs vary wildly, not only because it is difficult to decide on the appropriate boundaries for the product category but also because the market boundaries are constantly moving as companies change their product concept.

## Market Feedback and Product Definition

Sales of PDAs have disappointed *all* of the producers. Table 9-7 presents 1993 and 1994 estimates of future market size—which look huge. The problems with such estimates are multiple. Most obviously, the product categories are confounded and overlap; the estimates are based on extrapolations of current uses of related products—or at least products perceived to be related—and the technologies are still developing, so that future functionality may look quite different from current functionality. No one can really say whether such estimates are as wildly *under*stating the market, as the first predictions of computer usage did, or whether they are as wildly *over*stating the market, as the initial predictions for rates of PDA market penetration did. As EO's CEO, Bob Evans, noted of the original market forecasts in his company, they were "not credible." However, having nothing else to go on, the companies apparently believed there was indeed a market out there.

Managers in all of the companies in our study admitted that sales fell far below expectations. As table 9-8 indicates, Apple sold only eighty thousand to ninety thousand MessagePads. Analysts had predicted sales in the "hundreds of thousands."[46] In contrast, Apple had expected to ship 250,000 MessagePads during 1993 alone. EO sold less than 10 percent of what it expected.[47] Amstrad and Sharp will not say how many they sold, but managers in both companies said the sales were disappointing. The fact that Tandy lowered the price of the Zoomer by $200 suggests an attempt to stimulate a slow market.

The general message delivered to PDA producers by the market was therefore "No thanks"—or, at best, "Not yet." The question all the companies faced was how to redesign their product to appeal to a larger market segment. The most pressing problem in redesigning was how to continue development when the time-to-market pressures now

TABLE 9-7

## PDA MARKET PROJECTIONS

### Market Potential for PDAs and Functions of Current Offerings[1]

|  | EST. MARKET SIZE IN 1998 (IN BILLIONS) |
| --- | --- |
| Personal Communicator | $2.5 |
| Personal Agent (Pen) | $0.8 |
| Information Organizer | $0.6 |
| Electronic Book | $0.5 |
| Electronic Notebook | $0.4 |
| Entertainment | $0.8 |

### Handheld Computers and PDA Market Projections[2]

| OLD GENERATION HANDHELD (UNITS 000's) | PDAS (UNITS 000's) | TOTAL (UNITS 000's) |
| --- | --- | --- |
| 903 | 0 | 903 |
| 1,517 | 11 | 1,518 |
| 2,230 | 108 | 2,338 |
| 1,995 | 375 | 3,370 |
| 3,728 | 978 | 4,716 |
| 4,406 | 2,057 | 6,463 |

### Handheld Computers and Pen-Enabled Computer Market Projections[3]

| YEAR | HANDHELD COMPUTERS (IN MILLIONS) | PEN-ENABLED HANDHELD COMPUTERS (IN MILLIONS) |
| --- | --- | --- |
| 1992 | 4 | <1 |
| 1993 | 5 | <1 |
| 1994 | 6 | 1 |
| 1995 | 8 | <3 |
| 1996 | 13 | >6 |
| 1997 | 17 | 12 |

SOURCES:  1.  Link Resources, Corporation quoted in the *Wall Street Journal*, February 11, 1994.
2.  America Online.
3.  Mobile Hardware Conference Presentation. Gartner Group. 1993 Leslie Fiering.

traditional in the consumer electronics market required overlapping product design cycles. That is, the development cycles were shorter than the market feedback/learning cycles. EO's director of customer marketing, Wink Grelis, said that the company had learned from the 440 product that "A tablet-device-type of product is not something people relate to

TABLE 9-8

FIRST GENERATION PDA SALES

| Company/Product | Product Introduction | Sales From | Unit Sales |
|---|---|---|---|
| Apple Newton MessagePad 100 (or Sharp Expert Pad)[1] | 8/2/93 | 8/93–8/94[2] | 80–90K[3] |
| Casio Zoomer Z-7000 | 7/93 | 7/93–12/93 | 20K[4] |
| Tandy Zoomer Z-PDA 550 | 10/93[5] | 10/93–12/93 | 30K[6] |
| AST GridPad 2390 | 3/28/94[7] | | |
| Sharp Expert Pad | 6/93 | 6/93–12/93 | 158K[8] |
| Sharp LC Pencom Zaurus | 10/93 (for Japanese domestic market) | 10/93–3/94 | 200K |
| EO Inc. AT&T EO 440 and 880 | 7/93 | 7/93–12/93 | 4K[9] |
| HP 95/100LX | 6/91–6/92 | 6/91–4/94 | 390K |
| Motorola Envoy | Delayed[10] | | |
| Compaq Mobile Companion | Delayed until 1995[11] | Not selling yet | |
| Amstrad PenPad | 5/93 | Not available | |
| IBM Simon | Delayed 6/94[12] | Not selling yet | |
| Voice Powered Technology Voice Organizer[13] | 3/94 | Sales just starting | |
| Psion Series-3A | 6/93 | Not available | |

NOTES:

1. Discontinued when the Newton MessagePad 110 came out.
2. *Mobile Communications,* January 27, 1994.
3. *MacWeek,* February 21, 1994, p. 32.
4. *PC Week,* November 8, 1993, p. 32.
5. *Computer Reseller News,* June 14, 1993, p. 49.
6. *MacWeek,* February 21, 1994, p. 32.
7. *Infoworld,* March 28, 1994, p. 37.
8. *PC Week,* February 28, 1994, p. 25.
9. *PC Week,* February 28, 1994, p. 25.
10. In *PC Week,* February 28, 1994, p. 25; the introduction was predicted for 3/94.
11. Delaying introduction until late 1994, after support for a keyboard has been incorporated, because Compaq said consumers won't buy devices that rely on current handwriting technology. Sources however say that the device is already keyboard ready. *MacWeek,* February 21, 1994, p. 32. Conpac CEO Pfeiffer announced a further setback for the product, which will not be out until 1995. *Reuter European Business Report,* May 15, 1994.
12. Was being ramped up for production when a fax problem was discovered. Delayed indefinitely. *PC Week,* April 4, 1994, p. 31. Will come out in June 1994. *Christian Science Monitor,* April 22, 1994, p. 10.
13. *Infoworld,* April 18, 1994, p. 102. Voice Organizer is a digital voice recorder version of a PDA.

as much as communications."[48] However, as noted above, by the time that feedback was received, the next two products in the line were already well under way. Some very basic decisions made early in the first designs were affected. As researchers of the product development process have noted, there is usually a hierarchy of design in which early decisions constrain subsequent design options.[49] Therefore, companies that chose a strategy of rapid iterations were limited in their ability to approach the now much more precise product definition provided by the market.

Despite such constraints, the surviving companies appear to be responding to the market in several ways. Once PDAs were on the market, consumers and industry watchers could make intelligent (if somewhat conflicting) observations. Overall, organizer-type capabilities were rated as the most important PDA features across all respondent segments in some early surveys.[50] HP's 200LX emphasizes the personal organizer features more than HP developers originally thought necessary. On the other hand, industry observers have made such predictions as "PDAs will be purchased primarily for their communications capabilities. This will be the driving force behind the anticipated explosive growth of the PDA market in the mid-1990s."[51] Not surprisingly, we see that Apple's next MessagePad will be more communicative. Despite the apparent movement of computer/organizers toward more communication-centered devices, it is possible that before they truly converge, PDAs will divide more sharply into two market segments: calculator/organizer users, on the one hand, and users of smart cellular phones, on the other. It is still too early to tell.

Of the early entrants into the PDA market, only Psion initially addressed a feature that the early surveys identified as important: "Almost 40% of potential buyers desire voice recognition and/or voice recording operation of PDAs."[52] Latecomer Voice-Powered Technology's Voice Organizer is designed specifically around that feature. Of other early controversial features, handwriting recognition remains a dubious investment for most PDA producers: "Less than 25% of respondents prefer pen input for PDAs, while almost 54% still prefer keyboard input."[53] However, pen input does not necessarily mean handwriting recognition, and the products have numerous different approaches to using a pen for data and information entry. Finally, there is the issue of price. As figure 9-10 indicates, prices for each PDA producer's initial entrant ranged from $200 (if you consider the Voice Organizer as fitting in this product category) to $3,000 for the now defunct EO 880. The early market research showed that "the majority of potential PDA users expect products to be priced in the $1,000 range."[54] The price of many PDAs is determined by the number of add-on features, such as optional communication capabilities or software applications, but most current products are within that range. What this research does not address is how the potential user profile changes at lower prices. The companies have already found that the number of potential users at this price range is very limited. Consequently, most observers expect to see prices come down in subsequent product generations.

PDA producers not only are redesigning their products but also are redefining the markets for which the PDAs have utility. Moving away from mass markets, several companies indicate that they find more receptivity in vertical markets, in special niches. As Table 9-1 shows, Apple has moved from targeting a mass market toward more business focus. Observed Joseph Graziano, Apple's chief financial officer and acting general manager of the Personal Interactive Electronics Division: "We always knew that there'd be business users for the Newton. But our marketing message and approach at launch were wrong."[55] Recently Apple has begun experiments with vertical markets. For instance, twenty-eight physicians at two of Boston's most prestigious teaching hospitals are using MessagePads (increasingly referred to as Newtons) in their work on a research project called Constellation. In the first phase of the experiment, Newtons serve as electronic reference books; in the second, the Newton will be linked to hospital databases, enabling doctors to enter or retrieve patient information.[56] Moreover, HP has plans to ally with GeoWorks and Novell to make "information appliances" to supply the real estate market with multiple-listing information, and doctors and nurses with drug reference and patient information.[57]

## CONCLUSION

Competition in the PDA field was fierce and short-lived. Within the span of two years, major new products appeared on the market and then disappeared without a trace. Rapid turnover among product offerings and short product life cycles are not unique to the PDA business; to some degree, they characterize many other segments of the information technology industry. Still, the PDA experience was particularly extreme. The forces we have explored in this paper help explain the rapid pace of product development and the dynamics of competition in PDAs.

Considering the task taken on by PDA producers, one might have expected the industry to develop more slowly and deliberately. The great uncertainties regarding technology and market demand might well have

FIGURE 9-10

## PRICES OF PDA PRODUCERS' INITIAL (ENTRY) PRODUCTS

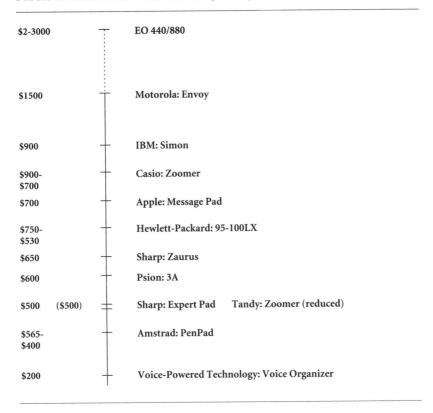

| $2-3000 | | EO 440/880 |
|---|---|---|
| $1500 | | Motorola: Envoy |
| $900 | | IBM: Simon |
| $900-$700 | | Casio: Zoomer |
| $700 | | Apple: Message Pad |
| $750-$530 | | Hewlett-Packard: 95-100LX |
| $650 | | Sharp: Zaurus |
| $600 | | Psion: 3A |
| $500 | ($500) | Sharp: Expert Pad    Tandy: Zoomer (reduced) |
| $565-$400 | | Amstrad: PenPad |
| $200 | | Voice-Powered Technology: Voice Organizer |

led to cautious product development, not the race to market that we observed. The fact that no company had all the skills needed to produce a PDA would have further slowed product development. And the absence of extensive communication networks and protocols in PDAs[58] should have given companies pause. Why didn't these factors slow the pace of product introduction in PDAs?

Our research suggests two reasons, one strategic and one organizational. First, the companies expected that important first-mover advantages would accrue to the product that first established itself in the market. This expectation was based on the well-known history of other information systems products in which technical standards were important, such as videocassette recorders and personal computers. We have not explored the extent to which this expectation on the part of the companies was justified. But everywhere we saw evidence that the players felt pressure to bring their products to market as early as possible, even if this meant that the first-generation product was not quite "ready."

The second reason for the rapid-fire introduction of new products in PDAs lay in the organizational structures and processes that the companies devised to pursue the perceived first-mover advantages. This has been our focus. We found that two types of mechanisms were important, corresponding to the main challenges facing product developers in PDAs —market uncertainty and technology convergence. To deal with market uncertainty, the competitors used market experimentation—a process for identifying customer needs through "real-time" feedback from actual products. To deal with technological convergence, the competitors used interfirm alliances—organizational structures that facilitated the combination of technical skills from disparate companies.

In sum, the perception of first-mover advantages defined the need for a race. But the race could not have taken place without the organizational mechanisms we studied. In the end, our mechanisms were successful in producing rapid innovation, but the first-mover advantages have not yet materialized. As a result, the competitors appear to have retreated to a more deliberate and measured process for introducing future products. They are likely to continue to experiment in the market and to use alliances to gain access to technologies, but both tactics will probably be used more selectively than in the past.

Precisely because the early years of the PDA industry were so turbulent, however, they contain valuable lessons for firms and managers in related sectors. The unforgiving nature of competition in these years brings the lessons into a sharp focus, as it were. We drew five lessons from our study.

The first lesson is that the process of "convergence" examined in this book represents much more than the merging of existing industries: *Convergence represents the creation of whole new products and markets.* This means that the process of convergence—whether in PDAs, in multimedia, in interactive TV, or in the development of Internet services— always brings with it great market uncertainties. The product concepts in these new fields may well consist of combinations of existing technologies, but market demand for these products is never a combination of customers from existing fields. Often, customer needs will have to be defined, identified, or even developed from scratch before the fruits of technological convergence can be enjoyed. Not only do we not know precisely who the customers are for the newly conceived products; we also do not know what they are willing to pay, what features they value most, and how they are best reached.

The second lesson we learned from PDAs regards how the competitors have coped with the challenges just outlined: *Market experimentation to identify customer groups and product features is critical in uncertain environments.* Some firms we studied hedged their bets and launched several versions of a product; through a process akin to Darwinian selection, they later found out which products were viable and which were not. Other competitors experimented vicariously—they observed customer responses to the products of rivals and then adjusted their own offerings accordingly. Still other vendors adopted the practice of market morphing —they incrementally changed their products based on customer feedback. In every case, however, the firms used actual products somewhat as trial balloons—they may have secretly hoped that they got the product "right" for their vaguely defined customers, but realistically they knew they were really gathering market information.

Our next two lessons concern the role of interfirm alliances in enabling the convergence of industries. As could be expected, technological convergence and alliance formation go hand in hand. What was perhaps not predictable was the degree to which alliance clusters became the driving force of competition. The proliferation of alliances in PDAs thoroughly reshaped rivalry in the industry. Every single PDA brought to market in the early 1990s was the product not of a firm but of a constellation of firms. Competition took place between these clusters, not between single firms. This meant that the way the firms in a cluster collaborated with each other determined how they competed as a group. The composition and structure of these clusters thus helped to shape their performance. This was lesson number three: *Convergence reshapes not only products and markets, but also the very unit of competition in an industry.* Alliances, in other words, are more than just linking mechanisms between firms; they are the glue that creates the new competitive units.

The rise of these new competitive units—call them alliance clusters, networks, virtual corporations, or constellations—dramatically changes the dynamics of competition in an industry. Our fourth lesson is that these *alliance clusters develop and interact according to a distinctive logic.* As we saw, the PDA clusters grew systematically by adding members responsible for learning, supply, and positioning. By using existing technologies from proven industry leaders, the clusters were able to speed up product development. The most innovative PDAs came from those clusters that relied the least on alliances for innovation. Even so, the clusters tended to imitate each other in their composition, strategies, and product offerings. These processes quickened the pace of product innovation and intensified rivalry in the industry. Paradoxically, collaboration in PDAs did not suppress competition but enhanced it. This is likely to be the case in other converging industries.

Convergence thus inevitably involves alliance formation as well as market experimentation. But this combination of processes is a potentially volatile mix. Our fifth and final lesson is therefore a warning to managers: *Converge at your own risk!* On the one hand, collaboration allows firms to be more flexible in responding to market feedback. But this may also mean that the composition of an alliance group is unstable —partners will be dropped and added in order to pursue new market experiments. Such instability is especially likely when a firm hedges its bets with multiple partners, a common pattern in uncertain markets.

Thus, while alliances can provide firms with flexibility, the firms may also need deep pockets to survive in a battle involving rapid market experimentation. As a general matter, alliance groups have looser commitments from members than do units of a large firm, making them inherently fragile in the experimentation process. Collaboration allows firms to acquire new resources quickly; all too often, however, it also reflects a firm's hesitancy in committing resources. Furthermore, alliance groups can suffer from a lack of direction when partners have different visions of the future.

Notwithstanding these drawbacks of alliances, the PDA experience suggests that the use of alliances in emerging markets is contagious. Indeed, group-based competition has spread rapidly in other emerging industries, such as RISC, multimedia services, and biotechnology. Because no firm has a dominant position or first-mover advantage in these businesses, nor all the capabilities needed for success, firms jockey for advantage by forming partnerships. As a result, when one firm forms an alliance, others often follow. The bandwagon then gathers its own momentum as firms begin *competing over partnerships,* hedging against the uncertain future with portfolios of alliances and forming preemptive alliances.

By the same token, market experimentation is risky and costly, but it, too, is unavoidable in emerging markets. The traditional tools of market research and product design simply do not work in these environments. The convergence of technologies may provide an opportunity for a new product, but it never guarantees a market. The object of competition in these markets is thus not to produce a better mousetrap, but to *find out before your rivals* whether customers are trying to trap mice.

Most of the firms involved in the PDA field are not used to the type of competition sketched here. Their industries of origin are usually more stable and mature, and they usually occupy positions of technological or market leadership. Their early experiences in the PDA field, however, have already taught most of them that success in this emerging business requires a change in strategy. We are convinced that, to succeed in environments such as this one, a firm needs to manage at least two processes better than its competitors: market experimentation and group-based competition. The pioneers in the PDA field learned these lessons the hard way; others will do well to learn from their experience.

## NOTES

1. Tom R. Halfhill, "PDAs Arrive but Aren't Quite Here Yet," *Byte*, October 1993, p. 68.

2. Christopher Barr and Michael Neubarth, "Pen Pals," *PC Magazine*, October 12 1993, p. 117.

3. Fumio Kodama, "Technology Fusion and the New R&D," *Harvard Business Review*, 70, no. 4 (1992): 70–78, points to the transformation of Fanuc from a producer of mechanical machinery into the world leader of computerized numerical controllers for machine tools as an example of a company that successfully fused expertise in mechanics with electronics and materials development. Similarly, Sharp has become a leader in liquid crystal displays by combining electronic, crystal, and optical technologies.

4. Hewlett-Packard's program in MC2 (measurement plus computing and communications) is promoted by the head of HP corporate laboratories, Joel Birnbaum, as a unique capability that will yield a crossbred series of totally new products. Looking ahead to all the possibilities created by digitization, Birnbaum predicted in 1993: "HP's going to be an almost totally different company 10 years from now." Quoted in Robert D. Hof, "Hewlett-Packard Digs Deep for a Digital Future," *Business Week*, October 18, 1993, p. 73.

5. Quoted in Joseph Weber, "Going over the Lab Wall in Search of New Ideas," *Business Week*, special issue, 1989, p. 132. At the time, Gussin was vice president for science and technology.

6. Dorothy Leonard-Barton, *Wellsprings of Knowledge: Building and Sustaining the Sources of Innovation* (Boston: Harvard Business School Press, 1995).

7. Benjamin Gomes-Casseres, *The Alliance Revolution: The New Shape of Business Rivalry* (Cambridge, Mass.: Harvard University Press, 1996).

8. Ibid.

9. EO's position in this chart lies a bit to the right of the pattern of the other observations. This is partly explained by the fact that AT&T was counted as an ally, and its contributions increased EO's "external dependence." In fact, AT&T controlled 51 percent of EO and, over time, gained increasing control over GO

and Pensoft, two critical EO allies. Thus, the location of EO on this chart may well belong further to the left.

10. Patrick Marshall, "Organized Time," *Infoworld*, April 18, 1994, pp. 81–102.

11. This three-part typology corresponds to the three theoretical approaches to joint ventures identified by Bruce Kogut, "Joint Ventures: Theoretical and Empirical Perspectives," *Strategic Management Journal*, July–August 1988, pp. 319–332. The typology is discussed further and applied in Benjamin Gomes-Casseres, "Computers: Alliances and Industry Evolution," in David B. Yoffie, ed., *Beyond Free Trade* (Boston: Harvard Business School Press, 1993); and Gomes-Casseres, *The Alliance Revolution*.

12. See Chapter 6 in this volume.

13. Microsoft could be expected to do the same, but its WinPad system was delayed.

14 Lindley H. Clark, "Intel to Sell Stake in VLSI, Partner in Chips," *Wall Street Journal*, August 5, 1994, p. B3.

15. Momenta Corporation, one of the first pen-based computer vendors, went out of business several years ago.

16. Estimates given us vary; however, managers at one of the companies investigating handwriting recognition estimated that cursive handwriting recognition would only work 70 percent of the time.

17. See Eric Von Hippel, *The Sources of Innovation* (New York: Oxford University Press, 1988).

18. The term originates from Dorothy Leonard-Barton, "Inanimate Integrators: A Block of Wood Speaks," *Design Management Journal*, 2, no. 3 (Summer 1991): 61–66; see also Leonard-Barton, Dorothy, Edith Wilson and John Doyle. "Commercializing Technology: Imaginative Understanding of User Needs," Technical note 694-102 (Boston: Harvard Business School, 1994).

19. For a detailed discussion of empathic design and other nontraditional methods of importing knowledge from the market, see Leonard-Barton, *Wellsprings of Knowledge*.

20. See Halfhill. 66–86, passim.

21. See Barr and Neubarth.

22. Volney Stefflre, "Stimulation of People's Behavior toward New Objects and Events," *American Behavioral Scientist* 8 (1965): 12.

23. Leonard-Barton, "Inanimate Integrators."

24. Michael Tchao, Apple's Newton Group manager of product planning and strategy, was at some pains to exclude some likely analogies: "We're not talking about Lotus 1-2-3 in the palm of your hand. We're not talking about pocket PageMaker. We're not talking about a little-bitty Microsoft Word with little-bitty keys and little-bitty menus. PDAs are defined as highly portable,

easy-to-use computing and communication devices aimed at the mass market." Quoted in Halfhill, p. 68.

25. Quoted in "First Newton—The Message Pad—Hits the Market," *Business Wire*, July 30, 1993.

26. Markos Kounalakis, *Defying Gravity: The Making of Newton* (Hillsboro, Oreg.: Beyond Words Publishing, 1993), pp. 01:70.

27. Personal interview with Dr. Herman Hauser, May 25, 1994.

28. Quoted in PR Newswire Association, online, July 30, 1993.

29. David Atkinson, AT&T vice president and general manager of personal communications, quoted in Stephanie Stahl, "A Personal Communicator Fiefdom," *Information Week*, August 23, 1993, p. 13.

30. Andrew Seybold, editor of *Outlook on Mobile Computing* newsletter, quoted in Stahl.

31. Personal interview with David Hennell, director of international marketing, Amstrad, May 17, 1994.

32. Among companies with relatively inexpensive product lines, test marketing in a limited geographic area has always been an important weapon in the marketer's arsenal. However, recently some companies have begun to perceive such limited testing as dangerous, giving competitors too much time for imitation or the opportunity to distort market feedback. For instance, if a competitor blitzes the region with promotions or coupons, consumer response to the new product may not be indicative of long-term buying intentions.

33. "What Makes Yoshio Invent," *The Economist*, January 12, 1991, p. 61.

34. Ibid.

35. Personal interview with Bob Evans, September 7, 1994.

36. Kounalakis, 01:46–01:48.

37. Evans interview.

38. David Atkinson, quoted in Stahl.

39. Roger Highfield, "Boxing Clever," *Esquire*, May 1993.

40. Interview with Dennis Ryan, September 7, 1994.

41. Personal interview with David Hennell and Cliff Lawson, Amstrad Inc., May 17, 1994.

42. Editorial, *MacWeek*, August 15, 1994, p. 110, and Dan Muse, Newton MessagePad Review, *MacWorld*, August 1994, p. 61.

43. Personal interview, Tim Williams, Hewlett-Packard, July 15, 1994.

44. See Barr and Neubarth.

45. See Everett M. Rogers, *Diffusion of Innovations* (New York: Free Press,1983).

46. John J. Keller, "AT&T's EO to Focus on Cellular Phones as Market for Data Devices Proves Slow," *Wall Street Journal*, February 1, 1994, p. B6.

47. Ibid.

48. Ibid.

49. Kim Clark, "The Interaction of Design Hierarchies and Market Concepts in Technological Evolution," *Research Policy* 14 (1985): 235-251.

50. BIS Strategic Decisions, "Forecasting the Market for Personal Digital Assistants," May 1993.

51. R. Martin, in America OnLine, Inc., Company Report (1993), pp 1–19.

52. BIS Strategic Decisions.

53. Ibid.

54. Ibid.

55. Mark Hall and Jon Swartz, "Graziano: Newton off the Rocks," *MacWeek*, August 15, 1994, p. 1.

56. Richard Saltus, "Pocket Computers Chip in to Help Doctors," *Boston Globe*, September 3, 1994, p. 21.

57. G. Christian Hill, "Motorola, Hewlett-Packard Stake out New Market," *Wall Street Journal*, March 7, 1994, p. B4.

58. See chapter 6.

## REFERENCES

Aharoni, Yair, ed. *Coalitions and Competition: The Globalization of Professional Business Services.* New York: Routledge, 1993.

Barr, Christopher, and Michael Neubarth. "Pen Pals." *PC Magazine,* October 12 1993, pp. 117–182.

Clark, Kim, "The Interaction of Design Hierarchies and Market Concepts in Technological Evolution." *Research Policy* 14 (1985): 235–251.

"First Newton–The MessagePad–Hits the Market." *Business Wire,* July 30, 1993.

Gomes-Casseres, Benjamin. "Computers: Alliances and Industry Evolution." In David B. Yoffie, ed., *Beyond Free Trade.* Boston: Harvard Business School Press, 1993.

Gomes-Casseres, Benjamin. *The Alliance Revolution: The New Shape of Business Rivalry.* Cambridge, Mass.: Harvard University Press, 1996.

Halfhill, Tom R. "PDAs Arrive but Aren't Quite Here Yet." *Byte,* October 1993, pp. 66–86.

Hall, Mark, and Jon Swartz. "Graziano: Newton off the Rocks." *MacWeek,* August 15, 1994, p. 1.

Highfield, Roger. "Boxing Clever." *Esquire,* May, 1993.

Hof, Robert D. "Hewlett-Packard Digs Deep for a Digital Future." *Business Week,* October 18, 1993, pp. 72–75.

Kodama, Fumio. "Technology Fusion and the New R&D." *Harvard Business Review* 70, no. 4 (1992): 70–78.

Kogut, Bruce. "Joint Ventures: Theoretical and Empirical Perspectives." *Strategic Management Journal,* July–August 1988, pp. 319–332.

Leonard-Barton, Dorothy. *Wellsprings of Knowledge: Building and Sustaining the Sources of Innovation.* Boston: Harvard Business School Press, 1995.

Nohria, Nitin, and Carlos Garcia-Pont. "Global Strategic Linkages and Industry Structure." *Strategic Management Review,* Summer 1991, pp. 105–124.

Rogers, Everett M. *Diffusion of Innovation.* New York: Free Press, 1983.

Saltus, Richard. "Pocket Computers Chip in to Help Doctors." *Boston Globe,* September 3, 1994, p. 21.

Stefflre, Volney, "Stimulation of People's Behavior Toward New Objects and Events." *American Behavioral Scientist* 8 (1965): 12.

Von Hippel, Eric. *The Sources of Innovation.* New York: Oxford University Press, 1988.

Weber, Joseph. "Going over the Lab Wall in Search of New Ideas." *Business Week,* special issue, 1989, p. 132.

"What Makes Yoshio Invent," *The Economist,* January 12, 1991, p. 61.

# CHAPTER 10

# BEYOND THE WATERFALL
## Software Development at Microsoft

Michael A. Cusumano
Stanley A. Smith

## INTRODUCTION

This paper analyzes the approach to software development followed at the Microsoft Corporation, the world's largest personal computer (PC) software company. Microsoft builds operating systems such as MS-DOS, Windows, and Windows NT; applications such as Microsoft Excel and Word (now usually packaged together in Microsoft Office); and new multimedia products and on-line systems such as the Microsoft Network. Inherent in our analysis of this company is a comparison with older software producers that have built operating systems and applications for mainframes, minicomputers, and workstations. Many of these older organizations have followed what has been called a sequential "waterfall" type of development process, which has both advantages (it can be relatively structured) and disadvantages (it is not very flexible to accommodate specification and design changes during a project). The reason for doing this comparison was to examine the effects on Microsoft of developing large-scale software products for the rapidly evolving PC software market. This challenge might have prompted Microsoft to become less unstructured or "hackerlike" and more like older software producers; on the other hand, it might also have prompted Microsoft to seek yet another development process that is structured but departs from waterfall-like practices in order to introduce more flexibility.[1]

The second section of this paper begins with a brief discussion of a stylized waterfall process, which includes such typical phases as requirements specification, design, implementation, testing, and product release. The waterfall model is widely considered to be the first well-defined development methodology, and the base upon which most current software development processes have been formed, particularly for formal project planning activities. The approach was probably first utilized on a large-scale project by IBM while developing the System/360 operating system in the 1960s. It represents a structured process and organization created for the purpose of developing large-scale software systems. But even though many firms have refined this process over many years, companies have continued to encounter numerous problems in software development, due both to a lack of effective process management and to inherent deficiencies in the waterfall process itself. As a result, many companies, including parts of IBM, have been moving away from certain elements of the waterfall process.

The third section presents the analysis of Microsoft's development approach, which we have labeled the synch-and-stabilize process. Since 1988–1989, the company has gradually been introducing techniques that add structure to software product development but also depart from the waterfall model. Many aspects of what Microsoft does resemble concurrent engineering and incremental development practices found in other software companies and in companies in other industries. We begin by describing the development life cycle, using the same terminology as in the waterfall model. Beyond this basic conceptualization of the development steps, however, we also attempt to describe more fundamental characteristics of the Microsoft process, such as approaches to project control, metrics, configuration management (how to manage the evolution of pieces of the product and various versions), process ownership, and process improvement initiatives.

The fourth section summarizes the similarities and differences in Microsoft compared with waterfall-type producers. In general, as its products have grown larger and more complex, Microsoft has moved closer to the approaches used by older companies with more formalized development processes. Nonetheless, there are important differences. In particular, Microsoft's synch-and-stabilize process allows the product specification to evolve during development. It also makes it possible for large teams to work like small teams through techniques that enable frequent synchronizations among the developers and periodic stabilizations of the code without relying on one large integration and test phase at the end of a project. These techniques help Microsoft compete on the basis of new product features with details that may change during a project. These techniques have also helped Microsoft build increasingly large and complex software systems, which it must continue to do as it expands into interactive video systems, video on demand, on-line network services, and other types of software products and services associated with the information highway and the Internet.

## SOFTWARE DEVELOPMENT PROCESSES AND PROBLEMS

### The Classic "Waterfall" Process

The waterfall process originated during the 1960s in firms building large-scale software systems for the U.S. defense and space industries as well as for commercial applications. These companies worked on multi-year projects and designed software for large computer (mainframe and mini-computer) systems that evolved relatively slowly. They modeled the waterfall process after hardware design projects, for which engineers could more easily (though not always completely) predict how pieces of a system would interact.[2]

The classic waterfall model views the optimal process for software development as a linear or sequential series of phases that take developers from initial high-level requirements through system testing and product shipment (figure 10-1). Designers begin by trying to write a specification that is as complete as possible. Next, they divide the specification into pieces or modules in a more detailed design phase, and then assign different individuals or teams to build these pieces in parallel. Each team tests and debugs (finds and fixes errors in) its pieces. Only in the last phase of the project, which could range from a few months to a few years for a large system, do the designers, developers, and testers try to put the pieces together and test the entire system. Usually, this process of integration and system testing requires reworking the modules and writing new code to correct problems in the operation or interactions of the pieces due to unforeseen problems as well as mistakes, miscommunications, or changes that have crept into the design of the parts during the project. If this integration work goes well, the team will ship the product when there are no serious bugs (errors or defects) remaining.

FIGURE 10-1

CONVENTIONAL WATERFALL DEVELOPMENT PROCESS

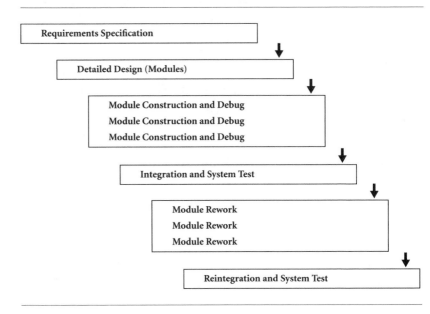

Coordinating the work of a large group of people building interdependent components that are continually changing requires a constant, high level of coordination and synchronization that departs from the simple sequence of activities prescribed in the waterfall model. How to enforce this coordination but still allow programmers the freedom to be creative is perhaps the central dilemma that managers of software development face.

The waterfall model works reasonably well in stable problem domains where product development consists mainly of adding incremental changes to an existing core of functionality. It is also suitable for projects where producers can control changes in design details and proceed to the end of a project or incorporate unplanned rework with little or no interference from customers or competitors. But the waterfall model is not a good framework to control the development process for products that have so much new content or so many uncertainties to resolve that changes in the design are inevitable and often desirable. In the PC software market, for example, both hardware technologies and customer requirements change very rapidly. In these types of cases, designers cannot write a specification at the beginning of the project that accurately captures what the optimal product design should be. Accordingly, product development cannot proceed in an orderly, sequential fashion from design to coding and then testing at the end of the project.

In cases of uncertain requirements or fast-moving markets, if designers try to create detailed specifications for the product and its pieces too early in the development cycle, the project team will end up building a product that does not meet customer needs very well or that is out of date before it is even shipped. If developers try to make changes in parts of the product as they go along, for example, due to interim feedback from customers or evolution in particular hardware or software technologies, or even just to add a feature that a competitor has just introduced, then the project may end up with pieces that no longer fit together. The integration effort and system testing fail. The project team then has to rework the pieces extensively—even though they thought they had finished coding. They may even have to throw much of the code away. With these types of difficulties, it is no surprise that so many software projects end up being late, over budget, and riddled with bugs, due to errors in the pieces as well as in how the pieces interact.

Researchers and managers have proposed alternatives to the waterfall since the 1970s in the form of more "iterative" approaches to product development. These include notions of "iterative enhancement" as well as the "spiral model" of software development.[3] These alternatives see developers moving around in phases, going back and forth between designing, coding, and testing as they go forward in a project. This type of iteration is, in fact, a relatively accurate description of what many, if not most, software developers experience in projects—but usually in an unplanned manner. Some companies refer to these iterations as "incremental builds," although they do not always incorporate these into formal project plans and checkpoints. Nor is it always clear in the iterative models when to stop the iterations or how to break up work into manageable pieces and phases.

Because most software projects require extensive iterations among specification, development, and testing activities, many companies have been moving away from the classic waterfall model in practice. Some companies also try to build software around reusable modules or objects, which means that developers need to begin with a detailed overview of the system objectives, then borrow from or build a library of reusable components as part of the design and development process. This type of activity requires a departure from the linear waterfall steps, although many companies known for pushing reusability tend to end with a single integration phase at the end of the project.[4] In short, we still find companies using elements of a waterfall process to plan and control software development, as well as other types of product development. At least until very recently, in cases of procurement for the U.S. Department of Defense, information system providers have had to follow, as well as document that they follow, a precisely specified waterfall process referred to as the development life cycle.[5]

## Waterfall Process Implications and Problems

The major advantage of the waterfall or life-cycle model is that it provides a structure for organizing and controlling a software development project. The single most important methodological need in this approach, however, is to identify user requirements accurately.[6] Most software projects pay inadequate attention to fulfilling this need.

Disadvantages associated with the waterfall include problems that occur if there is no iteration and feedback among phases, beginning with the need to define the system requirements specifications accurately. Unless there is iteration and feedback, there may be no way to improve initial imperfections in one of the later phases. Realistic life-cycle development processes are, therefore, iterative and interactive, and a company's software development process needs to accommodate this fact.[7]

The largely linear nature of activities defined in the classic waterfall model thus has important consequences. For example, waterfall projects generally include a certification step at the end of each phase to mark the completion of one phase and the beginning of the next. Projects can accomplish this through some form of verification and validation to ensure that the output of the phase is consistent with its input and also with the overall requirements of the system.[8] The goal of each phase is generally to produce a certifiable output. Many firms have found that reviews (formal meetings to uncover deficiencies in a product) are useful for certain key phases, such as requirements, design, and coding.

In a waterfall process, documents or code is the normal output of a phase, and output from one phase becomes the input for the next phase. Team members are not supposed to change outputs that the project has already certified.[9] In reality, however, requirements changes almost always happen. Software development projects thus need some mechanism for configuration control to ensure that team members make modifications in a controlled manner after evaluating the effect of each change on the product and progress of the project.

Companies have introduced many refinements to the waterfall process, as well as new programming tools and techniques to aid the software development process. Nonetheless, firms continue to report problems, especially in building large software systems for the first time. A 1993 list of common problems focuses on ten root causes of "runaway" projects and "missed objectives."[10] Runaway projects are characterized by significant overruns of schedule, resources, or funding; missed objectives consist of projects that do not meet customer expectations in some significant way:

1. Inadequate requirements statements

2. Lack of specific and measurable goals

3. Architecture design flaws and changes

4. Inadequate change-control systems

5. Inadequate project status reviews and reporting

6. Inadequate project metrics

7. Lack of open project communications

8. Lack of clear project milestones

9. Overly optimistic estimations of project feasibility

10. Various management difficulties.

This list is similar to lists compiled in the 1980s, 1970s, and 1960s, suggesting that the field of software engineering management has not made much progress.[11] Nonetheless, many firms have recently begun to depart from the waterfall style of management and to make other changes to improve their ability to control software projects, often in response to one or more disastrous projects.

Microsoft is one such company. It had a number of product recalls and extremely late projects during the 1980s and 1990s. A particularly important runaway project was the first version of Word for Windows. Microsoft started this in 1984 and ended up being off 500 percent in its original scheduling estimate.[12] Microsoft projects also typically generated hundreds and even thousands of bugs during the development process, too many of which the company did not catch prior to delivering products. By 1988–1989, many applications products were hundreds of thousands of lines of code, and the Windows operating system had grown to be more than a million lines of code. Microsoft could no longer build these products with small groups of programmers using ad hoc practices. As its customer base expanded to corporate users who demanded more reliable products, quality and delivery problems became unacceptable to Bill Gates and other top Microsoft managers. In addition, both retail customers and original equipment suppliers that ship computers with Microsoft operating systems and applications packages began to express concern that Microsoft was not utilizing quality processes to create its products, which had often become "mission-critical" for individuals and organizations.

The challenge Microsoft managers and developers began facing in the late 1980s was to introduce more structure and predictability into their loosely organized development process but still retain elements of the flexible and creative PC "hacker" culture. They viewed the traditional waterfall model as inadequate because it required too much structure: It demanded that teams determine and "freeze" a product's requirements at the beginning of a project, and that they build components that precisely followed this specification. Microsoft needed a different process that allowed team members to evolve product designs incrementally, responding to customer inputs, prototypes, competitors' products, and changes in the fast-moving PC hardware industry. We will now describe the process that Microsoft groups have been using since 1988–1989 to build products such as Excel, Word, and Windows NT. Other product groups have adopted versions of this approach, which we refer to as the synch-and-stabilize process, during the 1990s.

## MICROSOFT CASE STUDY

### The Company

Bill Gates and Paul Allen (who retired from Microsoft in 1983 but remains on the board of directors) founded Microsoft in 1975; the company went public in 1986.[13] Microsoft started by building programming languages, and now develops, markets, and supports a wide range of microcomputer software for business, professional, and home use. Its software products include operating systems, programming languages, application programs, communications programs, and an on-line network. Microsoft also develops and markets microcomputer-oriented books, hardware, and multimedia CD-ROM products.

Corporate headquarters are in Redmond, Washington. Total worldwide employment was about 17,800 in 1995, including 13,300 people in the United States. Research and development is based in the Redmond complex, with small satellite operations in Tokyo and in Vancouver, Canada. Diskette manufacturing takes place in Washington, Ireland, and Puerto Rico. Microsoft has direct and indirect marketing operations in thirty countries.

Microsoft is the leading PC software vendor on the basis of revenue, with 1995 sales of $5.9 billion. It is also one of the most profitable companies in the world. The company's revenues and profits have been positively affected by sales of upgrades, growth in worldwide personal computer sales, the success of the Windows operating system, the rapid release of new products and major new versions of existing products, and expansion of international operations to new areas.

## Leadership and Organization

Microsoft has a "communal" leadership instituted in 1992: the Office of the President. After a July 1995 reorganization, this includes, in addition to Bill Gates as Microsoft's chairman and chief executive officer, five senior managers who direct Microsoft's four operating groups. Group vice presidents Nathan Myhrvold (formerly head of advanced technology) and Pete Higgins (formerly head of desktop applications) jointly preside over the new Applications and Content Group. Group vice president Paul Maritz (formerly responsible for product and technology strategy) heads the new Platforms Group. These two groups build Microsoft's products and conduct research and development. Executive vice president Steve Ballmer is in charge of the Sales and Support Group, and Robert Herbold is head of the Operations Group and also serves as chief operating officer. Reporting to these group executives are division vice presidents and general managers. Below them are product unit managers, followed by functional team managers and then team leads in the product groups.

The Applications and Content Group has four divisions: desktop applications, consumer systems, on-line systems, and research. The Platforms Group also has four divisions: personal operating systems, business systems, developer and database systems, and advanced consumer systems. Most of these divisions contain their own marketing departments staffed by product planners and share a centralized usability lab (staffed by about thirty-five people) to test features and product prototypes. The Sales and Support Group has separate divisions for worldwide original equipment manufacturers (OEM) sales, product support services (PSS), international operations (mainly in Asia), advanced technology sales, strategic enterprise systems (special sales and consulting to large firms), North American sales, and European sales. The Operations Group includes finance, diskette production, manuals and book publishing (Microsoft Press), information systems, and human resource management.

Within the Platforms Group, the personal operating systems division produces Windows and MS-DOS. The business systems division produces Windows NT and Object Linking and Embedding (OLE), with a separate product unit for work-group applications (electronic mail and PC server systems). The developer and database systems division builds programming languages such as Visual Basic, programming support tools, and database products such as Access and FoxPro. The advanced consumer systems division contains groups for interactive TV systems and broadband communications and multimedia technologies. Within the Applications and Content Group, the desktop applications division contains the Office product unit. This supervises the Word and Excel product units and works closely with the graphics (PowerPoint) product unit to make sure that these three products function together properly in the Office applications suite. The division also builds Project, a popular project-management tool. The consumer systems division includes the Microsoft Home product groups, which build multimedia applications for home entertainment and education, and a combination word processor, spreadsheet, and database product for novices called Works. The online systems division develops and manages the new Microsoft Network. Research explores new product and programming technologies, and works closely with various product groups.

Within the product organizations, there are five major functions, each of which can have an individual manager for the larger products or can be combined for smaller products. These functions are program management, development, testing, marketing (product management), and user education. The functional groups in each product area define their own development processes as well as continually inject new ideas and improvements.

Program managers are responsible for consulting with developers and then writing specifications for the features of a new product. They also manage the product through all stages of development. In addition, program managers act as liaison to other dependent groups, and manage independent software vendor relationships for applications bundled with the product they manage.

Developers are responsible for feature design and coding. For each product, they form feature teams that work with one or more program managers. Recalc, charting, printing, and macros are examples of the eight feature teams on a former Excel project. Each feature team has a leader and several members (usually five to eight).

Testers are responsible for working with developers and testing products from the perspective of average users. They also organize into feature teams that match up with the development feature teams and individual developers. Testers start their work early in the development cycle by reviewing specifications as they evolve, and they continue all the way through final testing.

Marketing, called product management in Microsoft, involves marketing specialists as well as product planners. Marketing specialists study competing products, research customer needs, and prepare for the sale of new products. Product planners work with program managers to define vision statements for new products. These statements outline and prioritize basic feature ideas; they also clarify the objectives and target audience of the new product. Product planners also use focus studies and other mechanisms to get product input that is combined with input from sales and customer support during creation of the product requirements.

User education is responsible for producing manuals, electronic help files found in products, and other documentation for customers. Its members also determine what user training new products might require.

Beyond the formal organization and reporting structure, Microsoft has an informal "brain trust." This consists of more than a dozen senior managers and technical people spread throughout the organization. Bill Gates and other top executives call upon them to give advice or to take charge of particular projects and research efforts. In addition, Microsoft has companywide directors for functions such as product development, software development, and testing; they help groups share good practices, learn from their experiences, and adopt common methodologies and standards.

Microsoft's Sales and Support Group, which receives about twenty thousand phone calls per day, contributes significantly to product development and improvement. The more than two thousand people handling these phone calls log each customer inquiry, noting what product the call concerned and what type of problem the user encountered. Support staff members then generate a report summarizing information from these calls as well as customer suggestions, and send this to the development groups as well as to top executives (who avidly read the reports) each week. In addition, the support people have one team in place for each product, and a person on the team maintains direct contact with the developers, working with them on a consistent basis. For example, the product support team discusses customer calls, reads new product specifications, and begins preparing for customer support during beta testing of a new product.

## Culture

Microsoft's culture is evident in two of the company's most important goals: hire the best people possible, then give them private offices and good tools to do their jobs. Hiring the best people has been the focus within the company throughout its history. Microsoft recruits graduates from a variety of universities who have backgrounds in computer science and other technical fields, as well as experienced PC software developers. These new hires join product teams and usually stay with the same team for at least two development cycles (three to four years for applications, and longer for systems products). This is true for program management, development, testing, marketing, and the other functional groups. Staying with the product gives people a long-term investment in the product, ensures their familiarity with it, and helps them both understand process liabilities and benefits and learn from prior project experiences.

Bill Gates's presence and personality continue to have a significant influence in Microsoft. Many observers believe that the key reason for Microsoft's remarkable success is Gates himself. A technical visionary who is also the leader of the company and a skilled manager, he knows what to delegate and what to control. His involvement extends to reviews and input on the specifications for major products and their long-term development plans. The chairman and the people he has hired over the years are fiercely competitive, driven to achieving technical excellence, making and meeting aggressive commitments, and doing whatever it takes to ship products. Due to the aggressive schedules that are frequent in the company, significant stress, turnover, and "burnout" are common among employees. On the other hand, the work atmosphere is one of flexible hours, flexible dress, and open, honest relationships.

Changes in development methods provide some evidence of cultural changes through the years. The early development culture in Microsoft was one of small teams, ad hoc methods, and extreme individualism, with most products involving only three or four developers. The developers had ultimate control of the way they developed the product. A story that shows the extreme nature of that period is that of a developer who sat down and wrote the code for a new product, did not like the way the product worked, then started from scratch and completely rewrote it. He still did not like the product, so he sat down and started from scratch one more time.[14] The process involved his own vision of how the product should work and how the internals should be designed and coded.

When Microsoft moved from doing OEM work to developing products for the retail market, the culture changed with the addition of formal specification, testing, marketing, and support groups. IBM significantly influenced testing at Microsoft through the joint development work for the IBM PC. Microsoft also changed its product quality evaluation systems, project planning, security conditions, and other business processes. As quality and schedule mistakes began to mount in the company with the growing size and complexity of its products, developers changed the culture by adopting practices such as informal code reviews and more formal design and planning methods. The final significant influence has been the evolution of PC software to become "mission critical" applications for many companies and other organizations. Purchasers now demand that PC software suppliers have high-quality, repeatable processes in place to develop and support their products. As more systematization has become necessary in Microsoft, the company has increasingly tried to combine more structure in its development processes with enough flexibility to maintain the individual creativity and freedom of action needed to create leading-edge products.

## Product Description

Microsoft now has about two hundred separate products, most of them either systems or applications software. The company also sells some hardware products, such as a mouse and trackball pointing devices, and a keyboard, but these are a small part of the business.

Systems and language products generate about one-third of Microsoft's revenues. The Windows operating system is the major product offered in this area. Windows is a graphical user interface and operating system shell written for Intel-based PCs that works on top of the older MS-DOS operating system. Windows is easy to use, allows convenient data sharing, provides support for organizing and managing files created by applications programs, and allows switching between different application programs. It also lets programmers write larger applications than MS-DOS does. Estimates are that about seventy million users have adopted Windows since its introduction in the mid-1980s, with a majority adopting it after the 1990 introduction of version 3.0 and the 1992 introduction of version 3.1. Microsoft recently introduced another version, called Windows 95, which is widely expected to become the next standard for desktop PCs.

MS-DOS was the base operating system for the first IBM PC and has continued to be a standard for character-based PCs. The initial version came out in 1981, and updates have continued through MS-DOS 6.0 in 1993. This product still brings in a significant amount of revenue. Windows NT is the advanced product in the operating systems group, introduced commercially in July 1993. This is a 32-bit operating system designed for networking PCs and workstations at corporations and other sophisticated users. It also functions as a server for interactive television, video on demand, and on-line services provided through the Microsoft Network.

Applications products generate about 60 percent of Microsoft's revenues. These include an extensive range of products for Intel-based PCs and Apple Macintosh computers. Microsoft Excel, the company's spreadsheet application, competes with Lotus 1-2-3 for leadership in this category on Intel-based PCs and is the clear leader for the Macintosh. Microsoft Word, the company's word-processing application, competes with WordPerfect for leadership in this category on Intel-based PCs and is the clear leader for the Macintosh. Microsoft also offers Word and Excel in an integrated application suite called Microsoft Office, which costs about the same or less than just one of these programs cost when purchased individually only a few years ago. Office now accounts for about 70 percent of suite sales in the industry and more than half of Word and Excel sales. The standard Office suite includes PowerPoint for business graphics; a professional version contains an electronic mail program as well as the Access database management program.

## Review and Planning Cycle

The review and planning cycle is a logical point to begin our analysis of software development in Microsoft. The company splits the cycle into two portions, occurring in October and April. The result of the cycle is agreement among company executives on product rollouts and funding for the divisions.

The October review centers on presentations of three-year product plans. The product groups define the number of releases they are planning, explain why they are doing each release, and discuss interdependencies with other products. Bill Gates sits in on each division's dedicated review and on the final review in which all divisions present at once, to give everyone a common understanding of the product plans. Each product receives direction from Gates during this phase. He also interacts extensively with major product groups during the development process, usually through electronic mail and some personal visits and meetings.

After completing the October review, the marketing organizations create sales forecasts based on the product plans. The divisions then plan their budgets based on these forecasts. Managers look at the sales versus budget mix to determine how it compares with the profit model for the company. Based on this analysis, managers determine the head count for the fiscal year that begins in June. To our knowledge, Microsoft has never hit a point where managers limited the personnel needs of divisions due to head count or budget restrictions.

## Release Structure and Strategy

Product unit managers determine and gain approval for release plans for the individual products during the October review. In earlier years, product releases were more function-driven, based on the key features that product managers, program managers, and developers wanted to see in the next version. This has changed through the years to where the delivery date is now most important, except in the cases of operating systems (such as Windows 95), where product stability and reliability (quality) are most important. In applications and systems, groups make trade-offs in functionality to reach the target delivery date. Developers and the full product team determine the delivery date and commit to it, which raises their drive to make it. The transition from function-driven to date-driven releases happened during 1986–1988, and came after a long history of missing dates, a practice no longer considered acceptable by customers or Microsoft managers.

Product groups change a lot of code for each new release of a product, which makes it even more difficult to predict when a product will be ready to ship. Estimates are that groups change 50 percent of the existing product code for each new release. In addition, groups tend to add another 30 percent in new code for new functions in the release. The result is that code in Microsoft has an average half-life of only 1.5 years. For this reason, extensive automated regression tests are critical to development at Microsoft. Without them, groups could never test new products in time to meet the aggressive update schedules, which often call for a new product release every twelve or eighteen months, or faster.

## Development Process Overview

Some Microsoft product groups are further along in areas such as usage of metrics and adherence to review steps, but nearly all follow a relatively consistent high-level methodology for software development. Microsoft managers and developers first discussed elements of this process at a May

1989 retreat, where about thirty people in the company gathered to discuss ways to produce software with fewer defects. A memo from this retreat, dated June 1989, dealt with the subject of "zero defect code" and the strategy of building products daily. A 1989 "scheduling and methodology document" of about forty pages, drawn up by the old Office Business Unit, also discussed elements of the new Microsoft process. Neither of these documents circulated widely in the company, in part because of a general dislike within Microsoft to document processes in much detail because this may prevent change and improvement. Each group is free to define the details of its process. Nonetheless, most groups have adopted similar processes, and variations are relatively minor.

In general, Microsoft's development process has three main characteristics that differ from the more traditional waterfall process once used commonly at mainframe and minicomputer software producers. First, Microsoft divides the development cycle into three or four milestones, with each milestone containing its own coding, testing, and stabilization (debugging and integration) phases. Groupings of features determine the milestones. In general, projects try to do the most difficult and important features first, in case they run out of time later on. This milestone process contrasts with conventional life-cycle development, where projects try to write up as complete a specification as possible, then break up the work into parallel teams, followed by one large integration, system test, and stabilization phase after development. In fact, Microsoft (and many other firms) have found it difficult to specify and build all the pieces of a complex system, then try to put them together only at the end of the project. As a result, Microsoft puts pieces of a large system together three or four times during the development cycle, with refinements of the specifications as well as development, testing, debugging, and integration activities all done in parallel during each milestone. Microsoft's process thus resembles concurrent engineering as well as incremental styles of product development used in other industries.

Second, Microsoft projects assume that specifications will change during development, so they do not try to write a complete specification and detailed design document at the start of a project. They write a "vision statement" to guide developers and a functional specification from the user's point of view, but produce detailed specifications only for well-understood features, and allow project members to change the specifications as they deem necessary.

Third, Microsoft projects create a "build" of the product every day. (A build consists of checking pieces of code into a master file, and then putting the pieces together to see which functions work and which do not.) Not every developer has to check in code every day, but any developer who checks in code that conflicts with other features that have changed since the last build has to revise his or her code. The result is that developers try to check in their code as frequently as possible, usually about twice a week. This daily build process also helps developers evolve their features incrementally, as well as to coordinate or synchronize their changes with the work of other developers, whose features are often interdependent.

To develop products, Microsoft utilizes empowered teams that are responsible for all stages and the decisions required to get their product to market. The groups attempt to keep the teams small or arrange larger teams by product features to keep the small-team atmosphere. A full team that includes people from the five functional areas is in place for each product.

From a high-level viewpoint, the development teams are responsible for the following things: (a) producing a vision for the product that states what quality means for this product (bugs, performance, reliability, function); (b) producing specifications, designs, code, tests, and validations of the final packaged product; (c) product improvement with input from marketing, program management, Bill Gates, and anyone else with an opinion; (d) process improvement through usage of postmortem reviews along with midproject changes needed to get delayed or problematic products back on track; and (e) customer awareness via ties to the product support organization, monthly reports on problems, call logs on problems, and competitive analysis done by the product marketing groups.

Microsoft does not have an extensive set of formal development checkpoints, although most groups use a minimum of three in the product cycle: *schedule complete* (the functional specification is complete and approved), *code complete*, and *release to manufacturing*. The development team commits to the set of features or functions that will be delivered during the release, along with a schedule for the three checkpoints. Internally, it determines what is necessary to meet these three checkpoints. This may involve different combinations of design stages and reviews, along with different approaches to writing the actual product code. Groups also have other internal checkpoints and interdependency plans. Microsoft people do not see themselves as having significantly unique process concepts; instead, they feel that they utilize some new ways of putting good development concepts together.

Within Microsoft, investments for development have tended to follow, in order, people, specifications, tools, design and test plans, and code test cases. When problems arise during development, managers go through these investments in reverse order, in an attempt to fix the project. For example, they act starting from the bottom, making people changes only as a last resort. Microsoft managers have found that people changes are the most destructive in the long run, and should be avoided if at all possible. Recognizing this as a decision model appears to have been effective for negotiations and efficient problem-solving within the company.

## Requirements Process

The product marketing team in each product unit creates a vision statement for a new product or product version that defines its general direction (see figure 10-2). The statement describes the overall focus of the product, how to market it, the purpose of the next release, and the basic areas that the next release will address. Statements like "Fix the top twenty problems reported to the product support organization and add functions XX and YY" characterize statements of the basic areas to be addressed for a release. This type of input, fleshed out with some specification information, is what goes forward as a part of the April review input. Managers approve schedules during that review, and groups either proceed or change their general direction as a result of the review.

## Specification Process

The program manager owns and drives the specification for each release of a product. This person is responsible for soliciting inputs from all groups considered important for the product, especially the developers, who best know the code and what is technically feasible. Program managers utilize inputs to create a list of what to include in the product release.

Program managers write specifications from a user viewpoint. They show menus, commands, and dialogues that users will see, as well as error messages that can come up. They do not specify "how" to solve a functional requirement at the level of coding; developers will do that during the design stage. Even though they are incomplete during the specification stage, specs evolve during development and can be quite lengthy due to the amount of graphical presentation in them. For Excel, the spec is usually three hundred to five hundred pages, although it reached over a thousand pages in one recent version. A team from program management, marketing, development, testing, and user education continuously

FIGURE 10-2

## MICROSOFT'S "SYNCH AND STABILIZE" DEVELOPMENT PROCESS

Time: Usually 12- or 24-month Cycles

PLANNING PHASE

> VISION STATEMENT
>
> Example: Fifteen Features and Prioritization
> Done by Product (and Program)
> Management

↓

> OUTLINE AND WORKING SPECIFICATION
>
> Done by Program Managers with Developers
> Define Feature Functionality, Architectural Issues, and
> Component Interdependencies

↓

> DEVELOPMENT SCHEDULE AND
> FEATURE TEAM FORMATION
>
> A big feature team will have one program Manager,
> five Developers, five Testers

DEVELOPMENT PHASE

↓

> FEATURE DEVELOPMENT IN THREE OR FOUR MILESTONES
>
> Program Managers: Evolve the Spec
> Developers: Design, Code, Debug
> Testers: Test, Paired with Developers

STABILIZATION PHASE

↓

> FEATURE COMPLETE
> CODE COMPLETE
> ALPHA AND BETA TEST, FINAL STABILIZATION,
> AND SHIP
>
> Program Managers: Monitor OEMs, ISVs, Customer
> Feedback
> Developers: Final Debug, Code Stabilization
> Testers: Re-create and Isolate Errors

reviews the spec before holding the final review. Development groups generally do not use a formal review process during this stage, but most try to do a complete review of the specification that exists prior to starting development.

Development and testing groups are responsible for refining the spec during the development process. Developers flesh out details surrounding the functions, estimate the amount of work in person-months, and estimate the schedule for their individual pieces of the project. Testers provide early input on whether features seem testable, estimate the amount of work in person-months for their part of the schedule, and define what they need from development to test and support the product.

We noted earlier that Bill Gates still plays an important role in the specification process. Program managers are responsible for figuring out how to get his input for their products. They need to obtain this during the specification stage and get Gates to "buy in" to the spec. Each major product will have at least one formal review with him, and key products may have multiple meetings. During the meetings, Gates will set some key goals for the product that may relate to quality, cost, or function. Before a major product can move on to the implementation stage, it must have formal approval from Gates; this constitutes the "schedule complete" checkpoint. In the past, he personally reviewed every spec in detail; since then he has hired a full-time assistant to help review the specs and follow up with projects, as well as monitor competitors and their products.

An important aspect of the specification stage is the use of prototyping, done mainly using a Microsoft tool, Visual Basic. During the specification stage, program managers always build prototypes that include menus, commands, and dialogues, and serve as inputs to the spec. In some cases, the prototype may become the spec, and program managers will use it for the final meeting to get approval before starting implementation.

## Development Process

We noted earlier that Microsoft groups generally break a project into three or four milestones (figure 10-3). Product managers, with program managers, write up a vision statement that outlines and prioritizes features for the new product. Each feature has multiple functions and may require more than one milestone to complete. In general, however, product teams try to complete, for example, the first third of the most important features (or the most important functions in particular features) in the first milestone, the second third in the second milestone, and so on.

"Code complete" is the final step after the last milestone indicating that the team has finished design and coding work, and the product is ready for final testing. Individual developers and groups determine the processes and checkpoints necessary to meet the functional and schedule commitments.

*Design:* Developers need to do enough preliminary design work or analysis during the specification stage to make a solid estimate of the amount of effort and time required to complete each feature. Developers make individual estimates and view these as personal commitments, which encourages them to do a reliable job on the estimates and the early design work.

Microsoft does not have a formal set of design stages. It is up to the development team to determine what to detail during this step. Developers do much of this determination based on their experiences with prior releases. They deal with module structure, dependencies on other functions, input/output details, and other normal design stage considerations during this period. Developers may also hold design reviews for their work. They do not use any special specification languages or code generators.

*Coding:* PC and Macintosh products utilize much of the same code. Only about 10 to 15 percent of the code is unique for these two different platforms. Reused code between products amounts to only about 5 to 10 percent of all product code, although this is now changing. In the past, most reused code was for user interfaces, which have many standard elements. Microsoft has not usually developed code with reuse as the objective. Most reuse formerly happened through the general developer approach of "stealing what I can." As more Microsoft products have come to contain common features, like graphing and spreadsheet functions in Word, Excel, and other products, Microsoft has begun to design these features as large "objects" that one group will write once, then link and embed in numerous products. Microsoft calls this technology object linking and embedding (OLE), and has made it available as a commercial product. Groups do not widely use object-oriented (OO) programming languages like C++ for major products. New projects, however, including an object-oriented version of Windows NT,[15] are doing more work with C++ as a basic programming language. Parts of newly released products, such as some of the communications and network portions of Windows NT, are written in C++.

There is great allowance for individual coding styles, although most

FIGURE 10-3

## "SYNCH AND STABILIZE" DEVELOPMENT PROCESS, WITH MILESTONES

Time: Usually 2 to 4 months per Milestone

MILESTONE 1 (FIRST 1/3 FEATURES)

Development (Design, Coding, Prototyping)
Usability Lab
Daily Builds
Private Release Testing
Feature Debugging
Feature Integration
Code Stabilization (no severe bugs)
Buffer Time (20–50%)

MILESTONE 2 (NEXT 1/3)

Development
Usability Lab
Daily Builds
Private Release Testing
Feature Debugging
Feature Integration
Code Stabilization
Buffer Time

MILESTONE 3 (LAST SET)

Development
Usability Lab
Daily Builds
Private Release Testing
Feature Debugging
Feature Integration

Feature Complete
Code Complete
Code Stabilization
Buffer Time

Zero Bug Release
Release to Manufacturing

groups use a naming convention called "Hungarian," invented by Microsoft developer Charles Simonyi. This helps people read each other's code. At least one group, Windows NT, has a coding manual that serves as a rough style guideline.

Another important feature of development in Microsoft that corresponds to the idea of building prototypes and testing work under development is the utilization of internal "usability labs." Developers and some program managers use these labs to test how easy a particular feature or presentation of a feature is for the average person to understand. Microsoft internally has several rooms set aside as usability labs. A test consists of ten people brought in from "off the street" to try a feature under development. The lab staff videotapes the session and tracks the number of people who get the feature right on the first try. Most developers make very extensive use of the labs to prototype and test their features during development.

Code reviews have increasingly become part of the standard process at Microsoft. Various groups tried the reviews and found them so beneficial that most development teams decided to use them. But, in contrast with most companies that conduct code reviews in relatively large formal meetings, Microsoft code reviews usually have only one or two reviewers. Reviewers go through another person's code independently, usually in chunks of two thousand to five thousand lines at a time. Strong competition exists to find both defects and design mistakes during this stage.

The coding phase focuses on the "code complete" checkpoint after the last milestone. Developers estimate this date and all activities center around achieving it, even though it usually is not clear that a project has reached "code complete" until a month or more after this point, when it becomes certain that the code and features are indeed stable. The development manager polls all developers to determine whether they consider they are finished. When all are ready, the team declares "code complete," and testing can begin. After reaching the "code complete" target, the only code changes allowed are approved bug fixes.

Before "code complete," four other targets are part of the coding stage. *Private releases* go to testing or development groups with dependencies on the function. These are agreed to one-on-one between the developers and the individuals needing the code. *Visual freeze* is utilized for all products to allow screen shots to be taken for user documentation. The user education department drives these and negotiates the date with development. Typically, 20 to 30 percent change occurs after the freeze. *Functional freeze* is utilized to lock the text information used for documentation; not all products use this checkpoint. The user education department drives this and negotiates the date with development. Typically, 20 to 30 percent change occurs after the freeze. *Beta test release* signals confidence that the code is good enough to send to selected user sites for actual usage testing.

During the coding stage, developers continually tell testers which sections of the code are complete and which are incomplete. This communication allows targeted functional testing to begin as soon as possible. As a final step in development of the new code, developers run a mandatory suite of tests as internal checks for assertion testing of the code (assumptions made about conditions that will occur at specific steps that do not need code to check for them directly), and the usage of check routines available through debug menus.

***Daily Builds and Integration Testing:*** Developers keep all code modules in a master library on a central server. The master library contains the master version of the code from which the product is built. A library management tool exists on the server that allows developers to "check out" a master version of a module to work on with their PC. When developers finish making changes, they run a set of unit regression tests to validate the new function they have added. In addition, they must run a suite of preliminary integration tests to validate that base functions are not affected by the changed code. These tests are called quick tests, synch tests, or smoke tests, depending on the group. If all tests are successful, developers can do a "check in" to put the new version into the master library.

Most projects do daily builds of the master code. The builders then run build tests to ensure that the products will operate. Problems must be resolved immediately and everyone stops work until the guilty developer fixes the problem. Since teams do builds daily, tracing back to find the change that caused a problem is reasonably easy to do. Daily builds ensure that the product will function at all times and control the amount of churn in the system, which helps stability. For large integrated products that consist of separate products or components from different groups, or products that rely on different systems, such as Office or the Microsoft Network, Microsoft groups do daily builds of the components and weekly builds of the entire system.

## Testing Process

Unlike organizations that rely heavily on specification and design reviews to find defects as early as possible, Microsoft relies heavily on daily builds, automated testing, and manual testing by testers who work one-on-one with developers. Automated suites of tests available for developers to run prior to integrating their code are extensive and widely used. Test tools for developers and testers to test new functions also are available and are very useful.

Each of these items is helpful, but the most significant difference in Microsoft's approach from that of other firms is in the relationship between the testing and development groups. Testing is a functional group within the product development organization. There is no independent quality assurance organization; the testing managers report directly to the product unit general managers, not to the development managers. Testers also have a very close relationship with developers. Like the developers, they are involved with the product over multiple releases, and they are organized in feature testing teams that work in parallel with the feature development teams. Involvement starts at the spec stage and continues through the rest of the cycle.

Each developer creates what Microsoft calls a "private release" for the tester assigned to work with him or her. Developers may pass a private release of code to a tester that contains a new feature that is not fully developed and checked in. The tester will use it to improve and certify test cases; the developer can get bugs discovered early and recode as necessary. This coordination assists developers during development tests and assists testers for their final tests.

Microsoft carefully plans testing phases. Testing personnel do their own estimates of resources and schedules during the spec stage and commit to meeting the plan. They create formal test plans and review test cases. Developers participate in 70 to 80 percent of the test case reviews. Testers add automated tests from prior releases to the plan so that they can understand the total test coverage.

Final test is the main verification step that the testing organization runs. Microsoft tests products through customer-like usage and tracks results closely against the test plan. Testing includes documentation, tutorials, setup, hardware configurations, primary functions, and supporting utilities. Automated test cases are key to validating existing functions; testers use them extensively. They also measure performance against goals set for the product. Results from the final test are the most critical input to the decision to ship.

Most groups use three types of beta tests to stimulate awareness and excitement for a new product or feature (marketing reasons), and to get feedback and remove bugs (technical reasons). The three types of tests are narrow tests with a select set of customers that will utilize a new function or check compliance against specific goals; wide tests that attempt to catch rare cases not found on typical configurations; and internal distribution of the product to employees to get results similar to wide tests. Beta tests tend to get a very low response rate: 5 to 6 percent of users give feedback to development.

Developers have a set of scheduled checkpoints during the test phase at which they attempt to get the number of outstanding severe bugs down to zero. "Zero bug releases" is one set of checkpoints where development consciously attempts to drive known severe bugs down to the target of zero. Product groups tend to set multiple checkpoints like this during a test phase. "Release candidates" is an additional set of checkpoints and involves an attempt to build the final product. Although intended as a verification that the code will fit on the specified number of diskettes and that the build procedures work, this is also an attempt to freeze the code and test a solid product.

Projects make shipping decisions after final test. The senior (group) program manager organizes a committee that includes himself or herself as well as the development manager, the test manager, the product marketing manager, and a representative from the customer support organization. This committee recommends whether to ship the product, although the product unit manager is ultimately responsible for the shipping decision.

## Product Support

Separate support teams exist for each product. These teams are part of the sales and support organization, not of development. Their main responsibilities are to handle customer calls regarding the product and channel information from customer calls into the business units, to guide decisions on features or fixes for subsequent releases. When problems come in, the support organization logs them and creates problem reports that go to the development group on a weekly basis. Program managers, developers, and testers all carefully follow these problem reports and arrange for solutions. The development staff on the current product also handles all maintenance work, such as fixing bugs from the current release, and all or part of the team works on fixing problems when they come in.

## Process Usage and Compliance

Each product group is responsible for choosing the development process it will use, and nearly all groups utilize a version of the synch-and-stabilize process. The process originated primarily within the Excel group during 1989–1990, although other groups used aspects of it before then. There are also some differences in how groups building applications products, as opposed to systems products, utilize elements of the process. Nonetheless, the principles of synch-and-stabilize have gradually spread throughout the company's development groups as people have moved. Managers such as Dave Moore, the director of development, and Chris Peters, former head of the Office Product Unit, have encouraged groups to adopt "best practices" that have proved to work.

Over the last few years, as a result of these conscious efforts to "evangelize" best practices from the Excel group, Microsoft has rapidly progressed in usage of a more definable and repeatable process. Developers have recognized that these practices have become necessary as projects and products have grown enormously in size and complexity. Excel and Word each have at least ten program managers, thirty developers, and thirty testers, and both are a million or so lines of executable C code. The Office group overall (including Word and Excel as well as PowerPoint and a group developing common components) has about a hundred developers and an equal number of testers, and the total product is several million lines of code. Windows NT and Windows 95 each have teams of approximately two hundred developers, two hundred testers, and thirty to fifty program managers; their core products are between four and eleven million lines of code.

Customer demands have also been a key factor in accelerating the adoption of more solid and verifiable processes. As PC applications have become more central to organizations, customers have demanded in-process metrics and other indicators of quality before they will install new versions of products.

Microsoft does not handle process compliance via formal mechanisms, however. The pressure of the daily builds, milestone integrations, and program reviews is the main driver of compliance. Another mechanism is internal audits done by Dave Moore and other functional directors, who now include Moore's boss, Chris Williams, the director of product development, and Roger Sherman, the director of testing. Senior managers occasionally ask the functional directors to work with different groups, analyzing problems and the current status of projects, and to make recommendations for improvement. Managers use a formal "audit" to change things quickly. They use a "review" to take a more gentle approach to analyzing the development work (process or current status) and recommending actions to resolve the problems found.

## Project Management

In addition to writing down specifications with the help of developers, program managers keep track of schedules and coordinate with other groups that may be providing components to a particular project. Their job is difficult because they must rely on developers to write code but do not have direct authority over them; developers report to their own development team leaders and a development manager. Nonetheless, program mangers work closely with developers; one program manager is usually assigned to work with each feature team.

Beyond constant contact with the groups creating the product, there are two other mechanisms that are critical to project management. First, each of the functional groups, and the individuals in those groups, determine their own schedules. This means that people doing the actual work do all their own estimating. By having this relationship between estimates and work, individuals become very committed to meeting the schedules they set. One problem with this approach has been that developers usually are overly optimistic about how much time a job will take, leading to badly misscheduled projects or developer "burnout" as people try to catch up with a schedule that was unrealistic to begin with. New personnel also do not have much experience in creating estimates. As projects accumulate historical data on past work, however, developers are improving in their ability to make realistic estimates. The development leads also give assignments and schedules to new developers for the first several month after they join a project. In addition, teams now informally debate each member's estimates to improve accuracy.

Second, product groups utilize project reviews throughout the development process. Program managers schedule and run these reviews either weekly or monthly. Managers review everything associated with the project with each group as it reports its status. Monthly status reports also come from each functional area. Major program reviews on project status also are held with Bill Gates and other senior executives. Timing of these program reviews varies, depending on the strategic importance of the product.

## Change Control and Configuration Management

Microsoft has network servers to store source directories accessible by everyone in the company. Groups use password control to limit access to some of the source directory servers. They use network-based configuration control on everything associated with the products under development. Items in source directories include project documents such as specifications, code, tools, releases (current and previous), plans, and schedules. The parts can be "checked out," changed, and then "checked in" after changes are made. Forcing the parts to be checked out and back in places a level of control on all information related to a project.

Groups allow changes to requirements, specifications, and code during the development process. After checkpoints such as "schedule complete" and "code complete," the program managers take control of changes to specifications and code, respectively. By allowing approved changes, they let innovation continue to happen during coding and testing. When decisions are required for necessary changes, many groups use an informal decision model to determine the action necessary. The model, from highest priority to lowest, is (1) schedule and resources; (2) components, functions, or features of the product; (3) future extensibility and maintenance (these are bad for the long run but may be necessary); (4) product performance; (5) product reliability and quality. (This definitely is done only when no other options exist. The changes may be "not fixing" something that was previously planned.)

Tools on the system manage code changes. Source code must go through the "check out" and "check in" procedures. "Force outs" and "force ins" allow developers to check out source code when someone has previously done a standard "check out." The forces are managed through a function in the network control tool that compares changes to ensure that another developer has not altered the same lines of code. Before developers can check code back in, they must run "synch" tests that make sure the code does not degrade the system. Nearly all projects do daily builds on the total product, then run synch tests. Any problems discovered that hold up development are resolved by the developer who made the faulty change. Daily builds allow the product to be usable every day. In addition to the "check out" procedure, the project's senior managers must approve changes to code after "code complete."

Microsoft groups manage defects through a set of bug-tracking tools that run on the server. Team members enter bug reports into a database along with a description of how the problem can be re-created. Severity levels running from 1 (most critical, because it causes a system to crash) to 4 (not critical; may simply indicate a new function request) are assigned by the discoverer of the bug, although managers usually debate these levels for remaining bugs before moving on to another milestone or shipping a product. Development managers continuously monitor the database so that they can assign the problems to someone on the team when they are reported. Testing and program management also closely track the defects.

At the end of the development process, the change control process takes on an additional level of formality. The committee of four (one member each from development, testing, program management, and product support) meets daily to review all remaining problems and determine which ones to fix. Internal testing and beta tests both generate problem reports. Utilizing the committee review helps ensure that groups make decisions based on data rather than on emotions or pressures to ship. Approval requirements and the tracking capability provide a level of change management for bugs.

## Metrics

Data and metrics are important to resolving conflicts and making decisions on actions to take. Many company people told us that "Microsoft is data driven." Top management supports the usage of metrics because experience suggests that these help projects ship on time. The most watched and used metrics involve bugs. Tools are also in place and available to generate metrics and data. Some common metrics are bugs to date, bug severity mix, open versus fixed bugs to date, bugs found versus bugs fixed, clusters of defects, code churn, code test coverage, and customer problem calls versus units sold.

The bug metrics described above are very important during the development process. Groups also generate standardized queries and reports for management at defined intervals. Some project teams collect and use historical data as well, although Microsoft does not have a central companywide database for project metrics and data. If internal data does not exist for a product, groups may share data or use applicable external data. Some projects frequently use data that indicate how many bugs are likely to be in a product and how many should have been removed through each of the development stages.

## Process Improvement

New process ideas come largely from the teams themselves. Managers encourage teams to find "best practice" solutions to process problems, try them out, and talk about their experiences with other groups. The "best practices" information has come from the efforts of key project managers as well as the functional directors, to identify what works well in Microsoft's product units and what has worked well in other companies. Groups adopt improvements by trying new ideas and spreading information on the results; functional directors and other managers generally do not mandate that groups use particular processes or tools.

About two-thirds of all projects write postmortem review reports which can range to a hundred pages or more. Usually, the manager of each functional area (program management, development, testing, user education, product management) consults with team members and take responsibility for writing up the portion of the postmortem that relates to his or her part of the process. Each section generally contains three parts: what went well in the last project, what went poorly, and what the project should do next time. Groups debate and make process changes, and introduce them for the next release of the product. Since the teams tend to stay together for several years, the postmortem analysis is very effective and helps with process learning.

## Tools

Development environments consist of personal computers and a few workstations in offices connected to the local area network (LAN) server. Developers pick the hardware systems they wish to use; many have multiple systems in their offices because developers generally work simultaneously on both Windows and Macintosh versions of their products. The LAN has servers for each product developed and network servers that allow access to data throughout Microsoft. A corporate Management Information Systems (MIS) group manages at least six hundred servers, along with a worldwide network, in one building.

A good suite of specialized tools is available for automated testing. Microsoft groups have used these tools for several years, and have now progressed to event recorders and playback tools that make it possible to analyze all of the keystrokes and pointer movements of a user trying to accomplish a particular task. Automated test tools also run in multiple environments.

Developers and testers run automated tests "hundreds of times" during development. Testers continually add to this set of tests. Developers use "quick tests" before all "checkins" and after all daily or weekly builds. Testers run them frequently during the final test phase. Development has also supplied a variety of tools to assist in simulation of memory, data structure, system failure, and memory fill errors.

## Process Education

Microsoft offers orientation classes that describe their development cycle but the company does not have detailed formal process education classes. Most education is done within the team. Major product units have two-to-four-page documents that describe their products. Testing groups also have a series of brief documents that serve as checklists of job responsibilities. In addition, managers assign mentors to each new hire on their team; they help introduce the new hire to processes used in the company.

Managers generally expect technical personnel to undergo about two weeks of training each year. People use a combination of in-house courses, university seminars, and corporate or conference seminars to meet the objective. In-house training is available for corporate management skills, and product group training is available for technical skills.

## DISCUSSION

Table 10-1 presents key characteristics of the classic "waterfall" approach to software development as compared with Microsoft's synch-and-stabilize process. The latter relies primarily on daily builds for frequent synchronizations and on incremental milestones for periodic stabilizations of the products under development. We have based this stylized description of the waterfall process on our 1992–1993 analysis of IBM, Fujitsu, and Hewlett-Packard divisions building systems and applications software for mainframes, minicomputers, and technical workstations.[16] Some groups in these and other companies now build software by using processes that have significantly evolved from the base waterfall model, and have incorporated steps, such as more frequent builds and incremental development, that are similar to steps that Microsoft utilizes. We also believe, however, that Microsoft stands out for how it has institutionalized this style of software product development. More important, we believe that Microsoft's process is similar to, but more structured and repeatable than, approaches used at other PC software developers in the United States, such as Lotus, Borland, Novell-WordPerfect, and IBM's OS/2 group.

At a very high level of abstraction, the development life cycles appear to be similar across firms using a waterfall process versus a synch-and-stabilize process. Each utilizes common phases of requirements, design, coding, testing, delivery, and maintenance. Each spends significant effort on process support activities, such as release management, change management, metrics, and process improvement, although, in some respects, the development process seems less formalized at Microsoft. When we investigate in more detail, however, we see that Microsoft's development process has some important differences from the conventional waterfall model.

In comparing a small sample of companies, an important difference is where the products have evolved from and how quickly they continue to evolve. IBM, Fujitsu, and Hewlett-Packard, for example, all develop relatively stable operating systems for mainframes, minicomputers, and technical workstations that have multiple user groups on a single hardware platform. These development organizations have been in place and producing this type of software for many years. In contrast, Microsoft and other PC software companies develop products for a dynamic and relatively new set of markets. These companies themselves are relatively new and need to accommodate markets and hardware platforms that are rapidly evolving. As a result, one can argue that the PC software market requires more flexibility and creativity than the mainframe, minicomputer, or technical workstation software markets, even though some of these markets are merging to some degree, and PC software producers are introducing many of the same techniques and controls as their predecessors.

The basic problem that Microsoft has tried to address is that most of its projects now consist of teams with twenty to several hundred developers, and the larger teams are usually building components that are interdependent and difficult to define accurately in the early stages of development. In this situation, the teams must find a way to proceed that structures and coordinates what the individual members do while allowing them enough flexibility to define and change the product's details in stages as the project progresses.

As we have discussed, Microsoft's solution is to have development teams begin by outlining the product in sufficient depth to set priorities in terms of product features that they want to create, but without trying to decide all the details of each feature, as in a more conventional waterfall process. In other words, they do not lock the project into a set of features and details of features that they cannot later revise as they learn more about what should be in the product. The project managers then divide the product and the project into parts (feature and small feature teams), and divide the project schedule into three or four milestone junctures (subprojects) that represent completion points for major portions of the product. All the teams go through a cycle of development, testing, and fixing problems in each milestone phase. Moreover, throughout the project, the team members synchronize their work by building the product, and by finding and fixing errors, on a daily and weekly basis. When most serious problems are fixed, they stabilize (agree not to change) the most important pieces of the product and proceed to the next milestone and, eventually, to the shipping date.

In many ways, the synch-and-stabilize approach resembles prototype-driven product development processes that use a series of incremental design, build, and test cycles.[17] It also has elements of concurrent engineering to the extent that Microsoft groups refine specifications, start

TABLE 10-1

COMPARISON OF "WATERFALL" AND MICROSOFT DEVELOPMENT PROCESSES

| Activity | Classic "Waterfall" Process | Microsoft "Synch-and-Stabilize" |
|---|---|---|
| **Release Structure and Strategy** | Structured to occur at regular intervals, with support of hardware being a significant factor driving the content and schedule of a release. | Releases were based on function for initial and immediate follow-on releases. They have moved to a more predictable schedule-driven approach as products have matured. |
| **Planning Process** | All organizations utilize formal processes for well-defined development phases that proceed more or less sequentially, with a large integration phase at the end. | Development proceeds in broader phases. Projects have 3 or 4 milestones or subprojects, each with a full set of development, testing, and stabilization phases. |
| **Requirements** | Requirements and development phases are driven by product management groups with executives having final approval of contents and schedules. Organizations strive to meet the needs of diverse customer bases while expanding to new markets. Projects try to write as complete a specification as possible before proceeding to detailed design and coding. | Requirements and schedules are determined by a very small group that maintains control over the product as it matures. Projects do not try to write complete specifications up front, because they know these will change. Instead, they allow requirements to evolve through prototypes and continual input from developers, program managers, and users on what should be included in products. There is also a formal process to fix the top customer complaint areas in each release. |
| **Design and Coding** | Design and coding are manually done. Minimal usage of specification languages, automatic code generation, and object-oriented programming. Inspections are formally used by each, with very positive results. | There is less formal structure surrounding specific steps that must be carried out during development. These groups also have minimal usage of specification languages, automatic code generation, and object-oriented programming (though usage of the latter is rising). They are adopting design and code reviews due to positive early results. |
| **Testing** | In-house test groups are generally independent from the developers. The in-house groups are strong, with ratios ranging from 5 to 10 developers per tester. Beta and other customer tests are used by each for technical and marketing reasons. Few companies use software being developed in day-to-day operations. | In-house groups work more closely with developers than in the classic companies. There is a high ratio of testers to developers (nearly one to one). Beta tests are used for technical and marketing reasons. Personnel use their product's latest code levels on a continuous basis to get additional testing of the code. |

TABLE 10-1 continued

## COMPARISON OF "WATERFALL" AND MICROSOFT DEVELOPMENT PROCESSES

| Activity | Classic "Waterfall" Process | Microsoft "Synch-and-Stabilize" |
|---|---|---|
| **Process Usage and Compliance** | Process usage is dominated by the size of the products and the integration needs. Processes need to be used by all developers. The process is needed to predict schedules and quality. A strong use of metrics aids the checking of compliance. | There is more independence surrounding process choices. Fewer formal compliance measures are in place. A standard process is being introduced due to the need to predict schedules and control errors for the growing systems. |
| **Release Management** | This is a significant activity due to large size of product and number of people usually involved. Some companies have gone to an individual focused on "fighting fires" and ensuring decisions are made on a timely basis. Cross-functional groups are in place to support the individual. | Lead program managers are part of each product development group. Their focus is strictly on making sure the release gets done. They work closely with the product manager, managers of the specific development and testing groups, and all outside groups (support, manufacturing, subcon-tractors, etc.). |
| **Change Management** | This is done throughout the development phases with increased formality during coding and testing. Some companies have moved it all the way up to the requirements stage. Tools are in place to support change management. | Change management is done during the coding and testing stages to varying degrees. Loose controls are used during requirements and design stages. Change management appears to increase as products mature. |
| **Metrics** | These are used extensively to help manage the very large projects. Historical bases are in place, and progress results are compared against them. Metrics are used to manage schedules and quality. In-process metrics are being used extensively for design, coding, and testing stages. | Use of metrics is dependent on the maturity of the product and the historical base available. Microsoft is now using different metrics extensively for decision support on requirements and on escalations of decisions. |
| **Process Improvement** | This is extensively pursued. Causal analysis and defect prevention processes are used to remove sources of error injection. | This is used by the most mature organizations in the company. Postmortems are now a common and high-profile activity. Group continuity appears to be necessary for this to be effective. Projects are working to get more sharing and learning across groups. |

TABLE 10-1 continued

## COMPARISON OF "WATERFALL" AND MICROSOFT DEVELOPMENT PROCESSES

| Activity | Classic "Waterfall" Process | Microsoft "Synch-and-Stabilize" |
|----------|----------------------------|--------------------------------|
| **Tools** | Most companies have a well-established tool set to support change management, coding, and product builds. Most make investments in automated tools for testing. Networks are based on workstations, minicomputers, or mainframes. | Workstation-based networks are standard. Source code management tools are utilized, with a variety of languages and linkers employed. |
| **General** | The culture of the company and the formality of the development processes are tightly linked. | The culture of the company and the formality of the development process are tightly linked. Groups are finding the need to add structure to their development processes and have been continually doing that. |

building the product (coding), and do testing, debugging, and integration of components *in parallel,* rather than in distinct sequential phases. Many, if not most, software producers end up following this type of process as they run into problems during the first attempt at integration, but they often proceed in an ad hoc manner. What Microsoft has done is to introduce a concurrent, incremental, and iterative but structured approach to product development that offers several benefits to the development organization:

It *breaks down large products into manageable chunks* (a few product features that small   feature teams can create in a few months).

It *enables projects to proceed systematically even when they cannot determine a complete and stable product design* at the project's beginning.

It *allows large teams to work like small teams* by dividing work into pieces, proceeding in parallel but synchronizing continuously, stabilizing in increments, and continuously finding and fixing problems.

It *facilitates competition on customer input, product features, and short development times* by providing a mechanism to incorporate customer inputs, set priorities, complete the most important parts first, and change or cut less important features.

There are also some caveats with the Microsoft process that firms need to be aware of. First, when launching a new product, firms need to design the product architecture so that it can accommodate addition or subtraction of features in future versions of the product. Periodically, firms may want to go back and redo the product architecture, and this will require extensive planning at the beginning of the development process. Thus, the synch-and-stabilize process is primarily well-suited for "N+1" versions of a product, like the second or third versions of the Excel spreadsheet or the Windows NT operating system, rather than the very first versions or product versions that are almost completely new.

For example, Windows NT (which was about nine months late on a four-year development cycle) and Windows 95 (which was about eighteen months late on a three-year cycle) adopted this process only in the last year or two of development, after the projects had completed a set of features and functions on which to create daily builds. The Microsoft Network also went through more than a year of experimental planning, design, and development work before moving to frequent builds and milestone integrations.

Operating systems and network communications software also tend to have many interrelated functions that designers must analyze and plan before they start writing functional specifications and code, because these features and functions cannot be easily changed or cut late in a project. In addition, systems and communications software have to test nearly infinite numbers of user scenarios involving thousands of combinations of hardware and applications software; teams often require six months to a year or more to test these products in the field, to make sure that users will not run into a major bug (such as the one that plagued Intel's Pentium microprocessor). Windows 95, for example, was available in beta copies in June 1994, but Microsoft delayed the official commercial release until August 1995 in order to take extra time to test the product with four hundred thousand users. This time was necessary because Microsoft had trouble perfecting two new and highly complex architectural components: plug-and-play, which is supposed to detect and set up hardware peripherals automatically, and multitasking within certain memory limit targets, which allows the computer to run several applications programs simultaneously.

Second, projects can proceed with an evolving specification, but they can run into problems if they are dependent on components built by other projects, or build components for other projects to use. If these interdependencies exist, then projects must have coordinated schedules; they also need to establish standards for designing components and stable interfaces for integrating components, and add these to the specification process at the beginning of the project, with minimal changes thereafter. Microsoft managers have been encouraging projects to design components for other groups to share, and this has led to some delays when all projects were not tightly managed. For example, a recent version of Office was late because of delays in building OLE, which all the Office products use to share components, as well as Visual Basic, which serves as a macro language in the Excel product. Microsoft also had to coordinate changes and delays in Windows 95 as it built the Microsoft Network software.

Third, firms using a Microsoft-type synch-and-stabilize process need to commit extensive resources to testing the product as they build it, which also makes the process especially well suited to N+1 versions that have a stable core of features with which testers can test new features. On the other hand, the project should be able to reduce the total amount of resources needed for rework as well as for system testing and integration at the end of a project, because developers and testers have been designing, testing, fixing, and integrating features throughout the project.

Synch-and-stabilize also supports competition based on product features and incremental innovations, rather than product invention, which depends more on how well a company manages its research organization. Microsoft began to invest heavily in research only around 1991; hence, it has not invented many new product technologies, and has trailed competitors in introducing innovative products to market. For example, Intuit (which Microsoft wanted to acquire but did not, after opposition from the U.S. Department of Justice on antitrust grounds) has been the leader in personal finance software with Quicken, and Lotus has been the leader in office groupware with Notes. Novell has been the leader in corporate networking operating systems with NetWare. Several companies, including CompuServe, America Online, and Netscape have led in the introduction of on-line networks and Internet web browsers.

In all these areas, however, Microsoft has designed competing products in its research and development organization, and then used the process we have described in this paper to evolve these products incrementally by introducing new versions very frequently. Since this process makes it possible to synchronize the efforts of a large number of individuals and teams, we think it is well suited to building the complex software systems of the future. Microsoft groups need to understand, however, that complex new operating systems and network or Internet systems require more advanced planning and architectural design work than the company's stand-alone desktop applications products.

Finally, we should cite one additional area of concern for Microsoft as a company. It has now entered nearly every PC software market, both for home consumers and for corporate customers. It is unlikely that Bill Gates and other Microsoft managers, as well as Microsoft's development teams, can pay the same level of attention to two hundred products as they could to two or three products, in the early days of the company. Even a highly strategic project such as Windows 95 does not seem to have been well managed in its early stages; announced shipping dates were extremely optimistic, and the development team significantly underestimated the complexity of the tasks required to deliver this new product. Nonetheless, Gates has cultivated a talented "brain trust" to help him manage the company. Microsoft has also hired hundreds of experienced managers and researchers from universities as well as from other companies, and has acquired a dozen or more firms with a variety of new skills, such as multimedia software and communications technologies. These new people, as well as Microsoft's extensive financial resources and existing pool of technical experts, should help Gates and Microsoft compete effectively in desktop software as well as in the world of the information highway.

## NOTES

1. This study included IBM's AS-400 minicomputer systems group in Rochester, Minnesota, and the Federal Systems Company in Houston, Texas, which makes space shuttle software; Hewlett-Packard, which makes workstation operating systems; Fujitsu's mainframe operating systems development site at Numazu, Japan; and Lotus Development, which makes a variety of PC applications. For the full set of case studies, see Stanley A. Smith and Michael A. Cusumano, "Beyond the Software Factory: A Comparison of 'Classic' and 'PC' Software Developers," Sloan WP#3607-93/BPS (Cambridge, Mass.: Sloan School of Management, MIT, September 1993). For a full treatment of the Microsoft story, see Michael A. Cusumano and Richard W. Selby, *Microsoft Secrets: How the World's Most Powerful Software Company Creates Technology, Shapes Markets, and Manages People* (New York, Free Press/Simon & Schuster, 1995).

2. The first description of the waterfall model was by Winston W. Royce, "Managing the Development of Large Software Systems," in *Proceedings of IEEE Wescon* (Los Angeles: Western Electric Show and Convention, 1970).

3. See Victor R. Basili and Albert J. Turner, "Iterative Enhancement: A Practical Technique for Software Development," *IEEE Transactions on Software Engineering* SE-1, no. 4 (December 1975), pp. 390–396; and Barry W. Boehm, "A

Spiral Model of Software Development and Enhancement," *Computer,* May 1988, pp. 61–72. Discussions of iterative approaches to product development can also be found in literature on marketing and management of technological innovation, although mainly in the sense of probing customer needs in the initial conceptualization phase of product design. See, for example, Glen L. Urban and John R. Hauser, *Design and Marketing of New Products* (Englewood Cliffs, N.J.: Prentice Hall, 1980), and Eric von Hippel, *The Sources of Innovation* (New York: Oxford University Press, 1987).

4. For conventional approaches to reuse, see, for example, the discussions of Toshiba and NEC in Michael A. Cusumano, *Japan's Software Factories: A Challenge to U.S. Management* (New York: Oxford University Press, 1991). For an alternative approach that focuses on building a data architecture first, and then objects, see "Brooklyn Union Gas: OOPS on Big Iron," Harvard Business School Case 9-192-144 (1992).

5. See, for example, U.S. Department of Defense, "Defense System Software Development Standard," DOD-STD-2167-A (February 1988).

6. P. Sage and James D. Palmer, *Software Systems Engineering* (New York: John Wiley & Sons, 1990).

7. Ibid.

8. Pankaj Jalote, *An Integrated Approach to Software Engineering* (New York: Springer-Verlag, 1991).

9. Ibid.

10. Richard A. Sulack, "Advanced Software Engineering Management Core Competencies," presented at COMMON meeting, Spring 1993.

11. See Peter Naur and Brian Randell, eds., *Software Engineering: Report on a Conference Sponsored by the NATO Science Committee* (Brussels: NATO Scientific Affairs Division, 1969); Barry W. Boehm, "Software Engineering," *IEEE Transactions on Computers* C-25, no. 12 (December 1976), pp. 1226–1241; Richard Thayer, "Modeling a Software Engineering Project Management System," Ph.D. dissertation, University of California at Santa Barbara, 1979; C. V. Ramamoorthy et al., "Software Engineering: Problems and Perspectives," *Computer,* October 1984, pp. 191–209.

12. Geoffrey K. Gill, "Microsoft Corporation: Office Business Unit," Harvard Business School, case 9-691-033 (1990).

13. This section is based primarily on information obtained through an interview on March 15, 1993, with David Moore, director of development, testing, and quality assurance for Microsoft. Some information was obtained through materials received and interviews conducted during April and August 1993, and September 1994.

14. See Gill.

15. Elizabeth Corcoran, "Soft Lego," *Scientific American,* January 1993, pp. 145–146; and John Soat, "Object Oriented Technology: Where Microsoft Meets Berlitz," *InformationWeek,* March 1, 1993, pp. 44.

16. See Smith and Cusumano.

17. See, for example, Steven C. Wheelwright and Kim B. Clark, *Revolutionizing Product Development* (New York: Free Press, 1992).

CHAPTER 11

# MANAGING CHAOS
## System-Focused Product Development
## in the Computer and Multimedia Environment

Marco Iansiti

## INTRODUCTION

The environment created by the confluence of the computer, telecommunications, and media industries is characterized by chaotic levels of technical and market uncertainty. The needs of the nascent customer base, the number of competitors and alliances, and the range of technological possibilities are characterized by a complete lack of stability.

This extreme turbulence creates new challenges for organizations. These center on the need for extreme flexibility and responsiveness, particularly in the development of technology and the introduction of new products. This has created a new set of imperatives for the management of the product development process that contrast deeply with traditional models.

*I would like to thank Toshihiko Watari, Yuzo Shimada, and the members of the SX team at NEC, as well as Brett Monello, Zak Rinat, Ron Bernal, and the members of the Challenge team at Silicon Graphics for their thoughtful comments and assistance. In addition, I would like to thank Ellen Stein for her extensive help performing and analyzing the fieldwork. I would also like to acknowledge extensive discussions with Kim Clark, Rebecca Henderson, Gary Pisano, Susan Pope, Warren Smith, Marcie Tyre, Eric von Hippel, Jonathan West, and the participants in the Colliding Worlds Conference at Harvard Business School. Finally, I acknowledge the support of the Division of Research, Harvard Business School.

This paper focuses on the drivers of product development performance in this rapidly changing environment. Its foundations were laid in a four-year study of technology development in mainframes and supercomputers. The study demonstrated large differences in R&D performance among competitors in the development of advanced processor modules, computer subsystems whose design is characterized by high technical uncertainty. In this paper, I extend the findings to the current computer and multimedia environment by discussing detailed field-based observations of product development at Silicon Graphics, Inc. (SGI), a leading producer of workstations, supercomputers, and multimedia equipment.

The work shows that in uncertain environments, product development performance is linked to factors different from those identified in studies of product development performance in more traditional environments.[1] Traditional models for product development are largely aimed at controlling change and uncertainty in the evolution of technology and market needs.[2] Their focus is on developing a structured process with clearly defined and sequential phases, through which the future product is defined, designed, transferred to the manufacturing plant, and rolled out to the market. Performance is related to mechanisms that add clarity and stability to the project, such as a clear project definition phase, and a stable product concept and specification. The emphasis is on a process aimed at achieving focused and efficient project execution, involving strong project leadership, integrated problem-solving, and team-based organizational structures.[3]

Effective product developers in turbulent environments, such as Silicon Graphics, provide a contrast to these practices. Their fundamental idea is to embrace change, not to fight it, exhibiting a development process characterized by extreme flexibility and responsiveness. This hinges on the capability to gather and to respond rapidly to new knowledge about technical and market information *as a project evolves*.

In this and previous work, I have characterized this approach as "system-focused product development."[4] While the system-focused model also underlines the need for team-based organizational structures and close communication between functions, it emphasizes the imperative to manage change in the project's specification and product concept. Rather than execution and implementation, the model emphasizes the essential impact of the concept development stage, and keeps the product's specification fluid as late as possible in a development project. This ensures the best match between system and component technologies, as well as the maximum flexibility to respond to changes.

The paper begins by proposing a simple model for effective product development in an uncertain environment. It follows by discussing a cross-sectional study of processor development in the mainframe industry. This links R&D performance to the nature of the development process, exploring the validity of the model. The paper continues by describing the study of product development at Silicon Graphics, which enriches and deepens the framework. The paper concludes with a summary of the results. The appendixes are case studies of two particularly effective development projects, the SX-2 (drawn from the mainframe study) and the Challenge (drawn from the SGI study).

## PRODUCT DEVELOPMENT IN
## UNCERTAIN ENVIRONMENTS

Research on the management of product development has contributed to a much deeper understanding of the organizational structures, tools, and processes underlying R&D performance. Practitioners and academics have written about the product development imperatives of speed, productivity, and quality.[5] This research has also investigated the approaches needed to meet these challenges in a variety of environments, such as integrated problem-solving and simultaneous engineering, the impact of project teams, and the role of project leadership.

Most of the empirical work that underlies these findings, however, was conducted in environments characterized by relatively stable technological and market foundations, such as the automobile and the copier industries.[6] New managerial concepts, such as concurrent engineering, were developed to optimize the speed and efficiency of the development process and to arrive at a better product solution, not to react to turbulence in the environment.

The essence of traditional models of product development is summarized by figure 11-1(a), which identifies two basic development phases: concept development and implementation.[7] The concept development phase focuses on the specification of features, architecture, and critical technical components. It includes the examination of customer needs, and of technological possibilities and their translation into a detailed concept for the new product. The implementation phase includes all the activities aimed at translating the objectives outlined in the product concept into a detailed design, as well as transforming that design into a product that can be manufactured and shipped to customers.

Traditional product development models imply a clear separation

FIGURE 11-1

TWO MODELS OF EFFECTIVE PRODUCT DEVELOPMENT

(a)

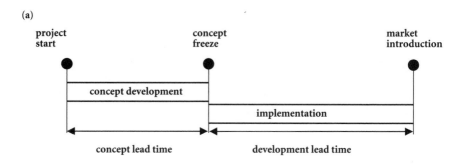

(b)

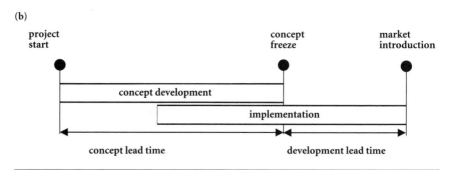

(a) is traditional or "element-focused" model.
(b) is the "system-focused" model.

between concept development and implementation, indicated in figure 11-1(a) by the "concept freeze" milestone. The idea is that a good project is characterized by extensive activities focused on the identification of customer needs and on technological feasibility, followed by the development of a detailed and thorough concept document. This concept document is then presented for approval. If approved, the concept is frozen and attention shifts to implementation. In this model, good projects are characterized by minimal changes after concept approval. The idea is that if the work is done "right," it should not be necessary to have to include late changes, which are inherently expensive.

As many authors have argued, development speed is a critical issue even in a stable environment, because it influences the ability to react to competitors, and has even been shown to be linked to resource utilization.[8] The right measure of speed is the *total* lead time, defined by the sum of the concept and development lead times shown in figure 11-1(a). If nothing changes in technology or market during the life of the project, there is no inherent benefit to delaying the "concept freeze" milestone, and the focus of the entire project should be to complete all stages as quickly as possible.

If we look at environments characterized by extreme turbulence, however, the situation changes. In this case, we expect that a lot of new technical and market information will emerge during the typical time scale of the project. I argue, therefore, that the emphasis should shift from the capability for focused and rapid project execution to the capability to react to newly discovered information during the course of the project itself. In figure 11-1(a) this translates into the ability to move the "concept freeze" milestone as close to market introduction as possible.

Speed, in a turbulent environment, is therefore a more subtle concept. Total lead time is clearly important, since it indicates the total time taken to fulfill the initial project objectives. However, the concepts "lead time" and "development lead time" are critical measures in their own right. Lead time is the "window of opportunity"[9] for including new information and for optimizing the match between technology and system.[10] Conversely, the development lead time indicates the time in which the window is closed, the product's architecture is frozen, and the project is unable to react to new information. This window of opportunity should be left open as long as possible. While the total lead time is the same in both cases, I would argue that the project described in figure 11-1(b) is preferable to that in figure 11-1(a), if the environment is turbulent. The shorter the development lead time, the greater the ability of the organization to respond to change.

The model in figure 11-1(b) indicates that concept development and implementation are a tightly linked set of activities, not sequential phases. To help shrink the development lead time, the product's concept and detailed design are being developed simultaneously. The project is characterized by frequent iteration of core concepts and details, rapidly moving up and down the hierarchy of design decisions.[11] While some of the up-front detailed design work will inevitably be wasted, the need to respond rapidly to unpredictable changes in technical or market environment makes iteration essential.[12]

Doing this well is not an easy task. As the rest of the paper will show, overlapping concept development and implementation effectively requires a critical set of capabilities rooted in individual skill, organizational managerial processes, and technical methodologies. I characterize this set of capabilities by the system-focused model of product development.

It is important to emphasize that this approach is quite different from concurrent engineering. Concurrent engineering models do *not* normally imply the simultaneous execution of conceptualization and implementation, but the joint participation of different functional groups in the execution of these separate and sequential sets of activities. Clausing, for example, divides the development process into four basic phases: concept, design, preparation for production, and production.[13] While acknowledging that the distinction between upstream and downstream activities is beginning to disappear, Clausing still emphasizes that there is a natural sequence to development tasks: "Concepts are selected before detailed designs."[14] A number of other authors emphasize a similar perspective.[15]

The system-focused model therefore goes beyond concurrent engineering or integrated problem-solving approaches. Whereas concurrent engineering fosters the joint resolution of different functional tasks in each stage of a project, the system-focused model actually implies overlapping the stages themselves: managing the joint evolution of system and technology, of a product's architecture and of its detailed design. I now shift to describing the empirical observations.

## EMPIRICAL FOUNDATIONS: A CROSS-SECTIONAL STUDY

My empirical work is divided in two basic parts. The first is a cross-sectional, field-based study of product development in high-performance computers. During the 1980s, the environment was characterized by very high levels of technical uncertainty, and the lessons drawn from my study of twenty-seven development projects therefore serves as a good model for the current computer and multimedia environments. These results set the stage for the second part, which is a longitudinal study of product development at Silicon Graphics, which is currently a leading manufacturer of computer and multimedia equipment.

### Empirical Approach

My cross-sectional empirical work was designed to investigate R&D performance in an environment characterized by high levels of technical uncertainty. The objective was to compare the approaches taken by a broad variety of organizations developing technology for a very similar set of products. The mainframe and supercomputer industry provided an appropriate environment for the study. The industry has a long history, characterized by technical excellence and strong emphasis on technology as a competitive weapon. While the measures of product quality and technical performance are well defined, the results achieved increased dramatically over the years through an impressive sequence of technological developments.

To obtain precisely comparable observations, I focused my inquiries on the development of technologies associated with the packaging and interconnect system of the mainframe processor, the "multichip module." Mainframe multichip modules form the core of the computer by housing and connecting its most critical integrated circuits. The greatest challenges in these projects are created by the combination of the uncertainties present in using new materials and techniques with the extreme complexity of the system architecture. The technical base for these products is quite turbulent, evolving rapidly during the course of a project.

I collected observations on most major projects performed by the leading competitors in the industry over the past fifteen years. The sample includes most leading companies in the computer and electronics industries, such as AT&T, Bull, DEC, Fujitsu, Hitachi, IBM, ICL, Mitsubishi Electric, NEC, Siemens, Toshiba, and Unisys, among others. In each company, one or more projects were analyzed in detail. I recorded the histories of each effort, tracking the dates of completion of each major step as well as the resources used. In addition, I gathered data on the basic characteristics of the organizations involved in the efforts, on the organizational structures and processes employed, and on the patterns of behavior of the managers and engineers. Furthermore, by discussing specific problem-solving examples, I captured individual approaches to technical problem-solving.

Table 11-1 summarizes the basic results for project performance; table 11-2 defines the variables. The most interesting column in table 11-1 exhibits the standard deviation in the observations. The column indicates that the variation in lead time and productivity figures is quite large. Productivity figures exhibited particularly large variation differences, with certain organizations employing more than three times the resources of other organizations in developing very similar products.

## Empirical Results

In other papers I have described how I used several analytical techniques to analyze and separate firms into two basic clusters, which I called "system focused" and "element focused."[16] The analysis was conducted at two levels: organizational process and problem-solving. The two levels of analysis (as well as several different analytical techniques) converged on a

TABLE 11-1

MEASURES OF PROJECT PERFOMANCE AND CONTENT
IN MAINFRAME MODULE DEVELOPMENT

| Project Perfomance (27 Projects) | Average | Standard Deviation |
|---|---|---|
| Total lead time (years) | 8.1 | 2.8 |
| Concept lead time (years) | 3.2 | 1.6 |
| Development lead time (years) | 4.8 | 1.9 |
| Person-years of activity | 347 | 386 |

TABLE 11-2

SUMMARY OF PRINCIPAL VARIABLE DEFINITIONS

| | |
|---|---|
| Total Lead Time | Time elapsed between the beginning of the project and market introduction. The project beginning is defined as the start of the first scientific investigations of new technologies specifically targeted for possible inclusion in the new design. |
| Concept Lead Time | Time elapsed between the beginning of the project and concept freeze. |
| Development Lead Time | Difference between Total Lead Time and Concept Lead Time. |
| Person Years of Engineering and Scientific Activity | Level of technical and managerial human resources used for the length of the entire project. Includes engineers, managers, scientists, and technicians internal and external to the firm. |

consistent definition for the two project clusters, focusing on the approach to concept development (or "technology integration") followed in the projects.[17] It is important to note that there are examples of Japanese, U.S., and European companies in both groups, indicating that the relationship is not strictly tied to geographical location.

Figure 11-2 shows the average lead times of system-focused and element-focused projects. It indicates that system-focused projects exhibit substantially shorter total and development lead times, compared with other projects. The difference in development lead time is particularly striking, indicating that system-focused organizations freeze the product concept much later than their competitors. The concept-development

FIGURE 11-2

AVERAGE LEAD TIMES FOR SYSTEM-FOCUSED AND ELEMENT-FOCUSED PROJECTS

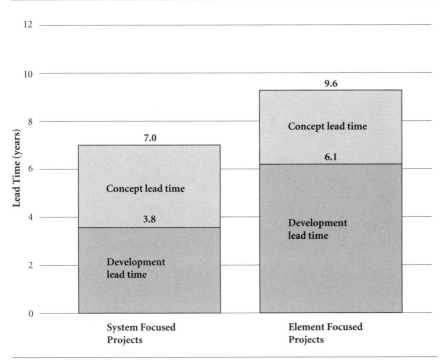

NOTE: The lighter shaded area indicates time spent in the concept development stage. The darker shaded area indicates time spent after the concept has been frozen.

phase makes up a much higher portion of the project for system-focused organizations. This behavior is consistent with the simple models described in figure 11-1, the element-focused group corresponding to figure 11-1(a) and the system-focused cluster to figure 11-1(b).

Figure 11-3 shows the average engineering resources used by system- and element-focused organizations. The data were corrected for differences in the content of each project, and should be interpreted as the person-years of engineering effort required by each project to conceptualize and develop an average processor module. System-focused projects are much more productive, using, on average, less than a third of the resources required by traditional projects.

Finally, I found distinct differences in the ability to transform technological possibilities into system-level performance. Figure 11-4 tabulates the difference in the ratio between system performance and

FIGURE 11-3

AVERAGE ENGINEERING RESOURCES USED IN THE SYSTEM- AND
ELEMENT-FOCUSED PROJECTS

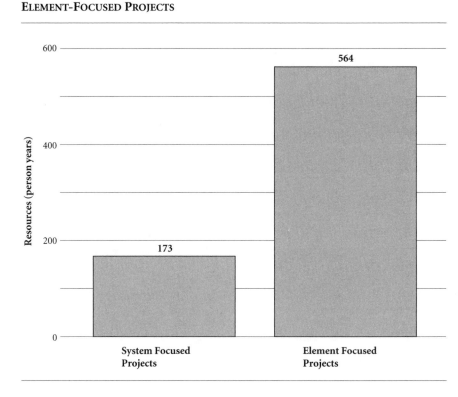

technological potential achieved in a group of six projects. The projects, selected from the overall sample, have very similar characteristics.

All of the products were based on a similar processor instruction set and were designed for comparable systems, making the comparison accurate and appropriate. System performance was given by the cycle time, an accurate measure of the speed of the processor subsystem. The technological potential was given by the electrical characteristics (the dielectric constant in figure 11-4[a]) and resistivity in figure 11-4[b]) and by the thermal characteristics (the power density in figure 11-4[c]). Figure 11-4 shows that the three system-focused projects (SF1, 2, and 3) consistently achieved a higher ratio of system performance to technological potential than the element-focused projects (EF1, 2, and 3).

The results show that the system-focused cluster of project was characterized by shorter development lead times than other projects, which is consistent with the model introduced in the section "Product Development in Uncertain Environments" (see figure 11-1). The system-focused

FIGURE 11-4

RATIO OF SYSTEM PERFORMANCE TO TECHNOLOGICAL POTENTIAL

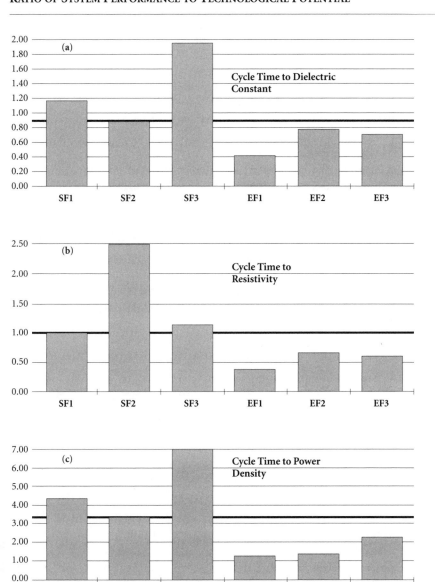

projects also achieved a higher degree of efficiency, shown by the higher level of R&D productivity. In addition, the results show that system-focused projects achieved higher effectiveness, obtaining a better leverage of technological potential into system performance. System-focused organizations also had a greater rate of overall technological improvement.[18]

## System-Focused Product Development

These substantial differences in R&D performance are related to fundamental differences in product development approach. Appendix I provides details on the development of the SX-2 supercomputer, as an example of a system-focused development project. The project is consistent with the simple model outlined in figure 11-1(b). Element-focused projects differed in a number of important characteristics. My observations fit into a pattern that is explained by different underlying product development models in an uncertain and rapidly changing technological environment.

In the element-focused approach, the concept development and implementation stages are clearly separated, as in the simple model shown in figure11-1(a). The process allows for flexibility and freedom in the early investigations, and is aimed at making sure that the concept includes the technical possibilities having the maximum theoretical impact on future product characteristics, within the constraint of feasibility. However, uncertainties regarding the impact of technology choice on the product and production system are not resolved before the concept is frozen. The implementation stage therefore wastes great resources attempting to account for newly discovered technical information while working within the rigid framework specified by the early concept development work. The result is an inefficient and ineffective match between technology and system.

In the system-focused approach, the emphasis is on discovering and capturing knowledge about the interactions between the new, uncertain technical possibilities and the system before committing to a particular concept. Substantial resources are therefore dedicated to the project before the concept is frozen, which is delayed as long as possible. In the SX-2 project shown in appendix I, the exploratory part of the project began in the late 1970s, but commitment to a particular system-level concept was delayed until August 1984, about one year before the product was shipped. Since detailed design had started in early 1981, this shows a considerable overlap between concept development and implementation. This allowed the latest information on technological possibilities, as well as the resolution of technical uncertainties through early implementation work, to be included.

As the NEC example shows, system-focused product development puts great emphasis on capturing knowledge about the interactions between basic technical decisions and the details of product and production system design. This knowledge is fed into the concept development stage, optimizing the match between technical choice and system performance. I observed in my study that a tightly knit group of individuals was responsible for concept development as well as for implementation (the "integration group" at NEC). Although they did not perform all design activities, they remained closely involved in the design process, providing conceptual guidance, setting basic specifications, and performing critical aspects of the product and process design. Helped by a high continuity of personnel between projects, knowledge about the interactions between the many elements of the system and its production process clearly accrued over time.[19]

## PRODUCT DEVELOPMENT AT SGI: A LONGITUDINAL CASE STUDY

### Empirical Approach

Studying product development at Silicon Graphics provides an opportunity to extend the concepts developed in the preceding section. The observations provide a rich description of effective product development in an uncertain environment. The challenges are even sharper than those found in the mainframe and supercomputer industries, since the company competes in an environment dominated by turbulence in *both* market and technology.

Silicon Graphics is a leader in the current high-performance server and graphics workstation industries, and is positioned to play a critical role in the evolving computer and multimedia environment. The company was founded about ten years ago and has enjoyed a very high growth rate since then. Its 1993 sales were in excess of a billion dollars, and are expected to double by the end of 1995.

Rather than a broad cross-sectional study, the empirical work carried out at SGI involved an in-depth focus on a single firm, performed over a two-year period. I examined three projects in some detail: the Challenge supercomputer server, described below, the Reality Engine graphics processor, and the Indy workstation. The data were gathered through extensive interviews conducted with almost every member of each project, over about a dozen visits that each lasted one or two days.

## R&D Performance

Before I describe SGI's development approach, it is useful to briefly analyze its R&D performance. The company is universally recognized as the technological leader in its primary graphics-oriented market segments. As with the system-focused projects described in the preceding section, the roots of the performance advantage is found not in superior component technologies but in a better match between component and system, as indicated in figure 11-5. It shows the system-level graphics performance (in objects moved per second) and computing performance (in SPECmarks) of a number of competitive systems, divided by the performance of the leading component (the microprocessor). The SGI product shows a clearly superior ratio of system to component performance.

Given the scope of this study, I did not gather systematic observations at SGI's competitors. However, information available from public sources,[20] and from interviews conducted with experts, indicates that SGI exhibits the highest level of R&D productivity and the shortest development lead times among industry leaders.

## Product Development At SGI: Key Features

The projects observed at SGI shared a number of critical features. The time line for the Reality Engine project, for example, can be superimposed almost exactly on the Challenge time line. The Everest project (described in appendix II) thus exemplifies a number of critical features of product development at SGI that appear quite consistent with the system-focused model. Everest aimed to develop a high-performance server to be used for scientific, business, and multimedia applications (such as digital interactive television).

First of all, SGI's development process stresses flexibility and responsiveness. It is universally expected that product specifications will evolve substantially over most of the life of a project. As an SGI architect described it:

> Some companies set certain "stakes" in the ground at the beginning of a project. At most large companies, you're married to that stake. At SGI, for every stake you put in the ground, there's a way to pull it back out.

FIGURE 11-5

RATIO OF SYSTEM TO COMPONENT PERFORMANCE, VARIOUS WORKSTATIONS

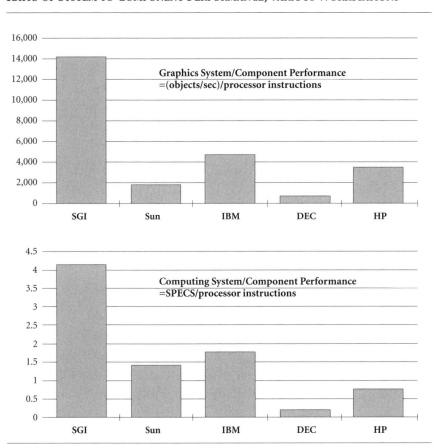

Another architect described the role that the specification played in one of the projects:

> It was a fairly fluid design. Good specs were set up in the beginning that provided certain envelopes you had to stay within. Some of the things considered fixed were the power outlets it would hook up to, the size of the box, that it not have to be in an air-conditioned room, and that it offer a five- to tenfold improvement in performance over the old products. Almost everything else could change.

SGI's development process acknowledges that surprises, both product- and market-related, are bound to arise during the life of a project. Some surprises are in the form of roadblocks, such as late delivery of key parts from vendors and a realization that new components do not perform as expected. Others can be viewed as positive surprises, if handled appropriately. For example, when a relatively inexpensive digital video camera appeared on the market during Indy's development period, SGI reacted quickly and incorporated digital video into the product.

At SGI, concept and specifications are left fluid until very late in a development project. Typically, the development lead time (defined as the time between concept freeze and shipping date) is only a small fraction of the total lead time. Appendix II provides a detailed time line of the Everest project, showing a substantial overlap in the concept development and implementation stages.

Several factors appear particularly important in enabling SGI to deal with so much change during the life of a project. First of all, activities performed at the start are critical. The early stages are driven by architects who have extensive experience on previous projects, and a good feeling for what is feasible. The group of architects draws a comprehensive block diagram of the system that serves as a blueprint for the project. However, this blueprint is not used as a rigid specification, and almost all of the detailed product objectives change repeatedly. Its main role is instead to identify the basic project modules and to highlight the most critical interactions between them. More than a detailed specification, the block diagram is used as an early road map for the project, identifying the most appropriate ways to partition project tasks and organize the project's activities.

The emphasis of concept development activities is clearly on architecture: on discussing how all individual components fit together at the system level, not only on exploring ways to stretch the potential contribution of individual components. This is reflected by the view of one of the leading component technologists, an ASIC design specialist: "We reach for performance using architectural enhancements."

Several methodologies and tools are critical to gather and react to new information rapidly. As a project progresses, the specification changes from a paper document to the actual software code representing the product design for computer simulations. This source code performs the function of a living specification; it is a complete representation of the electronics in the product, shared by all members of the project team. This enables the rapid verification of the system-level impact of individual technical choices. In addition, it serves to facilitate communication between team members and integrate individual efforts. All team members work on the same software body of design code. Any time a change takes place, each member is automatically notified via electronic mail.

Critical new information is discovered through the use of simulation as well as hardware models and mockups. Although not representative of the entire computer system, the mockups are very useful in investigating critical interactions between components. These methodologies create a very rapid testing cycle linking individual design choices and the performance of the entire system, facilitating their joint optimization.

SGI relies on several external sources to search for new, relevant information during the course of a project. The first of these is its lead customers. Team members repeatedly invite key customers to SGI, under nondisclosure agreements, to discuss the product in development and to try their latest software on it. Moreover, SGI relies on its ties with research institutions and universities for sampling the latest trends. Its relationship with Stanford's electrical engineering department is particularly close: Ph.D. students with potentially relevant dissertations are frequently hired by the company. Colleagues in other firms in Silicon Valley are another critical information source: "There is basically a group of twenty to thirty designers around the Valley that really understand this stuff; we all know each other well and constantly rely on each other for the latest news." Finally, SGI's vendor base (companies like NEC, Toshiba, and LSI Logic) is a critical source of technical information, particularly on the evolution of component technology.

These many sources of information are integrated by the team members, who use their broad experience base, combining a variety of backgrounds, to interpret the impact of changes. Typically, all key project architects have participated in several generations of development projects, some at SGI, and some elsewhere in the industry. As a result, they have a very rich understanding of how individual design choices will impact the product's system-level characteristics.

The broad experience base of the team members is also reflected in the later project stages. The critical "bring-up" stage is the clearest example. The essence of this stage is to use the flexibility of system software to work around possible problems with the relatively inflexible hardware design. Its success therefore hinges on the ability of team members to integrate software and hardware expertise. While some of this is accomplished through close communication and teamwork, individuals who have the broad experience of integrating hardware and software problems perform an essential role.

This need for breadth of experience in the development process is reflected in the career paths of individuals. The Everest project leader described his approach thus:

> I think it's best to start off inexperienced hardware engineers on simulation tasks, since these give you the best view of the entire system. As they build experience in that, we will shift them over to the design of components, such as the ASICs. Balancing the experience gathered by our engineers during their careers is probably our most crucial task.

The need to build on individual experience is reflected in SGI's approach to hiring and career development. SGI is constantly trying to hire the best available talent in the industry. In addition, it focuses on retaining critical individuals. Employee turnover is among the lowest in Silicon Valley.

## CONCLUSIONS

The multimedia and computer industries of the 1990s are fraught with uncertainty and turbulence. The capability to respond rapidly to evolving technical and market information through product development is of critical importance. The challenge reaches beyond the well-known pressures for short time to market, however. Major changes in standards, customer requirements, and technological possibilities may occur on a monthly or even a weekly basis, a time scale that is much shorter than even the fastest development project. Substantial change is therefore inevitable during the evolution of the project. In this type of environment, the capability to adapt to external and internal uncertainties during a project's evolution has become a critical source of competitive advantage.

I described two studies of product development that document how organizations have approached this challenge. The observations described are consistent in underlying the effectiveness of the system-focused model of product development. As expected, in a turbulent and uncertain environment, the system-focused approach was linked to significant advantages in development performance, such as higher R&D productivity, shorter development lead time, and a higher degree of leverage of technological potential into system performance. Projects following the traditional, or "element-focused," model, grown out of more mature environments, achieved much poorer performance levels.

The system-focused model centers on concept development. The early project stages should lay down a flexible path to the product's design. I noted the critical role played by the early "block diagram phase" at SGI, which investigates the modularity of the product and highlights the most important interdependencies. Similarly, early concept discussions at NEC's SX-2 project were critical in laying the groundwork for the rest of the project, highlighting the most critical technical problems to be solved. In both examples, the work defined a basic road map, partitioning project tasks to create the tightest problem-solving loops around the most critical interactions between design choice and system performance.

In addition, the concept development and implementation phases were tightly linked, occurring in an overlapped fashion. The development process proactively inquired into the uncertainties that characterize technology and market. Any resulting change in the product's concept was rapidly communicated and implemented in detailed design. Any inconsistencies discovered in the design, via prototyping or simulation, were then fed back to readjust the concept, changing the architecture at the system level, repeating the cycle.

Making the system-focused approach work hinges on a group of critical individuals, the "architects" at SGI and the "integration group" at NEC. These tightly knit groups drove the product development process. Although their main focus was on concept development, they remained involved in all aspects of the effort. The purpose is twofold: on the one hand, this maintains continuity and accountability; on the other hand, these individuals learn from the variety of rich experiences, becoming a critical repository of architectural knowledge in the firm.[21] They make up the engine for product development; while customers, vendors, research groups, or universities provide fuel by communicating possibilities, the architects turn the fuel into useful work by integrating these possibilities into new products. The engine accelerates over time: as the experience of the architects grows, so do the productivity and speed of the development organization.

Mastering the art of developing products in a chaotic environment is a critical source of advantage in the emerging computer and multimedia industry. An organization can consistently outperform its competitors by its ability to influence the market's direction with prompt responses to threats and opportunities. The capability to react quickly to technology and market changes can therefore turn into a truly proactive weapon. In the words of Ed McCracken, SGI's CEO:

> The source of our competitiveness in this industry is our ability to manage in a chaotic environment. But it's more proactive than that. We actually help create the chaos in the first place—that's what keeps a lot of potential competitors out.

## APPENDIX I: NEC'S SX-2 PROJECT

In June 1985, NEC entered the supercomputer business by introducing the SX-2, whose impressive design and performance stunned supercomputer and mainframe manufacturers (see figure 11-6 for a time line). In June 1990, it followed on the SX-2 project by delivering the first units of the SX-3, which became the world's fastest computer. Through these product introductions, NEC rapidly established itself as a technical leader in the industry.

NEC's entry into the supercomputer business had been envisioned in the late 1970s by a group of senior managers whose aim was to infuse technical competencies developed in the supercomputer. This goal was accomplished quickly, with a minimum of engineering resources and relatively low financial risk. To provide a detailed description of how this was accomplished, I will focus on a subsystem critical to the superior performance of NEC's supercomputers: the "multichip module," which houses the integrated circuits for the computer processor. The module was developed by using a number of new capabilities, including the application of polyimide materials.

Advances in polyimide material technology had their foundations in research performed in the late 1970s. In 1977, conscious of the pressure on conventional ceramic materials that future performance requirements would bring, NEC scientists—in joint ventures with two materials suppliers—began exploring the technical possibilities of polyimide materials for high-density packaging. The new materials had very attractive intrinsic properties that would allow faster transmission of signals and higher-density interconnection patterns, for example. They were not compatible with other characteristics of modern computer systems, however. Although they had been employed before in less sensitive computer applications (in circuit boards), they had never before been used in a structure as complex and compact as a supercomputer processor module.

As performance reports from the joint ventures came in, the promise of the new materials was gradually confirmed. Because NEC was a late entrant in the supercomputer industry, it was felt that challenging performance targets would have to be set to attempt to overtake industry leaders. The new materials fit these targets. However, the polyimide composition, properties, and fabrication process would have to be reengineered to fit with the properties of the rest of the module system. In addition, the rest of the module and its production process would have to be substantially redesigned to accommodate the stringent requirements

FIGURE 11-6

TIME LINE FOR NEC'S SX-2 PROJECT

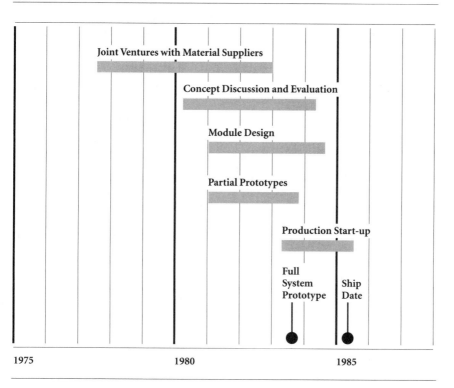

of the polyimide. The new material technologies would have to be integrated into the existing capability base of the organization.

Substantive concept discussions for the SX-2 supercomputer were started in 1980. The first customer, a Japanese university, had already been identified and was involved in setting the computer specifications. Two groups within NEC had been particularly active in the early discussions of new packaging concepts for the supercomputer: the central research and development laboratory, located in Kawasaki, and the integration group, located at the computer plant in Fuchu City. Both groups naturally became involved in the development of the new computer.

Members of the research and development group had been active in materials research for many years. The group was composed of about half a dozen scientists with expertise in material science and several years of research experience at NEC. Although they occasionally built functional experimental prototypes of packaging systems, most of their work was aimed at developing fundamental new techniques and approaches that would have application in novel systems. The objectives and approach of the integration group were quite different, since it was focused on designing a working, manufacturable product. Whereas the role of the R&D group was to research and offer a broad range of technical options, the integration group drove the investigations, selected the most promising alternatives, and integrated them into a manufacturable subsystem.

In 1980, the integration group of NEC's computer division was hard at work developing the packaging module for a new mainframe computer, the ACOS 1500. The group was quite small, consisting of about a dozen young engineers. Some had been out of university for only a few years, although many had been involved in the development of the previous-generation mainframe, the ACOS 1000 system. Some of the engineers had also been involved in the polyimide joint ventures on a part-time basis, and had strongly influenced the direction of the early research efforts.

For several generations, the integration group at NEC had driven the detailed design and development of packaging systems for high-end computers. The group's small size and the attention of the project managers had given members the chance to obtain broad exposure to a wide variety of tasks. Their approach involved continuous involvement by project members in the development project; there were no handoffs in the middle of the effort. Although a small number of production engineers (at most equaling the number of integration engineers) gradually became involved in the project, the tradition was that whoever started the project would see it through to the end. As a result, integration group members developed an intimate knowledge of existing production processes, system-level design considerations, and a wide variety of technical approaches. This put them in an ideal position to analyze the potential impact of the new approaches on the organization's existing capability base.

During 1981, managers and engineers of the two groups met repeatedly to discuss options for the supercomputer package. They had worked together several times previously and enjoyed a close, informal relationship. Members of the integration group naturally took leadership in setting the direction of future efforts, and they began to perform feasibility studies of new packaging concepts. They initiated discussions with members of the R&D laboratory and with materials suppliers, system engineers, and integrated circuit designers. Many possibilities were discussed and modeled; the most promising were investigated at the bench scale. At that time, the ACOS 1500 project was still going at full speed: the production process was being refined at the plant, and yield improvement activities had begun. Integration engineers working on the SX-2 project had retained some responsibilities for the ACOS 1500, and thus the same person often—sometimes on the same day—spent time in the plant refining the production process for the ACOS 1500 and working on feasibility studies for the SX-2. While generating a significant workload for the engineers, the practice created a seamless transfer of knowledge between projects.

In October 1982, the SX-2 project was officially approved by NEC senior management and the level of resource allocation was increased. The number of people involved from the integration group rose from five half-time engineers in 1981 to about a dozen engineers and ten technicians in 1982; their level of involvement in the SX-2 project increased as the ACOS 1500 project began to wind down. Between 1983 and early 1985, the allocation level of integration engineers and technicians remained about the same; the team was gradually joined by about a dozen production engineers from the Fuchu City plant. As the effort continued, confidence in the polyimide materials continued to grow.

During 1983, many models of the new packaging system were constructed to assess production yield. Great emphasis was put on quick-turnaround partial prototypes and models. For example, the yield of the polyimide thin films was investigated at each stage of the fabrication process, between the deposition of each layer. In this way, before the full prototyping process had begun, there were sufficient data (on yields, types of defects, causes of defects, and so forth) to give confidence in the eventual high yield of the process. Reliability testing, begun in November 1983 and continued in 1984, led to some changes in the composition of the polyimide. The first complete, fully representative prototypes were constructed in March.

More than one hundred modules were built. A batch was fabricated and tested until a major defect was encountered. Knowledge gained from analyzing the causes of the defect were then used in the construction of a second batch of prototypes, while the first batch, now only partially functional, was used to conduct additional tests. The integration group went through many such iterations. The approach was described as "thinking while running." A wide variety of design options was tested with the prototypes, gradually refining their design.

By midsummer 1985, the module's concept had finally stabilized, incorporating a number of novel techniques and approaches. The incompatibilities between the module system and the polyimide were resolved by the development of a number of specific technical competencies, including improved polyimide material compositions and many subtle improvements in the production process.

In early 1985, before the SX-2 project was completed, engineers in the integration group began working on adapting the new technical approach to the next generation of mainframes, the ACOS 2000, to be shipped at the end of 1986. Soon thereafter, the SX-3 project was also begun on an informal basis, with discussions about how the SX-2 concept could be extended to provide higher performance. As during the ACOS 1500, project engineers often were allocated to two projects at the same time, facilitating the transfer of knowledge from project to project.

The implementation of the SX-2 concept was completed in June 1985. The production process had been designed in detail, production workers had been trained, and the product had been shipped to the first customers. The ACOS 2000 was introduced on time at the end of 1986, exhibiting the fastest computer hardware in its industry segment. Early 1987 marked the official start and concept approval of the SX-3 project, the next-generation supercomputer. By this time, the bulk of engineers in the packaging group had participated in four or five projects, with full responsibilities ranging from concept investigations to product introduction. This level of experience was reflected in many of the design approaches taken by the organization.[22] The results were impressive: whereas the SX-3 retained essentially the same basic technologies developed in the SX-2 project, the new packaging module included forty times the number of transistors in the earlier model. The SX-3, introduced in 1990, surpassed existing supercomputer models in performance and cost.

The breadth of experience of the integration engineers, their intimate knowledge of the manufacturing system, the technical support of the R&D group and outside suppliers, and the high skill and extensive experience of the technicians all contributed to the design of a series of packaging modules that met aggressive performance specifications and was delivered on time. Furthermore, the projects themselves provided a critical base of experience to "refuel" all organizational subgroups that had participated and to prepare them for the next-generation efforts. The projects set up a strong technological platform for NEC. Even more important, they generated a rich knowledge base that would lay the foundation for future development efforts.

# APPENDIX II: SGI'S EVEREST PROJECT

Everest was the code name for the Challenge, a high-performance server and graphics workstation platform introduced in 1993. With a $40 million budget, the Everest project was the largest undertaking in SGI's history.

The project involved substantial changes in technology. Although SGI had experience with multiprocessor systems and had worked with the R4000 series MIPS (Millions of Instructions per Second) microprocessor in its Crimson product, it had never used the R4000 in a multiprocessor setting. The previous multiprocessor system, the Power series, had used the MIPS R3000 processor, which was not designed for multiprocessor environments. The R4000 was thus not only faster but also more suited for SGI's applications. To really make use of its speed, however, the product required the design of an architecture very different from previous product generations.

In addition, the project involved substantial changes in SGI's customer base. Unlike the Power series (the Challenge's predecessor), the Challenge series would be marketed explicitly for commercial applications. The charter for the development team was to provide "megaflops for the masses," with the intention of going after the larger-volume "bread and butter" markets from the beginning. An entirely new population of customers would be targeted—specifically, commercial applications such as banks and telecommunications companies. If SGI was successful, this new architecture would change the existing price–performance curve for high-end systems, bringing a new level of power to a population previously unable to afford such performance.

Critical decisions were made jointly by the "core" Business Team, a group of about twenty-five professionals who met frequently. They represented a wide range of expertise, and included members from hardware design engineering, product engineering, testing, software development (operating system and compilers), marketing, manufacturing, quality, and technical publications. The leader of the team had been the president of a supercomputer server start-up, and had extensive experience in computer system design.

The core of the Everest team was a group of "architects" who included both newcomers to SGI and old-timers. Each had worked on a number of supercomputer or server development projects (at least three or four product generations). The group consisted primarily of designers, although it also included individuals with extensive testing and manufacturing engineering experience.

The architects met on a daily basis from January 1991 through April 1991 to develop a basic block diagram of Everest's architecture (see figure 11-7). This phase involved discussions, mostly around a blackboard, characterized by arguments as to which architecture might maximize system performance with the least technical risk and effort. Most discussions focused on the nature of the "bus," the main conduit of information between the computer's processors and input/output devices. Because the R4000 was so much faster than the previous generation, the type of bus architecture used in the Power series computers would not be able to convey information rapidly enough.

By April the group had developed a reasonably stable block diagram of the new computer system and a document specifying its most critical technical features. These included a new bus architecture that had the potential to transfer information at 1.2 billion bytes per second—a rate more than a factor of ten higher than previous SGI designs. Along with increases in microprocessor speed and the number of processors, this would enable an increase in computing power of more than a factor of 100 over the fastest Power series system.

By April, the number of people on the team had reached almost its full complement. Many of the team members were spending much of their time working on Crimson, a single-processor workstation based on the R4000 processor. This was not wasted effort, as the software development manager explained:

> The work we did on Crimson had a real direct benefit on the Everest project. Crimson was actually the first system we designed around the R4000; Everest was only the first *multiprocessor* system. What we learned on Crimson was therefore immediately applicable when we came back to work fully on Everest, around the end of 1992.

During the late spring and summer of 1991, Everest's designers refined the product's specification and translated it into the programming source code for simulations. By the end of May, the team could run some fairly rough system-level simulations to test the performance of the new architecture. By late fall, the set of simulations encompassed the entire system electronics, from the ASIC logic at the chip level to the design of the circuit board. The programs were linked so that the entire computer system could be simulated as a single unit. SGI engineers could even test parts of the actual operating system to detect problems with logic timing and performance.

FIGURE 11-7

TIME LINE FOR THE EVEREST PROJECT

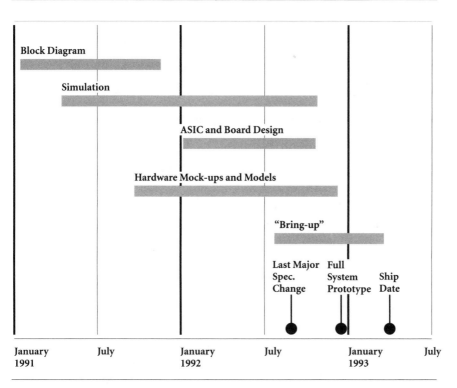

Although accurate, the simulation programs were relatively slow. Even though the Everest team used a large number of Power series servers linked together and running simultaneously, the simulation was still about fifty million times slower than the actual hardware would be. Hardware designers and testing engineers thus began building numerous physical models of the system. However, these prototypes included only some parts of the computer system in order to test for specific problem areas. In October, for example, testing engineers built a model of the Everest bus. Although it was not hooked up to actual chips (since their design was not yet finalized), the model was very useful in testing the signal integrity and noise properties of the bus design.

The idea was to uncover as many problems as possible and optimize the system's performance before committing to a (very expensive) complete and representative prototype.[23] Performance was not the only design target, however. Designers also added features to the system, such as the capability to interface with a variety of emerging networking standards. Furthermore, the team worked on adding several features to improve testing convenience and speed once the complete prototypes were finally assembled.

The design was left flexible until the last feasible moment, leaving open the opportunity to take account of late shifts in technology or market. For example, the team decided in December 1991 that the server market was looking even more attractive than originally expected. As a result, they decided to enlarge the scope of the Everest project to create a new product series designed specifically for commercial server applications. Before this point, the Challenge and Onyx[24] systems had been specified to share most hardware components. Now the Challenge series designs would include different chassis, input/output devices, and networking capabilities. This decision was made slightly more than a year before the shipping date of March 1993.

During the winter of 1991 and the spring of 1992, the team continued to refine the Everest's design based on the results of simulations and tests on partial models. The ASIC design was finalized, and LSI Logic was sent the specifications for the chips during the fall of 1992 (the last one was sent in November). The configuration of the basic Challenge systems was not finalized until August 1992. The system's networking characteristics, the size of its power supply, and the maximum number of processors were finalized in October; the graphics boards were finalized in November. The first complete system prototypes, including the full set of boards and ASIC devices back from LSI Logic, were put together in December 1992, about three months before the shipping date. One of the architects explained, "One thing we pride ourselves on is how late we make specification changes and still ship on time."

The assembly of the first batch of twelve complete Everest systems in the Mountain View facility in mid-December signified the beginning of the product's "bring-up" stage. Small groups of hardware designers, software developers, and manufacturing and testing engineers worked on each system, detecting and fixing any problems remaining with the hardware and software. Although some of the problems might still be in the design of the hardware, the simplest way to fix them was by adapting the software. For example, if it turned out that an ASIC chip had a bug in it, returning the chip to the vendor with a design change might cost as much as $100,000 and, much worse, two or three weeks. Fixing the problem by working around it instead—adapting the operating system software—might be done in a few hours. Doing this well necessitated close interaction between hardware designers and software developers. SGI devoted a team of two people (a software engineer and a hardware engineer) to work on each prototype. Each team would locate in the manufacturing facility until the product was shipped. This way, any improvement on a given prototype was quickly shared with the other teams working on the other prototypes located nearby on the shop floor. By March 31, 1993, SGI had shipped 254 Challenge servers to its lead customers.

The Everest time line shows a substantial overlap of conceptualization and implementation. The project involved major changes to the product concept made until the fall of 1992. This included changes in the CPU board, input/output subsystem, and graphics board. The last major change was in the graphics board, which was finalized in November 1992, a date I would define as the de facto "concept freeze" date. This translates into a "development lead time" of less than five months. This is only a small fraction of the "total lead time" of twenty-seven months.

The Challenge enjoyed great reviews. *Sun World* hailed it as a "dream machine." The magazine ran a number of performance benchmarks with competitive products, and concluded that the Challenge beat "the highest performing [Sun] SPARC server by a whopping 60%."[25] By early 1994, the Challenge product line was responsible for over $600 million of sales and more than its share of profits.

## NOTES

1. See, e.g., T. J. Allen, *Managing the Flow of Technology* (Cambridge, Mass.: MIT press, 1977); K. B. Clark and T. Fujimoto, *Product Development Performance* (Boston: Harvard Business School Press, 1991); Steven C. Wheelwright and Kim B. Clark, *Revolutionizing Product Development* (New York: Free Press, 1992); H. K. Bowen, Kim B. Clark, Charles Holloway, and Steven C. Wheelwright, eds., *The Perpetual Enterprise Machine* (New York: Oxford University Press, 1994); Don Clausing, *Total Quality Development* (New York: ASME Press, 1994); K. T. Ulrich and S. D. Eppinger, *Methodologies for Product Design and Development* (New York: McGraw-Hill, 1994).

2. See Clausing; Ulrich and Eppinger.

3. See, e.g., Wheelwright and Clark.

4. M. Ianitsi, "Science-Based Product Development: An Empirical Study of the Mainframe Computer Industry," Harvard Business School Working Paper no. 92083 (1993); and "Technology Integration: Managing the Technological Evolution in a Complex Environment," *Research Policy* (1994).

5. B. Uttal, "Speeding Ideas to Market," *Fortune,* March 2, 1987, pp. 62–66; G. Stalk, Jr., "Time—the Next Source of Competitive Advantage," *Harvard Business Review,* July–August 1988, pp. 41–51; Clark and Fujimoto; Wheelwright and Clark; Michael A. Cusumano and Kentaro Nobeoka, "Strategy, Structure and Performance in Product Development: Observations from the Auto Industry," *Research Policy* (1992):265–293; Clausing.

6. See, e.g., Clark and Fujimoto; Clausing.

7. M. Ianitsi and K. B. Clark, "Integration and Dynamic Capability: Evidence from Product Development in Automobiles and Mainframe Computers," *Industrial and Corporate Change* (1994).

8. Clark and Fujimoto argued that the faster the speed, the higher the productivity of resources.

9. See Marcie J. Tyre and Wanda J. Orlikowski, "Windows of Opportunity: Creating Occasions for Technological Adaptation in Organizations" (Sloan School of Management, MIT, 1991); Marcie J. Tyre and E. von Hippel, "Situated Trial and Error Learning in Organizations," Working Paper, Sloan School of Management, MIT, 1993.

10. Ianitsi, "Science-Based Product Development" and "Technology Integration."

11. K. B. Clark, "The Interaction of Design Hierarchies and Market Concepts in Product Development, *Research Policy* 14 (1985): 235–256.

12. E. von Hippel and Marcie Tyre, "How 'Learning by Doing' Is Done: Problem Identification in Novel Process Equipment," Working Paper no. BPS 3521-93, Sloan School of Management, MIT, 1993.

13. Clausing, *Total Quality Development.*

14. Ibid., 21.

15. See, e.g., Preston G. Smith and D. G. Reinertsen, *Developing Products in Half the Time* (New York: Van Nostrand, 1991), ch. 9; Christopher Meyer, *Fast Cycle Time* (New York: Free Press, 1993).

16. Ianitsi, "Science-Based Product Development" and "Technology Integration"; Ianitsi and Clark.

17. Ianitsi, "Science-Based Product Development."

18. See ibid.

19. See Ianitsi, "Science-Based Product Development" and "Technology Integration."

20. See, e.g., S. Prokesh, "Managing Chaos at the High-Tech Frontier," *Harvard Business Review,* November–December 1993: 134–145; Bernstein and Co. Analyst Reports (1992).

21. R. M. Henderson and K. B. Clark, "Architectural Innovation: The Reconfiguration of Existing Product Technologies and the Failure of Established Firms," *Administrative Sciences Quarterly* 33 (1990): 9–30.

22. These ranged from relatively major changes, such as a redesign of the cooling system, to account for the higher-performance specifications, to more subtle choices, such as the decision to define the pitch between chips to be the same as the pitch between pins at the bottom of the substrate, to allow for vertical connections and to minimize signal length and power dissipation.

23. A complete prototype could cost as much as a million dollars in components. In addition, it would require deciding on a final ASIC design, which implied commitment to several million dollars' worth of capital expenditure. A single engineering change in an ASIC design could require an expenditure of as much as $100,000 and delays of several weeks.

24. The Onyx was the graphics version of the product.

25. *Sun World*, January 1994.


# REFERENCES

Allen, T. J. *Managing the Flow of Technology*. Cambridge, Mass.: MIT Press, 1977.

Allen, T. J. "Organizational Structures, Information Technology and R&D Productivity." *IEEE Transactions on Engineering Management* EM-33, no. 4 (1986): 212–217.

Allen, T. J., M. L. Tushman, and D. M. S. Lee. "R&D Performance as a Function of Internal Communication, Project Management, and the Nature of Work." *IEEE Transactions on Engineering Management* EM-27, no. 1 (1980).

Bowen, H. K., Kim B. Clark, Charles Holloway, and Steven C. Wheelwright, eds., *The Perpetual Enterprise Machine*. New York: Oxford University Press, 1994.

Clark, K. B. "The Interaction of Design Hierarchies and Market Concepts in Product Development." *Research Policy* 14 (1985): 235–251.

Clark, K. B., and T. Fujimoto. "Overlapping Problem Solving in Product Development." In Kasra Ferdows, ed., *Managing International Manufacturing*. Amsterdam: North Holland, 1989.

Clark, K. B., and T. Fujimoto. *Product Development Performance*. Boston: Harvard Business School Press, 1991.

Clausing, Don. *Total Quality Development*. New York: ASME Press, 1994.

Cusumano, Michael A., and Kentaro Nobeoka. "Strategy, Structure and Performance in Product Development: Observations from the Auto Industry." *Research Policy* (1992): 265–293.

Henderson, R. M., and K. B. Clark. "Architectural Innovation: The Reconfiguration of Existing Product Technologies and the Failure of Established Firms." *Administrative Sciences Quarterly* 35 (1990): 9–30.

Iansiti, M. "Science-Based Product Development: An Empirical Study of the Mainframe Computer Industry." Harvard Business School Working Paper #92083. Cambridge, Mass.: 1993.

Iansiti, M. "Technology Integration: Managing the Technological Evolution in a Complex Environment." *Research Policy* (1994).

Iansiti, M., and K. B. Clark. "Integration and Dynamic Capability: Evidence from Product Development in Automobiles and Mainframe Computers." *Industrial and Corporate Change* (1994).

Meyer, Christopher. *Fast Cycle Time.* New York: Free Press, 1993.

Prokesh, S. "Managing Chaos at the Technological Frontier." *Harvard Business Review* November–December 1993, pp. 134–145.

Smith, Preston G., and D. G. Reinertsen. *Developing Products in Half the Time.* New York: Van Nostrand, 1991.

Stalk, G., Jr. "Time—The Next Source of Competitive Advantage." *Harvard Business Review* July–August 1988, pp. 41–51.

Tyre, Marcie J., and Wanda J. Orlikowski. "Windows of Opportunity: Creating Occasions for Technological Adaptation in Organizations." Cambridge, Mass.: Sloan School of Management, MIT, 1991.

Tyre, Marcie J., and E. Von Hippel, "Situated Trial and Error Learning in Organizations." Working Paper. Cambridge, Mass.: Sloan School of Management, MIT, 1993.

Ulrich, K. T., and S. D. Eppinger. *Methodologies for Product Design and Development.* New York: McGraw-Hill, 1994.

Uttal, B. "Speeding Ideas to Market." *Fortune* (March 2, 1987), pp. 62–66.

Von Hippel, E. "Task Partitioning: An Innovation Process Variable." *Research Policy* 19 (1990): 407–418.

Von Hippel, E. "The Impact of 'Sticky Data' on Innovation and Problem Solving." *Management Science* (1994).

Von Hippel, Eric, and Marcie Tyre. "How 'Learning by Doing' Is Done: Problem Identification in Novel Process Equipment." Working Paper #BPS 3521-93. Cambridge, Mass.: Sloan School of Management, MIT, 1993.

Wheelwright, Steven C., and Kim B. Clark. *Revolutionizing Product Development.* New York: Free Press, 1992.

# INDEX

ABC, 241
ACE consortium, 24
Acer, 89
Active Book Company, 338, 348
Advanced Computer Environment, 98
Advanced Intelligent Network (AIN), 177, 190
Advanced Micro Devices (AMD), 77, 79, 96, 97, 99, 343
Aegis operating system, 132, 133
Aiken, Howard H., 40, 42
Air Force, U.S., 48, 64
Air Touch, 173
Allen, Paul, 378
Alliance groups, PDA, 327–328, 363
and product development, 331–344
Alliances, multimedia industry's, 196–197
Allies, innovation and dependence on, 333–336

Amdahl, Gene M., 41, 59–60
Amdahl Corporation, 59–60, 68, 105
American Motors, 91
America On-Line, 170, 171, 343, 408
Ames, Edward, 202
Ampex Corporation, 59, 73, 248
Amstrad, 331, 333, 338, 348, 351, 354, 355
Amstrand, 88
Anchordoguy, Marie, 60, 75
Anderson, William F., 66
Apollo Computer, 13, 28, 70, 140–143
competition between Sun and, 130–132, 136–142
financial position of, 143–146, 147–148
Hewlett-Packard's acquisition of, 92, 93, 149
mainframe paradigm and, 128, 130, 134

product definition and design at, 132–134
workstations of, 31, 90–91, 92
Apple Computer, 4, 13, 16, 19, 93, 106
Apple Newton (see Apple Newton)
Apple II, 233
eWorld, 234
Macintosh, 16, 87, 99, 233, 234, 235
market feedback and, 356, 359, 360
market identification and, 346
"market morphing" and, 351, 352, 354–355
microcomputer revolution and, 81–89 passim
in the nineties, 108
PDA alliances and, 331–343 passim
PDAs of (see also Apple Newton), 23, 25, 27, 228, 230, 239, 255, 256–258

peripherals and, 95
semiconductors and, 97,
    98–99
Software Patent Institute
    and, 316
Apple Newton, 16, 23, 172,
    219, 238, 350
alliances to promote, 341
hospitals' use of, 360
initial product design of,
    347–348
innovation in
    development of,
    335–336
introduction of, 231–235
lessons for, from
    consumer electronics,
    255, 258–259
overpositioning of, 232,
    235, 239
ARM, 335, 338
ARM chip, 233, 238, 338,
    348
Armstrong, Edwin
    Howard, 241
Army, U.S., 66, 69
Arora, A., 302
ASICs, 233
AST Research, 89, 106, 107
Asynchronous transfer
    mode (ATM), 177
AT&T, 3, 20, 24, 43, 51,
    105, 419
acquisition of NCR by, 9,
    14, 105, 197
alliance with Olivetti of,
    342
breakup of, 8
EO of, 236–238,
    342–343
Hobbit, 236, 237–238,
    255, 342
long-distance network of,
    218

"market morphing" and,
    352
microcomputer
    revolution and, 88, 89
multimedia industry and,
    171, 178, 184, 187, 188
PCs of, 107
PDA alliances and, 338
PDAs of (*see also* AT&T
    EO), 25, 27, 228, 230,
    239, 255, 256–257, 348
RCA and, 240
RISC microprocessors
    and, 98
semiconductors of, 73,
    74, 75
–Sun technical alliance,
    145–147, 148–149
telecommunications and,
    60, 208
workstations and, 89–90,
    91–92
ATT McCaw, 173
Atlas I, 40, 47
Atomic Energy
    Commission (AEC),
    43, 48, 49
Automatic Data Processing,
    71–72
Automobile industry,
    computer industry
    compared to, 53,
    55–57

Backward compatibility,
    259–260
Baldwin, Carliss Y., 16, 25,
    28, 31, 123
Ballmer, Steve, 379
Bane, P. William, 9, 12,
    19–20, 31, 159
Bang and Olufsen, 193
Barney Harris Upham &
    Co., 134

BASF, 60
BASIC, 81, 83
BDC Computing
    Corporation, 73
Bechtolsheim, Andreas, 91,
    134, 135
Bell, Robert, 69–70
Bell Atlantic, 14, 173, 178,
    187, 188
Bell Laboratories, 73
Bell South, 172, 230, 238,
    338, 343
Bendix Aviation, 49, 69
Bertram, Jack, 93
Betamax (Beta), 249, 250,
    258
BINAC, 41
Biotechnology, patenting
    in, 306–317
Bipolar Integrated
    Technology, 92
Borland, 102
Bradley, Stephen P., 9, 12,
    19–20, 31, 159
Bresnahan, Timothy F., 21,
    32, 202, 265
Bricklin, Daniel, 81
Brock, Ron, 83
BRS Information
    Technologies,
    PATDATA database of,
    309
Bull, 60, 88, 419
Bundling, 26–27
Burroughs (Adding)
    Machine Company,
    47, 50–52, 65–66, 67,
    71, 265
merger of, 88, 105
Business structure,
    multimedia industry
    structure and,
    166–167
*Business Week*, 85, 251

CAA, 170
Cable, 174
CAD/CAM, 179
Caelus, 73
California Institute of
    Technology, 51
Canion, Ron, 86, 87, 96,
    107
Cannibalization, 28
Canon, 95
Cap Cities-ABC, 19
Casio, 27, 227, 338, 352,
    355
    PDAs of, 230, 231, 238
Cassette tapes, 245–248,
    259
Castro, Edwin de, 70
CBS, 242, 243, 244, 246,
    258
CBS Records, 253–254
Census Bureau, 41
Challenge, *see* Everest
    project
Chandler, Alfred D., Jr., 12,
    25, 30–31, 37
CHESS
    defined, 2–3
    strategy for digital
        convergence, 12–30
Chrysler, 53, 56
Cirrus Logic, 233
CISC products, 97
Claris, 259
Clark, Kim B., 16, 25, 28,
    31, 123
Client/server technology,
    271, 272, 275–278, 292
    attractions of, 278–280
    barriers to, 281
    differences in adoption
        behavior and,
        283–284
    hospital considering
        adoption of, 293

Coase, R., 302
COBOL, 126
Cocke, John, 90, 135
Collective competition,
    332–333
Collis, David J., 9, 12,
    19–20, 31, 159
Columbia Pictures, 9, 14,
    193
Commodore, 81, 82, 83, 88
Community Computer
    Corporation, 73
Compact discs (CDs),
    253–254
Compaq Computer, 24, 96,
    101, 106–107, 355
    microcomputer
        revolution and, 86–89
    semiconductors and, 97,
        98
Competitive access
    providers (CAPs),
    174–175, 187
Complements, convergence
    in, 204–205, 207,
    215–217, 221–222
    economic consequences
        of, 212–214
Compton, 32, 302, 316
CompuServe, 32, 171, 302,
    408
Compustat, 308
Computer Associates, 100,
    102
Computer Control
    Products, 67, 70
Computer industry, history
    of, 37–40
    dominance of System 360
        (second period),
        52–64
    mainframe competitors,
        64–68
    minicomputers, 68–71

service bureaus and
    software, 71–72
    at fifty, 103–110
    microcomputer
        revolution (third
        period), 80–89
    peripherals, 94–96
    semiconductors, 96–99
    software, 99–103
    workstations, 89–94
    military to commercial
        production (first
        period), 40–52
    peripherals and
        semiconductors
        (second period),
        72–80
ComputerLand, 84
Computer Research
    Corporation, 51
Computer Sciences Corpo-
    ration (CSC), 72
Computer systems, future
    of large, 292–295
Computervision, 94, 105
Conner, Finis, 95, 96
Conner Peripherals, 95, 96,
    107
Consumer electronics
    decade of, 227
    lessons for PDAs from,
        254–260
    lessons from, 239–254
    *See also* Personal digital
        assistants (PDAs)
*Consumer Reports*, 244
Content
    multimedia industry and,
        166, 168–169,
        182–183, 194
    producers, convergence
        and, 218
Control Data, 47–50, 51,
    52, 59, 98, 105

minicomputers of, 68
service bureaus and
software of, 71
suit against IBM by,
61–63, 64
supercomputers of, 64
Convergence, 94, 201–203,
221–222
applying framework of,
217–221
collaborative agreements
and, 219–221
in complements,
204–205
levels of analysis and,
205–206
other, 207–209
cooperation,
competition, and,
214–217
economic consequences
of, 212–214
process of, 362, 363–364
in substitutes, 203–204
along value chain,
209–212
*See also* Digital
convergence
Convex, 105
Copyright Act (1976), 307
Cornford, Dominic S.,
285
Corona, 85
Cortada, James, 45, 53
Council of Europe,
European Convention
on the International
Classification of
Patents for Invention
of, 310
Court of Appeals for the
Federal Circuit, U.S.,
307, 316
Coy, Wayne, 243

CPU (central processing
unit), 134, 135, 136,
238
Cray, Seymour, 49, 50, 64
Cray Research, 64, 68, 105,
274
Creative combinations, 3,
14–17
"Creative destruction," 14
Cross-sectional study, of
processor
development in
mainframe industry,
418–425
Customer-owned
communication
technologies, 208–209
Cusumano, Michael A., 29,
33, 100, 249–250, 371
Cypress Semiconductor, 92

D'Arezzo, James, 86
Darwinian selection,
349–350
Data Connection Network
(SS7), 177, 190
Data General, 68, 70, 71,
105, 124, 133
*Datamation*, 71, 88, 93,
103, 105
*Dataquest*, 77, 108
Davidson, 170
Decca Records, 250
Defense, U.S. Department
of, 376
Dell, Michael, 88–89
Dell Computers, 88–89,
106, 209
Deregulation, 7–8, 19–20
*Diamond* v. *Chakrabarty*,
306, 312
*Diamond* v. *Diehr*, 307
Diebold, 61
Digital convergence

CHESS strategy for,
12–30
defined, 2, 3–6
drivers of, 6–12
*See also* Convergence
Digital Equipment
Corporation (DEC),
13, 16, 40, 71, 81, 265,
419
mainframe paradigm
and, 124, 127
microcomputers and, 133
in the nineties, 105–106,
108
Open Software
Foundation and, 98,
101
Programmed Data
Processors (PDPs), of,
68–69, 70, 90, 108, 110
workstations and, 90–94,
148, 149
Digital Research, 83
Disney, 19, 31, 168, 187,
194, 195
Dolby system, 246–247
DOMAIN network
architecture, 132
DRAMs, 78, 79, 96, 107,
136
DuMont, Allen, 242
duPont, Pierre, 44

Eash, George, 245
Eckert, J. W. Presper, 40, 41,
47
Eden, 338
Electrodata, 51
Electronic Arts, 170
Electronic Data Systems, 72
E-mail, multimedia and,
166
Encyclopaedia Britannica,
27

Engineering Research
    Associates (ERA), 40,
    47, 49
Engstrom, Harold, 40
ENIAC, 40, 51
EO, 232, 236–238, 255, 348,
    356–359
    "market morphing" and,
    351, 352–355
    PDA alliances and, 338,
    342–343
EPROMs, 78, 79
Epson, 84, 95
ERM 1101, 40–41
Estridge, Philip D. "Don,"
    83, 84, 86, 100
Ethernet, 135
Evans, Bob, 351, 356
Everest project (Challenge),
    425, 426–430,
    437–441
Exley, Charles, Jr., 66
Externalities, exploiting, to
    set global standards, 3,
    21–25

Fairchild Camera and
    Instrument, 76, 77
Fairchild Semiconductor, 7,
    74, 76–77, 80, 87
Fall Comdex industry
    show, 355
Family Computer
    Communications
    Network System, 208
Federal Communications
    Commission (FCC),
    208, 212, 221,
    241–242, 243, 244
Federal Trade Commission,
    240
Ferguson, Charles H.,
    100–101
Ferranti, 50

First-mover advantages,
    258–259
Flamm, Kenneth, 42, 45–46,
    47, 53, 60, 69, 100
*Forbes,* 251
Ford, Henry, 53
Ford Motor Company, 50,
    53, 56, 67, 245, 259
Forrester, Jay, 40, 68
FORTRAN, 42, 126
*Fortune,* 84, 87
Fox Broadcasting, 15
French, Don, 81
Friedman, Andrew L., 285
Fujitsu, 3, 17, 60, 79, 98,
    419
    Amdahl and, 105
    mainframe paradigm
    and, 127
    microcomputer
    revolution and, 88, 89
    software and, 100, 102
    workstations and, 92

Galvin, Robert, 75
Gassée, Jean Louis, 232
Gates, William H., 83, 87,
    88, 98, 108, 378, 379
    on Apple Newton, 233
    characterized, 382
    development process
    and, 387
    Microsoft "brain trust"
    and, 381, 409
    review and planning
    cycle and, 384
    software and, 99–100,
    101, 102
    specification process
    and, 390
Gateway 2000, 89, 106
GEC Plessy, 233
General Electric (GE), 13,
    50, 52, 64, 67, 74

and FM radio, 240, 241
General Information
    Systems (GIS), 105
General Instruments, 49,
    191
General Magic, 178, 232,
    238, 343, 344
General Motors, 44, 53,
    55–56
GeoWorks, 343, 344, 350,
    360
Gilbert, R. J., 305
GO Corporation, 232, 236,
    238, 338, 342
Gomes-Casseres,
    Benjamin, 15, 33, 255,
    325
Gore, Al, 11
*Gottschalk* v. *Benson,* 307
Graham, Margaret, 250,
    251
Graphical User Interface
    (GUI), 171, 178,
    189–190
Graphics Interchange
    Format, 302
Graziano, Joseph, 360
Greenstein, Shane, 15, 31,
    201
Grelis, Wink, 357–359
Greyhound, 61
Groupe Bull, 107
Grove, Andrew, 17, 77,
    96
Groves, Leslie R., 47
Gussin, Robert, 326

Haanstra, John W., 57, 58
Hamilton, J. O., 316
Hardware
    from integration to
    separation of software
    and, in consumer
    electronics, 255–258

processing/storage,
179–180, 192
Harvard University, 40, 42,
81, 316
Hauser, Herman, 348
Heath Company, 88
Heller, Andrew, 93
Hennell, David, 348
Hennessy, John, 135
Herbold, Robert, 379
Hewlett-Packard (H-P), 13,
16, 40, 70, 71, 79, 231
acquisition of Apollo by,
92, 93, 249
handheld PCs of,
227–228
LX series of, 231,
334–335, 336, 338,
341, 348, 352, 355, 359
mainframe paradigm
and, 127
microcomputer
revolution and, 82, 85,
88, 133
in the nineties, 105–106,
108
Open Software
Foundation and, 98,
101
PDA alliances of, 333,
334–335, 336, 338,
339, 341–342
peripherals and, 95
RISC microprocessors
and, 98
software and, 102
workstations and, 90, 92,
93–94, 148
Higgins, Pete, 379
Hitachi, 60, 79, 89, 98, 102,
419
Hoff, Ted, 78
Honeywell, 13, 50–52, 64,
66, 67, 90

Computer Control
acquired by, 67, 70
Horizontal market model,
265–269, 270, 276
deficiencies in, 278,
286–292
successful adoption of,
292–295
Horizontal solutions, 3,
17–21
Hughes Aviation, 74

Iansiti, Marco, 29, 33, 413
IBM, 3, 9, 13, 16, 17, 419
AS/400, 28
challengers to, 47–52,
58–61, 64–68
failure to sustain
incumbent advantages
of, 27, 28
Justice Department's
antitrust suit against,
61, 63–64
losses of, 103–105
mainframe competitors
of, 64–68
mainframe paradigm
and, 124, 126–127
microcomputer
revolution and, 82–89,
133
Microsoft and, 383
minicomputers of, 71
modularitry and, 123,
124, 125
multimedia industry and,
191
in the nineties, 105–106,
107–108
OS/2, 26
PCs of, 28, 82–89, 106,
110, 209
PC standards of, 22, 24
PDA alliances and, 338

PDAs of, 230, 238
peripherals and, 213
position of, in computer
history, 38–40, 41–47,
57–64
semiconductors of, 73,
96, 97–99
software and, 100–103
Software Patent Institute
and, 316
System 360 (*see* System
360)
threats of "lockin" at, 22,
23
vertical market model
and, 265
vicarious
experimentation by,
355
workstations and, 90,
92–94, 148, 149
ICL, 50, 60, 419
IMSAI 8080, 80
Industrial Light and Magic
Unit of Lucasfilm, 207
Information Storage
Systems, 59
Information superhighway,
11, 159
convergence and cross-
section of, 218–219
software, 176–179,
189–192
*In re Wright*, 316
Integrated Service Digital
Network (ISDN), 177
Intel Corporation, 3, 7, 17,
39, 105, 191, 334
alliance with VLSI of, 343
dominance of, 31
microcomputer
revolution and, 80,
83–88
in the nineties, 107

PDA alliances and, 339,
    343, 344
Pentium microprocessor,
    25, 99, 407
semiconductors and,
    76–79, 96–99
software and, 100, 101
standards of, 24
threats of "lockin" at,
    22–23
workstations and, 90
X86 microprocessor, 23,
    149
Intellectual property, 32
    protection of, 301–303
    *See also* Patent(s)(ing)
Interactive shopping,
    multimedia and, 166
Intercomp, 73
Interexchange carriers
    (IXCs), 175–176,
    186–187, 189, 190, 195
Intergraph, 94
International Patent
    Classification (IPC),
    304, 308, 311, 312,
    313, 314
    versus USPTO, 310
Internet, 1–2, 3, 13, 32,
    177
    as creative combination,
    17
    managerial creativity for
    digital convergence
    and, 9–11
    rapid acceptance of, 12
    standards of, 24
    *See also* World Wide Web
Internet Explorer, 27
Intuit, 339
Iridium satellite network,
    161
Itel, 61
Iterative processes, 29

Jelinek, Mariann, 75
Jobs, Steven, 81, 87, 101
Johnson & Johnson, 326
Joint Environment for
    Digital Imaging
    (JEDI), 207
Joy, William, 91, 134, 136
Justice Department, U.S.,
    43–44, 51, 216, 221,
    408
    antitrust suit against
    AT&T by, 73–74
    antitrust suit against IBM
    by, 61, 63–64
JVC, 248–250, 253, 350

Kaleida, 99
Khanna, Tarun, 15, 31, 201
Khosla, Vinod, 91
Kilby, Jack, 74, 75, 76
Kildall, Gary, 83
Klemperer, P., 305
KMPG Peat Marwick, 9
Kuehler, Jack, 93
Kushan, J. P., 316

Labe, Peter, 134
Langlois, Richard, 81, 82,
    87
Las Vegas Consumer
    Electronics Show, 231,
    232
Lear Jet, 245, 246, 259
Learning alliances, 336, 337
    to shape product, 338
Learning Associates, 170
Leasco, 61
Leder, Philip, 316
Lentz, Edward, 315–316
Leonard-Barton, Dorothy,
    15, 33, 255, 325
Lerner, Josh, 32, 301,
    311–312
Levin-Townsend, 61

Lewis, Thomas S. W., 240
Lexmark, 107
Lexus, 218
Litton, 66
Local area networks
    (LANs), 190, 206, 207,
    208, 216, 401
    Novell and, 108, 179
Local (intra-LATA)
    transmission, 175, 176
Local loops, 186–188
Local telephone exchange
    companies (LECs),
    174–176, 184,
    186–188, 191, 195
"Lockin" and "lockout,"
    threats of, 22–23, 30
Long-distance (inter-
    LATA) transmission,
    175, 176, 188–189
Long-playing records
    (LPs), 245, 246, 247,
    253, 254
Lotus Development, 27,
    100, 102, 316, 355
    Notes, 408
    1-2-3, 384
    PDA alliances and,
    334–335, 338, 339,
    341–342
Lowe, William, 82–83, 84,
    100
LSI Logic, 92, 429, 440
Lubrano, David, 143

McCracken, Ed, 28, 431
MacDonald, Ray W., 65
McDonald's fast food
    chain, 81
McGahan, Anita, 32, 227
Machines Bull, 67
McNealy, Scott, 91, 92
Magnavox, 252
MAI, 61

Mainframe competitors,
64–68
Mainframe paradigm, 124,
126–128, 138
Apollo and, 128, 130, 134,
142
Management information
systems (MIS),
266–267, 271, 274,
276, 277, 289
and client/server
technology, 279–280,
281
at Microsoft, 401
Managerial creativity,
digital convergence
and, 8–11
Manhattan Project, 47
Manipulation, multimedia
industry and,
166–167, 176–180,
182, 189–192
Marconi Wireless
Telegraph Company,
240
Maritz, Paul, 379
Mark I, 40, 42
Market(s)
alignment, 330–331
feedback and product
definition, 356–360
identification, 344–347
new products for new,
328–331
Market experimentation,
PDA, 327, 328, 363
from market
identification to,
344–360
"Market morphing,"
351–355
Markulla, A. C., 87
Matsushita, 9, 78–79, 88,
95, 193–194

PDAs and, 234
videocassette recorders
and, 248–250, 259
Mauchly, John W., 40, 41,
47
MCA, 9, 251
MCI, 26
Friends and Family plan
of, 284, 293
Memorex, 59, 73, 95
Merges, Robert P., 32, 301,
305
Microcomputer revolution,
80–89
peripherals, 94–96
semiconductors, 96–99
software, 99–103
workstations, 89–94
Micron Technology, 79,
107
Microsoft, 7, 23, 33, 39,
108, 334
change control and
configuration
management at,
398–400
culture at, 382–383
desktop applications of,
287
development phase at,
390–394
development process
overview at, 385–388
dominance of, 27, 31
Excel, 378, 384, 388–390,
391, 396, 397
graphical user interface
and, 171, 178,
189–190
history of, 99–100,
378–379
interaction between
Justice Department
and, 216, 408

leadership and
organization at,
379–382
metrics at, 400
microcomputer
revolution and, 83–88
MS-DOS of, 384
multimedia industry and,
179, 191
and Netscape, 25
Network, 28, 407
patents and, 302
PDA alliances and, 339
process education at,
401–402
process improvement at,
400–401
process usage and
compliance at,
396–397
product description at,
383–384
product support at, 396
project management at,
397–398
release structure and
strategy at, 385
requirements phase at,
388
review and planning cycle
at, 384–385
semiconductors and, 98,
99
software and, 99–102
Software Patent Institute
and, 316
specification phase at,
388–390
standards of, 24
synch-and-stabilize
approach at, 3, 29–30,
372, 378, 402–408
testing phase at,
394–396

threats of "lockin" at,
    22–23
tools at, 401
and "waterfall"
    development process,
    371–372, 377–378,
    402
Windows 95 (*see*
    Windows 95)
Windows NT, 378, 384,
    391, 397, 407
Winpad, 350
Word, 378, 384, 391, 397
workstations and, 90
    Minicomputers, 68–71
MIPS, 92, 94, 98, 274, 437
MIT, 40, 41, 68, 70, 76
MITI, 60
MITS Altair, 80
Mitsubishi Electric, 419
MMU (memory
    management unit),
    135–136
Modified Final Judgment,
    212
Modular cluster, emergence
    of, 123–124
Modularity, 125
    birth of, in computer
    industry, 31, 124
    consequences of, 125–126
    -in-design, 125
    -in-production, 125
    -in-use, 125
    mainframe paradigm
    and, 126–128
    modular paradigm and,
    128–130
    power of, 147–150
    using aggressive financial
    strategy to exploit,
    141–142
Modular paradigm, 124,
    128–130

Sun and, 135, 136, 138,
    141, 147
Moore, Dave, 397
Moore, Gordon, 7, 77–78,
    83
Moore's Law, 7
Morris, Charles R.,
    100–101
Mosaic, 12
MOS Technologies, 81
MOSTEK, 79
Motorola, 106, 107–108,
    149, 339, 355
    microcomputer
    revolution and, 80, 81,
    83–84, 86
    microprocessors of, 131,
    135
    PDAs of, 230, 234, 238
    semiconductors and,
    74–80 *passim*, 97–99
Movies, on-demand,
    multimedia and, 166
MTV, 183–184
Multimedia industry,
    159–160, 194–197
    key success factors and
    firm capabilities in,
    181–194
    structure of, 160–167
    structure within
    industries in,
    168–180
Muntz, Earl, 245
Myhrvold, Nathan, 379
Mylonadis, Yiorgos,
    249–250

NASA, 70
National Bureau of
    Standards, 41
National Cash Register
    (NCR), 47, 50–52, 65,
    66–67

acquired by AT&T, 9, 14,
    105, 197
National Security Agency
    (NSA), 43
National Semiconductor,
    76, 77, 79, 81
National Television
    Systems Committee
    (NTSC), 243, 244
Naval Reserve, 68
Navickas, Leon, 348
Navy, U.S., 40, 52, 68, 74
NBC, 26, 241, 242, 243,
    258
NEC Corporation, 3, 4–5,
    79, 107, 419, 425
    mainframe paradigm
    and, 127
    microcomputer
    revolution and, 82, 88,
    89
    Silicon Graphics and, 429
    software and, 102
    SX-2 supercomputer of,
    424, 431, 432–436
Nelson, R. R., 305
Netscape, 12, 23–24, 25
Network effects, 256–257
Neumann, John von, 40
*New York Times,* the, 97,
    247
NeXt, 101
Nextel, 188
Nexus, 218
Nintendo, 194
Nintendo Network, 208
Nippon Electric Company
    (NEC), 52, 60
Norris, William, 40, 47, 48,
    49, 50, 69
Northrop Aviation
    Company, 41
Novell, 100, 101, 102, 287,
    360, 408

local area networks
    (LANs) and, 108, 179
Noyce, Robert, 76, 77
NV Philips, 92
NYNEX, 173, 188

OEMEC, 73
Office of Naval Research,
    42
Olivetti, 60, 76, 87, 88, 89
    AT&T's alliance with,
    342
    software and, 102
Olsen, Kenneth H., 68–69,
    106
Opel, John R., 58, 85
Open Software Foundation
    (OSF), 92, 98, 101,
    124, 148
Optical Data Company,
    301–302, 316
Oracle, 23, 100, 102, 178,
    191
Original equipment
    manufacturers
    (OEMs), 131, 249
Osborne, Adam, 81
Osborne (co.), 85
Ovitz, Michael, 170, 195

Packaging, multimedia
    industry and, 166,
    170–172, 182,
    183–186, 194
Packard-Bell, 70, 89, 106,
    107
Paddle, Chuck, 81
Palevsky, Max, 69–70
Parker, James, 49
*Parker* v. *Flook*, 307
Pasteur, Louis, 306
Patent(s)(ing), 32, 301–304
    in biotechnology and
    software, 306–317

scope, industry evolution
    and, 304–305
Patent and Trademark
    Office, U.S. (USPTO),
    302
    and patenting in
    biotechnology and
    software, 306–311,
    315–317
Patterson, David, 135
PDA Industry Association,
    239
PDAs, *see* Personal digital
    assistant(s)
Pennsylvania, University of,
    40
PepsiCo, 87
Peripherals, 72–80, 94–96
Perot, H. Ross, 72
Personal communication
    systems (PCS), 173,
    175, 187, 190
Personal computer (PC),
    82–89
    disk drives and, 95
Personal digital assistant(s)
    (PDAs), 9, 16, 21, 23,
    25, 219
    development and
    evolution of, 230–239
    early failure of, 32,
    228–229, 239
    emergence of, 325–326
    experience, lessons
    learned from, 360–365
    forthcoming battle for,
    238–239
    initial product designs of,
    347–348
    lessons for, from
    consumer electronics,
    254–260
    market
    alignment and, 331

characteristics of,
    326–328
    experimentation and,
    349–356
    feedback and, 356–360
    identification and,
    346–347
    prospects for, 229–230,
    260–261
Peters, Chris, 397
Pfeiffer, Eckhard, 86, 107
Philco, 50–51, 67, 74, 76
Philips Electronics, 24, 194,
    246, 251–252, 259
    compact discs and, 253,
    254, 255, 258
Pioneer Electronics
    Corporation, 252
Piore, Emanuel R., 42
Pitney-Bowes, 66
Poduska, William, 70, 90,
    143
Polygram Records, 194,
    253–254
Pooley, J., 303
Poqet PC, 231
Positioning alliances, 336,
    337
    to market product,
    341–343
President's Commission
    on the Patent System,
    307
Prime Computer, 13, 68,
    70, 71, 98, 105
    mainframe paradigm
    and, 124
    minicomputers and, 133
    workstations and, 90,
    94
    *See also* Computervision
Princeton University,
    Institute for Advanced
    Study at, 40

Processing/storage
   hardware, 179–180,
   192
Prodigy, 171
Product definition
   and design
   Apollo's, 132–134
   Sun's, 134–136
   market feedback and,
   356–360
Product designs
   and definition
   Apollo's, 132–134
   Sun's, 134–136
   initial, 347–348
Product development
   alliance groups and,
   331–344
   at Silicon Graphics,
   425–430, 431
   system-focused,
   424–425
   in uncertain
   environments,
   415–418
Product evolution,
   multimedia industry
   structure and,
   161–166
Programmed Data
   Processor (PDP),
   68–69, 70, 90
Project Stretch, 43, 44
Psion, 231, 355, 359
Pugh, Emerson, 43, 58

Quantum, 95, 96, 107

Radio, FM, thirty-year
   struggle to establish,
   240–242
RadioMail, 339, 344
Radio Shack, 81, 82, 88
RAMs, 78

Rand, James Henry, 47, 48,
   49, 50
Raytheon, 51–52, 74
RCA, 13, 43, 50, 52, 59, 75
   cassette tapes and, 245,
   246
   color television and,
   242–245, 258, 259
   FM radio and, 240–242,
   258, 260
   Sperry-Rand's acquisition
   of computer business
   of, 64, 65
   vacuum tube
   technologies of, 74
   videocassette recorders
   and, 248, 249, 259
   videodisc players and,
   250–252
Reception stage interaction
   (RSI), 218, 219,
   220–221
Regional Bell Operating
   Company (RBOCs),
   220
Remington Rand, 41, 47,
   48
Remington Typewriter
   Company, 47
Remodularization, impact
   of, on competitive
   performance,
   136–141
   *See also* Modularity
Reverse engineering, 302
RISC microprocessor, 25,
   40, 98, 135, 149
   collective competition
   and, 332
   PDAs and, 238, 328, 343
   workstations and, 90–94
Rochester Plan, 173, 175
Rolm, 9, 235
Rosenberg, Nathan, 202

Rosenbloom, Richard S.,
   249–250

SAGE program, 43, 68
Sakoman, Steve, 348
Saloner, Garth, 21, 32, 265
Samsung, 107
Sanders, W. Jeremiah, 77
Santa Cruz Operation, 98,
   102
Sanyo, 350
Sarnoff, David, 241, 242,
   243–244, 260
Saxenian, Annalee, 76, 78
Scale
   economies, 3, 26
   and scope, 25–28
Schlumberger, 76
Schoonhoven, Claudia B.,
   75
Schumpeter, Joseph, 14
*Scientific American*, 14
Scientific Data Systems
   (SDS), 67, 68, 69–70
SCI Systems, 84
Sculley, John, 4, 16, 87,
   347–348, 351
   and PDAs, 231, 232, 233
Seagate Technology, 95, 96,
   107
Sears Business Centers, 84,
   89
Seattle Computer Products,
   83
Securities and Exchange
   Commission, 146, 318
Securities Data Company,
   308
Sega, 182, 194
Sega Channel, 207
Selby, Richard W., 100
Selden, 305
Semiconductors, 72–80,
   96–99

Service bureaus, 71–72
"Seven Dwarfs," 64
Shapiro, C., 305
Sharp, 16, 89, 193, 227, 352
 PDA alliances and, 335,
  338, 343
 PDAs of, 230, 231,
  233–234, 238–239
 Zaurus of, 238–239, 349,
  350, 352
Sherman, Roger, 397
Shockley, William, 74, 76
Shugart, Alan, 95
Shugart Associates, 95
Siemens, 50, 60, 102, 234,
  235, 253, 419
Siemens-Nixdorf, 94
Silicon Glen, 87, 92
Silicon Graphics, Inc.
 (SGI), 13, 16, 28, 105,
  106, 414
 Everest project
  (Challenge) of, 425,
  426–430, 437–441
 semiconductors and, 98
 system-focused product
  development strategy
  at, 3, 29–30, 33,
  425–430, 431
 video games and, 207
 workstations and, 94
Silicon Valley, 77, 80, 86,
  236, 303, 429, 430
 birth of, 76
Simonyi, Charles, 393
Sinclair, 85
Singer, 66
Skytel, 234
Sky TV, 15
Sloan, Alfred P., 44
Smith, Stanley A., 29, 33,
  371
SmithKlein Beckman, 315
Sobel, Robert, 242, 243

Software, 71–72
 effect of microcomputer
  revolution on, 99–103
 information
  superhighway,
  176–179, 189–192
 from integration to
  separation of
  hardware and, in
  consumer electronics,
  255–258
 patenting in, 306–317
 traditional manipulation,
  179, 189
Software Patent Institute,
  316
Sony, 9, 14, 24, 75, 78–79,
  89
 compact discs and, 253,
  254, 255, 258
 MTV and, 184
 PDAs and, 238
 purchase of Columbia by,
  193
 terminals and, 193–194
 videocassette recorders
  and, 248–250, 258
 Walkman, 248
SPARC, 149
Sparks, "Sparky," 86
Sperry, Elmer, 48
Sperry-Rand Corporation,
  47–50, 52, 64–65, 67,
  69
 merger of, 88, 105
Spork, Charles, 77
Sprague, Peter, 77
Sprague Electric
  Equipment, 77
Sprint, 173, 220
Stac, 302
Standard diffusion model,
  272, 273, 275–276
Stanford University, 429

 Graduate School of
  Business, 271
Stock market crash
  (October 19, 1987),
  145
Storage Technology
  Corporation, 59, 73
Substitutes, convergence in,
  203–204, 207, 215,
  216–217, 221–222
 economic consequences
  of, 212, 214
"Substitution economics,"
  165
Sullivan, P. H., 303
Sun Microsystems, 13, 23,
  40, 98, 106
 –AT&T technical alliance,
  145–147, 148–149
 competition between
  Apollo and, 130–132,
  136–142, 143
 financial position of,
  143–146, 147
 hypergrowth at, 142
 Java, 24
 modular paradigm and,
  130, 135, 136, 138,
  142, 148–150
 and Open Software
  Foundation, 149
 product definition and
  design at, 134–136
 workstations of, 16, 25,
  31, 90–94
*Sun World*, 441
Supply alliances, 336, 337
 to assemble capabilities,
  338–339
Supreme Court, U.S., 306,
  307
SX-2 supercomputer, 424,
  431, 432–436
Sylvania, 74

Synch-and-stabilize
approach, 3, 29–30,
372, 378, 402–408
System-focused processes,
3, 28–30
System-focused product
development strategy,
3, 29–30, 33, 425–430,
431
System 360, 43, 48, 50, 51,
108
competitive strength of,
45–46
description of, 38–39, 44
dominance of, 31, 39,
52–64
mainframe competitors
and, 64–68
minicomputers and,
68–71
service bureaus and
software and, 71–72
System 360/370, 39, 58, 59,
60, 64, 72
global spread of, 80

Taligent, 99
Tandem, 98, 102, 105
Tandon, 84, 95
Tandy, Charles, 81
Tandy Corporation, 230,
338, 352, 355
microcomputer
revolution and, 81–82,
83, 88, 89
Tchao, Michael, 348
TCI (Telecommunications,
Inc.), 14, 15, 187, 207,
220
TDK Electronics, 246
Technological maturity,
328–330
Teldec, 250
Telefunken, 250, 253

Television, color, 242–245
Telex, 59
Terminals, multimedia
industry and, 167,
180, 182, 192–194, 196
Texas Instruments (TI), 45,
50, 86, 92, 233
microcomputer
revolution and, 80, 85
semiconductors and,
74–80 *passim*, 99
Time Warner, 15, 24, 207,
220
Timex, 85
Toshiba, 24, 79, 88, 89, 419
PDAs and, 234, 235
RISC microprocessors
and, 98
Silicon Graphics and,
429
software and, 102
Traditional manipulation
software, 179, 189
Trajtenberg, Manuel, 202,
311
Tramiel, Jack, 81
Transitron, 74
Transmission, multimedia
industry and, 166,
172–176, 182,
186–189
Transmission stage
interaction (TSI), 218,
219, 220–221
Triology Systems
Corporation, 60
Tymsharing, 72

UHF channels, 243, 258,
260
U-Matic, 248–249
Unisys, 88, 94, 105, 302,
419
UNIVAC, 41, 47, 48

UNIX International (UI),
149
UNIX operating systems,
25, 28, 40, 98
Apollo and, 132, 133, 134,
137–138, 144
Sun and, 135, 136, 137,
138, 146, 149–150
workstations and, 90, 91,
92, 93
US West, 173, 220

Vadasz, Leslie L., 32, 227
Value chain, convergence
along, 209–212
Vanderslice, Thomas, 143
Venture Economics, 308
Vertical market model,
265–269, 270, 291
dissatisfaction of buyers
with, 285–286
Very-large-scale-integrated
(VLSI) chips, 58, 60,
79
VHF channels, 243, 244
VHS (Video Home
System), 249–250, 258
Vicarious experimentation,
355–356
Videocassette recorders
(VCRs), 248–250
Videodisc players,
250–252
Video game industry,
207–208
VLSI Technology, 233, 343
Voice-Powered Technology,
359
"Vulture capitalism," 80

Wal-Mart, 26, 89
Wang, An, 70
Wang Laboratories, 13,
70–71, 265

"Waterfall" development
process, 371–372,
373–376, 402
implications and
problems of, 376–378
Watson, Thomas J., Jr., 42,
43, 44, 63
Watson, Thomas J., Sr., 42,
43, 47
Western Digital, 107
Western Electric, 73
Westinghouse Corporation,
74, 240, 258
Whirlwind Computer
Project, 40, 41, 68
Wide area networks
(WANs), 208
Williams, Chris, 397
Williams, James C., 76

William Shockley's
Laboratories, Inc., 76
Windows 95, 22, 26, 27, 30,
171, 383
development of, 18–19,
407, 409
Network and, 28
product stability and
reliability of, 385
teams for, 397
Wireless, 8, 173–174, 180
terminal technology, 172
Wireline, 174–175, 180
WordPerfect, 27, 102
Workstations, 89–94
World Book, 27
World Intellectual Property
Organization, 310
World War I, 48

World War II, 31, 40, 46,
48, 51, 74
World Wide Web (WWW),
11–12, 17, 21, 218
browser software of, 23,
27
Wozniak, Steve, 81, 87

Xerox, 67, 70, 95
Xerox PARC, 16

Yang, C. Y., 316
Yoffie, David B., 1, 32, 227

Zander, Edward, 133
Zenith, 84, 88
Ziff start–up Interchange,
171
Zilog, 81–82, 83

# ABOUT THE CONTRIBUTORS

*Carliss Y. Baldwin* is the William L. White Professor of Business Administration at the Harvard Business School. Her research includes design practice, industry structure, and financing in the computer industry. She has published papers and articles on such topics as modularity in design, and capital budgeting systems. Professor Baldwin serves as a director of the Federal Home Loan Bank of Boston and the Thermolase Corporation, and is an associate editor of *Financial Management*.

*P. William Bane* is a vice president and group head of Mercer Management Consulting, Inc., in Washington, D.C. His current practice activities include identifying profitable growth strategies in the converging industries of communications, content, and computing, particularly the economic and organizational transitions faced by telephone companies as they convert from copper-based public networks to "intelligent" broadband and wireless infrastructures.

Mr. Bane was previously a vice president and director of the Boston Consulting Group and was founder, chairman, and CEO of ManageWare, a venture-capital funded PC software developer and marketer.

*Stephen P. Bradley* is the William Ziegler Professor of Business Administration and chair of the Competition and Strategy unit at the Harvard Business School. His current research centers on the impact of technology on industry structure and competitive strategy; current projects include facilitating business strategy in the telecommunications, finance, pharmaceutical, and electronics industries, and working with public agencies to analyze the impact of public policy on the competitive structure of such industries.

Professor Bradley has written books on such subjects as applied mathematical programming and management of bank portfolios, and is the co-editor, with Jerry A. Hausman and Richard L. Nolan, of *Globalization, Technology, and Competition* (HBS Press).

*Timothy F. Bresnahan* is a professor of economics and codirector of the Stanford Computer Industry Project at Stanford University. His current research centers on competitive analysis, information technology industries, and the strategic use of information technology. He has published a wide variety of empirical industry studies in such journals as the *Journal of Political Economy* and the *Brookings Papers on Economic Activity*. Professor Bresnahan's most recent book, coedited with Robert Gordon, is *The Economics of New Goods*.

*Alfred D. Chandler, Jr.,* is the Isidor Straus Professor of Business History, Emeritus, at the Harvard Business School, where he began teaching in 1970. He has written many books on the history of business and management including the prizewinning *Strategy and Structure: Chapters in the History of the Industrial Enterprise; The Visible Hand: The Managerial Revolution in American Business;* and *Scale and Scope: The Dynamics of Industrial Capitalism.*

*Kim B. Clark* is the dean of the Harvard Business School and the Harry E. Figgie, Jr., Professor of Business Administration. Dean Clark's research interests include technology, productivity, product development, and operations strategy. He has studied technological innovation and competition in a variety of industries, including automobiles, steel, semiconductors, computers, and advanced ceramics. His most recent publications, co-authored with Steven Wheelwright, include *Leading Product Development* and *Revolutionizing Product Development.*

*David J. Collis* is an associate professor in the Competition and Strategy unit at the Harvard Business School. His expertise is in global competition and corporate strategy, and his research includes an international comparison of the role of the corporate office in large multibusiness corporations. Professor Collis consults to several large U.S. and European corporations and has published work in the *Harvard Business Review, Strategic Management Journal, European Management Journal,* and in *Beyond Free Trade* (HBS Press). He is a co-author, with Cynthia Montgomery, of the forthcoming book, *Corporate Strategy.*

**Michael A. Cusumano** is a professor of management at the Massachusetts Institute of Technology Sloan School of Management. He specializes in competitive strategy and technology management in the computer software, automobile, and consumer electronics industries, and does much of his work on technology-based Japanese companies and comparisons with U.S. firms. He works as a consultant in software development management.

Professor Cusumano has written over fifty articles and papers on such topics as software engineering, video-recorder product development, manufacturing innovation, and product development in the auto industry, and has authored three books. His most recent book, written with Richard W. Selby, is *Microsoft Secrets: How the World's Most Powerful Software Company Creates Technology, Shapes Markets and Manages People.*

**Benjamin Gomes-Casseres** is an associate professor of international business and the director of the Master's program at the Graduate School of International Economics and Finance at Brandeis University. He specializes in alliance strategy and management, particularly in global, high-technology industries, and is a frequent speaker and consultant on alliance management to companies in the United States and worldwide. He has published in the *Harvard Business Review,* the *Sloan Management Review,* and various scholarly journals and edited volumes. His most recent book is *The Alliance Revolution: The New Shape of Business Rivalry.*

**Shane Greenstein** is an associate professor of economics at University of Illinois at Urbana/Champaign, where he teaches microeconomics, the economics of technology, and the economics of regulation. His research interests include the economics of high technology, particularly buyer benefits from advances in information technology, structural change in information technology markets, standardization in electronics markets, investment in digital infrastructure, and government procurement of computers.

Professor Greenstein is also a faculty research fellow in the productivity group of the National Bureau of Economic Research and a columnist on computing economics for *IEEE Micro*. He has written many chapters and articles on his research topics.

*Marco Iansiti* is an associate professor in the Technology and Operations Management unit at the Harvard Business School. His area of expertise is microelectronics, with emphasis on the development, fabrication, and testing of very small electronic circuits. His research focuses on the management of technology and product development, and he has been involved in studies of effective development practice in industries such as microelectronics, steel manufacturing, software, and automobiles. His current study is on product in environments characterized by extreme market and technological turbulence, focusing on software, multimedia, and workstations.

Professor Iansiti consults to several Fortune 500 companies and serves on the board of the Corporate Design Foundation. He has authored numerous chapters, cases, and articles, which have appeared in such journals as the *Harvard Business Review*, the *California Management Review*, and *Research Policy*.

*Tarun Khanna* is an assistant professor at the Harvard Business School, where he teaches in the Competition and Strategy unit. Professor Khanna's research includes a comparative study of product development activities in the high-end computer industry in the technological evolution and understanding the structuring and management of collaborative arrangements among firms, and on understanding the strategy issues associated with management of multiproduct, diversified companies. He has written many articles on this topic and is the author of *Foundation of Neural Networks*.

*Dorothy Leonard-Barton* is the William J. Abernathy Professor of Business Administration at the Harvard Business School, where she teaches classes on new product and process development, manufacturing, technology strategy, and technology implementation. She is also a faculty member of Harvard programs on Enhancing Corporate Creativity and Managing International Collaboration.

Professor Leonard-Barton's major research interests and consulting expertise are in technology development and commercialization. She is currently undertaking an international study of these topics in the multimedia industry. Her most recent book is *Wellsprings of Knowledge: Building and Sustaining the Sources of Innovation* (HBS Press 1995).

***Josh Lerner*** is an assistant professor in the Finance area and the Entrepreneurial Management Interest Group at the Harvard Business School. His research focuses on the structure of venture capital organizations and their role in transforming scientific discoveries into commercial products. He also examines how intellectual property shapes high-technology industries. His work has been published in a variety of academic journals, including the *Journal of Finance,* the *Journal of Financial Economics,* the *Journal of Law and Economics,* and the *Rand Journal of Economics.*

***Anita M. McGahan*** is an assistant professor in the Competition and Strategy area at the Harvard Business School. Professor McGahan's research focuses on the evolution of competitive strategy. Her academic publications include studies on the brewing, consumer electronics, insurance, and pharmaceutical industries. She has also conducted case studies on companies in the automobile, wheelchair, telecommunications, and network software industries. Her current research involves large-scale statistical studies on the evolution of advantage among firms in a cross-section of industries.

***Robert P. Merges*** is a professor at the Boalt Hall School of Law, University of California at Berkeley, where he teaches intellectual property and contracts. Professor Merges is also a special consultant to the Antitrust Division of the Department of Justice on intellectual property issues and a consultant to numerous public and private agencies. His scholarly interests include the economic aspects of intellectual property rights, especially patents, on which he has written numerous articles and chapters.

***Garth Saloner*** is the Robert A. Magowan Professor of Strategic Management and Economics, associate dean for academic affairs, and director for research and curriculum development at the Graduate School of Business at Stanford University. His research focuses on issues of strategic management, competitive strategy, industrial economics, and antitrust economics. Currently, Professor Saloner's research is devoted to issues of competitive strategy arising from standardization and compatibility, especially in the information technology industries.

***Stanley A. Smith*** is a senior programmer with IBM Corporation in Austin, Texas. His work has centered around operating system design and development for System/38, AS/400, and OS/2. His most recent work has involved the incorporation of object-oriented and Internet technology into operating systems. As part of his thesis in the management of technology area at MIT, Mr. Smith worked with Michael Cusumano on what has formed the base of chapter 10.

***Leslie L. Vadasz*** is a senior vice president and a board member of Intel Corporation, where he has worked since 1968 in such capacities as director of engineering, general manager of the Microcomputer Component Division, and general manager of the Systems Group. Currently, he is responsible for corporate business development with the orientation toward investments and acquisitions of businesses and technologies that will extend Intel's growth. Mr. Vadasz is a fellow of the IEEE.

***David B. Yoffie*** is the Max and Doris Starr Professor of International Business Administration at the Harvard Business School, where he has been a member of the faculty since 1981. Professor Yoffie's research focuses on business strategy as well as international competition in high technology industries. He is a director of Intel Corporation, the National Bureau of Economic Research, Evolve Software, and Bion, Inc. A widely published author, Professor Yoffie has written and edited six books, including *Beyond Free Trade: Firms, Governments, and Global Competition* (HBS Press) and *Strategic Management in Information Technology.* In addition, Professor Yoffie has written more than seventy-five cases and articles on international trade, firm strategy, and global competition in high-technology industries.